Educators' Work Integrated Learning Experiences

Iman C. Chahine · Lalini Reddy
Editors

Educators' Work Integrated Learning Experiences

Stories from the Trenches

🖄 Springer

Editors
Iman C. Chahine
University of Massachusetts Lowell
Lowell, MA, USA

Lalini Reddy
Cape Peninsula University of Technology
Cape Town, South Africa

Research Unit Self-directed Learning
(SDL), North-West University
Potchefstroom, South Africa

ISBN 978-3-031-65963-8   ISBN 978-3-031-65964-5 (eBook)
https://doi.org/10.1007/978-3-031-65964-5

© The Editor(s) (if applicable) and The Author(s), under exclusive license to Springer Nature Switzerland AG 2024

This work is subject to copyright. All rights are solely and exclusively licensed by the Publisher, whether the whole or part of the material is concerned, specifically the rights of translation, reprinting, reuse of illustrations, recitation, broadcasting, reproduction on microfilms or in any other physical way, and transmission or information storage and retrieval, electronic adaptation, computer software, or by similar or dissimilar methodology now known or hereafter developed.
The use of general descriptive names, registered names, trademarks, service marks, etc. in this publication does not imply, even in the absence of a specific statement, that such names are exempt from the relevant protective laws and regulations and therefore free for general use.
The publisher, the authors and the editors are safe to assume that the advice and information in this book are believed to be true and accurate at the date of publication. Neither the publisher nor the authors or the editors give a warranty, expressed or implied, with respect to the material contained herein or for any errors or omissions that may have been made. The publisher remains neutral with regard to jurisdictional claims in published maps and institutional affiliations.

This Springer imprint is published by the registered company Springer Nature Switzerland AG
The registered company address is: Gewerbestrasse 11, 6330 Cham, Switzerland

If disposing of this product, please recycle the paper.

Introduction

In the heart of a bustling city, a young engineering student named Sarah embarked on her journey of work-integrated learning that would forever change her perspective on education. She had spent years in lecture halls, diligently taking notes and acing exams, but something was missing. She yearned for real-world experience to complement her theoretical knowledge.

One summer, Sarah secured an internship at a cutting-edge robotics company. On her very first day, she found herself in a room filled with engineers huddled around a colossal robot, their brows furrowed in concentration. This robot, they explained, was designed to inspect and maintain infrastructure in hazardous environments, such as nuclear power plants and underwater pipelines.

The seasoned engineers handed Sarah a toolbox and said, "You'll be working on the robot's sensory systems today." Her eyes widened with a mixture of excitement and trepidation. It was her responsibility to ensure that this behemoth of technology could "see" and "feel" its surroundings accurately.

Over the weeks that followed, Sarah inspected the intricacies of sensors, learning not just from textbooks but from the engineers who had spent years perfecting their craft. She found herself crawling into tight spaces within the robot's chassis, fine-tuning sensors, and calibrating data points. She would often lose track of time, her hands covered in grease and her mind consumed by the fascinating challenges that real-world engineering presented. Immersed in her work, Sarah faced numerous challenges. There were moments of frustration when lines of code just wouldn't cooperate and instances of self-doubt when the deadline seemed impossible to meet. Yet, it was precisely these challenges that fueled her desire to succeed. Her work-integrated learning experience wasn't just about acquiring technical skills; it was about resilience, teamwork, and problem-solving.

As the summer internship drew to a close, Sarah realized the profound impact of work-integrated learning. It was not just about acquiring skills, but about embracing the mindset of a problem-solver. She had learned that textbooks could only teach you so much; real learning happened when you grappled with the unpredictable intricacies of the real world.

Sarah returned to her university with a newfound enthusiasm, eager to apply the lessons she had learned during her work-integrated learning experience. She knew that her academic journey had been transformed from a mere quest for grades to a passionate pursuit of knowledge with real-world relevance. Sarah's journey with work-integrated learning didn't just transform her résumé; it transformed her entire perspective. Through this immersive experience, she not only honed her technical skills but also learned the value of persistence, creativity, and collaboration. Sarah's anecdote became a testament to the power of work-integrated learning, a hands-on education that not only equips students with skills but ignites their passion and prepares them to tackle the complex challenges of the world beyond the classroom.

In the ever-evolving landscape of education, the role of a teacher is not only to impart knowledge but also to continually learn and adapt, showing the world that when knowledge meets real-world application, the possibilities are limitless (Dean, 2023). This dynamic interaction between being a teacher and a learner finds its most innovative expression in the realm of work-integrated learning (WIL). This book volume, *Educators' Work Integrated Learning Experiences: Stories from the Trenches*, explores the multifaceted experiences of educators in the context of WIL, offering a profound insight into the challenges, triumphs, and transformative processes they undergo.

Within the pages of this book, you will embark on a journey that spans diverse dimensions of education, from online excursions and immersive experiences to reflective practices and culturally oriented instruction. Spanning 16 chapters, each segment of this festschrift is a unique portal, inviting readers to embark on a journey through distinct realms of lived experience, self-discovery, and contemplation. The chapters in this book are not mere narratives; they are voyages of encounters, each exploring a distinct facet of the intricate tapestry of teaching and learning within a WIL context.

We begin our journey with Chapter "The Changing Faces of Work Integrated Learning," which serves as a comprehensive introduction to the concept of work-integrated learning, examining its theoretical underpinnings and practical applications in the educational landscape. The author explains that WIL encompasses activities that bridge theory and practice, ranging from low to high levels of engagement. As WIL primarily involves authentic experiences within a structured curriculum, focusing on graduate outcomes and career paths, real-world partnerships maximize WIL benefits. The author further describes how case studies can be instrumental in illustrating the advantages of engaging in WIL, including career clarity, industry ties, enhanced skills, and improved academic performance for students. There is also significance to professional development and how employers can benefit from access to fresh ideas, specialized resources, and improved image, making WIL integration crucial for future-proof curricula.

Chapter "Learning to Work, Working to Learn: Using Immersion Experiences to Guide Culturally Oriented Mathematics Instruction" explores cultural immersion field experiences for pre-service teachers, emphasizing the development of intercultural competencies through the study of mathematics as a cultural activity. It discusses examples of such experiences in diverse global and local contexts, including interactions with Ndebele women in South Africa and Gullah Geechee Sweetgrass weavers. The chapter also presents a Cultural Immersion Mathematics Project involving elementary preservice teachers, demonstrating how these experiences help recognize, interact with, and understand mathematics as a cultural practice. Additionally, the chapter offers specific strategies to promote intercultural competence and enhance culturally oriented mathematics instruction alongside cultural immersion field experiences.

The journey continues in South Africa, where Chapter "Work-Integrated Learning and Self-directed Professional Learning in a Rural Setting: What Do Pre-service English FAL Teachers Need from Their Mentor Teachers?" explores the significance of work-integrated learning (WIL) for pre-service teachers' preparation in aiming to make them competent educators. While the South African government policies like the Minimum Requirements for Qualification in Teacher Education outline necessary competencies, and that WIL involves mentorship by experienced teachers, the authors describe how pre-service teachers' perspectives are often overlooked, hindering their self-directed professional growth. The chapter presents a study, which focused on pre-service English FAL teachers in a rural setting, investigating their needs during WIL. Using qualitative methods, the authors reveal areas where mentor teachers are essential: lesson planning, classroom management, learner-centered teaching, providing support and feedback, and fostering self-directedness.

In the context of South Africa's massified university education, Chapter "Being and Becoming a Teacher Educator in an Online Work-Integrated Learning Excursion for Future Super Teachers" explores the nuances of being a teacher educator in the digital age. It offers profound insights into the transformational processes that mold future educators. By focusing on the reflective self-study of a novice teacher educator's experience facilitating teacher preparation in an online virtual excursion, Chapter "Being and Becoming a Teacher Educator in an Online Work-Integrated Learning Excursion for Future Super Teachers" showcases the educator's strengths and limitations, emphasizing the importance of reflective practices. The study offers valuable insights into the challenges faced by novice lecturers in online teaching contexts and highlights the significance of ongoing professional development in this area.

In Chapter "Exploring Reflective Practice as a Supportive Professional Development Tool for Novice Teachers: A Narrative Inquiry," reflective practice, a cornerstone of effective teaching, takes center stage as the author explores how novice teachers can harness the power of self-reflection as a tool for continuous professional development, ensuring their growth as educators. The author further examines the potential of reflective practice as a self-support mechanism for novice teachers, aiming to understand its role in their professional development. Drawing on personal experiences, the research embarks on the reflective journey of the author as a novice teacher, utilizing narrative inquiry as the methodological approach. The study's central focus is on the phases of teacher development, emphasizing the impact of reflection on professional growth. The study emphasizes the significance of reflective practice, induction support, and teacher agency in enhancing professional development. The findings underscore the need for policy changes, particularly in South Africa, emphasizing the importance of teacher retention and promoting a culture of collegiality and support within the teaching profession. The study's contribution lies in its narrative approach, providing valuable insights for in-service and pre-service teachers, promoting the integration of reflective practices into teacher education programs, and suggesting implications for work-integrated learning contexts.

In response to the critical discourse surrounding teacher quality and effectiveness, especially in the context of South Africa, Chapter "A Self-study from the Work Integrated Learning Trenches: The Achilles Heel Stories" narrates challenges faced in the trenches of work-integrated learning. By unearthing the vulnerabilities and strengths of educators, and providing valuable lessons for both novice and experienced teachers alike, the study delves into the lived experiences of teacher educators through collaborative self-study. Grounded in Wenger's Community of Practice framework, this study examines the dialogues and reflections between teacher educators from different provinces in South Africa, revealing key challenges such as policy adherence, numerical pressures, the impact of COVID-19, and the inadequacies in language preparation. The study emphasizes the crucial role of language in achieving quality education and highlights the gaps in understanding its significance in global educational initiatives. By narrating their experiences, the teacher educators offer valuable insights for policymakers, faculty leaders, and curriculum designers, contributing to informed decisions regarding the enhancement of work-integrated learning within teacher education programs. This chapter provides immersed cases of work-integrated learning in diverse contexts, fostering a deeper understanding of the challenges faced by teacher educators and preservice teachers alike.

Examining the role of young learners in work-integrated settings, Chapter "Children's Participation in Work Integrated Learning in Early Childhood Education" highlights the importance of early childhood education in shaping the future generation of educators and learners. The chapter further addresses a gap in existing research by alluding to the fact that while much research has focused on the experiences of pre-service teachers during WIL, little attention has been given to how children engage in these learning environments. The chapter emphasizes the need to understand how children perceive and experience lessons during WIL, providing insights into their perspectives. The authors advocate for a reimagining of the role of both young and older children in WIL, offering suggestions for policymakers and higher education institutions. Additionally, the chapter calls for empirical studies to explore the impact of children's participation, specifically focusing on gathering feedback on how children experience lessons taught by both pre-service and in-service teachers

Chapter "Unveiling First-Year Student Teachers' Experiences: An Excursion Programme Rooted in Playful Learning for Active and Critical Learning" probes into the initial steps of future educators, chronicling the experiences of first-year student teachers in an excursion program, shedding light on the transformative impact of early exposure to real-world teaching environments. This chapter discusses the challenges of teacher preparation programs and the high attrition rates among novice teachers due to the theory-practice divide in the teaching profession. The author argues that many educational institutions fail to adequately prepare student teachers for the complexities of teaching. To address this issue, particularly in a South African context, the chapter describes a synchronous virtual work-integrated learning (WIL) excursion program rooted in playful learning pedagogy. The program was aimed at fostering active and critical learning experiences for first-year student teachers. This chapter contributes to the theme of work-integrated learning in online teaching and learning environments by presenting the outcomes of a synchronous virtual WIL excursion program for undergraduate students.

Maintaining the focus on WIL in teacher preparation programs, Chapter "Examining Collaborative Mentoring to Improve the Professional Learning of a Pre-service Teacher During Work Integrated Learning Practicum Experience: A Case Study of Practice" addresses the absence of national policies regulating the involvement of schools and higher education institutions (HEIs) in South Africa's Initial Teacher Education (ITE) programs, specifically during the practicum period. The focus is on the lived experience of a pre-service teacher (PST) engaged in collaborative mentoring with a university lecturer and a mentor teacher (MT). The study explores how this collaborative mentoring approach influences the PST's professional learning (PL) during the practicum period. Employing an interpretive case study design with multiple methods, the research aims to understand the dynamics of the mentor-mentee relationship within a work-integrated learning (WIL) environment and assess the effectiveness of collaborative mentoring. The findings highlight the need to address the disconnect between university and school programs and advocate for the establishment of collaborative mentoring programs in South Africa's ITE.

Chapter "Variations in South African Novice Mathematics Teachers' Lived Experiences and Reflections on Multiple Solutions Problem-Solving: Implications for Work-Integrated Learning" focuses on South African in-service teachers' and pre-service teachers' challenges with geometry problem-solving, specifically in the context of multiple solution tasks (MSTs). The research explores teachers' reflections and perceptions regarding the importance of MSTs and investigates their struggles with solving these tasks. The authors indicate that while novice teachers acknowledged the importance of MST problem-solving in geometry and recognized it as a critical skill, they struggled to produce complete and accurate multiple solutions. Limited knowledge and inadequate prior experiences with Euclidean geometry problems were cited as obstacles hindering their ability to generate comprehensive solutions. The study highlights the need for improved teacher training in MST problem-solving and its integration into work-integrated learning (WIL) programs. WIL, combining theoretical learning with practical experience, offers students the chance to apply creative and innovative problem-solving techniques in real-world contexts. Integrating MST problem-solving into WIL can better prepare future mathematics educators, equipping them with critical thinking and creative problem-solving skills essential for teaching mathematics effectively.

The candid and authentic portrayal of the life and experiences of teachers in the educational trenches crosses geographic boundaries with Chapter "Work Integrated Learning in the Forest: The Journey of a Science Educator," where the author shares her educational journey participating in the Harvard Forest's Schoolyard Ecology

Long Term Ecological Research (LTER) Program in the Northeastern region of the USA. Transporting the reader to the heart of nature, the author shares how outdoor and experiential learning in forest environments enriches work-integrated learning experiences, fostering a deep connection between learners and the natural world. The program involves teachers and students collecting ecological field data in their schoolyards. The author discusses their involvement in three specific projects related to forest composition, invasive species, and climate change. Using a work-integrated learning (WIL) perspective, the author examines their experiences, practices, and perspectives in this context. Employing a self-study design, the chapter explores how participation in the program shifted the author's self-perception as an educator, improved their confidence in designing transformative learning experiences, and transformed relationships with students. Through qualitative data analysis, five main themes emerge: increased content knowledge, enhanced confidence in designing impactful learning experiences, limitations due to standardized testing and school schedules, exposure to technical skills through authentic data sets, and the joyful nature of experiential outdoor learning for both educators and students.

In Chapter "Learning Through Teaching: A Year in an All-Girls Engineering Class," the author, a second-career teacher with an engineering background, narrates her experiences while teaching an all-girls engineering class in a high school setting. The purpose of the study is to investigate the effectiveness of teaching methods in an all-girls engineering class compared to mixed-gender classes. The teacher, concerned about the declining number of girls enrolling in engineering classes, conducted action research and self-study to understand how teaching practices could be modified to engage and retain female students in the field of engineering. The study employed self-study methodology, focusing on self-initiated and focused inquiry into teaching practices. The research questions centered around the effectiveness of the teacher's pedagogy in an all-girls engineering class compared to mixed-gender classes and how teaching methods needed to change to meet the educational needs of girls in engineering. Several themes emerged from the study, which culminated in a set of adjustments in the teacher's practices, including providing explicit instructions, reducing competitive elements, incorporating humanitarian-focused projects, fostering a supportive learning environment, and offering recognition for achievements. The study highlights the importance of tailoring teaching methods to meet the specific needs and preferences of female students in engineering classes.

Exploring the intersections of mind, body, and environment, Chapter "Full Circle: A Personal Journey of Work-Integrated Learning and Self-Directed Discovery" investigates the embodied experiences of learners in work-integrated settings, shedding light on the intricate connections between physical presence and cognitive processes. In this chapter, the author shares a personal journey deeply rooted in STEM fields, influenced by family experiences and early exposure to technical elements. Despite not following a conventional educational path, the author's life experiences sparked a passion for education, leading to a career in teaching and later, pursuing doctoral studies. The chapter aims to explore two significant stories: one focusing on educational experiences shaping the author's expertise, and the other highlighting their impact on future educators. The writing draws upon thematic frameworks like work-integrated learning (WIL) and Embodied, Situated, and Distributed (ESD) cognition, emphasizing experiential learning and the influence of multi-sensory experiences on education. The chapter delves into the author's doctoral research findings, examining their implications for developing courses for both in-service and pre-service elementary teachers.

In a detailed narrative, Chapter "The Unlimited Benefits of Work-*Integrated* Learning: Reflections, Shifts, and Other Transformations by an Educational Leader, Improvement Scientist, and Math Pun Enthusiast" recounts the author's educational journey and professional growth as a math educator, emphasizing his involvement in initiatives aimed at enhancing STEM education. He highlights his experiences with Work-Integrated Learning (WIL) during his doctoral studies, where he applied theoretical knowledge to real-world scenarios at their high school. The author probes into the process of developing and implementing initiatives, such as restructuring the math curriculum, conducting extensive research, and using data analysis techniques. Through his work-integrated learning experiences, he describes how he gained insights into effective educational leadership, enabling him to make data-driven decisions, engage in research-focused endeavors, and transform his school environment. The narrative concludes with the author's commitment to continuing their educational initiatives, drawing on the valuable lessons learned through WIL.

The author in Chapter "Math and Maths: Diversifying U.S. Math Instruction with Work-Integrated Learning Through Inclusive Math Pedagogies from England and Spain" shares insights from their immersion experience in math instruction in England, emphasizing the need for intentional international exchanges and ongoing dialogues on learning, particularly in mathematics education. The author's goal is to establish a global pedagogical collaboration involving US students, teachers, and communities, connecting with nations that share similar educational values. During their stay in England, the author visited various schools to explore effective math practices. The chapter focuses on key questions about lesson delivery, curriculum programs, teaching strategies, addressing learning differences, and identifying beneficial practices for US students. The author discusses the similarities and differences between elementary schools in England and the USA, analyzing what can be adapted into American math instruction and what may not be suitable. Additionally, the chapter highlights the methods and tools incorporated into the author's own teaching practices based on the international experience. The author's future plans involve continued collaboration with England and expanding the network globally to enhance math teaching and learning, fostering meaningful connections and mutual understanding among students and educators worldwide

Final Chapter "Work-Integrated Learning in a Value-Based Course" offers a nuanced perspective exploring the intersection of the social, spiritual, and scientific aspects of teaching with work-integrated learning, offering a holistic perspective on education that goes beyond the traditional boundaries of classrooms. The author discusses the urgent need for human values education in the face of rising social issues such as violence and crime. The Sri Sathya Sai Institute of Educare in South Africa offers Sri Sathya Sai Education in Human Values (SSSEHV) certificate courses, emphasizing core values like truth, love, peace, right conduct, and non-violence.

Initially conducted face-to-face, the course transitioned to a blended format and eventually moved fully online due to the COVID-19 pandemic, utilizing platforms like Google Classroom and Zoom. Despite initial challenges, the online courses have expanded globally, facilitated by mentors. The author describes how the integration of interactive elements enhanced engagement, emphasizing the ripple effect of positivity and core human values through the principle of resonance, as learners spread these values to their communities.

As you delve into the pages of *Educators' Work Integrated Learning Experiences: Stories from the Trenches*, you will witness the transformative power of education, the resilience of educators, and the limitless potential of work-integrated learning in shaping the future of teaching and learning. Each chapter is a testament to the dedication, passion, and innovation that educators bring to their profession, serving as an inspiring beacon for all those embarking on their own journeys in the world of teaching.

Iman C. Chahine
Lowell, USA

Reference

Dean, B.A. (2023). The value of work-integrated learning for preparing the future teaching workforce. In Winslade, M., Loughland, T., Eady, M.J. (Eds.), *Work-Integrated Learning Case Studies in Teacher Education*. Springer, Singapore. https://doi.org/10.1007/978-981-19-6532-6_2

Contents

The Changing Faces of Work Integrated Learning 1
Lalini Reddy

Learning to Work, Working to Learn: Using Immersion
Experiences to Guide Culturally Oriented Mathematics Instruction 13
Alesia Mickle Moldavan

Work-Integrated Learning and Self-directed Professional
Learning in a Rural Setting: What Do Pre-service English FAL
Teachers Need from Their Mentor Teachers? 39
Mosebetsi Mokoena and Tshepang J. Moloi

Being and Becoming a Teacher Educator in an Online
Work-Integrated Learning Excursion for Future Super Teachers 67
Gordon Keabetswe Sekano and Adri Du Toit

Exploring Reflective Practice as a Supportive Professional
Development Tool for Novice Teachers: A Narrative Inquiry 87
Cisca de Kock

A Self-study from the Work Integrated Learning Trenches: The
Achilles Heel Stories 101
Zelda Barends and Carisma Nel

Children's Participation in Work Integrated Learning in Early
Childhood Education 127
Naseema Shaik and Andile Mji

Unveiling First-Year Student Teachers' Experiences: An Excursion
Programme Rooted in Playful Learning for Active and Critical
Learning 141
Neal T Petersen

Examining Collaborative Mentoring to Improve the Professional Learning of a Pre-service Teacher During Work Integrated Learning Practicum Experience: A Case Study of Practice 169
Cisca de Kock

Variations in South African Novice Mathematics Teachers' Lived Experiences and Reflections on Multiple Solutions Problem-Solving: Implications for Work-Integrated Learning 183
Sfiso Cebolenkosi Mahlaba and Iman C. Chahine

Work Integrated Learning in the Forest: The Journey of a Science Educator 209
Tara M. Goodhue

Learning Through Teaching: A Year in an All-Girls Engineering Class 231
Mariel Kolker

Full Circle: A Personal Journey of Work-Integrated Learning and Self-Directed Discovery 251
Karin A. Loach

The Unlimited Benefits of Work-*Integrated* Learning: Reflections, Shifts, and Other Transformations by an Educational Leader, Improvement Scientist, and Math Pun Enthusiast 269
Michael Strandberg

Math and Maths: Diversifying U.S. Math Instruction with Work-Integrated Learning Through Inclusive Math Pedagogies from England and Spain 283
Amy Bride

Work-Integrated Learning in a Value-Based Course 301
Maggie Perumal

The Changing Faces of Work Integrated Learning

Lalini Reddy

Abstract Work Integrated Learning (WIL) is an umbrella term for a range of pedagogical activities that are designed to enhance the integration of theory and practice. WIL extends across a continuum from low to high levels of authenticity and engagement. WIL describes experiences that are (1) authentically engaged with the practices and experiences of the workplace, (2) located within an intentional discipline-centered curriculum, and (3) a focus on graduate learning outcomes and career pathways. Although this book focuses primarily on the teaching practice modality of WIL, the other modalities are discussed as additional options for teachers to include in the education programs or other disciplines. Each WIL modality is found to require careful designing in order to maximize the rich potential for student learning per discipline. WIL is a valuable mechanism for demonstrating authentic learning and providing evidence of student outcomes. The full benefits of WIL are only realized when the experiences are connected to a real-world context through dynamic and flexible partnerships with external organizations. Two case studies show the benefits of Community Service Learning and Workplace Based Learning. The need for the development of future-proof curricula with the inclusion of WIL is the need of the hour.

Keywords Modalities of WIL · Workplace-based learning · Community service learning

1 Introduction

Work-integrated learning (WIL) is an umbrella term for a range of approaches that integrate theory with the practice of work. In 2007, the promulgation of the new Higher Education Qualifications Framework (HEQF) in South Africa introduced

L. Reddy (✉)
Centre for Community Engagement and Work-Integrated Learning, Cape Peninsula University of Technology, PO Box 1906, Bellville 7535, Cape Town, Western Cape, South Africa
e-mail: reddyl@cput.ac.za

the term 'Work-Integrated Learning' (WIL) into a Department of Education document for the first time (DHET, 2018). According to Zegwaard and Rowe (2019) "an educational approach involving three parties—the student, educational institution, and an external stakeholder—consisting of authentic work-focused experiences as an intentional component of the curriculum." Work-integrated learning (WIL) is a well-theorized pedagogical practice that facilitates students' learning through connecting or integrating experiences across academic and workplace contexts (Andrews & Ramji, 2020). Kolb (1984) described this experiential learning as "the process whereby knowledge is created through the transformation of experience."

The role of the university in today's world is about more than just earning a degree (Garwe, 2020). With current competitiveness and struggling economies, the student needs to get prepared for the big world of employment after graduation. Work-integrated learning is an innovative learning development program that is specifically integrated into a degree or diploma curriculum, and which counts towards your final qualification (Lukins, 2022).

Education has evolved. The work environment has also changed drastically especially as we embrace the fourth industry revolution (4IR) and artificial intelligence (AI) technologies (Reddy, 2023b). Trends in the future world of work impact the nature of WIL. Universities are required to transform curricula into future-proof curricula (Rampersad & Zivotic-Kukolj, 2018). The purpose of the chapter is to expose readers to a wide variety of modalities of WIL for consideration with their curricula. The author also provides more in depth reflections on two modalities from her diverse experiences with Work-Integrated Learning (WIL).

2 Modalities of WIL

There are various modalities in which WIL may be integrated into curricula. The intended purpose of the qualification may determine which modality/ies may be used. This chapter reflects briefly on the following modalities: *Experiential Learning (EXPL), In-Service Training (IST), Workplace-based learning (WPBL), Work-Directed Theoretical Learning (WDTL), Work Project Based Learning (WPJBL), Work-Directed Theoretical Learning (WDTL), Work Project Based Learning (WPJBL, Work Simulation, Immersion (IMM), WIL Excursion (EXC), Teaching Practice (TP), Clinical Practice (CP), Community Service Learning (CSL), and Technopreneurship.* Brief reflections on these modalities are provided.

2.1 Experiential Learning (EXPL)

Since Kolb introduced his Experiential Learning Model in the 1970's (1984), the details of the experiential learning model continue to be refined. The fundamentals of all experiential learning theories are the same: in experiential learning, students are given the time and space to actively participate in the process of learning by engaging their senses in real situations (Kolb & Kolb, 2005).

Despite substantial support for the role of experience as a cornerstone of learning, it must be noted that learning is not an automatic result of experience (Beard & Wilson, 2013). Instead, deliberate engagement with an experience (e.g., critical reflection on aspects of experience) is required for effective experiential learning (Beard & Wilson, 2013). Experiential learning can be facilitated in postsecondary education through work-integrated learning, which is a broad term that encompasses various learning opportunities centered on the integration of academic learning and practical application in a chosen work environment (HEQCO, 2016).

According to Beard (2023) "experiential learning is holistic, as embodied, embedded, enacted, relational, and extended, and that learning is not only socially and culturally "constructed," but also biologically, psychologically, emotionally, sensorily, cognitively, spiritually, and conatively (intention to act/action/behaviors) constructed." Students can engage in experiential learning anywhere. It depends on a 'Learning Experience Designer' who creates opportunities for example for children to 'do, sense, feel, and think'. These experiences contribute to the development of the "human sense of self, as a person belonging, becoming, and being in the world."

Prestholdt and Flecher (2018) assessed students pre and post-experiential learning in the realm of biology in Tanzania, the bio-diverse field site for human and ecological history. Biology and non-biology students were treated to a powerful first-hand understanding of the interdependent and dynamic connections between animals and their environment. There was heavy participation of both the faculty and the students while in Tanzania, as well as peer-to-peer learning and pre-trip classroom preparations. In this rich environment, there was no barrier between students and the wildlife. The results showed a significant increase in learning by the non-Biology students post the EXPL experience.

2.2 In-service Training (IST)

In-service training includes educational activities that aim to increase the student's level of efficiency and increase their knowledge, experience, and skills so that they can better fulfill their future duties and responsibilities. In an international study (Finland, Malaysia, Tanzania), carried out the the Department of Planning, Monitoring and Evaluation in South Africa (Mabogoane, 2021), the following need improvement with in-service training: Post-training follow-up and support at school and classroom level; Collaborations and peer-engagement offer opportunities for both new and experienced teachers to learn together in a supportive environment, Collegiality: Management support, peer support and mentorship, Guidelines for the selection of teachers to attend out-of-school CPD are essential, Objective reporting regime, with monitoring and risk management plans, Targeting and expenditure tracking: Value for money and to flag cost overruns, Causal link between higher qualifications and school-based efficiencies, and Sustainability: Enhanced by building-in incentives

(Mabogoane, 2021). Overall responsibility for reporting, communication strategy, monitoring and evaluation strategy needed improvement in order to determine the effectiveness of in-service training.

2.3 Workplace-Based Learning (WPBL)

This is an educational component of an occupational qualification that provides students with real-life work experiences where they can apply academic and technical skills and increase the prospect of employability (DHET, 2018).

Work-based learning (WPBL) experiences involve students engaging with professionals in workplace environments. WBL can take many forms, from job shadowing to apprenticeships, but these authentic experiences educate our students in a vastly defining way. Students develop clarity for their postsecondary learning and career goals (Association for Career & Technical Education, 2024). Graduate employers regularly rate strong interpersonal, negotiation and teamwork skills as highly desirable attributes of university graduates. WPBL experiences embedded in curriculum set a best practice standard to meet these expectations and produce employable, work ready graduates (Reddy, 2023a).

The benefits to employers include the opportunity to recruit new graduates, complete a technical task at a low cost, bring in new and fresh ideas, have access to university expertise and specialized resources, and improve corporate image.

2.4 Work-Directed Theoretical Learning (WDTL)

According to the CHE WIL Good Practice Guide (CHE, 2011), the theory covered in the classroom should align disciplinary demands with workplace relevance. Other ways of introducing industry-relevance theory in the classroom are the use of industry guest lectures, authentic examples, or case studies from the world of professional practice in setting learning and assessment tasks. Often assessors are drawn from the workplace to form part of a panel to assess students' work.

2.5 Work Project Based Learning (WPJBL)

Project-based learning is a student-centered pedagogy that allows students to acquire deeper knowledge through active exploration of real-world challenges and problems. Students investigate and respond to a complex question, challenge, or problem systematically.

Tamim and Grant (2013) discussed project-based learning as a constructivist approach to learning and suggested its use in in-service training or student-centered learning environments. They explained, "Students' interest, critical thinking abilities, presentation skills and communication skills, and their ability to work effectively on a team were enhanced when they worked on a WPJBL activity." In addition, students could enjoy a sense of success and accomplishment as they moved "from novices to experts in the domain of knowledge, and that they blended some of their learning abilities in the production of the artifacts." It is important for novice teachers to note that teachers in PjBl struggle in managing the project environment, in scaffolding, and in assessment.

2.6 Work Problem-Based Learning (WPBL)

Problem-based learning is a student-centered pedagogy in which students learn about a subject through the experience of solving an open-ended problem found in trigger material from the workplace. The process promotes the development of other desirable skills and attributes. This includes knowledge acquisition, enhanced group collaboration, and communication relevant to the workplace. In light of the digital technologies and automation that have crept into most workplaces, placing students in the workplace to experience these new environments can only augur well. This, however, comes with challenges when class sizes are very large and finding suitable workplaces for all students may be problematic. My experience has found that significant effort needs to be placed on developing close and trustworthy partnerships with industry (Reddy, 2023b).

2.7 Work Simulation

A job simulation, or work simulation, is an employment test where potential employees are asked to complete tasks expected from them on the job. For example, for a secretary position, a job simulation might include typing a dictation or completing forms. This modality may be most effective with technology -based courses.

2.8 Immersion (IMM)

Glocal immersion (cross-country study abroad programs) and excursion (in-country, off campus) experiences are two fundamental options that afford teachers the capability to (1) grow holistically (cognitively, interpersonally, and intrapersonally); (2) shift perspective and appropriately adapt their behavior to cultural differences and commonalities; (3) self-construct substantive content and pedagogical knowledge using self-directed learning approaches in real life situations; and (4) demonstrate the flexibility to embrace malleable mindsets to address intercultural problems within educational contexts.

Williams and Nunn (2016) discuss the power struggles that occur in immersion programs in South African communities, such as that in a rural called Makuleke. The authors contend that "Unequal power relations are an enduring dilemma of this kind of work even when the intention is to "join in community" with others to learn, create, and build relationships side by side for mutually beneficial purposes." It is thus important for WIL practitioners to mitigate the power differential between us and our community partners, in Makuleke. Cross-cultural exchanges should demonstrate respect for village knowledge and language.

2.9 WIL Excursion (EXC)

An excursion is a short trip or outing to an industry, geographical environment or social setting, typically to experience a real-life work setting and with the intention of a prompt return: a work excursion.

Stellenbosch University (2018) students enjoyed an "excellent opportunity to explore South Africa's rich geological history, when they visited outcrop spanning from the Archean (i.e., Barberton outcrop and mines) through to the Permian-aged Karoo coal fields. This also exposed students to field mapping techniques, and they were able to concisely record all geological observations and field relationships in their notebooks. The following feedback was received from one student, S. Teek.: "I believe that was the most valuable learning experience I have had since I have been at varsity. … In my opinion fieldtrips are the best way to formulate your own understanding…".

2.10 Teaching Practice (TP)

Teaching practice is a period that a student teacher spends teaching at a school as part of his or her training i.e., practice teaching. Most of the Chapters in this book discuss Teaching Practice as a WIL modality.

In a study at a South African University, the "data revealed that education preservice teachers need to pay attention to (1) flexibility in time of course participation, (2) flexibility in content in the course, (3) flexibility in instructional approaches and learning materials, and lastly (4) flexibility in course delivery and logistics." (Heeralal & Bayaga, 2011)

Hlengiwe and Nzimande (2023) found that mentors play a significant role in preservice teacher mentees. They reported that "Mentees were able to establish positive mentoring relationships with their mentors, which were influenced by many factors such as professionalism and prior interaction. However, in certain experiences, where participants faced challenges establishing professional relationships with some of their mentors", these experiences could be used as learning curves.

2.11 Clinical Practice (CP)

Clinical practice means the act of providing all forms of medical and health care, including patient consultations, and the act of performing clinical investigations involving patients, including as a means of training. Each country has their own set of guidelines for clinical practice, and these may differ for each profession. Common, however, are the Ethical Guidelines when working with patients.

2.12 Community Service Learning (CSL)

The Community Service Learning Program offers students opportunities to connect classroom learning with real-life experiences in the community (Houngbo, 2023).

Although there may be various challenges experienced by students, lecturers and community organizations, service learning can impart "high-demand skills to graduate students by transforming how students learn and move from knowledge into ideas and ultimately action, and by offering opportunities for developing higher-order reasoning and critical thinking" (Levkoe et al., 2014). Planning for Change: Community Development in Practice is an eight-month graduate SL course in the Department of Geography and Program in Planning at the University of Toronto. The geography and planning courses presented an ideal pedagogical opportunity to implement SL. In order to produce engaged citizens upon graduation, practical learning opportunities to address community concerns, equip students to be socially responsible. Whilst SL has a shared focus on both service and learning, the skills and knowledge are also beneficial for employability. Student progress in the course was assessed as part of a mutual learning process whereby self-evaluations around specific themes of their work, such as communication with their community partners, was appraised. The partners also provided feedback to instructors and students on these same themes. Thus a "full range of feedback and on the quality of assignments, participation, and final projects, the instructors jointly determined the final grade." (Levkoe et al., 2014)

2.13 Technopreneurship

Technopreneurship refers to a new breed of entrepreneurship. It involves promising creative, driven, persuasive, and tech-savvy individuals. Unlike entrepreneurship, however, technopreneurship is never a one-man show. Technopreneurship is not a product but a process of synthesis in engineering the future of a person, an organization, a nation, and the world. Strategic direction or decision-making processes are becoming more demanding and complex. This requires universities and on-site professional development programs and training to produce strategic thinkers who will have the skills to succeed in a rapidly changing global environment (Reddy, 2023b).

In many post-schooling and higher education institutions, entrepreneurial workshops and advocacy efforts strongly connect with transformative power in terms of social mobility. In South African communities, innovative business models equip young and old(er) entrepreneurs with knowledge, skills and increased societal resilience to sustain their efforts in making a sustainable mark on society. Entrepreneurship thus has the power to inspire social enterprise development. In South Africa, we want graduates to be job makers rather than job seekers (UNISA Western Cape, 2023).

3 Case 1—Community Service Learning Project

The qualification is the SSEHV (Sathya Sai Education in Human Values) value-based education certificate course for teachers and other interested persons. The course aims to catalyze the unfolding of human values in students engaged in WIL which may result in character transformation and social service. The students were required to design and implement a service project in the community and report on the outcomes and the impact of this project on them, the recipients (target audience), the environment, and others. The challenges were also presented and how these were overcome was reflected upon.

A SSEHV student in a far North African country chose to adopt a community in a rural area 300 km from her hometown. She carried out a detailed needs analysis of the area and gained the confidence of the local community and school. She used the SSEHV teaching techniques with the teachers and community members. Projects on social service, SSEHV education, and medicare training ensued. To support the SSEHV program at the school, she provided educational resource materials for the library. Guidelines were established to help teachers integrate SSEHV into the daily curriculum. The SSEHV student followed up on how teachers were applying the SSEHV in their classrooms.

Together with the local community, the students and a few volunteers took the initiative to renovate a well for water supply, sanitation, and plantations. This project continued long after the student graduated with the SSEHV Introductory Certificate. An irrigation system and planting of trees; construction of corridors and installation of libraries in classrooms; social service projects including coordination and organization of green spaces and educational gardens in the school and design and distribution of Green Bags have been completed. The local authorities, inspired by the SSEHV student's civic engagement, sponsored a Medical Caravan to provide general medical check-ups to determine the health status of 421 children. This rural area has limited access to health facilities and doctors. The caravan was a blessing and the realization of a fervent wish of the school committee came true with the help of the SSEHV student doing her WIL project. The Ministry of Health and a local NGO set out to identify and provide necessary treatment to the children who required dental and eye care. Students and teachers of the public school said that the atmosphere of the school has become much more relaxed and agreeable since the adoption of the SSEHV program in the school. Such is the transformative power of a community service project on the student and the community.

Parent's comments: "In my point of view, this program is very helpful to our children. It aims to teach our children many values that they need in their life. I think it is very important to have a meeting between the parents and the SSEHV program coordinator to extend this good program to more schools. We are sure we will get a good society with these values." Teacher's comments: "Human values have always been important for me as they are part of my culture and my religious teachings. I have always tried to include them and teach them to my students. However, the SSEHV program provides me with tools and methods that are easily accepted by the students." A learner stated: "I am very thankful to everyone and especially the SSEHV teacher trainer who helped my school be a better place for me to learn and live."

As an SSEHV trainer and assessor myself, at a poorly resourced East African school, I found the school principal to be the ideal role model for the SSEHV program. Despite limited resources and his being in a wheelchair, he inspired the students and other teachers to engage in silent sitting, prayer, storytelling, group activity, and song. He integrated values into secular subjects. I witnessed this transformation in the school children when they were able to lead these value-based techniques in the muddy walled single large without floors.

4 Case Study 2—Workplace-Based Learning—WIL in a University Diploma

In a previous role as a lecturer in charge of workplace-based learning for the final year students of the Diploma in Biotechnology, I have placed many students in industry for over twenty years. The nature of the industry varied from chemical to food, health, agricultural, and industrial sectors. The students undertook routine work in quality control, sampling, processing, and product development. During my monitoring visits to the students in industry and meetings with their industry supervisors, I noticed the gradual development of the student's knowledge, communication and technical skills, attitudes and values of responsibility, and willingness to learn. These positive changes occurred in all students irrespective of their previous performance in their earlier theoretical subjects. This demonstrated the immense poof transformation that workplace-based learning has on students and how they are prepared for employment.

5 Benefits of WIL and Factors that Make WIL an Ideal Learning Environment

In today's world, university is about more than just earning a degree. It's also about getting yourself prepared for the big world of employment awaiting you after graduation. WIL is a vehicle for economic development as it promotes employability and business growth. South African universities of technology acknowledge that with an increasingly complex global economy, all learners must be prepared with intellectual, technical, and social skills needed to compete and contribute meaningfully towards socio-economic development as espoused in the National Development Plan (NDP).

The factors that foster the development of students engaged in various modalities of WIL include the following: the physical environment of the workplace, the infrastructure, the multidisciplinarity of work, the work etiquette, the workplace norms, communication protocols, teamwork, company goals, corporate work ethic and values, dedication, and innovation.

According to Lukins (2022), the opportunity to work in a genuine business setting, develop your sense and awareness of workplace culture, enhance your soft skills support an advancement of your theoretical knowledge, and can help you manage your future career aspirations and decisions. Students can boost their employment prospects, build a flourishing network of contacts, increase their awareness of global challenges and industry issues, broaden their perspectives make a positive impact, and offer solutions to real-life problems.

6 Recommendations

The world of work is changing therefore graduates need to be prepared for the future world of work (Zegwaard et al., 2023). There is a need now, for visionary curriculum experts in educational institutions to respond with a future-proof curriculum that includes WIL (Reddy, 2023b).

Employment trends, the interface between humans and machines, the needs of our communities, and the expertise and skills demanded from our graduates, are some of the reasons why we need to re-curricula (Kay et al., 2019). At a South African university of technology, Vision 2030 prompts staff to prepare students for the future, get students ready for the world of work, produce a future generation of scholars, engage in regionally relevant research, and promote socio-cultural and economic growth.

Academics need to spend time in the workplace themselves to become familiar with the latest and future fit trends in their disciplines. Various modalities of WIL should be included as well as resources to promote student entrepreneurship. Processes need to be in place to promote engagement between employers, government, community, and universities around curriculum design and delivery (Kay et al, 2019). Skill-driven curriculum is an option to be used. Research-driven curricula should emerge from market trends (Zegwaard & Rowe, 2019). The dual education model of a 50/50 split curriculum between university and industry may be considered.

Lastly, models for authentic assessment of WIL should be developed to include the critical knowledge, skills, attitudes, and values developed during WIL. Work ethic, ability to work in multidisciplinary teams, digital literacy, critical and strategic thinking, and problem-solving capabilities are some important areas for assessment.

References

Andrews, J., & Ramji, K. (2020). Connecting work-integrated learning and career development in virtual environments: An analysis of the UVic Leading Edge. *International Journal of Work-Integrated Learning, Special Issue, 21*(5), 643–656.

Association for Career and Technical Education. (2024). Work-Based Learning. Retrieved from https://www.acteonline.org/wp-content/uploads/2022/10/WBL_Fact_Sheet_Final.pdf

Beard, C. M. (2023). *Experiential learning design: Theoretical foundations and effective principles.* Routledge Taylor & Francis Group.

Beard, C. M., & Wilson, J. P. (2013). Experiential learning: A handbook for education, training and coaching, *Business & Economics,* 1–331.

CHE. (2011). Work integrated learning good practice guide, *Council for Higher Education,* 1–92.

DHET. (2018). Sector education and training authorities, workplace based learning programme agreements regulations, *Government Gazette Republic of South Africa,* 1–34.

Garwe, E. C. (2020). Does the timing of work integrated learning affect graduate employability outcomes? *South African Journal of Higher Education 34*(5), 192–209. https://doi.org/10.20853/34-5-4225

Heeralal, J., & Bayaga, A. (2011). Pre-service teachers' experiences of teaching practice: Case of South African university. *Journal of Social Sciences, 28*(2), 99–105. https://doi.org/10.1080/09718923.2011.11892933

HEQCO. (2016). *A practical guide to work integrated learning.* Higher Education Quality Council of Ontario, Canada. Retrieved from https://heqco.ca/wpcontent/uploads/2020/03/HEQCO_WIL_Guide_ENG_ACC.pdf

Hlengiwe, S. L., & Nzimande, N. (2023). Pre-service teachers' experiences of mentoring relationships during teaching practice. *International Journal of Sciences and Research, 79*(1), 67–87. https://doi.org/10.21506/j.ponte.2023.1.5

Houngbo, G. F. (2023). *The world needs a strong and sustained dose of social justice.* International Labour Organisation. https://www.ilo.org/global/about-the-ilo/how-the-ilo-works/ilo-director-general/statements-and-speeches/WCMS_868098/lang--en/index.htm

Kay, J., Ferns, S., Russell, L., Smith, J., & Winchester-Seeto, T. (2019). The emerging future: Innovative models of work-integrated learning. *International Journal of Work-Integrated Learning, 20*(4), 401–413.

Kolb, D. A. (1984). *Experiential learning: Experience as the source of learning and development* (pp. 1–23). Prentice Hall.

Kolb, A. Y., & Kolb, D. A. (2005). Learning styles and learning spaces: Enhancing experiential learning in higher education. *Academy of Management Learning & Education, 4*(2).

Levkoe, C. Z., Brail, S., & Daniere, A. (2014). Pedagogy and transformative learning in graduate education/ learning in graduate education: A service-learning case study. *Canadian Journal of Higher Education RCES, 44*(3), 68–85.

Lukins, S. (2022). Benefits of work-integrated learning. Retrieved from https://www.topuniversities.com/student-info/careers-advice/9-fantastic-benefits-work-integrated-learning

Mabogoane, T. (2021). Rapid review of teacher in-service training in South Africa. Department of Planning, Monitoring and Evaluation, South Africa.

Prestholdt, T., & Flecher, V. (2018). The value of experiential learning: A case study with an interdisciplinary study abroad course. *Bioscene, 44*(2), 17–23.

Rampersad, G., & Zivotic-Kukolj, V. (2018). Work-integrated learning in science, technology, engineering, and mathematics: Drivers of innovation for students. *International Journal of Work-Integrated Learning, 19*(2), 193–204.

Reddy, L. (2023a). *Digital solutions for WIL.* UWC Digital Horizons Symposium, Cape Town, South Africa.

Reddy, L. (2023b). *Preparing future-proof curricula to boost the economy and contribute to social cohesion: A Western Cape, South African perspective.* World Association for Co-operative Education, Canada.

Stellenbosch University. (2018). *Undergraduate field trips.* Retrieved from https://www.sun.ac.za/english/faculty/science/earthsciences/prospective-students/undergraduate-programme/field-trips

Tamim, S. R., & Grant, M. M. (2013). Definitions and uses: case study of teachers implementing project-based learning. *Interdisciplinary Journal of Problem-Based Learning, 7*(2), 72–101. https://doi.org/10.7771/1541-5015.1323

UNISA Western Cape. (2023). Sustainable Development in Communities Supporting entrepreneurial initiatives through capacity building and community engagement. In *9th Annual academic development symposium—Cape Town, South Africa.*

Williams, J. M. & Nunn, L. M. (2016). Immersive practices: Dilemmas of power and privilege in community engagement with students in a rural South African village, *Engaging Pedagogies in Catholic Higher Education (EPiCHE), 2*(1). https://doi.org/10.18263/2379-920X.1009. https://digitalcommons.stmarys-ca.edu/epiche/vol2/iss1/5

Zegwaard, K. E., Pretti, T. J., Rowe, A. D., & Ferns, S. J. (2023). Defining work-integrated learning. In K. E. Zegwaard & T. J. Pretti (Eds.), *The Routledge international handbook of work-integrated learning* (3rd ed., pp. 29–48). Routledge.

Zegwaard, K. E., & Rowe, A. D. (2019). Research-informed curriculum and advancing innovative practices in work-integrated learning. *International Journal of Work-Integrated Learning, Special Issue, 20*(4), 323–334.

Learning to Work, Working to Learn: Using Immersion Experiences to Guide Culturally Oriented Mathematics Instruction

Alesia Mickle Moldavan

Abstract Cultural immersion field experiences can provide opportunities for preservice teachers to develop their intercultural competencies while studying mathematics as a cultural activity. In this chapter, examples of cultural immersion field experiences in diverse global–local contexts are first reported. Thereafter, personal experiences of working alongside Ndebele women in South Africa and Gullah Geechee sweetgrass weavers are reflected upon. A Cultural Immersion Mathematics Project of elementary preservice teachers' experiences is shared. This shows how to develop preservice teachers' skills to recognize, interact with, and understand mathematics as a cultural practice. Furthermore, specific strategies that can be used alongside cultural immersion field experiences to promote intercultural competence and advance culturally oriented mathematics instruction are recommended.

Keywords Cultural immersion · Cultural diversity · Cultural competency · Mathematics education · Teacher education · Instructional assignment · Mathematical activities

1 Introduction

Teacher education should prepare intercultural teachers who are responsive to diverse school contexts (Smolcic & Katunich, 2017). One way to support teachers in developing their understanding of culture is through structured immersion experiences in culturally different communities. While international and "study abroad" opportunities can offer insights into unfamiliar linguistic, socioeconomic, and cultural contexts, cultural immersion field experiences can also occur locally outside the school community. Teacher educators can use such places to enhance their curriculum and show ways that preservice teachers can use culturally different spaces to promote intercultural learning (Cushner & Mahon, 2009), even for use within their future

A. M. Moldavan (✉)
Georgia Southern University, Savannah, GA, USA
e-mail: amoldavan@georgiasouthern.edu

classrooms. Furthermore, such opportunities can motivate teachers and students to see school content in use, thereby making meaningful connections to real-life applications to shape intercultural attitudes and worldviews (Leung et al., 2014).

This chapter explores several questions. Firstly, what does it mean to engage in cultural immersion field experiences offering work-integrated learning opportunities for preservice teachers? Secondly, how can these experiences be used to develop preservice teachers' skills to recognize, interact with, and understand mathematics as a cultural practice? Thirdly, what specific strategies can be used alongside cultural immersion field experiences to promote intercultural competence, thereby advancing culturally oriented mathematics instruction that encourages global awareness, fostering a more informed and well-rounded worldview? To address these questions, existing literature is examined, and personal experiences are shared from the lens of a mathematics teacher engaging in immersion experiences in diverse global–local contexts to acknowledge how such authentic learning shaped work as a mathematics teacher. These experiences have been used to guide mathematics instruction and expose future teachers to learning opportunities, connecting theoretical concepts to practice-based mathematics tasks. The purpose of this chapter is to (a) inform educational stakeholders of the impact cultural immersion field experiences have in both K-12 and teacher education, (b) encourage strategic participation in such experiences to integrate learning and practice, and (c) argue that cultural immersion field experiences can serve as a catalyst for preparing teachers for cultural challenges they may encounter during work-integrated learning experiences as well as enhancing culturally oriented mathematics instruction to develop deeper understandings of mathematics through real-life applications.

2 Valuing Cultural Immersion Field Experiences for Teachers

Cultural immersion field experiences can be described as first-hand, community-based learning opportunities whereby participants authentically engage with practices in real-life settings to develop awareness and appreciation for different cultures (Addleman et al., 2014). Such experiences may vary in purpose, structure, and length. While it is recognized that experiences that are very involved and longer in length may seem more effective (Sleeter, 2008), even a few hours immersed in informal settings can be just as influential, especially for preservice teachers. Moreover, while structure can guide immersion, both formal and informal experiences can be beneficial when connected to a discipline-centered curriculum considering cultural funds of knowledge (Moll et al., 1992). By engaging in these experiences, participants can learn about specific cultures, challenge their beliefs and biases, and develop new understandings outside dominant and familiar cultures (Wiest, 1998).

Cultural immersion field experiences can provide work-integrated learning opportunities to study mathematics in everyday practice. Students and teachers often struggle to bridge cultural connections between school mathematics and real-life applications (Brown et al., 2019). Cultural immersion field experiences can allow students to work alongside "mathematicians" in diverse global–local contexts to help develop a deeper understanding of how everyone uses mathematics and, therefore, are doers of mathematics (Bishop, 1988a; Cobb & Hodge, 2007). Furthermore, such immersion experiences can be used to see mathematics as cultural knowledge (Bishop, 1988b) and as a human endeavor providing insight into various cultures from diverse communities (Swetz, 2009). Additionally, students can use these immersion experiences to develop their mathematical identities and sense of self as mathematicians, which is crucial to increasing motivation to learn mathematics and develop cultural competence (Yu et al., 2022).

Cultural immersion field experiences can also equip students with the skills to engage in hands-on problem-solving, eliciting critical thinking connected to workplace learning practices. Critical thinking skills can promote a deeper understanding of self that can shape one's personal and professional identity (Campbell et al., 2019; Reid & Dawes, 2022). Student success in mathematics, along with mathematics mindset, identity, and self-efficacy, can be used to make informed decisions about one's identity and sense of self (Hay, 2020). Furthermore, criticality can encourage individuals to question their ethics and critical moral agency (Zegwaard et al., 2017; Zegwaard & Pretti, 2023). A better understanding of how individuals see themselves as doers of mathematics with a critical responsibility can spark interest in mathematics-related career opportunities (Cribbs et al., 2021), increasing interest in mathematics in higher education.

While K-12 students can benefit from cultural immersion field experiences, so can preservice teachers by connecting relevant teaching and learning experiences (Doppen & Diki, 2017). Furthermore, it can be used to build inclusive and collaborative relationships with community partners to advance research and professional practice (Harfitt & Chow, 2018). Having mutually beneficial partnerships can build the capacity for networks between institutions, schools, and communities. Additionally, access to community expertise and resources can be used to guide culturally oriented mathematics instruction that fosters awareness of community contributions, creating more informed citizens. Thus, there is a need to prioritize cultural immersion field experiences in teacher education to prepare culturally competent and internationally minded teachers.

3 Steppingstone Stories from the Trenches

While understanding the existing literature to support cultural immersion field experiences is important, personal connections to the work can be informative. I had several opportunities to engage in cultural immersion experiences during my roles as a teacher and a teacher educator. I share my experience through a collection of three short stories. The first story recounts an experience from my graduate studies when I traveled to South Africa to study Ndebele beadwork, including the isometries present in the intricate art. The second story details my experience studying Gullah Geechee sweetgrass baskets and the mathematics explored in such work (e.g., counts of coiled rows, concentric circle patterns, bilateral and rotational symmetry). The third story provides insights into my current work engaging preservice teachers in cultural immersion field experiences in surrounding communities during mathematics methods courses.

I acknowledge that these stories were inspired by learning opportunities afforded to me as I began my teaching career. While in my graduate studies, I was privileged to engage in cultural immersion field experiences that offered work-integrated learning opportunities to study mathematics. I traveled to South Africa, Brazil, and Jamaica. These experiences challenged me to reflect on how I used mathematics and viewed mathematics as a cultural activity. I also used these experiences to develop cultural sensitivity and awareness toward others. My cultural immersion field experience in South Africa played a particular role in who I am today as a teacher and researcher in mathematics education (Moldavan, 2021). Next, I share how this immersion experience exposed me to the mathematics of Ndebele beadwork and the intricate geometric designs of jewelry, dolls, and clothing. I also report how I used my experience to enhance my mathematics instruction, mainly when teaching geometry to high school students.

4 Cultural Immersion in Indigenous Contexts

Studying mathematics in indigenous communities has been historically critiqued for marginalizing the contributions of those communities, especially in the context of mathematics as scientific knowledge (Chahine, 2011). Chahine (2013) attributes this historical deduction to a "limited view of what counts as mathematics on one hand and to a lack of understating of living indigenous practices on the other" (p. 2). Providing teachers with firsthand experiences to immerse themselves in indigenous cultures through work-integrated learning can encourage studying various mathematical ideas used in the daily practice of unconventional contexts. Furthermore, individuals can use these experiences to reflect on their lens and knowledge of mathematics, often grounded in Eurocentric pedagogical concepts reflective of colonizing practices that seep into the teaching and learning practices found in higher education institutes. As Arney (2022) and Dorasamy and Rampersad (2018) note, a critical lens is imperative for cultural immersion to advocate for a relational understanding to guide transformative experiences. Thus, when working with cultures different from one's own, it is essential to consider ways to create respect, responsibility, and reciprocity that will honor the Indigenous philosophies of ways of doing while also recognizing the need to give back and honor the communities that welcomed one (Ramji et al., 2021). Therefore, work-integrated learning experiences can guide

Fig. 1 Working alongside a Ndebele woman to weave a straw mat

learning goals and critical reflection (Buchanan et al., 2022) that challenges perceptions regarding indigenous mathematical knowledge, informs practice-based knowledge integrated into workplaces and formal learning settings, and develops a broader appreciation for culture across borders.

While engaged in my graduate studies, I participated in a course focused on teaching indigenous mathematical knowledge systems through cultural immersion in an indigenous context in South Africa (Moldavan, 2021). I visited Mapoch Ndebele Village, known for its community that still lives and practices its traditional ways of life (Powell, 1995). While in the village, I worked closely with the Ndebele women to study their daily practices, like weaving beads, mats, and baskets. Figure 1 depicts a photo of me learning how to weave a straw mat from a community member. She taught me how she weaves each straw strand between a colored string wrapped around a heavy weight like a battery. The string is woven using colored patterns and counts to create intricate designs similar to the mat we were sitting on. She shared how she can finish a doormat in about a day, but a larger mat may take up to a week.

The Ndebele women are also known for painting colorful, geometric murals on their village's homesteads. The murals' colors and patterns have symbolic meanings, often denoting the power and status within the home. The decorated homesteads also communicate ceremonies and announcements, such as marriage, grief, protests, and prayer. The symbolic art is typically made with paint pigments added to clay and cow dung. Thick black lines and bright colors create designs incorporating flowers, animals, and people, depicting stories passed down from generations, typically from mother to daughter. Figure 2 is an example of a painted mural with green and yellow razor blades painted on a homestead. Ndebele women also paint various canvases to share their stories, as seen in Fig. 3.

The paintings, beadwork, and other material artifacts revealed insight into tribal customs and traditions (Plummer & Chahine, 2014) and an understanding of how community members used mathematics. I learned from the Ndebele women that counting and patterns were vital in creating products to sell. Additionally, the Ndebele women needed to know how much their items were worth and make the necessary

Fig. 2 Murals painted on a homestead in the Ndebele village

Fig. 3 Two Ndebele women painting

monetary exchanges when selling their products. Figure 4 shows an example of a Ndebele woman creating beadwork to sell, and Fig. 5 shares some of her handmade products.

This cultural immersion taught me how to connect the observed beadwork with my teaching. When teaching high school geometry, I looked for real-life connections to teach rigid transformations, also known as isometries. I used sample bracelets made alongside the Ndebele women to relate the placement of beads in a strip pattern design to that on a Cartesian plane. A motif within the pattern could be analyzed using transformational symmetry rules. Concepts of translations, reflections, and rotations could be illustrated with the mathematical ideas inherent in Ndebele weaving artifacts while teaching about Ndebele heritage. My students were interested in learning about the Ndebele culture and the mathematics concepts studied.

Fig. 4 A Ndebele woman making a bracelet

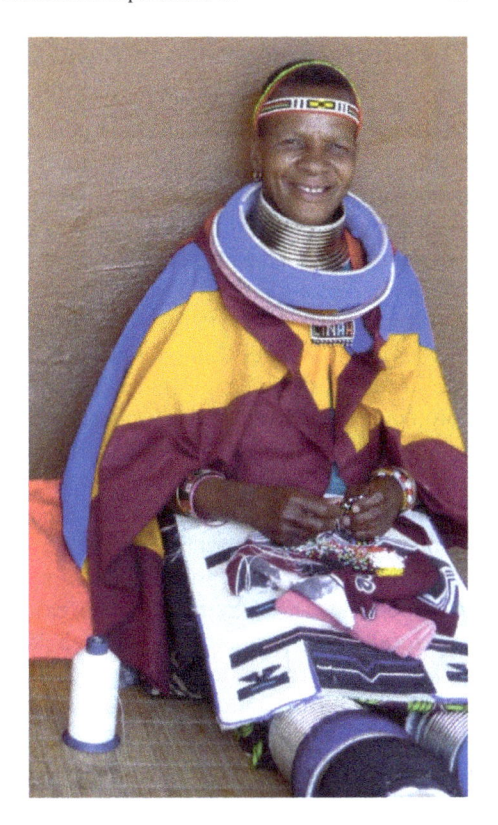

Fig. 5 Ndebele beadwork for sale on a straw mat

5 Cultural Immersion in Local Contexts

While immersion in international contexts made cultural connections new and exciting, I realized I did not have to travel far to learn about a new culture. During another graduate course, I had the opportunity to visit Charleston, South Carolina, where I was intrigued by the local marshes and how community members used materials gathered from the land (e.g., sweetgrass, pine needles, palmetto palm, bulrush) to make sweetgrass baskets. Through research, I learned that sweetgrass baskets were made by members of the Gullah Geechee community.

The Gullah Geechee Cultural Heritage Corridor stretches from Wilmington, North Carolina to Jacksonville, Florida along the eastern coast of the United States in the Lowcountry marshlands. The Gullah or "Geechee" community has preserved its traditions for nearly 400 years by sharing its Creole cuisine and artifacts made by the remaining 300,000 descendants of enslaved Africians from West Africa (Coakley, 2005; Cross, 2008). The Gullah inhabitants were known for bringing their rice farming skills to the coastal region. Their sweetgrass baskets were used as "fanners" to winnow rice, a process of tossing rice into the wind to separate the hull from the grain. Through time, Gullah weavers constructed baskets of different sizes for various uses, such as storing household items and food. Today, the sweetgrass baskets are used for similar purposes, but Gullah weavers also sell them to share their ancestral heritage and make a living. Figures 6 and 7 show examples of sweetgrass baskets and other accessories like palmetto roses, symbolizing everlasting love, made by Gullah weavers.

Fig. 6 Example sweetgrass baskets

Learning to Work, Working to Learn: Using Immersion Experiences … 21

Fig. 7 Palmetto roses in a sweetgrass basket

During my day's immersion experience in Charleston, South Carolina (Moldavan, 2020), I visited local markets and interviewed vendors along Highway 17 to learn about the sweetgrass baskets. I also took a sweetgrass basket-making class led by a Gullah weaver to show me the labor-intensive process of basketry (see Fig. 8). The class served as a work-integrated learning experience, providing an entry to active learning (O'Shea et al., 2022). I related the weaving artistry to my previous experiences working alongside the Ndebele women, linking similarities across the crafts. I used this experience to develop an appreciation for the Gullah weavers' critical thinking skills and artistic creativity. I also observed for myself the various ways they used mathematical ideas to engage in their cultural activity.

For instance, to start a sweetgrass basket, a weaver uses approximately four stalks of dampened pine needles to tie a center knot. This knot is then used as the center

Fig. 8 A Gullah weaver making a sweetgrass basket

point to add coiled rows. Next, a weaver gathers dried sweetgrass to bundle together and thread into the center knot with a "sewing bone," a filed metal spoon, fork, or nail. A thin palmetto palm is made to pass through the bundle to keep the grass tightly bound and eliminate holes in the basket. The palmetto palm's placement is typically a fingernail's length apart from the previously made pass. The angle of the palmetto palm can reveal the weaver's dominant hand, as an angle of northeast to southwest is made by a left-handed weaver and an angle of northwest to southeast is made by a right-handed weaver. The coloring and design found in the baskets reflect varying grasses (e.g., pine needles, bulrush) that are strategically "fed" into the bundle. After the weaver makes their desired sized base of the basket, the weaver begins to gradually stack the coils to "turn up" the sides of the basket, adding to the depth and the design. Decorative accents (e.g., handles, knots, lids) can also be added to the basket to enhance its design or add to its functionality. To plan for making the decorative accents, the Gullah weavers must count coiled rows, understand concentric circle patterns, and consider bilateral and rotational symmetry.

Learning the basketweaving process showed me how the Gullah weavers use mathematics to count coils, create patterns, add accents (e.g., handles, curves, ears, knots) using rotational symmetry, and calculate the "turning up" depth for volume requirements. These mathematical concepts can be used to address various geometry standards: drawing and identifying lines, angles, and shapes by their properties; identifying line-symmetric figures and drawing lines of symmetry; solving real-life and mathematical problems involving angle measure, area, surface area, and volume; and apply theorems about circles. Connecting these mathematical concepts to sweetgrass baskets offers students a unique opportunity to see mathematics in the intricate designs of the sweetgrass baskets, thereby developing a deeper understanding of mathematics and providing a glimpse into the history of the Gullah's weaving traditions and contributions.

6 Assigning a Cultural Immersion Mathematics Project

To understand mathematics as a cultural activity, it can be helpful for preservice teachers to study mathematics as it is used in real-life applications and cultural practices. When preparing for my elementary mathematics methods course, I looked at my assigned reading journal reflections and began wondering what more I could do to ensure my preservice teachers had experiences to guide more meaningful reflections that interested them and possibly related to their future students. I began considering a Cultural Immersion Mathematics Project that would encourage preservice teachers to study a culture different from their own and participate in an immersion field experience. I thought such an assignment might encourage preservice teachers to develop their understanding of mathematics and how it is used in unconventional contexts different from the ones they commonly interact with. It might also serve as a model for how they could engage their future students in understanding how mathematics is embedded in everyday life. I took the risk and eagerly developed the assignment's expectations.

When I first began conceptualizing the Cultural Immersion Mathematics Project, I reflected on my experiences in South Africa and the Gullah Geechee Cultural Heritage Corridor. Learning about how the community members of Ndebele and Gullah Geechee used mathematical ideas to participate in cultural activities would not be the same if only viewed through pictures or as text on paper. It was through visiting contexts and being actively immersed that the pictures and text would make sense and contribute to understanding the community members engaged in their practice. Therefore, such a project would need to ask participants to engage in active learning and observe their culture of choice but do so in a way where they would also have to interact with members of the culture. Participants would engage through active participation in an activity and see for themselves where mathematical ideas play a role in the activity. They would also engage in conversations with community members, understanding from an insider perspective how mathematics is a human endeavor shaped by cultural practices (Bishop, 1988a; Swetz, 2009). Thus, there was little way to observe passively during work-integrated learning.

When considering what to have my preservice teachers reflect on, I thought of the following elements:

1. Description of the Local Community
2. Active Observation and Participation
3. Connections to School Mathematics
4. Developing an Understanding of Mathematics as a Cultural Practice

I share my reasoning below to provide more context for what these elements would entail and why these elements are necessary components to consider in a cultural immersion project embedding ideas of work-integrated learning. For the details and prompts for the finalized Cultural Immersion Mathematics Project, see the Appendix.

6.1 Description of the Local Community

When asked to describe the local community, the preservice teachers had to clearly identify the population they studied. They were asked to reflect on how the culture of the population was different from their own, including descriptions of visible differences (e.g., race, dress, gender) and "invisible" differences (e.g., sexual orientation, beliefs). While describing the differences, they were also asked to note their perceptions of this population before going into this experience. Perceptions could include stereotypes and assumptions with recognition of who and what might have influenced their thoughts about this population. A statement addressing why they selected that particular population was also requested. The preservice teachers had to make a case for why they wanted to study the population in the local community and how this experience might help them learn more about students' cultural backgrounds. They were encouraged to share their concerns and ask for support if they perceived any challenges they might face while engaged in the learning experience.

It is also important to note that it would be necessary to help preservice teachers generate ideas for their cultural immersion. While some preservice teachers may have grown up in the university's surrounding community, some are from outside the state and the country. Encouraging preservice teachers to venture off their university grounds may place them in spaces they did not even know existed around them. However, when they enter surrounding schools to do their field experiences, they will need to be familiar with the communities where their students live. Thus, this cultural immersion field experience may provide an early entry point into local communities that preservice teachers will engage with as they continue their certification program. So, what are some contexts to consider for a cultural immersion project? I shared the following list to get preservice teachers thinking:

1. Historical organizations, museums, and parks
2. Community cultural events and meetings
3. Places of worship and religious studies
4. Charity events and mission shelters
5. Places of work and shared hobbies

While this list is not exhaustive of communities with shared cultural practices, it can be used as a starting point to familiarize oneself with different people and workplaces to immerse oneself. I also shared with my preservice teachers the importance of providing insight into who they are and their purpose in seeking entry into the community. Unfortunately, many communities that have been negatively critiqued, stereotyped, and "othered" may feel especially vulnerable when people who do not share a similar cultural identity wish to "study" their cultural practice. Moreover, while this is a learning opportunity for the preservice teachers, it might also be perceived differently by a community that may not know the purpose of the cultural immersion and how information learned may be disseminated to the public. Thus, I encouraged my preservice teachers to share the assignment with community members and ensure all aspects of the assignment's goals were made known. As guests in someone else's space, my preservice teachers had to consider ways to share information about themselves and create a safe space for community members to ask questions. They were expected to respect the privacy and anonymity of the community members and make the members aware of the respect for confidentiality.

6.2 Active Observation and Participation

As for reflecting on the active observation and participation element, the preservice teachers were asked to detail how they connected with the population and immersed themselves in the community. Notes could include how they learned about the community, including their research, and their correspondence with a community member to learn of upcoming meetings and events. This part of the project would encourage preservice teachers to study their interested community and interact with community members outside their comfort circles. Challenging oneself to engage with populations different from them can be intimidating, so this part of the project can help preservice teachers build confidence in their communication with different populations and develop their networking skills.

Once immersed in the community, the preservice teachers had to describe what they observed and did during their visit. In particular, the preservice teachers were asked to describe the culture of the community and how they saw mathematics used by community members in cultural activities and practices. If the use of mathematics was not apparent to them, they might have had to inquire through dialogue with community members. See Table 1 for sample cultural immersion dialogue questions that could be used or modified to guide conversations. Additionally, I reminded the preservice teachers that it was necessary to note whom they had conversations with within the community and what role that individual has in the community. Gathering this information can be insightful in learning about an individual's culture and the lens they bring to the shared information.

6.3 Connections to School Mathematics

As the preservice teachers continued to explore how mathematics played a role in their observed cultural activity, they were tasked with brainstorming ways to connect school mathematics content and standards to their work-integrated learning. The purpose of bridging this connection was to help preservice teachers recognize ways mathematics is used in real-life applications and, more specifically, to understand mathematics as a cultural activity. Since this assignment was shared with preservice teachers seeking elementary teacher certification, the connections to school mathematics were related to the content addressed in grades K–5. To help guide this element of the assignment, the preservice teachers could ask community members how school mathematics plays a role in their cultural activities and practices. Some of the questions noted in Table 1 could be referenced when speaking with community members to learn about their perspectives.

6.4 Developing an Understanding of Mathematics as a Cultural Practice

For the last element of this assignment, the preservice teachers were asked to reflect on how their understanding of mathematics as a cultural practice evolved through this assignment. Some considerations to guide this reflection include reflection on their perception and newfound knowledge of the cultural activities and practices of the

Table 1 Cultural immersion dialogue questions

General Cultural Wonderings

1. What cultural activities and practices are important to your community?
2. What cultural activity are you engaging with today?
3. What makes this cultural activity important to your community?
4. What historical events are associated with this cultural activity?
5. What are community members' views and attitudes toward this cultural activity?
6. Are there instances where this cultural activity has been stereotyped or discriminated against? How so, and what are these instances?
7. Is there another culture that engages in a similar cultural activity? How does this cultural activity differ from other similar cultural activities?

Mathematical Ideas in Cultural Activities and Practices

1. What are the attitudes and beliefs of mathematics to engage with community-related cultural activities and traditions?
2. How would you describe the use of mathematical ideas in this cultural activity?
3. What mathematical skills and strengths are needed to participate in this cultural activity?
4. How do community members view mathematics as essential to this cultural activity?
5. How do community members view themselves as mathematicians?

Cultural Connections to School Mathematics

1. What role does school mathematics play in the community?
2. What are common attitudes and beliefs toward school mathematics?
3. How do community members connect school mathematics to cultural activities and practices?
4. What concepts from school mathematics are needed to engage in cultural activities and practices?
5. What school mathematics skills are highly respected or needed? What skills are least respected or needed?

community. Reflecting on what was learned throughout this experience can influence future interactions with community members or other communities different from the preservice teachers' cultural backgrounds. Preservice teachers can consider what key information would help someone outside of the community relate to the culture of the community. The preservice teachers can compare how they now see their culture as similar and different from the community studied. They can also reflect on how this learning experience might be used to learn about students' cultural backgrounds.

6.5 Lessons Learned from My Preservice Teachers

This cultural immersion field experience showed me how a short, informal immersion can influence learning about local communities, including the mathematics practiced and how what was learned can be used to guide culturally oriented mathematics instruction. When I first presented the Cultural Immersion Mathematics Project to my preservice teachers, they expressed varying interests and concerns. While I had several preservice teachers who liked using this assignment to learn about a culture different from their own, the thought of immersing oneself in an unfamiliar culture rather than just reading a text or reviewing pictures provoked some anxiety. Immediately, some preservice teachers began to panic about what culture they would study. For instance, one preservice teacher noted, "When assigned this project, I was honestly stressed because I had no idea what other culture I would observe." Part of this panic was attributed to the preservice teachers concerned about the role of mathematics in cultural activities. Some preservice teachers began to share ideas about professions that require known mathematical skills, such as accountants, financial analysts, and engineers. While these are communities with known practices that use mathematics, I pushed my preservice teachers to think beyond commonly known professions that use mathematics to contexts where mathematics may not be as obvious, at least at this moment in time to them.

To guide planning and ease some anxiety, we began brainstorming historical organizations, museums, and parks in the university's surrounding community. The goal of looking into these places would be to provide research opportunities to learn about the community and network with members of those spaces. My university's setting is in Savannah, Georgia in the United States. Hence, there are many historical organizations (e.g., Georgia Historical Society, Coastal Heritage Society), parks (e.g., Forsyth Park, Wormsloe Historic Site, Bonaventure Cemetery), and museums (e.g., military, forts, railroad, maritime, historic architectural houses, gardens) with a rich history recognizing members of the community. These sites could be used to become familiar with local communities with historical ties to various cultures that inform present-day communities, events, and gatherings. We also thought of charity events and mission shelters (e.g., Old Savannah City Mission, Inner City Night Shelter) as well as places of worship and religious studies. Being a historic landmark along the eastern coast known for Georgia's largest port, Savannah is home to many historic places of worship (e.g., First African Baptist Church, Congregation Mickve Israel) and picturesque cathedrals (e.g., Cathedral of St. John the Baptist). Preservice teachers could explore these religious sites to learn about religious and cultural ties. Other ideas include visiting community cultural events (e.g., St. Patrick's Day Festival, Savannah Jewish Cultural Arts Festival, Savannah Music Festival), the Savannah College of Art and Design exhibitions, and local vendors in Forsyth Farmers' Market or along River Street.

Once the preservice teachers identified communities of interest, they had to think of the questions they would ask and the cultural activities they might engage in alongside community members. While there was some resistance to getting hands-on in spaces with people they did not know, the preservice teachers also liked the idea of getting out in the field, with a push from this assignment, to see mathematics used in non-school settings. Since work-integrated learning and cultural immersion field experiences can help preservice teachers draw upon cultural worlds to develop meaningful learning experiences (Smolcic & Katunich, 2017), such activities can be used to explore mathematics and better understand how mathematics is used in everyday practice. Furthermore, it allows preservice teachers to connect to school mathematics and students' cultural backgrounds to help them learn more about themselves and others.

Despite the brainstorming efforts to connect with various communities with organizational, religious, and mission ties, most preservice teachers immersed themselves in profession-related communities. The professions included electricians, pump specialists, chefs, estimators, and associates at home improvement stores, to name a few. These spaces provided opportunities for preservice teachers to explore professionals who use mathematics in ways many knew nothing about. While notes of how these professional spaces differed from spaces of familiarity and experience (e.g., daycares, educational organizations, schools), there were still links to knowing someone who helped them gain entry into the space. For instance, four preservice teachers contacted their spouses or family members (e.g., sister, father). Two other preservice teachers connected with neighbors and friends to visit them on the job. The other preservice teachers went to spaces they were already connected with in some way to learn about other cultural ties among community members. For instance, one preservice teacher was a server at a restaurant. She shared how she was unfamiliar with the kitchen side of the business, so she connected with the head chef to learn about running the kitchen, placing supply orders, and creating the restaurant's menu. It is important to note the preservice teachers' ties to the communities because it signifies the scaffolds and modifications needed when administering this assignment to encourage looking beyond profession-related communities. Next time, I plan to spend more time scaffolding research to support preservice teachers better as they investigate various communities. For instance, a list of contacts could be provided to help bridge the connection, or a list of questions that might be asked of the community members could receive feedback to build confidence, especially since little ties to friendly faces made entry into these spaces intimidating. Nevertheless, it is encouraging to note that the preservice teachers connected the communities they studied to their students. They discussed how these professions are common in some rural communities on the outskirts of Savannah, where they hoped to seek employment.

When reflecting on how mathematics played a role in the communities, the preservice teachers successfully made various observations. Two preservice teachers connected with head chefs. While one chef ran the kitchen at a popular restaurant along Savannah's River Street, the other ran a locally Black-owned bakery. The preservice teacher reported that the pastry chef shared how: "baking and pastries in her culture are staples when attending Sunday dinners, parties, funerals, and holidays. Recipes are passed down from ancestors that stem back to slavery, and her pie recipe is an example of a cultural dish." Both chefs shared with the preservice teachers how they had to plan for their products, such as the number of dishes and pastries. They used mathematics to determine the pricing of their food and the number of products needed to sell to be profitable. The preservice teachers examined recipe binders and the formulas to convert recipes to bulk orders. Measurements were also referred to when considering dish consistency, especially when measurements were noted on the menu (e.g., ounces of meat). When planning for mathematics tasks, one of the preservice teachers said they would help students make no-bake cookies and cut up desserts into fractions to help students gain a real-world understanding of the mathematics chefs use. The preservice teacher ended her reflection with the following:

> During this Cultural Immersion Mathematics Project, my understanding of mathematics as a cultural practice evolved because I never realized how much mathematics is incorporated into the kitchen. However, after talking with the chef, I realized that mathematics is one of the main reasons a bakery can run successfully. Before working on this assignment, I thought of mathematics as something we learn in school that we may use now and again. I now know that such things as "culinary math" and formulas are used in a bakery. There is so much more to mathematics and who uses it.

Similarly, two preservice teachers conducted their immersion experience with electricians. When discussing what interested one of the preservice teachers about the community, she said, "This community is different from mine because I am a wood builder and not an electrical builder, which is a space I could benefit learning from." She recounted how, in a conversation with the electrical builder, he shared that he used mathematics in almost every aspect of his work in the community. He mentioned pipe bending, measuring the lengths of wires and receptacles, and calculating amperages. He noted that pipe bending is typically done at 30°, 45°, and 90° angles. When creating a 45° angle, the offset must be 2 inches from the start of the pipe and the multiplicity 1.4 times from the starting point. He uses a measuring tape and calculator to calculate lengths, often adding and subtracting whole numbers and fractions. Mathematics is essential for him because it is necessary for electricity and safety. The preservice teacher used what she learned from the community to generate a mathematics task that considered community-related word problems, such as where to install meter bases, how to calculate the size of thermal heaters, and how to calculate amperage to ensure not overloading a circuit breaker. She noted, "Many students ask where they will use mathematics. Now, I have a job that can be referenced. This assignment makes me want to dig deeper into other careers and show students that mathematics has a purpose in life."

Another preservice teacher visited a lumber facility, where the culture of the community is to "produce as much lumber as necessary to create a profit without being wasteful." The preservice teacher shared how she talked with millworkers who specialized in cutting big timbers. They must determine how many logs are needed to create sellable lumber that meets shipping and buyers' expectations. Calculations often involve averaging log sizes and estimating how many board feet they can make by multiplying that average by the number of logs. While this preservice teacher expressed how this assignment helped her learn more about a family member's culture away from home, she also noted how she could have used more guidance to connect the mathematics observed to specific state standards and learning goals. She said:

> Usually, you see mathematical concepts presented and then have to connect them to real-life applications. This assignment challenged me to do the reverse, which I had little experience doing. I see why it is important for teachers to know how to do it because that makes mathematics more relevant to why you need to learn it and how to talk about it with your students.

Another preservice teacher visited a pump specialist that works with well drillers, farmers, and golf course owners to calculate irrigation needs. Mathematics is used to determine pump sizes, calculate gallons per minute in wells, and pump levels, to name a few. The preservice teacher used work-integrated learning to design a mathematics task targeting a fifth-grade volume-related standard using multiplication and addition operations to solve real-world problems. Students had to help a farmer with irrigation troubles. If the crops could not get the needed water to survive, food supplies would be reduced for the local community. Her mathematics problem addressed a submersible pump and the volume of water from a well needed to supply a specific crop area. The preservice teacher noted: "It is important for elementary students to understand how mathematics helps solve real-world problems, such as water irrigation for food. The more places students can see mathematics used, the more students can make connections between mathematics and their lives."

In speaking with a small family-owned construction company, another preservice teacher learned the role of an estimator. The preservice teacher targeted the community because she recognized that "the construction industry is a culture of its own. There are phrases used that only people in the construction industry know." She continued to note:

> In my culture, I use mathematics to measure food and buy groceries. I don't use it to build a house. As a homemaker, I can understand how to use a recipe to make a meal, but I don't understand how to read blueprints to build a house.

She learned how mathematics was used by an estimator who shared calculations with framing and siding crews. She created a mathematics task inviting the estimator to speak about his work and share example blueprints with students in her second-grade classroom. The students could look at the blueprints to help calculate materials using addition and subtraction. Furthermore, students would be asked to draw a picture of a room to meet length requirements. She could then discuss future connections in later grades with calculations involving perimeter. The preservice teacher shared, "I learned how mathematics is used in different professions like construction. Understanding mathematics is at the core of cultures' practice. Mathematics is more than being used in cooking and grocery shopping."

The last preservice teacher visited a home improvement store because she saw it as a cultural place shared by community members like her sister. However, she has not learned about her sister's community members, whom she describes as vital in making the store function and helping others with home improvement projects. She created a field trip experience for her mathematics task, as she found it important for students to visit these stores. During her upbringing, she had limited opportunities to visit stores like this one. She saw this field trip as an opportunity to get students out in the community and learn about places to work later in life. She created a handout for kindergarten students to reference as they toured the store. Students would have to count the shopping carts in the checkout lines. They would then visit the paint department and make comparisons of different-sized paint canisters. Students would predict which canisters held more paint and check for themselves. Students would then visit the appliance department and discuss how important measurements were to fit appliances in kitchen spaces. They would work with the associate to complete a mathematics problem calculating the cooktop size to fit inside a kitchen island. After the appliance department, students would visit the flooring department and predict how many tiles they would need to cover a sample floor space. They would then count the tiles to confirm their predictions. When the students returned to school, they would be asked to draw a picture of how they saw mathematics being used at the home improvement store. She would tell her students, "Mathematics is practiced all the time. We use the mathematics studied in school to help others in our community, just like the associates at the store."

The Cultural Immersion Mathematics Project encouraged preservice teachers to learn about their local communities. I knew assigning this assignment to my preservice teachers would generate mixed excitement and anxiety. The excitement centered around the opportunity to learn new skills and study a new culture through work-integrated learning. Those exhibiting anxiety were concerned with entering a new space, encountering "culture shock," and maybe being "othered" in the process. It is natural for someone to enter a new space, and in turn, that space causes them to become anxious, confused, and isolated. These opportunities challenge preservice teachers to become aware of their surroundings and ask about others, which are important skills to learn about their future students. They can use these experiences to adapt to unpredictable situations, solve problems, think critically, and respond to teachable moments.

When immersion experiences also introduce a new language, preservice teachers can learn the importance of non-verbal communication, body language, and visuals to aid with communication. Learning a new language requires overcoming language barriers, often limiting or preventing participation. Students entering communities that might not speak their native language may experience language barriers, and it is the responsibility of teachers to break down these barriers. What better way than to have one's own experience in a similar situation to reflect on? This also extends to learning customs and etiquette, which vary across cultures.

While I hoped this assignment would encourage preservice teachers to learn more about their community, I also hoped it would encourage personal growth. Understanding the importance of respect and appreciation toward culture is needed when learning about communities. The same applies to understanding the role of mathematics in cultural activities and practices. When preservice teachers can relate their cultural immersion experiences to school mathematics, mathematics learning becomes more relevant and meaningful for students. Students can also become more creative in connecting mathematics to daily practices.

The Cultural Immersion Mathematics Project allowed me to learn from my students and the local community. In thinking about my next steps, I wish to create an open repository of my preservice teachers' reflections and mathematics tasks so that others can benefit from learning about these experiences. I hope that having some examples to inspire future iterations of this assignment will enrich the received reflections and mathematics tasks. I also hope to study how preservice and in-service teachers use the resources to guide their mathematics tasks in the classroom. Findings from studied implemented resources will also guide modifications to the assignment's expectations so others can benefit in their contexts.

7 Leveraging Learning to Guide Work (Culturally Oriented Mathematics Instruction)

The work of a teacher must be meaningful for both the teacher and their students. In mathematics education, there is a need for rigor and relevance in student learning experiences connected to the curriculum (National Council of Teachers of Mathematics, 2014). Mathematics teaching and learning can (and should) go beyond the "typical" classroom. Cultural immersion field experiences can serve as a catalyst for work-integrated learning. While immersion can be done globally through international travel and study abroad programs, it can also extend to local contexts. Both opportunities prepare intercultural teachers (Smolcic & Katunich, 2017). This chapter recounted my journey in developing and becoming an intercultural mathematics teacher and teacher educator. As I close this chapter, I circle back to the guiding questions driving this work.

8 Cultural Immersion Field Experiences for Preservice Teachers

There are many reasons why engaging preservice teachers in cultural immersion field experiences is important. As a participant in cultural immersion field experiences, I had an opportunity to study my cultural identity and learn about others through active learning. I used these experiences to develop an understanding of intercultural issues and engage in critical thinking to reflect on my cultural awareness and sensitivity. Before these experiences, I had limited life experiences interacting in different cultural spaces. However, as a teacher, I knew I would need to use my experiences and skills to understand students' cultural backgrounds. It would be challenging to honor students' cultural backgrounds concerning the mathematics studied if I had limited intercultural competencies. The same applies to the preservice teachers I now work with as a teacher educator.

Providing cultural immersion field experiences for preservice teachers with the aid of a Cultural Immersion Mathematics Project, for example, offers a backdrop for preservice teachers to critically reflect on and reimage the role culture plays in mathematics. Furthermore, such experiences allow preservice teachers to study their cultural identities, privileges in particular spaces, and how their worldviews impact assumptions about others (Addleman et al., 2014). The preservice teachers shared positive experiences, expanding their cultural awareness through work-integrated learning. While it may have been uncomfortable at times to engage in a context as an "outsider," the sense of being an "outsider" could be used to empathize with students with culturally different backgrounds from the rest of the class or school. Such an experience can also encourage speaking to and learning from others and heightening one's sense of privilege in a community. Reflecting on one's privilege and observing how others perceive that privilege can help one understand how others are marginalized in systems (Brown et al., 2019). Such realizations can dismantle oppressive systems and attitudes, thereby recognizing one's ethics and critical moral agency (Zegwaard et al., 2017; Zegwaard & Pretti, 2023). While this assignment may need to be further modified to push preservice teachers to develop these realizations more deeply, it does encourage preservice teachers to consider cultural contexts about their future students and how such realizations can influence their beliefs, attitudes, and behaviors when considering the impact of their role as teachers. Through cultural immersion field experiences, those engaged are pushed to think critically and self-reflect, shaping one's personal and professional identity (Reid & Dawes, 2022). Individuals can become culturally competent professionals through self-reflection guided by experiential learning (Arthur & Achenbach, 2022; Canfield et al., 2009).

9 Understanding Mathematics as a Cultural Practice

While the Cultural Immersion Mathematics Project focuses on connecting mathematics to observed cultural activities and practices, the preservice teachers still develop intercultural awareness. They then use this awareness to inform their practice of teaching mathematics from a well-rounded worldview, thereby making connections that mathematics is a cultural activity and a global human endeavor (Bishop, 1988b; Swetz, 2009). Preservice teachers need structured learning opportunities to develop the skills to recognize, interact with, and understand mathematics as a cultural practice (Cobb & Hodge, 2007; Yu et al., 2022). While experiences abroad are great, they can also be designed at the local community level, making cultural immersion field experiences accessible to all.

10 Strategies to Promote Intercultural Competence and Advance Mathematics Instruction

The Cultural Immersion Mathematics Project was designed to offer opportunities for students to turn to their local communities to learn more about the mathematics around them. The communities studied were open and flexible to encourage a personalized and meaningful experience for the preservice teachers. With the open nature of the assignment, the preservice teachers had to research to learn about their local communities. Then, they needed to connect with community members to educate themselves about the community's cultural activities and practices. While some guiding questions were shared, the preservice teachers had to use intercultural skills to understand others and communicate their ideas effectively.

To support preservice teachers in developing their intercultural skills, they must have opportunities to engage in different cultural situations. It is through unfamiliar situations that they can comprehend and adapt their perspectives of different ideas (Wiest, 1998). Communicating with active listening, open-mindedness, and empathy can allow one to develop cultural competencies (Leung et al., 2014). Additionally, they can use these communication skills to develop confidence, resourcefulness, adaptability, and sense of initiative to learn about others, such as their students who share different cultural backgrounds.

Thus, to promote preservice teachers in developing their intercultural competence, teacher educators need to model instruction and design assessments that encourage responding to cultural connections. Some strategies that can be considered are as follows:

1. Activate prior experiences and perceptions to examine and critique cultural awareness and identity.
2. Make learning contextual and relevant.
3. Leverage the voices and experiences of community members to shape learning.
4. Use intercultural skills to build relationships and networks.
5. Recognize culture to inform culturally oriented instruction.

These strategies can be beneficial when cultural connections guide culturally oriented mathematics instruction. Although mathematics is integral to cultural activities and practices, linking mathematics to culture can be hard when connecting school mathematics (Brown et al., 2019). When presenting cultural immersion field experiences in teacher education, preservice teachers must be invited to participate alongside the community members to have hands-on experiences (rather than just observational experiences) while developing relationships with community members (Smolcic & Katunich, 2017). Preservice teachers must be challenged to share information about the community they engage with. In the context of mathematics education, preservice teachers must also be challenged to describe how they see mathematics being used in the community and reflect on how their understanding of mathematics as a cultural practice has evolved. Sharing these experiences in K-12 settings and teacher education can inform educational stakeholders of the impact cultural immersion field experiences have on teachers and students. To benefit from cultural immersion field experiences, strategic expectations of participation in such experiences must be made to integrate learning and practice. Doing so provides an example of how cultural immersion field experiences can serve as a catalyst for preparing teachers for the cultural challenges they may encounter during work-integrated learning experiences. Such experiences can also enhance culturally oriented mathematics instruction to develop a deeper understanding of mathematics through real-life applications. Thus, encouraging future teachers (and their future students) to engage in cultural immersion field experiences sets the foundation for using education to learn how to work in diverse settings, thereby supporting one's ability to learn about diverse cultures.

Appendix

Cultural Immersion Mathematics Project

You have an opportunity to learn more about the local community, paying particular attention to a distinctive culture different from yours and how community members use mathematics daily. You are asked to spend approximately 60 min participating alongside the community members, engaging in hands-on experiences and interactions (e.g., dialogue) to learn about cultural activities and how they use mathematics in their practices. In a 4–5 page reflection, you will reflect on the following:

Description of the Local Community

- Describe the local community visited and the population you engaged with.
- Include a rationale for why you selected that particular community and how its distinctive culture differs from yours. Include descriptions of visible differences (e.g., race, dress, gender) and "invisible" differences (e.g., sexual orientation, beliefs).
- Reflect on your perceptions of this population before going into this experience. Perceptions could include stereotypes and assumptions with recognition of who and what might have influenced your thoughts of this population.
- Make a case for why to study this population in the local community. Reflect on how this experience might help you learn more about students' backgrounds and ways of incorporating the backgrounds of local community members in your classroom. Be sure to note any perceived challenges you might face while engaged in this learning experience and ask for support if needed.

Active Observation and Participation

- How did you learn of and connect with the community and its members?
- What research did you do prior to your cultural immersion? What information is of critical importance to understanding the culture of the community?
- Describe the cultural activity you observed. How does the cultural activity represent the culture of the community?
- How did you actively participate with community members in the cultural activity? What conversations did you have, and with whom did you have these conversations?
- How did you see school mathematics being used by community members? How do the community members describe the "mathematics" they use? Does the "mathematics" described align with your idea of school mathematics?

Connections to School Mathematics

- How might you connect elementary mathematics content (grades K–5) to the mathematics observed in the cultural activity?
- What state standards and learning goals can be related to the cultural activity?
- What might be an example mathematics task that you could create to help students learn about the cultural activity connected to elementary mathematics content?

Provide a rough outline/description of the mathematics task. Be sure to note the associated state standards and learning goals.

Developing an Understanding of Mathematics as a Cultural Practice

- How has your understanding of mathematics as a cultural practice evolved through this assignment?
- How did your cultural immersion experience impact your perception of the cultural activities and practices of the community? How might this impact influence your future interactions with members of this community or other communities different from your cultural background?
- How do you now see your culture as similar and different from the explored culture of the community members?
- How might you use this learning experience to help you learn about students' cultural backgrounds?

References

Addleman, R. A., Nava, R. C., Cevallos, T., Brazo, C. J., & Dixon, K. (2014). Preparing teacher candidates to serve students from diverse backgrounds: Triggering transformative learning through short-term cultural immersion. *International Journal of Intercultural Relations, 43*, 189–200. https://doi.org/10.1016/j.ijintrel.2014.08.005

Arney, N. D. (2022). A relational understanding of learning: Supporting Indigenous work-integrated learning students. *International Journal of Work Integrated Learning, 23*(2), 153–167.

Arthur, N., & Achenbach, K. (2002). Developing multicultural counseling competencies through experiential learning. *Counselor Education and Supervision, 42*, 2–14.

Bishop, A. J. (1988a). *Mathematical enculturation: A cultural perspective on mathematics education*. Kluwer.

Bishop, A. J. (1988b). Mathematics education in its cultural context. *Educational Studies in Mathematics, 19*, 179–191. https://doi.org/10.1007/BF00751231

Brown, B. A., Boda, P., Lemmi, C., & Monroe, X. (2019). Moving culturally relevant pedagogy from theory to practice: Exploring teachers' application of culturally relevant education in science and mathematics. *Urban Education, 54*(6), 775–803. https://doi.org/10.1177/0042085918794802

Buchanan, S., Eady, J. J., & Dean, B. A. (2022). Exploring the importance of intentional learning goals on work-integrated learning placement. *International Journal of Work-Integrated Learning, 23*(1), 113–127. https://www.ijwil.org/files/IJWIL_23_1_113_127.pdf

Campbell, M., Russell, L., McAllister, L., Smith, L., Tunny, R., Thomson, K., & Barrett, M. (2019). A framework to support assurance of institution-wide quality in work-integrated learning. *Australian Collaborative Education Network*. https://research.qut.edu.au/wilquality/wp-content/uploads/sites/261/2019/12/FINAL-FRAMEWORK-DEC-2019.pdf

Canfield, B. S., Low, L., & Hovestadt, A. (2009). Cultural immersion as a learning method for expanding intercultural competencies. *The Family Journal: Counseling and Therapy for Couples and Families, 17*(4), 318–322. https://doi.org/10.1177/1066480709347359

Chahine, I. C. (2011). An ethnomathematical encounter: A cultural immersion of mathematics teachers in the daily practices of craftsmen in the Old City of Fez-Morocco. *International Study Group on Ethnomathematics Newsletter (ISGEm), 5*(2), 11–13.

Chahine, I. C. (2013). Mathematics teachers' explorations of indigenous mathematical knowledge systems through immersion in African cultures. *CEMACYC, I*, 1–10.

Coakley, J. V. (2005). *Sweetgrass baskets and the Gullah tradition.* Arcadia Publishing.
Cobb, P., & Hodge, L. L. (2007). Culture, identity, and equity in the mathematics classroom. In N. S. Nasir, & P. Cobb (Eds.), *Improving access to mathematics: Diversity and equity in the classroom* (pp. 159–171). Teachers College Press.
Cribbs, J., Huang, X., & Piatek-Jimenez, L. (2021). Relations of mathematics mindset, mathematics anxiety, mathematics identity, and mathematics self-efficacy to STEM career choice: A structural equation modeling approach. *School Science and Mathematics, 121*(5), 275–287. https://doi.org/10.1111/ssm.12470
Cross, W. (2008). *Gullah culture in America.* Blair Publishing.
Cushner, K., & Mahon, J. (2009). Intercultural competence in teacher education—Developing the intercultural competence of educators and their students: Creating the blueprints. In D. K. Deardorff (Ed.), *The SAGE handbook of intercultural competence* (pp. 304–320). SAGE.
Dorasamy, N., & Rampersad, R. (Eds.). (2018). *Critical perspectives on work-integrated learning in higher education institutions.* Cambridge Scholars Publishing.
Harfitt, G. J., & Chow, J. M. L. (2018). Transforming traditional models of initial teacher education through a mandatory experiential learning programme. *Teaching and Teacher Education, 73*, 120–129. https://doi.org/10.1016/j.tate.2018.03.021
Hay, K. (2020). What is quality work-integrated learning? Social work tertiary educator perspectives. *International Journal of Work-Integrated Learning, 21*(1), 51–61.
Leung, K., Ang, S., & Tan, M. L. (2014). Intercultural competence. *Annual Review of Organizational Psychology and Organizational Behavior, 1*, 489–519. https://doi.org/10.1146/annurev-orgpsych-031413-091229
Moldavan, A. M. (2020). Weaving geometry into sweetgrass baskets. *New York State Mathematics Teachers' Journal, 70*(3), 91–95.
Moldavan, A. M. (2021). Unraveling the mathematics of Ndebele beadwork: Transformations on an indigenous Cartesian plane. In I. C. Chahine & J. de Beer (Eds.), *Evidence-based inquiries in ethno-STEM research: Investigations in knowledge systems across disciplines and transcultural settings* (pp. 57–74). Information Age Publishing.
Moll, L. C., Amanti, C., Neff, D., & Gonzalez, N. (1992). Funds of knowledge for teaching: Using a qualitative approach to connect homes and classrooms. *Theory into Practice, 31*(2), 132–141. https://doi.org/10.1080/00405849209543534
National Council of Teachers of Mathematics (NCTM). (2014). *Principles to actions: Ensuring mathematical success for all.* NCTM.
O'Shea, M., Vitale, C., Spong, H., Boyer, D., & Hurriyet, H. (2022). Active learning through work-integrated learning frames exploring student and academic experiences. In J. Keengwe (Ed.), *Handbook of research on active learning and student engagement in higher education* (pp. 45–65). IGI Global.
Plummer, A., & Chahine, I. C. (2014). Mathematics lessons from "a place of light." *Mathematics Teacher, 108*(4), 254–257. https://doi.org/10.5951/mathteacher.108.4.0254
Powell, I. (1995). *Ndebele: A people and their art.* Cross River Press.
Ramji, K., Kines, L., Hancock, R. A., & McRae, N. (2021). Developing and delivering a culturally relevant international work-integrated learning exchange for Indigenous students. *International Journal of Work-Integrated Learning, 22*(3), 307–321.
Reid, L., & Dawes, T. (2022). Cultural identity transforming work-related learning. *International Journal of Work Integrated Learning, 23*(2), 323–333.
Sleeter, C. E. (2008). Preparing White teachers for diverse students. In M. Cochran-Smith, S. Feiman-Nemser, D. J. McIntyre, & K. E. Demers (Eds.), *Handbook of research on teacher education: Enduring questions in changing contexts* (3rd ed., pp. 559–582). Routledge and Association of Teacher Educators. https://doi.org/10.4324/9780203938690
Smolcic, E., & Katunich, J. (2017). Teachers crossing borders: A review of the research into cultural immersion field experience for teachers. *Teaching and Teacher Education, 62*, 47–59. https://doi.org/10.1016/j.tate.2016.11.002

Swetz, F. J. (2009). Culture and the development of mathematics: An historical perspective. In B. Geer, S. Mukhopadhyay, A. B. Powell, & S. Nelson-Barber (Eds.), *Culturally responsive mathematics education* (pp. 11–41). Taylor and Francis.

Wiest, L. R. (1998). Using immersion experiences to shake up preservice teachers' views about cultural differences. *Journal of Teacher Education, 49*(5), 358–365.

Yu, M. V. B., Hsieh, T., Lee, G., Jiang, S., Pantano, A., & Simpkins, S. D. (2022). Promoting Latinx adolescents' math motivation through competence support: Culturally responsive practices in an afterschool program context. *Contemporary Educational Psychology, 68*, 102028. https://doi.org/10.1016/j.cedpsych.2021.102028

Zegwaard, K. E., Campbell, M., & Pretti, T. J. (2017). Professional identities and ethics: The role of work-integrated learning in developing agentic professionals. In T. Bowen & M. T. B. Drysdale (Eds.), *Work-integrated learning in the 21st century*. International perspectives on education and society (Vol. 32, pp. 145–160). Emerald Publishing Limited. https://doi.org/10.1108/S1479-367 920170000032009

Zegwaard, K. E., & Pretti, T. J. (Eds.). (2023). *The Routledge international handbook on work-integrated learning*. Routledge.

Work-Integrated Learning and Self-directed Professional Learning in a Rural Setting: What Do Pre-service English FAL Teachers Need from Their Mentor Teachers?

Mosebetsi Mokoena and Tshepang J. Moloi

Abstract Work-integrated learning (WIL) is vital in preparing pre-service teachers to become competent, dynamic, and effective in the classroom. To realize this, initial teacher education (ITE) programmes and government policies such as the Minimum Requirements for Qualification in Teacher Education (MRTEQ) stipulate various competencies that pre-service teachers must embody and adhere to once they join the teaching profession. This requires universities to devise quality teacher education programmes that sufficiently and effectively prepare pre-service teachers to meet, adapt and cope with workplace demands. Supervision or mentoring of pre-service teachers by qualified and experienced in-service teachers in schools forms an integral part of work-integrated learning in many countries, including South Africa. Mentor teachers are expected to induct and introduce pre-service teachers to the realities of classroom teaching, work ethic, and the teaching profession in general. However, the voices of pre-service teachers remain largely neglected when determining the kind of support and identifying areas in which they need to be developed during WIL in schools. This situation compromises the aim and quality of WIL and pre-service teachers' abilities to undertake self-directed professional learning. Despite this, the research focusing on what pre-service teachers of English first additional language (English FAL) in a rural setting need from their mentors to enhance self-directed professional learning remains largely scant. By adopting the transformative paradigm, this chapter explores the developmental and pedagogical needs of pre-service English FAL teachers to enhance self-directed professional learning during WIL in schools. This qualitative study followed a convenience sampling and generated data through semi-structured interviews and focus-group discussion of eleven pre-service English FAL teachers in their third year of study towards a Bachelor of Education Degree (B.Ed.) at one rural university. An inductive approach to data analysis was followed. Framed within critical pedagogy; the study found that

M. Mokoena (✉)
University of the Witwatersrand, Johannesburg, South Africa
e-mail: mosebetsi.mokoena@wits.ac.za

T. J. Moloi
Cape Peninsula University of Technology, Mowbray Campus, Cape Town, South Africa

pre-service English FAL teachers have developmental and pedagogical needs. They need their mentor teachers to assist in the following areas: lesson planning, classroom management, learner-centered teaching, support and constructive feedback, and self-directedness.

Keywords English FAL · Mentor teachers · Rural schools · Self-directed professional learning · Work-integrated learning

1 Introduction

Continuous developments and rapid changes in the world of work have become common in the twenty-first Century. One noticeable change is the demographic diversity of teachers and learners in many schools across the globe. Teachers and learners from multicultural, multilingual, and multinational backgrounds occupy many classrooms in developing countries, such as South Africa. This situation calls on higher education institutions, such as universities, to offer initial teacher education (ITE) programmes that prepare pre-service teachers for the realities of a twenty-first-century school. While they equip them with skills to teach effectively, these programmes must be responsive to the needs of the pre-service teachers (Moosa & Rembach, 2018). To realize this, the South African government, through the Department of Higher Education and Training (DHET), introduced the Minimum Requirements for Qualification in Teacher Education (MRTEQ). The policy document spells out the areas in which newly qualified teachers must be competent. This aligns with a need to develop dynamic, flexible, and knowledgeable teachers in South African schools (DBE, 2011; Moosa & Rembach, 2018).

It is, therefore, important for ITE programmes to be aligned with the prescripts of MRTEQ. To this effect, pre-service teachers are expected to attend teaching practicum (TP) as part of the work-integrated learning (WIL) experience (DHET, 2015). Zegwaard et al. (2023) describe WIL as an approach to developing and empowering pre-service teachers. These teachers are often placed in schools that provide adequate training and mentoring. Effective mentoring by mentor teachers (in-service teachers) is significant for developing pre-service teachers and the success of WIL programmes (Du Plessis, 2013; Winchester-Seeto et al., 2016). Through mentoring, in-service teachers can induct and expose student-teachers to the realities of classroom teaching, work ethic, and the teaching profession in general (Moosa & Rembach, 2018). In addition, mentor teachers play a pivotal role in supporting pre-service teachers' emotional and identity development (Du Plessis, 2013).

Although mentoring plays such an important role in teacher development, pre-service teachers, such as those of English FAL, continue to experience challenges during TP. The blurring of expectations and roles features predominantly in WIL pedagogy. University lecturers and mentor teachers hold diverging views regarding the roles and expectations of pre-service teachers in schools. Similar observations are common between mentors and pre-service teachers (Moosa & Rembach, 2018). In some instances, the roles of all these stakeholders remain mismatched (Winchester-Seeto et al., 2016). In other instances, limited resources for effective mentoring, especially in rural schools, add to the problems (Muyengwa & Jita, 2021). Moreover, Dlamini (2018) argues that pre-service teachers are inadequately prepared to teach in rural schools.

Without intervention, various studies caution about the negative impact of this misalignment on pre-service teachers' WIL experience and the quality of ITE programmes (Dlamini, 2018; Du Plessis, 2013; Moosa & Rembach, 2018). This situation compromises the aim and quality of WIL programmes and pre-service teachers' abilities to undertake self-directed professional learning. Despite the urgency to address these challenges, Winchester-Seeto et al. (2016) point to the scarcity of research that aims to enhance understanding of the stakeholders' roles and expectations during TP. In addition, research focusing on what pre-service teachers of English FAL in a rural setting need from their mentors to enhance self-directed professional learning remains largely scant.

This chapter addresses these gaps by exploring the areas in which English FAL pre-service teachers in a rural setting need to be developed to enhance self-directed professional learning during WIL. In our view, the voices of pre-service teachers remain largely neglected when determining the kind of support and identifying areas in which they need to be developed during WIL in schools. We argue that this critical task is often delegated to other stakeholders such as universities, faculties, and mentor teachers. From pre-service teachers' perspectives, the chapter challenges this bureaucratic approach to WIL by posing the question: What do pre-service English FAL teachers need from their mentor teachers to enhance self-directed professional learning during WIL? This question informs the study's overall objective: to explore the developmental and pedagogical needs of English FAL pre-service teachers in a rural setting to enhance self-directed professional learning during WIL. Exploring issues from pre-service teachers' perspectives may help alleviate confusion, lack of sense of belonging, and unmet developmental and pedagogic needs that they often experience during WIL in rural schools.

The chapter is structured in the following manner: First, there is a review of the literature regarding work-integrated learning, self-directed professional learning, and the student voice. Next, the theoretical framing for this study is discussed. The research questions and methodology follow the discussion. After that, the findings and discussion are presented. Conclusion and recommendations are provided after the discussion on the implications of this study.

2 Understanding Work-Integrated Learning

Since its genesis in the early 1900s in the United States (US), work-integrated learning (WIL) continues to enjoy widespread recognition and use worldwide. The popularity of this approach lies in its emphasis on applying and integrating theory and practice

(Zegwaard et al., 2023). According to McRae and Johnston (2016), gaining work-related experience in a workplace environment, integrating academic and workplace learning, and developing skills applicable to the workplace are some of the critical features of the global WIL framework. For Groenewald (2007), the effective implementation of WIL requires that structured learning, appropriate job-related training, and other job-related learning opportunities be available in the workplace. Moreover, this means that different organizations are required to ensure supportive relationships, promote autonomous and aided learning and practicing, encourage conceptual and reflective practices, and facilitate the mastery of skills through activities that encourage reflection and constructive feedback (Bogo, 2015; Hay, 2020). Generally, WIL helps students develop generic and work-related skills. Also, participating in WIL improves students' confidence and ability to navigate academic and career directions (Khampirat et al., 2019). Furthermore, WIL improves students' cognitive skills and problem-solving abilities. Additionally, it improves students' competence and assists them in developing specialized and professional knowledge (Van Vuuren, 2020). In their study, Dressler and Keeling (2004) categorize the benefits of WIL. As an academic benefit, students exude increased knowledge of the discipline or subject matter. Noticeable improvement in communication skills and willingness to take the initiative illustrates personal growth. Students also gain professional identity from WIL while they simultaneously develop positive work values and ethics. Jackson et al. (2023) add that through WIL, students gain experience and professional socialization, enhancing their employability chances.

Although there is no universal definition of WIL (Zegwaard et al., 2023), attempts have been made to describe WIL in ITE programmes in many universities worldwide. It has been used as an overarching term to describe pre-service teachers' performance and completion of work-related tasks (Varty & Sovilla, 2023). In some instances, WIL has been defined as an educational approach aiming to expose pre-service teachers to occupational learning and link this to authentic workplace practices (Du Plessis, 2015). In other instances, it has been described as a practicum involving workplace learning in which pre-service teachers immerse for a specific period while mentored by an experienced mentor teacher (DHET, 2011). For instance, a four-year education programme requires pre-service teachers to immerse themselves in WIL programmes for over 30 weeks to obtain a teaching qualification (DHET, 2015). Successful implementation of WIL in the field of education needs to meet several requirements. WIL programmes must form part of the curricula presented at HEIs. In other words, WIL activities must be inherent requirements for a student to obtain a teaching qualification. The learning context in which pre-service teachers participate in WIL must be schools. In the end, pre-service teachers are expected to familiarize themselves with the realities of the classrooms in which they are expected to teach (DoE, 2007). These are the right places where they can link and put theory and knowledge into practice in real-time. While at schools, pre-service teachers must perform and practice relevant tasks and activities that form a core part of the teaching profession (Zegwaard et al., 2023).

WIL features predominately in the curricula of HEIs because it facilitates students' transition from these institutions to the workplace (Khampirat et al., 2019;

Schonell & Macklin, 2019). The WIL programmes have since become integral to (ITE) programmes (Jagals, 2020; Wang et al., 2023). The inclusion of these programmes comes as a response to the perception that the ITE programmes offered at universities and colleges have largely remained theoretical and, at times, obscured by the realities and demands of the workplace. The WIL programmes also integrate classroom learning and workplace application (Matoti & Junqueira, 2012; Rowe & Zegwaard, 2017). In other words, they empower pre-service teachers to link theoretical learning from the lecture halls to applying authentic work-focused tasks (lesson planning, lesson instruction, classroom management, etc.), requirements, and practices (Zegwaard et al., 2023). Participation in these programmes assists education students (pre-service teachers) in developing the necessary competencies to become effective teachers (Singh & Mahomed, 2013).

In the South African context, WIL operates within several policy and organizational frameworks. The MRTEQ (2018) policy spells out the types of knowledge critical for teachers' competency and professional development (DHET, 2018). These include disciplinary knowledge, pedagogic, practical, fundamental, and situational learning (DHET, 2015). As a result, the learning-in-practice component features prominently in many WIL programmes in South African universities. In this regard, pre-service teachers participate in structured, supervised, and formally assessed school-based activities for a specified period (Van Vuuren, 2020). The South African Council for Educators Act (Act no. 31 of 2000) prescribes the professional teaching standards that in-service and pre-service teachers must adhere to (SACE, 2018). These involve regulating the conduct of these teachers in relation to learners, colleagues, and other stakeholders in the field (SACE, 2018). Similarly, the National Education Policy Act (1996) outlines specific roles and competencies of teachers (Republic of South Africa, 1996). It is, therefore, important to design WIL programmes that prepare pre-service teachers, such as English FAL teachers, to perform these roles and uphold high professional teaching standards.

3 Preparing Pre-service English FAL Teachers in the Context of Rurality

In the context of education, WIL takes the form of teaching practice to enable pre-service teachers to gain skills and competencies over a specified period ranging from weeks to over three months (Omodan, 2022). These teachers are expected to attend and apply the theoretical knowledge to an authentic classroom situation (Dube et al., 2021). During this period, they also engage learners in differentiated instruction, higher-order learning and critical thinking (Mafugu, 2022). However, pre-service teachers face a myriad of challenges during teaching practice, especially in rural communities and schools (Omodan, 2022). In many cases, these challenges are serious and severe for pre-service teachers in rural contexts compared to their urban counterparts (Mitra, 2018). It is important to note that South Africa is said to have a dual system of education. One is characterized by abundant resources, adequate infrastructure, qualified teachers, and good-performing learners. The other consists of poorly resourced, underdeveloped, understaffed schools and overcrowded classrooms. This dichotomy indicates the vastness of the school contexts in which pre-service English FAL teachers are expected to engage in WIL programmes (Van Vuuren, 2020).

Considering the latter system of education, it is critical to understand the challenges faced by learners who pre-service English FAL teachers are expected to teach during teaching practice. The majority of these learners are not proficient in the English language. In other words, they also struggle to develop oral and academic proficiency (Bravo & Cervetti, 2014). According to Cummins (1983, 1996), language proficiency can be categorized into Basic Interpersonal Communicative Skills (BICS) and Cognitive Academic Language Proficiency (CALP). Learners in rural schools often perform poorly and possess inadequately developed language skills (Van der Merwe, 2022). For instance, speaking remains underdeveloped in many English FAL classrooms resulting in learners who struggle to express themselves (Dincer & Yesilyurt, 2017; Mthembu et al., 2021). Besides speaking, learners in English FAL classrooms struggle with reading and writing (Mhlongo et al., 2018). The latest results of the Progress in International Reading and Literacy Study (PIRLS, 2021) reveal that 81% of learners in the 4th Grade fail to read for meaning (Mullis et al., 2023). In other cases, they read below grade level due to in-service and pre-service teachers' ineffective reading comprehension instructional practices in English FAL classrooms (Olifant et al., 2023). Moreover, learners' writing skills remain underdeveloped, thus affecting their writing proficiency (Mhlongo et al., 2018; Ngubane et al., 2020).

Similarly, pre-service English FAL teachers from rural backgrounds bring challenges to teaching practice. The majority of them are non-native speakers of English, and this affects their exposure to the English language and their proficiency in the language (Suryasa et al., 2017). As a result, they possess limited communication skills that impede them from acquiring WIL competencies (Dwesini, 2017). In their study, Mncube et al. (2021) report teachers' difficulty in expressing themselves in English. Van der Merwe (2022) reports that pre-service teachers also struggle with teaching strategies and lesson design. Learners' backgrounds limit teachers' use of English during the lessons (Mncube et al., 2021). They also face challenges with learning from their mentor teachers and understanding the main aspects of language teaching. Finally, the pre-service English FAL teachers face difficulties understanding how learning occurs in the classroom. It is not unexpected that pre-service teachers of English FAL are generally less satisfied with their WIL experiences (Schonell & Macklin, 2019).

Amid these challenges and shortcomings, developing specific skills and competencies is critical for pre-service English FAL teachers to succeed in WIL programmes (Gribble et al., 2017). This makes mentoring an integral part of WIL activities in many universities (Mahomed & Singh, 2022; Wang et al., 2023). Producing pre-service teachers who are responsive to the learning needs of rural learners makes mentoring by experienced teachers appropriate and relevant for WIL programmes

(Mentz & De Beer, 2020). Mentor teachers are regarded as subject specialists whose mentoring focuses on lesson preparation, facilitation and assessment of learning, and classroom management (Matoti & Junqueira, 2012). Kram (1985) adds that mentor teachers provide career-related and psycho-social support to pre-service teachers. For this to happen, it is essential for pre-service teachers and mentor teachers to build a positive relationship during WIL. Pre-service teachers find this kind of relationship helpful in developing WIL skills (Singh & Mahomed, 2013; Wang et al., 2023). For instance, the study by Matoti and Junqueira (2012) reveals improvement in the classroom management skills of pre-service teachers who relate positively with their mentor teachers. The success of this relationship largely depends on the mentor teachers' approachability, accessibility, knowledge, communication and listening skills, confidence, commitment, attitude and genuine care for the pre-service teachers (Singh & Mahomed, 2013). In their study, Shapley and Bush (2000) summarize the main functions of mentoring in educational and WIL contexts. These include providing support to enable pre-service teachers to cope with the demands of the teaching profession, supporting pre-service teachers' pedagogical development, and promoting the retention of these teachers. Additionally, mentoring enhances the pre-service teachers' application of theory to teaching practice, thus, developing practical teaching skills (Ngibe et al., 2019; Singh & Mahomed, 2013). Moreover, pre-service teachers often view their mentors as role models who help them navigate the realities of the classroom environment (Smith-Rug, 2014). The findings of Castañeda-Trujillo and Aguirre-Hernández's (2018) study indicate that mentor teachers enhance pre-service English FAL teachers' sense of awareness in the school environment.

However, in South Africa, the urban–rural divide affects the quality of mentoring pre-service English FAL teachers receive (Mahomed & Singh, 2022). In this regard, Robinson (2015) avows that pre-service teachers receive poor mentoring during WIL in rural schools. In their respective studies, Ramsaroop and Gravett (2017) and Nkambule and Mukeredzi (2017) allude to mentor teachers' reluctance and unwillingness to mentor the pre-service teachers. Van Vuuren (2020) highlights the HEIs' failure to appoint appropriate mentors as another factor hindering effective mentoring and assessment of pre-service teachers during WIL. This author further opines that the inaccessibility and seclusion of the areas in which some rural schools are located often deter other HEIs' stakeholders from mentoring pre-service teachers effectively during WIL. Besides, the lack of clear communication between HEIs and rural schools about mentor and pre-service teachers' roles and expectations exacerbates these challenges (Mahomed & Singh, 2022).

Despite the challenges, undertaking WIL in rural contexts also ignites the pre-service teachers' passion for gaining knowledge, understanding and capacity to work with rural communities (Green et al., 2022). In addition, immersing these teachers in rural experiences equips them with the ability and skills to teach in varying educational contexts instead of only teaching in the so-called elite schools (Taylor, 2019). After developing these skills, they might be interested in assuming teaching posts in rural schools; thereby alleviating the challenges of teacher shortages that often plague these schools. In this case, Miller (2012) affirms that rural schools often view pre-service teachers' exposure to and immersion in rural experiences favorably during recruitment. Furthermore, exposure to these experiences also helps to lessen the feelings of professional and personal isolation after accepting permanent appointments as teachers of English FAL in rural schools (Cuervo & Acquaro, 2018).

In summary, WIL and mentoring equip pre-service teachers with the skills to transfer theoretical knowledge from the lecture hall to the real classroom. By their nature, WIL and mentoring provide temporary support to the pre-service teachers in their journey to becoming dynamic and competent teachers of English FAL. While engaging in WIL programmes, they are expected to initiate activities to augment their learning and WIL competencies as part of their professional development. This makes self-directed professional learning (SDPL) another integral part of WIL programmes in educational contexts (Petersen et al., 2020).

4 Locating the Nexus Between WIL and Self-directed Professional Learning

The teaching profession and professional development are inseparable. As a result, starting from the pre-professional age, a teacher's life involves participating in a series of developmental programmes and initiatives (Sariyildiz, 2017). Gebhard (2009) distinguishes two perspectives that dominate the discourses on teacher development programmes, such as teaching practice (WIL). On the one hand, the training perspective focuses on equipping the pre-service teachers with specific skills, techniques, and behaviors they must master. Creation and provision of opportunities that enable pre-service teachers to decide, learn and reflect on their decisions about their teaching philosophies and practices remain central to the developmental perspective. Similarly, Sawyer (2001) explains that a deficit approach, which emphasizes pre-service teachers' content knowledge, has since been superseded by a technical approach that advocates for school-based professional development (WIL). To affirm this, Richards and Farell (2005) observe a shift in teacher development and professional learning in HEIs towards self-directed approaches, such as self-directed professional learning (SDPL).

Therefore, by participating in teaching practice (WIL), pre-service teachers can engage and reflect on their learning as future professional teachers (Thabane, 2022). Although the WIL programmes in which pre-service teachers participate appear organized and tailor-made by HEIs, it is critical for the pre-service teachers to direct and facilitate their development and professional learning (Slavit & McDuffie, 2013). According to researchers (Garrison, 1997; Mushayikwa & Lubben, 2009), self-directed professional learning (SDPL) has occurred naturally in ITE programmes, such as WIL, for quite some time. In the WIL context, SDPL requires pre-service teachers to initiate the means to achieve mastery of WIL competencies. This involves having the ability to set learning goals independently, a desire to achieve the goals, and an open mind to accept support from others in the school environment (Bhatt, 2021). Furthermore, effective SDPL demands that pre-service teachers are able to plan, practice, and engage in self-monitoring and assessment (Thabane, 2022) throughout WIL. Shurr et al. (2014) outline several steps of SDPL. Conducting a self-assessment is the first step in the SDPL process. In other words, pre-service teachers need to assess their skills and abilities during WIL. This assists them in identifying the competencies they may need further development. After this, evaluating self-assessment and determining objectives becomes critical. Here, the pre-service teachers devise plans to address the challenges related to the WIL competencies. Recruiting support follows. In this case, the pre-service teachers reach out to the mentor teachers for support and guidance. Then, pre-service teachers review the initial goals and monitor their progress towards achieving the desired competencies. In addition, appropriate adjustments are made where necessary. Finally, towards the end of the WIL programme, the pre-service and mentor teachers review and acknowledge success and improvement in the teaching competencies due to self-directed professional learning.

The intersection between WIL and SDPL benefits pre-service teachers in several ways. Integrating WIL and SDPL enables pre-service teachers to gain confidence, build skills, and reflect on the progress towards attaining the essential competencies (Khampirat et al., 2019; Thabane, 2022). Through school, community, and universal reflections, SDPL improves WIL in several ways. Pre-service teachers engage in systematic self-reflection at the school level, focusing on their capabilities, content, and pedagogical knowledge gained from HEIs. This type of reflection involves pre-service teachers' identifying and recognizing the competencies that require improvement and devising the strategies to address these challenges. Community-based reflection requires pre-service teachers to build, sustain, maintain and strengthen the relationship with community members. At the universal level, pre-service teachers reflect on their relationship with national and international colleagues in the field (Shurr et al., 2014).

Also, both WIL and SDPL are critical in sustaining and enhancing pre-service teachers' learning in ITE programmes (Mushayikwa & Lubben, 2009). Besides improving the quality of education (Bhatt, 2021), WIL and SDPL regard pre-service teachers' willingness to take the initiative as central to professional development and growth (Mushayikwa & Lubben, 2009; Shurr et al., 2014). In this case, pre-service teachers identify their learning needs, devise various strategies, identify resources, and evaluate or attain professional development during WIL activities. During these activities in the contexts of WIL and SDPL, mentor teachers guide, motivate and instill confidence in the pre-service teachers (Slavit & McDuffie, 2013). In addition to empowering the pre-service teacher with knowledge, WIL and SDPL assist in reducing the mismatch between the expectations, roles, learning activities, and teacher classroom practice (Mushayikwa & Lubben, 2009). Ultimately, this nexus between WIL and SDPL enhances pre-service teachers' sense of ownership of the professional development process (Maw et al., 2021).

Without incorporating SDPL in the WIL activities, pre-service English FAL teachers cannot explore various ways of developing professionally (Castañeda-Trujillo & Aguirre-Hernández, 2018). Azano and Stewart (2015) lament the limited research on preparing pre-service teachers for rural schools in their study. Without an intervention, Eckert and Petrone (2013) warn about pre-service teachers' increased chances of perpetuating the deficit views of rurality and rural people. On the contrary, SDPL has been found to create a platform for teachers in deprived (rural) contexts, such as pre-service English FAL teachers, to have a voice in and take control of their professional development. It exposes and prepares them for the real complexities of English teaching (Castañeda-Trujillo & Aguirre-Hernández, 2018), especially in rural contexts. This may be important in reducing high teacher attrition and reluctance to work in rural schools (Kadel, 2023). This is also important because pre-service English FAL teachers face continuous challenges when engaging in WIL and SDPL. Often mentor teachers are unprepared and unavailable to offer much-needed guidance (Mafugu, 2022).

Ultimately, WIL aims to facilitate pre-service teachers' transition from HEIs to vastly diversified school contexts. According to Wolhuter (2016), about 80% of South African schools are considered dysfunctional. To function effectively in this category of schools, pre-service English FAL teachers need support to engage in SPDL after obtaining a teaching qualification at HEIs (Petersen et al., 2020). According to Kennedy (2016), due to intense scholarship, the theoretical basis for understanding how students learn has been established. However, the reverse is true about understanding how teachers (including pre-service teachers) learn. For instance, understanding how pre-service English FAL teachers need to be supported during WIL for the purposes of SDPL remains unexplored (Green et al., 2022). In most cases, external stakeholders such as universities, faculties, university supervisors, and mentor teachers often assume their developmental needs. This often results in the pre-service English FAL teachers' struggle to adapt to the realities of language teaching, decide on suitable pedagogic practices, and ultimately respond to the learning needs of learners in rural contexts (Mncube et al., 2021).

To address these challenges, researchers (Anjum et al., 2023; Castañeda-Trujillo & Aguirre-Hernández, 2018; Thabane, 2022) accentuate the need to include the voices of pre-service teachers not only to empower them but also to facilitate their success in directing their professional development.

5 Positioning the Student Voice in Teacher-Professional Learning

Despite its recent prominence in HEIs globally, student voice remains a nebulous and slippery concept with unclear origins (Cook-Sather, 2006). Seale (2014) laments the weak conceptualization of student voice in these institutions. To date, there is no universally accepted definition of this term (Cook-Sather, 2006). However, several attempts have been made to explain student voice in the educational context. Bovill et al. (2011) refer to student voice as a theory and practice which intends to enable students to become agents who actively participate in the analysis and revision of curricula and educational practice. In the definition of this term, Mitra (2008) alludes to students' control of the curriculum and the ability to express their thoughts about classroom instruction and pedagogy. Other researchers (Baroutsis et al., 2016; Conner, 2022) associate having a voice with students' active engagement and participation in decision-making processes concerning power relations, educational policies, and autonomy in their learning environments.

Active participation is a critical component of the student voice in HEIs. It moves the student voice beyond being listened to by authorities, including university educators and school mentor teachers (Hopkins, 2014). Listening to students must lead to developing a partnership between pre-service teachers and these authorities (Kidd, 2012). Moosa and Rembach (2018) opine that listening to pre-service teachers enhances the stakeholders' understanding of students' mentoring experiences during WIL. Through active participation, the student voice also transcends the simplistic practice of venting frustrations to the authorities (Mitra, 2008). On the contrary, it involves acknowledging students' capacity and power to make choices and influence decisions (Cook-Sather, 2014). In this regard, active participation through student voice empowers pre-service teachers to initiate and influence the discourses around curriculum change, adaptation and delivery (Strydom & Loots, 2020). In this regard, Warwick et al. (2019) assert that it is important to ensure that students' views are considered and implemented-that their impact in effecting fundamental changes is evaluated. To achieve this, students are taken through dialogue, reflection and discussion in which they participate actively as co-researchers with a significant voice (Fielding & McGregor, 2005).

Furthermore, Hart (1992) proposes the ladder of participation model to describe how students can initiate, take action, and participate in decision-making through student voice. Student voice and participation are represented in the eight rungs of the ladder. The high tokenism levels make student voice and participation non-existent in the first three rungs (Baroutsis et al. (2016). In other words, pre-service English FAL teachers comply with the pre-scripts of WIL programmes without any challenge. In cases where they may attempt to challenge the views of university educators and mentor teachers, their ideas are often neglected. In rungs four and five, students are dictated to, and they do not control the decision-making process. In other words, pre-service English FAL teachers' influence on decision-making remains minimal. This means their 'voice' is simply 'heard' without any impact on WIL pedagogy and programmes; thus, their participation remains limited. Increased levels of participation and student voice characterize the remaining three rungs. Student-initiated and led actions with shared decision-making are central to rungs seven and eight (Hart, 1992). Pre-service English FAL teachers engage in self-initiated activities and share ideas about their professional learning with university educators and mentor teachers. According to MacBeath et al. (2003), it is important to recognize students' learning experiences and solicit student voices about their experiences. This helps to empower pre-service teachers and enhances student–teacher relationships (Conner, 2022).

Student voice in HEIs benefit students in several ways. It enhances conditions to enable students to engage in learning. Through student voice, effective lesson design is likely to occur in good learning environments (Geer & Sweeney, 2012). These environments give students a sense of belonging and recognize them as competent individuals with the abilities and awareness to effect fundamental changes in educational programmes (Mitra, 2004). During WIL programmes, pre-service English FAL teachers collaborate with university educators and mentor teachers to address challenges affecting their professional development (Mitra, 2008). This collaboration transforms teacher professional learning, and pre-service teachers become critical of the educational practice (Cook-Sather, 2018; Mayes et al., 2021; Treacy & Leavy, 2023). Treating students as partners in learning results in them receiving the appropriate support during WIL activities (Robinson & Taylor, 2007).

Mitra and Gross (2009) report high levels of motivation and engagement when students 'have a voice'. This positively impacts pre-service teachers' academic and developmental outcomes (Mitra, 2018). The development occurs when students' voices and experiences are interrogated in educational and teacher-professional learning programmes (Mockler & Groundwater-Smith, 2015). Collecting and recognizing experiences enhance university educators' and mentor teachers' understanding of how students learn and areas in which they need to be supported during WIL (Robertson, 2017). According to Kidd (2012), student voice makes pre-service teachers appreciate the value of listening. In turn, they gain the confidence, knowledge and skills to support learners once they assume teaching positions in schools (Enright et al. (2017).

Although student voice proves beneficial, it is often received unfavorably in educational settings. At HEIs, the student voice is often perceived negatively and received with negative attitudes by the authorities (Tuhkala et al., 2021). Other researchers (McLeod, 2011; Black & Mayes, 2020; Skerrit et al., 2021) contend that fear and anxiety remain the impetus for the negativity towards the student voice. Sometimes, the rigidity and hierarchical nature of institutional policies hinder the development and inclusion of student voice academic programmes, such as WIL. Unsurprisingly, students are still excluded from the curriculum decision-making processes (Carr & Sztajn, 1996; Enright et al., 2017). In school settings, besides instilling fear and anxiety among teachers, including mentor teachers, student voice is perceived to be emotionally challenging (Skerrit et al., 2021). As a result, student voice remains under-researched, under-utilized, and missing in professional learning programmes such as WIL in many HEIs (Treacy & Leavy, 2023). Mayes et al. (2021) postulate that there are challenges in translating student voice into pre-service teachers' professional learning. The little communication from the HEIs and the conspicuous absence of students' voices in WIL programmes lead to the misaligned roles and expectations of mentor and pre-service teachers (Winchester-Seeto et al., 2016; Muyengwa & Jita, 2021). The lack of effective partnerships between HEIs and rural communities amplifies this problem further (Du Plessis, 2013). Sometimes, WIL programmes are perceived as unresponsive and irrelevant to classroom realities (Moosa & Rembach, 2018). Ultimately, these factors lead to high rates of exodus of teachers from the education system (Kadel, 2023).

Amid these challenges, there is a continuous call for including student voice in WIL programmes in many HEIs. For language teacher education, pre-service

English FAL teachers' reflection can contribute to developing a curriculum responsive to the needs of students and the broader society (Castaneda-Trujillo & Aguirre-Hernandez, 2018). In this regard, Cook-Sather (2006) argues that student voice challenges the power dynamics that often characterize educational programmes, such as WIL. McLeod (2011) equates student voice to representation, empowerment and emancipation. Also, Carr and Sztajn (1996) add that student voice creates a space for students in the power structure of educational programmes. This voice also empowers pre-service teachers to initiate their professional learning and development (Mushayikwa & Lubben, 2009) and to circumvent what Treacy and Leavy (2023) call de-contextualized and abstracted professional learning and development of pre-service teachers.

Finally, including student voice can also help address the perpetual alienation of pre-service teachers from marginalized and rural backgrounds (Baroutsis et al., 2016). In other words, including student voice in WIL programmes, especially in the rural context of South Africa, responds to calls "…for emancipatory agenda in educational research to create space for marginalized groups to influence decisions" (Moloi & Mokoena, 2023, p. 170). In this chapter, we endeavored to create a space for pre-service English FAL teachers from a rural university to express their developmental needs to their mentor teachers. This was premised on the view that the voices of pre-service teachers remain largely neglected when determining the kind of support and identifying areas in which the pre-service teachers need to be developed during WIL in schools. This is contrary to the common practice where these needs are assumed by the faculty, university educators, and mentor teachers. In other words, this approach affords them the opportunity and power to influence decisions about their institution's WIL pedagogy and programmes. Hopefully, with such data in place, all the stakeholders can begin to see WIL as a collaborative effort, developing effective competencies and SDPL skills among the pre-service English FAL teachers in a rural setting.

6 Theoretical Framing: Critical Pedagogy

The empowerment and emancipatory agenda driving this study make critical pedagogy an appropriate lens for this chapter. As a theory, Critical Pedagogy (CP) originates from the dialogic and reflective works of Socrates and Pluto (Guilherme, 2017). In addition, the notions of transformative and liberating education contributed significantly to the advancement of critical pedagogy. In particular, education is liberating when it creates a space where social issues such as dominance, oppression and marginalization are challenged in various contexts. However, this cannot happen if all stakeholders are not empowered to recognize and challenge an unjust system (Jeyaraj, 2019). For this to happen, CP accentuates critical thinking and conscientization. In other words, pre-service teachers must become critical and aware of their actions, biases and oppression. This also includes being aware of the oppression of others and their personal experiences of oppression and injustice. In the context of WIL, it is important for the authorities (faculty, university educators and mentor teachers) to realize that in its current form, WIL pedagogy neglects the voices of the pre-service English FAL teachers. On the contrary, WIL programmes and pedagogy are based on the presumed developmental needs of the pre-service teachers from the perspectives of policymakers, faculties and mentor teachers. CP seeks to challenge and transcend these communication boundaries between the WIL authorities and pre-service teachers (Kevser & Aydin, 2021).

Transformed WIL programmes are appropriate for self-directed professional learning and the co-construction of knowledge. In these programmes, pre-service teachers must be taken through several domains, such as qualification, socialization, and subjectification. The first domain pre-service teachers gain knowledge and WIL competencies. Socialization allows them to learn norms, values and ethics related to the teaching profession. At the same time, subjectification teaches critical thinking and the ability to engage in self-directed initiatives aimed at challenging and changing unjust practices, such as the ones in WIL programmes. Furthermore, CP appreciates the role of critical reflection, action and dialogue when addressing social problems (Kavenuke & Muthanna, 2021). The transformative nature of CP requires that students and their teachers collaborate in constructing knowledge (Kavenuke & Muthanna, 2021; Smith & Seal, 2021). Through the semi-structured interviews, the pre-service teachers could reflect on their experiences during WIL programmes critically. This reflection empowered them to initiate steps towards meaningful self-directed professional learning guided by dialogue and collaboration between themselves and their mentor teachers.

At the center of student voice and CP are the notions of empowerment and emancipation of the marginalized members of society. Specifically, they often focus on personal experiences and disempowerment (Bourke & McDonald, 2018). In the context of WIL, pre-service English FAL teachers, especially in rural settings, remain 'voiceless' and 'powerless'. However, the CP and student voice combination created a platform for these teachers to express their developmental needs to their mentor teachers. This gives a sense of ownership and power to the pre-service English FAL teachers to have their 'voices' heard and have the power to influence decision-making about mentoring during WIL programmes.

7 Study Methodology

Eleven (11) pre-service teachers of English FAL in their third year of study towards a Bachelor of Education Degree (B.Ed.) at one rural university consented to participate in this study. Five (5) males and six (6) females of African origin were conveniently sampled to participate in the triangulated semi-structured interviews and focus-group discussions to generate qualitative data and improve the overall reliability of this data. Guided by prompts and probes, semi-structured interviews were used to gain insights into the pre-service English FAL teachers' experiences of WIL. In addition to being free from the interviewer's control, this type of interview allowed the participants to express their feelings (Cohen et al., 2007). On the other hand, focus-group discussion augmented the insights gained from the semi-structured interview. Open-ended questions guided the discussion and allowed for flexible interaction among the participants. Furthermore, they empowered the pre-service English FAL teachers to have a voice and influence decisions about WIL programmes (Gibbs, 2012).

8 Data Analysis

For analysis of all data, the study adopted the thematic approach to elicit meaning, gain understanding and develop empirical knowledge relevant to the aim of this study. The researchers followed an inductive approach to data analysis. In doing this, we adopted the guidelines recommended by Braun and Clarke (2006). These included: familiarization with the data, identifying significant codes, formulating meanings, clustering themes, developing a detailed description, producing a fundamental structure and seeking verification of the basic design as the processes in analysis. Throughout, the utterances of the participants were quoted verbatim for analysis.

9 Findings and Discussions

Data from the semi-structured interviews and focus group discussion revealed that pre-service English FAL teachers experienced challenges during WIL in rural a setting. To a large extent, these challenges and experiences informed their developmental needs during WIL. These needs are categorized into the following themes: lesson planning, classroom management, teaching aids, updates and feedback, and self-directed teaching.

9.1 Findings: Pre-service English FAL Teachers' Developmental Needs During WIL

9.1.1 Theme A: Lesson Planning

Pre-service teachers are taught lesson planning as part of their English FAL curriculum at the university under study. In the English Teaching modules, they are taught how about different components of a constructively aligned lesson plan. The module also introduces them to designing lesson plans in line with the prescripts of the Curriculum and Assessment Policy Statement (CAPS). English FAL teachers are required to plan for a two-week cycle in which various language skills are integrated

(DBE, 2011). As stated before, most of the information the pre-service English FAL teachers receive during lectures is purely theoretical. They experienced challenges applying this knowledge in an authentic classroom situation during WIL. As a result, they raised the following developmental needs:

> **PT1:** *I would like him/her to help me with the introduction. For example, how to link prior knowledge with new knowledge.*
> **PT5:** *I would like the mentor teacher to teach me how to structure a good lesson plan…he can support me by giving me the guidelines for the lesson plan.*
> **TP11:** *I would like my mentor teacher to guide me on using specific learner assessments and learner performance data as appropriate.*

The above extracts reveal that the pre-service English FAL teachers experienced challenges designing, structuring and implementing lesson plans during WIL. This involves their inability to use introduce lessons and decide on assessment methods. As a result, they need mentor teachers to assist with all these aspects of lesson planning. The participants also added the following:

> **PT9:** *I would also like my mentor teachers to help me conduct English lessons using different strategies…and to ask questions that are fair to all learners.*
> **PT3:** *I wish my mentor teacher to help me by providing me…with a strong background in content knowledge, pedagogical theory and teaching methods.*

Apart from these components, pre-service English FAL teachers experienced challenges in selecting the appropriate teaching strategies.

9.1.2 Theme B: Classroom Management

Pre-service teachers are taught classroom management during teacher preparation as part of their coursework. They learn about various classroom management theories, strategies and models (O'Neill & Stephenson, 2012). They expect to become competent in creating a classroom environment characterized by rules and effective disciplinary interventions to curb disruptions (Girardet, 2018). However, the participants had a bad experience with classroom management during WIL. Their utterances were captured as follows:

> **TP11:** *I would like my mentor teacher to assist me with classroom management. I have struggled a lot with managing my classroom in previous schools, especially dealing with learners who regularly disrupt the classroom while I am busy teaching.*
> **PT6:** *I will like my mentor teacher to teach me how to deal with my shyness since I am an introvert…teaching me how to handle misbehaving learners during the class.*
> **PT8:** *I would like my mentor-teacher to help me with class management strategies and how to manage discipline in the classroom.*

From the above extracts, pre-service teachers struggle to transfer and utilize information about various classroom strategies, techniques and models in an authentic classroom situation. In other words, they need their mentor teachers to provide them with effective and tried and tested strategies instead of relying on what they learnt in their coursework. This need becomes more urgent in light of the fact that lack of discipline is a major challenge in South African schools (Foncha et al., 2015).

9.1.3 Theme C: Learner-Centered Teaching

During teacher preparation, pre-service English FAL teachers are expected to familiarize themselves with the prescripts of the CAPS document. One of these involves ensuring learner-centered teaching in English FAL classrooms. This approach is characterized by learners' active participation and the teacher's facilitative role during the teaching and learning process (Du Plessis, 2020). While undertaking WIL at different schools, pre-service English FAL teachers are expected to use various methods to promote active learning during lesson delivery. Fink (2003) identifies observation, performance, and reflection as methods of lesson delivery. All these methods promote learners' active participation when completing tasks and constructing knowledge while the teacher facilitates the process. The participants experienced challenges during WIL. Below are their responses:

> **PT4:** *I struggled a lot when it comes to making learners participate in activities or even respond to questions. Mostly, I am the one who is talking and doing everything. I don't how I can get all my learners to participate in the lesson. I wish my mentor teacher to help me with the relevant strategies to teach learners English FAL so they easily adapt to the content.*
> **PT6:** *I would like my mentor to help me with how I must interact with learners, especially those who need special attention, and how I am going to accommodate them in the classroom without leaving them behind.*
> **PT10:** *I need the educator to provide me with teaching materials like books and advise me on what teaching aids I can utilize at school*

The preceding responses indicate that the participants experienced challenges with implementing learner-centered teaching in English FAL. These challenges emanate from the participants' inability to use different strategies and techniques to promote active learning. Furthermore, they struggled to select and use resources to accommodate varying learning styles in their classrooms. Based on these experiences, they need their mentor teachers to guide them on these issues during WIL.

9.1.4 Theme D: Support and Constructive Feedback

Mentor teachers are regarded as subject specialists (Matoti & Junqueira, 2012). In the context of WIL, mentor teachers guide, motivate and instill confidence in the pre-service teachers (Slavit & McDuffie, 2013). They also provide career-related and psycho-social support to pre-service teachers (Kram, 1985). Based on the following extracts, the participants did not gain these benefits during WIL, impacting their SDPL endeavors.

> **TP11:** *I also need my mentor teacher to help me with the information about the curriculum, availability of instructional materials, and planning.*
> **PT3:** *Support me by engaging me in ongoing conversations about my practice and encourage me to ask questions...should support me by giving me advice about good practice, what works and what doesn't work, and explain why!*

From the extracts above, the participants need their mentor teachers to guide them in professional development. In addition, they need to learn from their mentor teachers about the latest developments related to the curriculum and the teaching profession in general. Apart from seeking support, the participants stated the following:

> **PT4:** *I wish him to be available when I need some input and guidance and to have one-on-one sessions with him/her based on my progress as a student teacher.*
> **PT7:** *I would like my mentor to be open with me...being honest by showing guidance will help.*

Pre-service English FAL teachers also need sincerity from their mentor teachers. The need here for mentor teachers to provide constructive feedback that enhances learners' self-directed professional learning.

9.1.5 Theme E: Self-directedness

Fostering self-directedness among pre-service teachers is essential for achieving success in WIL programmes. Du Toit-Brits and Van Zyl (2017) maintain that it is important for these teachers to become self-directed to create conditions conducive to self-directed learning in their classrooms. In other words, it leads to pre-service teachers' academic development and success in instilling self-directed learning skills in their learners (Gunes, 2023). These skills enable them to devise strategies to set and achieve learning objectives (Du Toit-Brits & Van Zyl, 2017). In addition, high levels of self-directedness in learning lead to career success (Guglielmino & Guglielmino, 2000). Consequently, as Mentz (2014) observes, pre-service teachers' ability to take responsibility for their learning complements the acquisition of theoretical knowledge. Based on their experiences, the participants in this study expressed similar developmental needs from their mentor teachers. The assertions were as follows:

> **PT1:** *In my previous school, my mentor would sit with me from the first day until the day I left without ever allowing me to teach on my own. I think I was treated more as an assistant than a teacher. This time around, I would like my mentor teacher to support me by giving me opportunities to teach learners without his/her intervention during the lesson and review my delivery afterwards.*

PT3: *My mentor teacher could help me learn and work independently during teaching practice by giving me a chance to learn the school environment as a whole, …encourage me to take part in teaching and learning.*

PT4: *He must be present during my presentation then after, I wish he/she could give me a space with my learners to see how capable I am when it comes to teaching English FAL*

PT10: *He/she can sit in on my lessons and, at the end…tell me about the areas I need to improve and give me pointers*

The above extracts show that the participants experienced challenges which impeded their efforts to achieve self-directedness during WIL programmes. Seemingly, mentor teachers' reluctance to allow them to teach and learn independently led to negative experiences of WIL in schools. As a remedy, pre-service English FAL teachers need their mentors to engage in behaviors that promote self-directedness.

10 Discussions

This study explored the areas in which English FAL pre-service teachers in a rural setting need to be developed to enhance self-directed professional learning during WIL. The findings indicated that pre-service English FAL identified lesson planning as an area of concern. This challenge emanated from the inability to transfer what they learned in English coursework to practice in an authentic classroom. These findings concurred with other national and international studies (ElDeen & El-Sawy, 2018; Dube et al., 2021). Another area of development has been found to be classroom management. Pre-service English FAL teachers struggled to manage learners' ill-discipline and disruptive behavior during teaching practice. This continued despite receiving information during teacher preparation coursework about various strategies they could employ to deal with these challenges in the classroom. Similarly, in their study, O'Neill and Stephenson (2012) also found that the participants were not adequately prepared to manage misbehavior in the classroom. Similarly, Mafugu (2022) alluded to an existing gap between the school environment and the development of pre-service teachers' pedagogical skills. In this regard, the study found that pre-service teachers were not adequately prepared. The study also found that pre-service English FAL teachers need assistance with implementing learner-centered approaches in their teaching. In their study, Adebola and Tsotetsi (2022) found that this challenge originated from pre-service teachers' limited exposure to learner-centered teaching during preparatory training at HEIs. Moreover, the findings indicated that pre-service English FAL teachers need support and constructive feedback from their mentor teachers. Although the provision of constructive feedback and support by mentor teachers has been reflected in many studies (Slavit & McDuffie, 2013), the need to be updated by the mentor teacher about the developments in the field of education was peculiar to this study. This aspect is often left out and is intended to instill self-directed learning among pre-service teachers. Finally, the results indicated that pre-service English FAL teachers need assistance in attaining high levels of self-directedness in professional learning development. In this case, they highlighted mentor teachers' behaviors that often inhibited self-directedness in the classrooms. This finding is surprising considering mentor teachers' experience and familiarity with the prescripts of the CAPS curriculum.

11 Implications of the Study

This study has far-reaching implications for the nature of WIL programmes in general and the teaching practice of pre-service teachers of English FAL. The results of this study may ignite the possibility of considering the subject-specific WIL practice in place of the generic one in schools. The current practice is informed by the presumed developmental needs of pre-service teachers of English FAL, and it is void of student voices and lived experiences. Informed by the critical pedagogy and student voice, universities may re-design their WIL programmes in line with their student teachers' actual developmental needs and lived experiences. This approach, we believe, may assist in enhancing pre-service teachers' sense of belonging within an environment that requires self-directed professional learning.

12 Conclusion and Recommendations

Based on the research question, this study provides a deductive conclusion and recommendations to enhance pre-service English FAL teachers' self-directed professional learning during WIL. The study concludes that pre-service English FAL teachers need assistance with lesson planning, classroom management, learner-centered teaching, support and constructive feedback, and high levels of self-directedness to enhance their WIL experiences and self-directed professional learning in a rural setting. Informed by these findings, the study recommends that the WIL authorities (universities, faculties, university educators, and mentor teachers) at HEIs and schools need to create a platform where student voice is accommodated. Such an arrangement may allow pre-service teachers to express themselves and guard against these authorities assuming their developmental needs. For instance, pre-service teachers in rural settings lack the technological tools to access the information necessary to enhance their professional learning during WIL. Consequentially, they struggle to acquaint themselves and keep themselves abreast with developments relating to the teaching methods and approaches within their areas of specialization, such as English FAL. A student-voice platform can also provide customized learning opportunities for pre-service English FAL teachers. They can learn about recent developments relating to pedagogical issues, such as lesson planning, classroom management, and the use of learner-centered approaches during WIL. In addition to supporting autonomy and flexibility, these learning opportunities are necessary to overcome the challenges that are specific and unique to rural schools. For example, pre-service teachers are often subjected to poor-quality mentoring and support, which also leads to exploitation by mentors during WIL (Floncha et al., 2015). When their voices are heard, pre-service English FAL teachers can reflect regularly on their progress and work collaboratively with mentors, other student-teachers, and the local community to have their developmental and pedagogical needs met. This may also help improve pre-service English FAL teachers' pedagogical skills (i.e., providing support and constructive feedback, and classroom management) to reduce the gap between theory and practice (Mafugu, 2022) and enhance their understanding of the culture, language variations, and social dynamics of the communities in which they are placed for WIL. Finally, the platform enables the WIL curricula to create space for rural education and teaching (Mukeredzi, 2021). In this regard, pre-service teachers can learn about the value of resource-sharing and improvisation in the contexts (rural schools) characterized by resource deficiencies.

References

Adebola, O.O., & Tsotetsi C.T. (2022). Challenges of pre-service teachers' classroom participation in a rurally located university in South Africa. *Journal of Educational and Social Research, 12*(5), 210–221. https://doi.org/10.36941/jesr-2022-0135

Anjum, S., Farooq, U., & Akbar, G. (2023). Gender differences in primary school teachers' perceptions of self-directed professional learning. *Research Journal of Social Sciences & Economics Review, 4*(1), 72–81. https://doi.org/10.36902/rjsser-vol4-iss1-2023(72-81)

Azano, A. P., & Stewart, T. T. (2015). Exploring place and practising justice: Preparing pre-service teachers for success in rural schools. *Journal of Research in Rural Education, 30*(9), 1–12.

Baroutsis, A., McGregor, G., & Mills, M. (2016). Pedagogic voice: Student voice in teaching and engagement pedagogies. *Pedagogy, Culture & Society, 24*(1), 123–140. https://doi.org/10.1080/14681366.2015.1087044

Bhatt, S.P. (2021). Self-directed professional development: EFL teachers' understanding. *International Journal of Language and Literacy Studies, 3*(4), 196–208. https://doi.org/10.36892/ijlls.v3i4.737

Black, R., & Mayes, E. (2020). Feeling voice: The emotional politics of 'student voice' for teachers. *British Educational Research Journal*, 1–17. https://doi.org/10.1002/berj.3613

Bogo, M. (2015). Field education for clinical social work practice: Best practices and contemporary challenges. *Clinical Social Work Journal, 43*, 317–324.

Bourke, R., & MacDonald, J. (2018). Creating a space for student voice in an educational evaluation. *International Journal of Research & Method in Education, 41*(2), 156–168.

Bovill, C., Cook-Sather, A., & Felten, P. (2011). Students as co-creators of teaching approaches, course design, and curricula: Implications for academic developers. *International Journal for Academic Development, 16*(2), 133–145. https://doi.org/10.1080/1360144X.2011.568690

Braun, V., & Clarke, V. (2006). Using thematic analysis in psychology. *Qualitative Research in Psychology, 3*(2), 77–101. https://doi.org/10.1191/1478088706qp063oa

Bravo, M. A., & Cervetti, G. N. (2014). Attending to the language and literacy needs of English learners in science. *Equity & Excellence in Education, 47*(2), 230–245. https://doi.org/10.1080/10665684.2014.900418

Carr, A. A., & Sztajn, P. (1996). Hearing unheard voices: Teacher education as conceptualized by pre-service teachers. *Teacher Education Quarterly, 23*(2), 35–44.

Castañeda-Trujillo, J. E., & Aguirre-Hernández, A. J. (2018). Pre-service English teachers' voices about the teaching practicum. *HOW, 25*(1), 156–173. https://doi.org/10.19183/how.25.1.420

Cohen, L., Manion, L., & Morrison, K. (2007). *Research methods in education* (6th ed.). Routledge.

Cook-Sather, A. (2006). Sound, presence, and power: "Student voice" in educational research and reform. *Curriculum Inquiry, 36*(4), 359–390. https://doi.org/10.1111/j.1467-873X.2006.00363.x

Cook-Sather, A. (2014). The trajectory of student voice in educational research. *New Zealand Journal of Educational Studies, 49*(2), 131–148. http://search.informit.com.au/fullText;dn=842480978608459;res=IELNZC

Cook-Sather, A. (2018). Perpetual translation: Conveying the languages and practices of student voice and pedagogical partnership across differences of identity, culture, position, and power. *Transformative Dialogues: Teaching & Learning Journal, 11*(3), 1–7.

Conner, J. O. (2022). Educators' experiences with student voice: How teachers understand, solicit, and use student voice in their classrooms. *Teachers and Teaching, 28*(1), 12–25. https://doi.org/10.1080/13540602.2021.2016689

Cuervo, H., & Acquaro, D. (2018). Exploring metropolitan university pre-service teacher motivations and barriers to teaching in rural schools. *Asia-Pacific Journal of Teacher Education, 46*(4), 384–398. https://doi.org/10.1080/1359866X.2018.1438586

Cummins, J. D. (1996). *Negotiating identities: Education for empowerment in a diverse society*. California Association for Bilingual Education.

Cummins, J. (1983). Bilingualism and special education: Program and pedagogical issues. *Learning Disability Quarterly, 6*(4), 373–386. https://doi.org/10.2307/1510525

Department of Basic Education. (DBE). (2011). National curriculum statement, curriculum and assessment policy statement (CAPS): Government Printing works.

Department of Higher Education and Training. (2011). National Qualifications Framework Act (67/2008): policy on the minimum requirement for teacher education qualifications. *Government Gazette, 553*(34467), 1–64. http://www.dhet.gov.za/Teacher%20Education/Policy%20on%20Minimum%20Requirements%20for%20Teacher%20Education%20Qualifications%20(2011),%2022%20July%202011.pdf

Department of Higher Education and Training (DHET). (2015). National Qualifications Framework Act, 2008 (Act no. 67 of 2008): Revised policy on the minimum requirements for teacher education qualifications (Notice 111) *Government Gazette*, 38487.

Department of Higher Education and Training. (2015). Revised policy on the minimum requirements for teacher education qualifications government printer.

Department of Higher Education and Training (DHET). (2018). *The minimum requirements for teacher education qualifications* (Unpublished draft).

Department of Education (DoE). (2007). The National Policy Framework for teacher education and development in South Africa. *Government Gazette*, 29832. Government Printer.

Dincer, A., & Yeşilyurt, S. (2017). Motivation to speak English: A self-determination theory perspective. *PASAA, 53*, 1–25.

Dlamini, M. E. (2018). Preparing student teachers for teaching in rural schools using work integrated learning. *The Independent Journal of Teaching and Learning, 13*(1), 86–96.

Dressler, S., & Keeling A. E. (2004). Student benefits of cooperative education. In: R. K Coll, C. Eames (Eds.), *International Handbook for Cooperative Education* (pp. 217–236). World Association for Cooperative Education.

Dube, M. C., Ulienya, C., & Mncube, D. W. (2021). University supervisors' perceptions on preservice teachers' lesson planning during teaching practice: The case of a South African University. *International Journal of Innovation, Creativity and Change, 15*(5), 497–511.

Du Plessis, E. (2020). Student teachers' perceptions, experiences, and challenges regarding learner-centred teaching. *South African Journal of Education, 40*(1), 1–10.

Du Plessis, E. (2013). Mentorship challenges in the teaching practice of distance learning students. *The Independent Journal of Teaching and Learning, 8*, 29–43.

Du Plessis, A. E. (2015). Effective education: Conceptualizing the meaning of out-of-field teaching practices for teachers, teacher quality and school leaders. *International Journal of Educational Research, 72*, 89–102.

Du Toit-Brits, C., & Van Zyl, C. M. (2017). Embedding motivation in the self-directedness of first-year teacher students. *South African Journal of Higher Education, 31*(1), 50–65. https://doi.org/10.20853/31-1-824

Dwesini, N. F. (2017). The role of work integrated learning in enhancing employability skills: Graduate perspectives. *African Journal of Hospitality, Tourism and Leisure, 6*(2), 1–9.

Eckert, L. S., & Petrone, R. (2013). Raising issues of rurality in English teacher education. *English Education, 46*(1), 68–81.

ElDeen, H., & El-Sawy, A. (2018). The relevance among preservice English teachers' preparation courses, their views about teaching and their real teaching behaviors (a case study). *Journal of Language Teaching and Research, 9*(3), 510–519. https://doi.org/10.17507/jltr.0903.09

Enright, E., Coll, L., Chroinin, D. N., & Fitzpatrick, M. (2017). Student voice as risky praxis: Democratizing physical education teacher education. *Physical Education and Sport Pedagogy, 22*(5), 459–472. https://doi.org/10.1080/17408989.2016.1225031

Fielding, M., & McGregor, J. (2005). *Deconstructing student voice; new spaces for dialogue or new opportunities for surveillance.* Paper presented at the annual meeting of the American Educational Research Association, Montreal.

Fink, A. D. (2003). *Creating significant learning experiences: An integrated approach to designing college courses.* San Francisco: Jossey-Bass.

Foncha, J. W., Abongdia, J. F. A., & Adu, E. O. (2015). Challenges encountered by student teachers in teaching English language during teaching practice in East London, South Africa. *International Journal of Educational Sciences, 9*(2), 127–134. https://doi.org/10.1080/09751122.2015.11890302

Garrison, D. R. (1997). Self-directed learning: Toward a comprehensive model. *Adult Education Quarterly, 48*(1), 18–33.

Gebhard, J. G. (2009). The practicum. In A. Burns & J. C. Richards (Eds.), *The Cambridge guide to second language teacher education* (pp. 250–258). Cambridge University Press.

Geer, R., & Sweeney, T. A. (2012). Students' voices about learning with technology. *Journal of Social Sciences, 8*(2), 294–303. https://doi.org/10.3844/jssp.2012.294.303

Gibbs, A. (2012). Focus groups and group interviews. In J. Arthur, M. Waring, R. Coe, & L. V. Hedges (Eds.), *Research methods and methodologies in education* (pp. 186–192). Sage.

Girardet, C. (2018). Why do some teachers change and others don't? A review of studies about factors influencing in-service and pre-service teachers' change in classroom management. *Review of Education, 6*(1), 3–36. https://doi.org/10.1002/rev3.3104

Green, E., Hyde, S., Barry, R., Smith, B., Seaman, C. E., & Lawrence, J. (2022). Placement architectures in practice: An exploration of student learning during non-traditional work-integrated learning in rural communities. *International Journal of Environmental Research and Public Health, 19*, 1–17. https://doi.org/10.3390/ijerph192416933

Gribble, C., Rahimi, M., & Blackmore, J. (2017). International students and post-study employment: The impact of university and host community engagement on the employment outcomes of international students in Australia. In L. T. Tran & C. Gomez (Eds.), *International student connectedness and identity: Transnational perspectives* (pp. 15–39). Springer.

Groenewald, T. (2007). Towards a definition for co-operative education. In R. K. Coll, & C. Eames (Eds.), *International handbook for co-operative education.* Waikato Print.

Guglielmino, P. J., & Guglielmino, L. M. (2000). Moving toward a distributed learning model based on self-managed learning. *SAM Advanced Management Journal, 66*(3), 36–43.

Guilherme, A. (2017). What is critical about critical pedagogy? *Policy Futures in Education, 15*(1), 3–5. https://doi.org/10.1177/1478210317696357.

Güneş, H. (2023). Self-regulated learning skills of pre-service English language teachers. *European Journal of Education Studies, 10*(2), 113–121. https://doi.org/10.46827/ejes.v10i2.4661

Hart, R. (1992). Children's participation: From tokenism to citizenship. Innocenti Essay 4. UNICEF/ICDC. http://www.unicef-irc.org/publications/100

Hay, K. (2020). What is quality work-integrated learning? Social work tertiary educator perspectives. *International Journal of Work-Integrated Learning, 21*(1), 51–61.

Hopkins, E. A. (2014). Supporting pre-service teachers to enhance the effectiveness of their classroom practice through engaging with the 'voice' of their pupils. *Teacher Development, 18*(1), 15–28. https://doi.org/10.1080/13664530.2013.852131

Jackson, D. Dean, B. A., & Eady, M. (2023). Equity and inclusion in work-integrated learning: Participation and outcomes for diverse student groups. *Educational Review*, 1–23. https://doi.org/10.1080/00131911.2023.2182764

Jagals, D. (2020). The value of work-integrated learning for professional teacher development programmes in open distance learning. In J. De Beer, N. Petersen, & H. I. Van Vuuren (Eds.), *Becoming a teacher: Research on the work-integrated learning of student teachers* (pp. 1–41). NWU Self-Directed Learning Series.

Jeyaraj, J. J. (2019). Possibilities for critical pedagogy engagement in higher education: Exploring students' openness and acceptance. *Asia Pacific Education Review, 21*, 27–38.

Kadel, P. B. (2023). Prospects and practices of induction for novice teachers. *Journal of Practical Studies in Education, 4*(2), 1–5. https://doi.org/10.46809/jpse.v4i2.63

Kavenuke, P. S., & Muthanna, A. (2021). Teacher educators' perceptions and challenges of using critical pedagogy: A case study of higher teacher education in Tanzania. *Journal of University Teaching & Learning Practice, 18*(4), 1–17.

Kennedy, M. M. (2016). How does professional development improve teaching? *Review of Educational Research, 86*, 945–980.

Kevser, O., & Aydin, S. M. (2021). Teachers' approaches to the principles of critical pedagogy: A mixed-method study. *Psycho-Educational Research Reviews, 10*(2), 128–141.

Kidd, W. (2012). Relational agency and pre-service trainee teachers: Using student voice to frame teacher education pedagogy. *Management in Education, 26*(3), 120–129. https://doi.org/10.1177/0892020612445684

Khampirat, B., Pop, C., & Bandaranaike, S. (2019). The effectiveness of work-integrated learning in developing student work skills: A case study of Thailand. *International Journal of Work-Integrated Learning, Special Issue, 20*(2), 127–146.

Kram, K. (1985). *Mentoring at work: Developmental relationships in organizational life*. Scott Foresman.

Mafugu, T. (2022). Science pre-service teachers' experience with mentors during teaching practice. *EURASIA Journal of Mathematics, Science and Technology Education, 18*(11), 1–11. https://doi.org/10.29333/ejmste/12476

Mahomed, C. C., & Singh, P. (2022). Leading collegially: Shifting paradigms for effective student teacher mentoring during work-integrated learning. *South African Journal of Education, 20*(4), 1–12. https://doi.org/10.15700/saje.v42n4a2101

Matoti, S. N., & Junqueira, K. (2012). An assessment of student teachers' experiences of work-integrated learning at a South African Institution of higher learning. *Journal of Social Sciences, 31*(3), 261–269. https://doi.org/10.1080/09718923.2012.11893035

Mayes, E., Black, R., & Finnerman, R. (2021). The possibilities and problematics of student voice for teacher professional learning: Lessons from an evaluation study. *Cambridge Journal of Education, 51*(2), 195–212. https://doi.org/10.1080/0305764X.2020.1806988

Maw, S. M., Hlaing, S. S. & Hlaing, N. T. (2021). A study of self-directed learning readiness and self-directed professional development practices of teachers. *Journal of the Myanmar Academy of Arts and Science, xix*(9A), 521–534.

MacBeath, J., Demetriou, H., Rudduck, J., & Meyers, K. (2003). *Consulting pupils: A toolkit for teachers*. Pearson.

McLeod, J. (2011). Student voice and the politics of listening in higher education. *Critical Studies in Education, 52*(2), 179–189. https://doi.org/10.1080/17508487.2011.572830

McRae, N., & Johnston, N. (2016). The development of a proposed global work-integrated learning framework. *Asia-Pacific Journal of Cooperative Education, 17*(3), 337–348.

Mentz, E. (2014). Preparing pre-service teachers to support self-directed learning. Accessed May 10, 2023. http://www.p21.org/news-events/p21blog/1477-mentzpreparing-pre-service-teachers-to-support-self-directed-learning.

Mentz, E., & De Beer, J. (2020). Self-directed learning in teacher education: Lessons from Finland. In J. De Beer, N. Petersen, & H. I. Van Vuuren (Eds.), *Becoming a teacher: Research on the work-integrated learning of student teachers* (pp. 157–188). NWU Self-Directed Learning Series.

Mhlongo, H. R., Pillay, P., & Maphalala, M. C. (2018). The experiences of the further education and training (FET) phase learners involved in a programme for developing writing skills. *Journal of Gender, Information and Development in Africa 7*(1). https://doi.org/10.31920/EFE_7_1_18

Miller, L. C. (2012). Situating the rural teacher labor market in the broader context: A descriptive analysis of the market dynamics in New York State. *Journal of Research in Rural Education, 27*(13), 1–31. http://jrre.vmhost.psu.edu/wp-content/uploads/2014/02/27-13.pdf

Mitra, D. L. (2004). The significance of students: Can increasing "student voice" in schools lead to gains in youth development? *Teachers College Record, 106*(4), 651–688.

Mitra, D. L. (2008). Amplifying student voice. *Educational Leadership, 66*(3), 1–7.

Mitra, D. L., & Gross, S. J. (2009). Increasing student voice in high school reform: building partnerships, improving outcomes. *Educational Management Administration & Leadership, 37*(4), 522–543. https://doi.org/10.1177/1741143209334577

Mitra, D. (2018). Student voice in secondary schools: The possibility for deeper change. *Journal of Educational Administration, 56*(5), 473–487.

Mncube, D. W., Mkhasibe, R. G., & Ajani, O. A. (2021). Teaching in English across the curriculum: A lived experience of the novice teachers in selected rural FET schools in South Africa. *International Journal of Higher Education, 10*(6), 72–82. https://doi.org/10.5430/ijhe.v10n6p72

Mockler, N., & Groundwater-Smith, S. (2015). Seeking for the unwelcome truths: Beyond celebration in inquiry-based teacher professional learning. *Teachers and Teaching, 21*(5), 603–614. https://doi.org/10.1080/13540602.2014.995480

Moloi, T. J., & Mokoena, M. (2023). Using student voice as a strategy to palliate student unrest. In: C. T. Tsotetsi, & B. I. Omodan (Eds.), *A compendium of response to student unrest in African universities*. South Africa: Axiom Academic Publishers.

Moosa, M., & Rembach, L. (2018). Voices from the classroom: Pre-service teachers' interactions with supervising teachers. *Perspectives in Education, 36*(1), 1–13. https://doi.org/10.18820/2519593X/pie.v36i1.1

Mthembu, B., & Pillay, P. (2021). Strategies that learners employ in acquiring speaking skills in English Second Language (ESL) in township schools. *Gender and Behaviour, 19*(1), 17454–17464. https://www.ajol.info/index.php/gab/article/view/210243

Mukeredzi, T. G. (2021). Teacher preparation for rurality: A cohort model of teaching practice in a rural South African school. In S. White & J. Downey, (Eds.), *Rural education across the world*. Springer.

Mullis, I. V. S., von Davier, M., Foy, P., Fishbein, B., Reynolds, K. A., & Wry, E. (2023). PIRLS 2021 international results in reading. Boston College, TIMSS & PIRLS International Study Center. https://doi.org/10.6017/lse.tpisc.tr2103.kb5342

Mushayikwa, E., & Lubben, F. (2009). Self-directed professional development-Hope for teachers working in deprived environments? *Teaching and Teacher Education, 25*, 375–382. https://doi.org/10.1016/j.tate.2008.12.003

Muyengwa, B., & Jita, T. (2021). Contexts of work-integrated learning in schools for pre-service teachers: Experiences of field placement in Zimbabwe. *International Journal of Work-Integrated Learning, 22*(1), 107–119.

Ngibe, N. C. P., Pylman, J., Mammem, K. J., & Adu, E. O. (2019). Turning pre-service school experience challenges into strengths. *Journal of Human Ecology, 66*(1–3), 33–44. https://doi.org/10.31901/24566608.2019/66.1-3.3150

Ngubane, N. I., Ntombela, B., & Govender, S. (2020). Writing approaches and strategies used by teachers in selected South African English first additional language classrooms. *Reading & Writing: Journal of the Reading Association of South Africa, 11*(1), 2079–8245. https://doi.org/10.4102/rw.v11i1.261

Nkambule, T., & Mukerdzi, T. G. (2017). Pre-service teachers' professional learning experiences during rural teaching practice in Acornhoek, Mpumalanga Province. *South African Journal of Education, 37*(3), 1–9. https://doi.org/10.15700/saje.v37n3a1371

Olifant, T., Cekiso, M. P., & Boakye, N. (2023). Investigating English first additional language educators' reading comprehension practices in selected schools in Gauteng, South Africa. *South African Journal of Education, 42*(2), 1–10. https://doi.org/10.15700/saje.v42n4a2094

Omodan, B. I. (2022). Challenges of pre-service teachers in rural places of teaching practice: A decolonial perspectives. *International Journal of Learning, Teaching and Educational Research, 21*(3), 127–142. https://doi.org/10.26803/ijlter.21.3.8

O'Neill, S., & Stephenson, J. (2012). Does classroom management course influence pre-service teachers' perceived preparedness or confidence? *Teaching and Teacher Education, 28*, 1131–1143. https://doi.org/10.1016/j.tate.2012.06.008

Petersen, N., De Beer, J., & Mentz, E. (2020). The first-year student teacher as a self-directed learner. In J. De Beer, N. Petersen, & H. I. Van Vuuren (Eds.), *Becoming a teacher: Research on the work-integrated learning of student teachers* (pp. 115–152). NWU Self-Directed Learning Series.

Ramsaroop, S., & Gravett, S. (2017). The potential of teaching schools in enabling student teacher learning for the teaching profession. *Journal of Curriculum Studies, 49*(6), 1–18. https://doi.org/10.1080/00220272.2017.1325516

Republic of South Africa. (1996b). National Education Policy Act, 27 of 1996, date of commencement: 24 April 1996. In C. Brunton & Associates (Eds.), *Policy handbook for educators* (pp. A2–A95). Education Labour Relations Council, Universal Print Group, Pretoria.

Richards, J. C., & Farrell, T. S. C. (2005). *Professional development for language teachers: Strategies for teacher learning.* Cambridge University Press.

Robertson, J. (2017). Rethinking learner and teacher roles: Incorporating student voice and agency into teaching practice. *Journal of Initial Teacher Inquiry, 3*, 41–44.

Robinson, M. (2015). Teaching and learning together: The establishment of professional practice schools in South Africa: A research report for the department of higher education and training. Stellenbosch University.

Robinson, C., & Taylor, C. (2007). Theorizing student voice: Values and perspectives. *Improving Schools, 10*(1), 5–17. https://doi.org/10.1177/1365480207073702

Rowe, A. D., & Zegwaard, K. E. (2017). Developing graduate employability skills and attributes: Curriculum enhancement through work integrated learning. *Asia Pacific Journal of Cooperative Education, Special Issue, 18*(2), 87–99.

Sariyildiz, G. (2017). Novice and experienced teachers' perceptions towards self-initiated professional development, professional develop activities and possible hindering factors. *International Journal of Language Academy*, 248–260.

Schonell, S., & Macklin, R. (2019). Work integrated learning initiatives: Live case studies as a mainstream WIL assessment. *Studies in Higher Education, 44*(7), 1197–1208.

Shapley, K. S., & Bush, J. (2000). Mentoring beginning teachers: The implications of contextual conditions. In D. T. Pan, S. E. Mutchler, K. S. Shapley, J. Bush, & R. W. Glover. *Mentoring beginning teachers: Lessons from the experience in Texas* (Policy Research Report). Southwest Educational Development Laboratory. https://www.govinfo.gov/content/pkg/ERICED463572/pdf/ERIC-ED463572

Shurr, J., Hirth, M., Jasper, A., McCollow, M., & Heroux, J. (2014). Another tool in the belt: Self-directed professional learning for teachers of students with moderate and severe disabilities. *Physical Disabilities: Education and Related Services, 33*(1), 17–38.

Singh, P., & Mahomed, C. C. (2013). The value of mentoring to develop student teachers' work-integrated learning skills. *International Business & Economics Research Journal, 12*(11), 1373–1387.

Skerritt, C., Brown, M., & O'Hara, J. (2021). Student voice and classroom practice: How students are consulted in contexts without traditions of student voice. *Pedagogy, Culture & Society.* https://doi.org/10.1080/14681366.2021.1979086

Slavit, D., & McDuffie, A. (2013). Self-directed teacher learning in collaborative contexts. *School Science and Mathematics, 113*(2), 94–105. https://doi.org/10.1111/ssm.12001

Smith, A., & Seal, M. (2021). The contested terrain of critical pedagogy and teaching informal education in higher education. *Education in Science, 476*(11), 1–6.

Smith-Rug, T. (2014). Exploring the links between mentoring and work-integrated learning. *Higher Education Research & Development, 33*(4), 769–782. https://doi.org/10.1080/07294360.2013.863837

South African Council of Educators (SACE). (2018). *SACE professional teaching standards (PTSs).* https://www.sace.org.za/assets/documents/uploads/sace_36738-2019-03-06SACE%20Draft%20PTS%20for%20Gazette%2028082018%20(00000003).pdf. Accessed 30 May 2023.

Strydom, F., & Loots, S. (2020). The student voice as a contributor to quality education through institutional design. *South African Journal of Higher Education, 34*(5), 20–34.

Sawyer, R. D. (2001). Teacher decision making as a fulcrum for teacher development: Exploring structures for growth. *Teacher Development, 5*(1), 39–58.

Suryasa, W., Prayoga, I. G. P. A., & Werdistira, I. (2017). An analysis of students motivation toward English learning as a second language among students in Pritchard English Academy. *International Journal of Social Sciences and Humanities, 1*(2), 43–50.

Taylor, N. (2019). Inequalities in teacher knowledge in South Africa. In N. Spaull & J. D. Jansen (Eds.), *South African schooling: The enigma of inequality—A study of the present situation and future possibilities* (pp. 263–283). Springer.

Thabane, R. W. (2022). Mentoring student teachers for self-directed professional learning through the use of E-portfolios during teaching practice. *Education and New Developments.* https://doi.org/10.36315/2022v1end040

Treacy, M., & Leavy, A. (2023). Student voice and its role in creating cognitive dissonance: The neglected narrative in teacher professional development. *Professional Development in Education, 49*(3), 458–477. https://doi.org/10.1080/19415257.2021.1876147

Tuhkala, A., Ekonoja, A., & Hamalainen, R. (2021). Tensions of student voice in higher education: Involving students in degree programme curricular design. *Innovations in Education and Teaching International, 58*(4), 451–461.

Van Canh, L. (2013). Great expectations: The TESOL practicum as a professional learning experience. *TESOL Journal, 5*(2), 199–224. https://doi.org/10.1002/tesj.103

Van Vuuren, H. J. (2020). The journey of becoming a professional teacher: Policy directives and current practices. In J. De Beer, N. Petersen, & H. I. Van Vuuren (Eds.), *Becoming a teacher: Research on the work-integrated learning of student teachers. NWU Self-Directed Learning Series* (Vol. 4, pp. 1–41). AOSIS. https://doi.org/10.4102/aosis.2020.BK215.01

Van der Merwe, D. (2022). Preparing pre-service teachers to guide and support learning in South African schools. *South African Journal of Childhood Education, 12*(1), 1–10.

Wang, J., Gill, C., & Lee, K. H. (2023). Effective mentoring in a work-integrated learning (WIL) program. *Journal of Teaching in Travel & Tourism, 23*(1), 20–38. https://doi.org/10.1080/15313220.2022.2056561

Warwick, P., Vrikki, M., Færøyvik Karlsen, A. M., Dudley, P., & Vermunt, J. D. (2019). The role of pupil voice as a trigger for teacher learning in lesson study professional groups. *Cambridge Journal of Education, 49*(4), 435–455.

Winchester-Seeto, T., Rowe, A., & Mackaway, J. (2016). Sharing the load: Understanding the roles of academics and host supervisors in work integrated learning. *Asia-Pacific Journal of Cooperative Education, 17*(2), 101–118.

Wolhuter, C. (2016). The education system of South Africa: Catapulting the country into the twenty-first century. In K. Horsthemke, P. Siyakwazi, E. Walton, & C. Wolhuter (Eds.), *Education studies: History, sociology, philosophy*. Oxford University Press.

Zegwaard, K. E., Pretti, J., Rowe, A. D., & Ferns, S. J. (2023). *Defining work-integrated learning: The Routledge international handbook of work-integrated learning* (3rd ed.). Routledge.

Being and Becoming a Teacher Educator in an Online Work-Integrated Learning Excursion for Future Super Teachers

Gordon Keabetswe Sekano and Adri Du Toit

Abstract This chapter reports on the professional development of novice teacher educators in an online work-integrated learning (WIL) excursion for future teachers. A self-study research design was used to explore how a novice teacher educator participating in an online WIL excursion, developed professionally through reflecting on their roles and experiences. A reflective journal, feedback from colleagues and participants, and video recordings were used to gather qualitative data, which were subsequently thematically coded in order to find key patterns and themes. The findings indicated both strengths and areas for improvement in the novice teacher educator's social, communication, and technological roles in the online educational setting. The implications for further research underscore the importance of integrating peer feedback, reflective practices, and qualitative methodologies to support the development of novice teacher educators in online educational settings.

Keywords Novice educators · Online learning · Reflective practice · Teacher educators · Work-integrated learning (WIL)

In this self-study, the first author was the primary researcher. Being a novice in the field, he however required substantial support in two key areas: in designing and conducting the research, and in organising the information into a manuscript. The second author took on both roles, and provided significant guidance throughout the process. As a result, both authors made substantial contributions to the writing of the manuscript.

G. K. Sekano (✉) · A. Du Toit (✉)
Research Unit Self-directed Learning, North-West University, Potchefstroom, South Africa
e-mail: gordon.sekano@nwu.ac.za

A. Du Toit
e-mail: dutoit.adri@nwu.ac.za

© The Author(s), under exclusive license to Springer Nature Switzerland AG 2024
I. C. Chahine and L. Reddy (eds.), *Educators' Work Integrated Learning Experiences*,
https://doi.org/10.1007/978-3-031-65964-5_4

1 Introduction and Rationale

Massification of university education, with increasing "emphasis on widening participation, throughput, and lecturer accountability" (McMillan & Gordon, 2017, p. 778), implies that university teacher educators must continuously reflect on and reconsider their practices as part of efforts to align their practices with these obligations. For teacher educators, this becomes an even more complex task, as they have to prepare students as future teachers by facilitating "learning related to the different roles of the teacher, for example, the teacher as a facilitator of learning, critical reflective practitioner, agent promoting social justice and being an inclusive teacher" (De Beer et al., 2020, p. 194). Teacher educators' reflections on and about teaching often change and shape the teacher educators themselves, resulting in them developing profound insights into practice through their own praxis (Loughran, 2005).

Reflective self-study is a research methodology where teacher educators (both experienced and novice) analyze their own viewpoints and experiences critically in order to become more self-aware, and comprehend how their own biases could affect their research (Vanassche & Kelchtermans, 2015). According to Berry (2010, p. 10), "[t]eacher educators who adopt a self-study perspective understand well that they are navigating a changing and complex terrain." Reflection can contribute meaningfully to the transition from being a novice teacher educator to becoming a more experienced scholar. McMillan and Gordon (2017) report a lacuna in the literature about how novice teacher educators understand their learning environment, enabling them to thrive and develop professionally. To address this gap, the current chapter reports on the case study of a novice teacher educator's critical reflective thinking on his contextual strengths, and the limitations of facilitating teacher preparation in an online virtual excursion, which is a compulsory component of work-integrated learning (WIL) at the university where the study was conducted.

The aim of this self-study was to explore my own strengths and limitations as a teacher educator in the context of an online virtual excursion reflectively. The purpose of the reflective self-study was to develop insight into additional avenues I need to pursue as part of my professional development, to overcome my limitations, and to enable me to guide and facilitate the preparation of future teachers for a complex profession better. An additional purpose was to delineate my strengths as a teacher educator, which could then serve as a foundation upon which I may construct further scholarship and professional development in this field.

These professional development objectives were intended to contribute to attaining the broader university goals of increasing student participation and throughput, as well as lecturer accountability (in this case, that of the teacher educator), as recommended by McMillan and Gordon (2017). The overarching goal of the current research was to contribute to the existing scholarship on professional development and preparation of novice teacher educators to prepare future teachers for a complex career, especially in contexts where online excursions are utilised.

I therefore share my story of how my lived experiences as a novice teacher educator in a teacher preparation excursion contributed to my professional development as a young teacher educator. I believe that others might gain insight from my experiences to help them overcome similar issues to succeed—or even thrive—in higher education.

At North-West University (NWU), where I started my academic career as a novice researcher, work-integrated learning (WIL) is a compulsory component of the first year of the four-year Bachelor of Education (BEd) qualification. Within the larger WIL programme, a compulsory annual excursion contributes to student teachers' preparation for their future careers. This excursion:

- focuses on the application of theory in authentic education contexts;
- addresses specific teaching competencies identified for teacher training in related training programmes;
- develops practical and contextual skills and knowledge that will make the teacher–student employable in schools;
- provides a real context in which the theoretical, practical, interpersonal and reflexive competencies of the teacher–student are developed in an integrated manner, and;
- provides structured opportunities for experiential teaching strategies within teaching practice through supervised and assessed teaching practice and work-based learning (Du Toit & Petersen, 2023).

Some years, the excursions in the WIL programme are offered as virtual or online experiences. In online WIL excursions, the programme intends to foster online interaction in a safe space that takes students out of their comfort zone, to bring them closer to the Vygotskyan "zone of proximal development [ZPD]" (Vygotsky & Cole, 1978, p. 86). The excursions aim to contribute to students' development as 'future super teachers', a motivational term coined to inspire students toward greatness (De Beer et al., 2022). Developing students as 'super teachers' was the leitmotif for the excursions, and students were "encouraged to identify their own 'super-powers' as teachers, and … their own strengths and growth opportunities" (De Beer et al., 2022, p. 234).

As I had limited online teaching experience at that early stage in my lecturing career and had never participated in such excursions in the WIL programme, I viewed the opportunity to participate as a way to contribute to my professional development as a teacher educator. This view was particularly based on the five foci bulleted above for these excursions. I believed that these would add to my understanding of the breadth and depth of teacher preparation required in these programmes.

2 Theoretical Underpinnings of Reflective Practice in Teacher Education

Teacher education and reflective practice have become almost inextricably linked (LaBoskey, 2010). The research reported here was theoretically underpinned by Dewey's (1933) contextualization of reflection, as explained by Rodgers (2002). Rodgers (2002, p. 842) presents four criteria that could serve "as a starting place for talking about reflection, so that it might be taught, learned, assessed, discussed, and researched, and thereby evolve in definition and practice". Her four criteria contribute to meaningful, deep reflective practices and, in brief, state that reflection ...

- contributes to meaning-making, and leads to deeper understanding through linking experiences and ideas;
- is rooted in scientific enquiry, following a rigorous, systematic and organised manner of thinking;
- is not individualistic but includes interaction with others; and
- requires that a person value both his or her own intellectual growth and that of others.

Based on these four criteria, reflection explains how "human beings learn from their experiences to improve themselves and their society" (LaBoskey, 2010, p. 629). Using these criteria to scaffold reflection as part of self-study "will [therefore] not only be informative to the individual conducting the research but also meaningful, useful and trustworthy for those drawing on such findings for their own practice" (Loughran, 2005, p. 6). A reflective self-study, based on these four criteria, was therefore deemed appropriate for exploring my own strengths and limitations in order to contribute insights, which subsequent scholars and novice teacher educators could use for the construction of meaning-making.

Openly examining personal experiences might encourage others to reflect on their abilities and areas for growth. Common challenges can be identified, and strategies for overcoming such challenges can be shared to provide valuable guidance.

3 Relevant Concepts from the Literature

Certain key concepts, identified from the literature, contributed to my exploration, meaning-making, and understanding in the self-reflective study on which this chapter reports. Firstly, I outline the requirements for teacher preparation in South African higher education. I then describe how WIL, as one of these requirements, was facilitated as an online excursion in the teacher preparation programme of one South African university to contribute to the preparation of future 'super teachers'. The focus then shifts to the roles of teacher educators in teacher preparation programmes. The discussion concludes by emphasizing the importance of carefully preparing novice teacher educators for the important roles they have to fulfil in teacher education, through well-structured professional development programmes.

3.1 Teacher Preparation in South Africa: Exploring Key Concepts and Reflective Practices in the Context of the NWU

In general, teacher education programmes aim to develop and expand the knowledge, skills, and perspectives of student teachers (Burn et al., 2022). Teacher education is nevertheless often much more complex than this. In South Africa, for example, teacher preparation is guided by the policy on the minimum requirements for teacher education qualifications (Republic of South Africa [RSA], 2011). The above policy on minimum requirements provides a foundation for the extended breadth and depth of learning needed to ensure future teachers are exceedingly well prepared (RSA, 2011). The "notion of integrated and applied knowledge" encapsulates all learning associated with the policy on minimum requirements, which emphasises not only "*what* is to be learned [but also] *how* it is to be learnt" (RSA, 2011, p. 9) (emphasis added). Practical learning is outlined in the policy on minimum requirements as one of the core types of learning contributing to the "acquisition, integration and application of knowledge for teaching purposes" (RSA, 2011, p. 11). In this context, practical learning is underpinned by learning *from* practice and learning *in* practice, to close the gap between teacher education and the reality of teaching in a classroom. Work-integrated learning (WIL) includes aspects of learning *in* practice, such as preparing lessons and reflecting on these, as well as learning *from* practice, for example when observing other teachers in action (RSA, 2011). It is therefore clear why WIL forms an integral part of all teacher preparation programmes in South Africa.

The drastic limitations placed on face-to-face contact brought about by the Covid pandemic resulted in the restructuring of WIL excursions presented in an online learning environment so that students would not miss out on the extended learning opportunities embedded in this programme. The WIL programme was restructured to be offered in a synchronous online environment using the Zoom platform, which allowed students and teacher educators to "interact in real time, through videoconferencing software that includes video, audio, and instant messaging" (Grammens et al., 2022, p. 2). The processes and implementation of these adaptations to WIL at NWU are described in detail in a book edited by De Beer et al. (2023). Evident from the compilation of studies in this book, is that—although there were many benefits as part of the teacher preparation programme—it was a steep and often difficult learning curve for teacher educators. Similarly, Burn et al. (2022, p. 442) describe how "some teacher-educators saw new technologies [such as online learning] as offering opportunities" for facilitating learning using alternative approaches; however, it "resulted in a steep learning curve for [other] teacher-educators". Furthermore, Burn et al.

(2022) note that teacher educators had to revise how they could "enable student-teachers to build relationships and work collaboratively". That meant that we, as teacher educators, had to reflect, reconsider, plan, revise, and re-implement aspects of the excursion in an effort to optimise the online learning experience and process for the students. To this extent, authors such as Burgueño et al. (2022) highlight the motivational role, which teacher educators play in shaping future teachers. Likewise, I became increasingly aware of the potential of my real influence on the students, and the various roles I was expected to fulfil in the online environment, while facilitating important learning content.

3.2 Content Included in Our Work-Integrated Learning Programme

To guarantee that WIL experiences are relevant and in line with curriculum goals, educational institutions must include current and relevant learning as part of the WIL programme. In keeping with the 'super teachers' leitmotif of the excursions, the content included in our WIL excursions are, therefore, aimed at supporting student teachers in self-reflection to identify their own 'super-powers' as future teachers (De Beer et al., 2022). Current and relevant content topics that are necessary to strengthen teacher education in South Africa are purposely included to contribute 'tools' to our future super teachers' 'toolboxes'. In other words, the WIL programme content is selected to contribute meaningfully to the preparation of the student teachers "to enable them to face challenging realities in their future classrooms" (Du Toit & Petersen, 2023, p. 2). Some examples of the content in our WIL programme, and how it is intended to prepare these future teachers for their careers, include:

- using real-world examples of injustices that have taken place in South African classrooms, to prepare student teachers for critical reflection toward social justice and help them to avoid similar situations by creating inclusive spaces in their future classrooms where a sense of belonging can be fostered (Du Toit & Petersen, 2023; Kruger & Mdakane, 2023);
- using game-based learning to bring home the breadth of diversity (socio-economic, cultural, linguistic, and more) which future teachers may expect in their classrooms, and how they could become inclusive practitioners (Bunt et al., 2023);
- explaining and demonstrating the use of shoestring approaches—that is, using affordable or freely available resources creatively to support the teaching–learning process, especially in under-resourced schools (Du Toit & Petersen, 2023);
- developing entrepreneurship education as part of the South African school curriculum, to enable future teachers to merge this critical content with existing subject content, as part of efforts to ameliorate youth unemployment in this country (Du Toit, 2023).

The inclusion of this content will guarantee that our students graduate from university with the knowledge, insights and abilities required to succeed in their future careers in the South African context.

3.2.1 Elements of Online and Work-Integrated Learning

Online learning and WIL have become essential aspects of the ever-changing educational landscape because they help students prepare for the working world by bridging the knowledge gap between theory and practice. This integration is in line with the movement in pedagogy towards experiential learning approaches, where the emphasis is on problem-solving situations and real-world experiences in addition to traditional classroom settings (De Beer et al., 2022). The central goal of WIL, as expressed in the creative curriculum designs of Du Toit and Petersen (2023), is to bridge the gap between theory and practice by allowing students to apply academic theories in real-world contexts. Several elements are included in the WIL programme to contribute to attaining this goal. These elements include teaching–learning of content, guided facilitation in the learning process, and utilizing appropriate teaching–learning strategies, such as those mentioned above by De Beer et al. (2022) to prepare student teachers for real-world application thereof. These same elements must be included when WIL is offered in online settings. Creative and innovative adaptations are, therefore, necessary to ensure that the content, facilitation, and teaching–learning strategies utilized in online WIL mirror those used in face-to-face (in-person) settings, without loss of quality (Du Toit & Petersen, 2023). Adaptations that were made to these elements for the online environment include presenting the content as small, interactive videos; facilitating students' learning process in online break-away rooms, followed by synchronous, large-group discussions; and using (or sometimes demonstrating) play-based and experiential teaching–learning strategies as part of our online facilitation. Du Toit and Petersen (2023) further highlight that creating a sense of belonging for students participating in the online environment remains a key element to maintain in online WIL excursions.

Nonetheless, a thorough grasp of the roles and skills needed by educators in these settings is essential for the effective execution of online WIL experiences. Effective online teaching techniques necessitate that educators handle the instructional, social, managerial, and technical domains skilfully, according to Baran et al. (2011). The complex job of the teacher educator highlights the necessity for educators to manage learning processes, build a welcoming online community, provide crucial technical assistance, and develop and lead learning activities that encourage active engagement. These skills are essential for making sure that WIL experiences occurring online are worthwhile, interesting, and helpful in reaching the intended learning objectives. Furthermore, as Grammens et al. (2022) point out, adding synchronous components to online WIL activities adds complexity that calls for teachers to be adaptable in their communication and teaching techniques, underscoring the importance of honing these skills for the success of WIL programmes.

The Roles of Teacher Educators in Online Learning Baran et al. (2011) conducted a comprehensive literature review to analyze the roles and competencies of online educators with the extensive purpose of promoting online educators' reflection. More recently, Grammens et al. (2022) conducted another systematic literature review on the roles of educators in online learning environments, starting with the framework of roles identified by Baran et al. (2011). Grammens et al. (2022) particularly intended to expand the original framework by exploring the roles of online educators in synchronous settings and by refining and clarifying the roles in the original framework of Baran et al. (2011). An amalgamation of the key roles and core competencies of online educators developed by Baran et al. (2011), as adapted by Grammens et al. (2022), are presented in Table 1. Based on the findings of the latter study, there was significant overlap between the 'pedagogical', 'facilitator', and 'instructional designer' roles included in Baran et al.'s (2011) original framework. Grammens et al. (2022) therefore opted to merge these three roles into the 'instructional role' only, as shown in Table 1. In addition, Grammens et al. (2022) added the 'communication role' to include aspects of the synchronicity and complexity of real-time interaction in online environments (Table 1).

The same roles and competencies are important for teacher educators in higher education. Care should however be taken that the aspects of learning *in* practice and learning *from* practice are adhered to in order to enable the attainment of the goals of the WIL programme. The original aim of Baran et al. (2011), namely to promote reflection in online educators, should also not be disregarded, as reflection is critical for personal growth and professional development.

3.3 *Novice Teacher Educators' Roles and Expectations*

Novice lecturers—and particularly novice teacher educators—are individuals who are beginning their careers as educators in higher education institutions (HEIs) after gaining some teaching experience in high (i.e. secondary) schools (Kember & Leung, 2020). The authors further state that, in high schools, novice teacher educators have a set curriculum that they must follow, and they are often in control of their classrooms (Kember & Leung, 2020). After joining an HEI, novice lecturers generally face many challenges in their initial years of teaching, especially challenges related to their three key roles and responsibilities, namely teaching, research, and community service (Ibrahim et al., 2013). Unlike in the school environment, novice teacher educators in HEIs are expected to be researchers, scholars, and mentors to their students, in addition to their teaching responsibilities (El-Hussein & Cronje, 2019). They are also responsible for designing their courses, teaching materials, and assignments. Novice teacher educators are also expected to create courses that align with the goals of their departments, institutions, and national standards (Jonsén & Fossland, 2021).

Table 1 Teacher roles and competencies required for effective synchronous online teaching

Key roles for online educators	Core competencies developed for each role
Instructional designer (*including pedagogical and facilitator roles*)	• Organising the learning process • Stimulating active learning • Designing and recreating learning tasks and materials • Implementing assessment • Providing feedback • Meeting students' personal learning needs • Motivating students
Social	• Building an online learning community • Being considerate of cultural differences • Building a teacher–student relationship • Contributing to the development of student interaction
Manager	• Leading and controlling the learning programme • Establishing and monitoring protocols and rules • Managing equipment • Organising and planning the learning programme
Technical role	• Providing technical support • Having knowledge of using different technical tools • Understanding the affordances and limitations of various online tools • Having and maintaining a positive attitude towards utilising online learning • Encouraging and using safe digital behaviour
Communicative role	• Facilitating and encouraging communication • Pedagogically mastering the different communication channels • Selecting the most appropriate channels for various scenarios • Exhibiting and using good communication skills

Source Adapted from Baran et al. (2011) and Grammens et al. (2022)

Bathmaker and Avis (2007) reveal that the challenges novice teacher educators experience in their professional development journey could cause them to feel disempowered, which could negatively affect the development of their teacher identities, especially in the early years of their career. Difficulty in developing a strong and positive identity could negatively affect a novice teacher educator's sense of self within the context of the teaching and academic profession (Conklin, 2020). In turn, such negative experiences affect teacher educators' own praxis, something that is especially pertinent in the case of novice lecturers involved in teacher preparation, which necessitates careful construction of learning experiences that student teachers, in turn, could transfer into school contexts (Burke, 2020). It is therefore important that novice teacher educators understand their roles and responsibilities, and that they reflect on and plan their professional development in the tertiary organisation to be(come) effective instructors. Conklin (2020) notes that novice teacher educators could facilitate their adaptation to their new roles and expectations by means of engaging in reflection. In the next section, the utilization of reflective self-study as a research methodology for the present chapter is presented.

4 Methodology

The question that guided this reflective case study was:

> What are my strengths and limitations as a teacher educator in the context of an online virtual excursion, and how do these strengths and limitations contribute to my professional development?

Following the so-called Self-Study of Teacher Education Practices (S-STEP) research design, reflective self-study was used to design and implement the research on which this chapter reports. The starting point for self-study is one's own lived experiences and understanding how meaning is made based on lived practices (Vanassche & Kelchtermans, 2015). According to LaBoskey (2015, p. 97), "self-study was developed specifically by and for teacher educators", underscoring its appropriateness for the current investigation. LaBoskey recollects that a cluster of teacher educators who formed a special interest group (SIG) of the American Educational Research Association (AERA) in 1993 coined the name Self-Study of Teacher Education Practices (S-STEP) for their SIG (LaBoskey, 2015). S-STEP has since been used extensively to design and implement reflective self-study research, especially by (but not limited to) teacher educators (Dobbs et al., 2022).

S-STEP utilizes various research methods and frameworks, including case studies, and employs qualitative data sources (Peercy & Sharkey, 2020). S-STEP is not limited by a single method or design but has five identifying characteristics. S-STEP research is namely self-initiated, focused, interactive (or collaborative), based on qualitative methodology, and utilizes exemplar validation (Pinnegar et al., 2010). In the current study, as a novice teacher educator, I initiated the research to explore my professional development in which I was both a practitioner in the excursion and the researcher. The study focused on exploring my strengths and limitations as a teacher educator in the context of an online virtual excursion. I did not rely solely on my own reflections but also on peer feedback, participant observations, and relevant literature.

S-STEP literature has drawn attention to the crucial role of colleagues, peers and students as participants, and sources of knowledge, criticism, and guidance (Trumbull & Cobb, 2000). I included interactions and feedback from a more experienced colleague (the second author), as well as from many of the 1340 students who participated in the online virtual excursion I facilitated. My own comments and those of others were in the form of qualitative data—using a reflective journal and informal communication, both in person and during online interactions (as explained in detail in the next paragraph). Exemplar validation, according to Pinnegar et al. (2010), refers to how I collected data, analyzed it, and made meaning of it. According to these authors, the trustworthiness of self-study relies on "ontology rather than epistemology", follows a process that "is empirically grounded in dialogue rather than the scientific method" and "is grounded in a study of personal practice in the space between self and others in the practice" (Pinnegar et al., 2010, p. 204).

Data for this case study were collected from my own reflective journal, notes from meetings with facilitators after the excursion, video recordings of the excursion, and formal and informal conversations with colleagues. Having data from various sources enabled me to compare my journey from *being* a teacher educator to *becoming* a teacher educator in an online WIL excursion for future super teachers. My ability to concentrate on everyday events made keeping a reflective journal helpful. Each entry had a date and accompanying contextual information. Thematic coding was employed to analyse the data, allowing for the identification of meaningful patterns, concepts, and recurring ideas. The initial codes were organised into themes that represented my social role, communication role, and technical role as an online teacher educator. Through rigorous review and comparison of the data, the emergent themes were refined and defined to depict my experiences accurately. The iterative process of data analysis, coupled with triangulation for validation, ensured the reliability and credibility of the themes, providing valuable insights into the growth and development of novice teacher educators in online educational settings, as explained by Creswell and Creswell (2018). I carefully examined the information, distinguished what was significant from what was not, and categorized it into strengths and areas for improvement or where professional development would be needed, as discussed below.

5 Findings and Discussion

As a novice teacher educator, participating in the online WIL excursion for the first time in 2022, I encountered several obstacles in my role as an online educator. I followed the S-STEP research design to explore the challenges I faced, and the ways I managed to overcome them. Based on the steps for reflective teacher educator self-study, I report my experiences in line with three of the five key roles for online educators listed in Table 1, namely the social, communication, and technical roles of the facilitator as described by Baran et al. (2011) and Grammens et al. (2022). The other two roles, that is, the role of instructional designer and the managerial role (Table 1), are not discussed in the findings of this case study, as I was not involved in the 2022 WIL excursion planning or management. Through this discussion, I offer insight and recommendations that could potentially benefit other novice teacher educators in the field of online education, particularly in the context of WIL, which will contribute to attaining the goals set for these excursions. As the university continually endeavours to appoint young (often novice) lecturers and thereby offer them opportunities to grow and develop professionally in its programmes, the contribution of my reflections in this regard could be meaningful for novice lecturers in the same situations.

5.1 My Social Role as an Online Teacher Educator

I attended 8 of the 12 excursion sessions conducted in 2022, mainly in the capacity of a participant-observer, as described by Nieuwenhuis (2010). I was asked to join random virtual rooms and witnessed students' discussions and interactions in their small breakaway rooms. In my reflective journal, I noted that most students appreciated my presence during their breakaway sessions when they had to discuss common issues. In my social role, I supported student groups in refocusing their attention on the issues to be discussed, and I provided guidance for them to explore ideas in a less structured format. One student, for example, mentioned, "we were lost during the first task and did not know where to start, but Mr Sekano came to our rescue". This comment supports my notes that, in my social role, I contributed guidance in the students' online learning process. These findings align with the literature where various researchers advocate the need for online teachers (or in the current case, a teacher educator) to establish a supportive and interactive learning community among students (Burgueño et al., 2022; Burn et al., 2022). It is thought that the presence of the online teacher educator—whether overt or covert—affects how students view and engage with online learning (Ou et al., 2004). The core competency of contributing to developing student interaction in an online environment afforded some students a meaningful learning experience. This aligns with excursion and WIL principles that emphasize the significance of collaborative learning and community engagement in enhancing student teachers' learning experiences. Moreover, the researcher's role as a participant-observer in the WIL excursion aligns with the experiential learning aspect of WIL, where students and teacher educators actively participate in real-world settings to support the integration of theory and practice (Du Toit & Petersen, 2023).

Data collected from my reflective journal revealed that I had learned the importance of building relationships with my students to facilitate a positive and productive learning environment. For example, on 3 May 2023, I noted how I had made an effort to learn students' names and inquire about their interests and concerns in order to build rapport with them during breakaway sessions. After addressing them by name and showing genuine interest in their comments, I noticed a significant improvement in their level of comfort and engagement in the excursion. Building these relationships helped create a positive and productive online learning environment where students felt valued and connected. According to research by Chen et al. (2015), lecturer–student relationships are critical to student engagement and achievement. By establishing a rapport with these first-year students, I contributed to creating a supportive community where students felt comfortable asking questions and seeking guidance. My purposeful social interaction contributed to students feeling more comfortable, or in a better position for learning in the social and interpersonal planes of learning, in line with similar reports on the same excursions by Du Toit and Petersen (2023). Additionally, as is evident in video recordings of the WIL excursions, allowing students to work cooperatively and collaboratively in small groups could foster a sense of teamwork and enhance students' self-directed learning, as reported by De Beer et al. (2023), which aligned with the overarching goals for teacher preparation at the study university. These findings are supported by Johnson and Johnson (2013, 2019), who found that cooperative learning could improve student engagement and knowledge retention. The collaborative approach to learning mirrors the principles of WIL, where students are encouraged to work in teams, interact with industry professionals, and gain hands-on experience to bridge the gap between theory and practice. Overall, my experience as an online teacher educator has taught me that effective facilitation of learning in online environments involves more than just delivering 'content' (as described earlier in the chapter); it also requires a focus on building relationships and creating a sense of community among students.

One of the key strengths identified from the meetings with facilitators after the excursion is my ability to contribute to students' sense of belonging, by providing them with insights into the teaching profession and suggestions for improvement, informed by my own experiences as a schoolteacher. For example, sharing my personal experiences motivated students and provided them with feedback in terms of effective classroom management and student engagement, in line with suggestions by Grammens et al. (2022). Creating a sense of belonging for students was a key objective of the WIL excursions, as reported by Du Toit and Petersen (2023); therefore, this is a significant finding. In addition, I had to put aside my own feelings and reactions to see the situation through the students' eyes (i.e. had empathy), and carefully managed my own emotions by staying calm and rational amidst a few stressful or problematic circumstances during the excursion (i.e. showed poise under pressure). This I noted in my reflective journal, and was also reported on by Du Toit and Petersen (2023, p. 6) as "tensions" experienced in these excursions. This finding is consistent with previous research that highlights the importance of creating a supportive and inclusive learning environment for future teachers (see De Beer et al., 2020). According to the literature review, Baran et al. (2011) emphasize that the roles of teacher educators in online learning require a combination of technical, pedagogical, and interpersonal skills, as well as a deep understanding of the online learning environment and the needs of the students. These personal strengths therefore served as a foundation on which I could construct my own growth and development as part of becoming an experienced teacher educator and scholar (Burgueño et al., 2022).

5.2 My Communication Role as an Online Teacher Educator

As I looked back at video recordings of the excursion, I realized that my communication role as an online teacher educator was not as effective as it could or should have been. According to research by Venter (2019), online communication can be challenging due to the absence of nonverbal cues, which are essential for conveying emotions and intent. In my experience, I struggled to connect with the students during the session, which sometimes led to misunderstandings and confusion. Likewise, Du Toit and Petersen (2023, p. 13) emphasize the importance of optimizing "interactions between learners and content through efficient communication channels while designing an educational online environment in order to optimise learning in the ZPD [zone of proximal development]." Additionally, while I endeavoured to provide constructive feedback to the participants, it was not always delivered in a way that was "constructive" or "supportive" (Du Toit & Petersen, 2023, p. 7). One possible reason for this could be that I am still developing my academic language and the appropriate terminology, and I had to think quickly during the discussions. My vocabulary was therefore inadequate at times, as I had noted in my journal. This, in turn, negatively affected my confidence to participate in the discussion. I was so focused on getting through the material that I did not take the time to ask my students questions or encourage them to participate. According to Sadler and Good (2021), not providing constructive or supportive feedback during online teaching and learning could have several disadvantages, including reduced motivation, poor performance, and a lack of student engagement. This made some of the sessions feel impersonal and disconnected, which is not the kind of learning environment I wanted to create. To address these issues, I have since focused on improving my communication skills, such as active listening and clear messaging, and developing my academic vocabulary to ensure that my students can understand and engage with the material effectively on a tertiary level. Grammens et al. (2022, p. 5) also identified "encouraging communication" as one of the competencies that are important for effective teaching in online environments. These authors argue that teachers who can communicate clearly, listen actively, and provide timely feedback could help create a positive and engaging learning environment for their students, whether they are teaching asynchronously or synchronously online (Grammens et al., 2022).

Concerning my communication roles, the reflective journal highlighted that my proficiency as an online teacher educator was hampered by insufficient use of formal academic language and a deficiency in self-confidence during presentations. Additionally, from the notes of the meeting with other facilitators, I also noticed that I tended to dominate the conversation at times. While this was not intentional, it did "limit the opportunity for other participants to contribute their ideas and insights" (Martin, 2009, p. 77). I believe I could benefit from taking a step back and allowing others to take the lead in discussions. These limitations indicate that I need to explore additional professional development opportunities to learn and apply new knowledge and skills during my professional growth, as recommended by Kabashi et al. (2021), particularly to strengthen my listening skills. This will strengthen my abilities as a teacher educator and set an example of preferred teacher behaviour for the student teachers in the WIL excursion to adopt for use in their future classrooms. For instance, increasing my self-confidence might enable me to talk with greater authority and clarity, which in turn might help audiences comprehend and respond better to my message (Martin, 2009). According to Gao and Gao (2021), this, in turn, could create a pleasant overall presentation experience for the students and myself.

5.3 *My Technical Role as an Online Teacher Educator*

Formal and informal conversations with colleagues regarding knowledge of using different technical tools and providing technical support in online learning have taught me the importance of flexibility, patience, ongoing learning, and learning from mistakes. Technical issues can be frustrating for an online teacher educator, and it can be tempting to act on frustrations or with impatience when trying to troubleshoot issues. From the conversations with colleagues, I have learned, however, that remaining patient and empathetic could help to create a positive learning environment and promote a sense of collaboration between my students and myself. This is a beneficial skill to have as a teacher educator, and models preferred teacher behaviour for the student teachers in the WIL excursion—again something they could adopt for use in their future classrooms (Uunona & Goosen, 2023). Furthermore, when faced with technical challenges during online sessions, my behaviour set an example for my students. This is something I always have to keep in mind during interactions with students. These findings are similar to those in a study by Yu et al. (2019), who found that patience, empathy, flexibility, and adaptability were important factors in successful online teaching.

Data from the notes in my reflective journal also reveal that I have learned that understanding the affordances and limitations of various online tools is essential for effective online teaching, which is a requirement for the facilitation of effective online learning (Uunona & Goosen, 2023). For example, during my technical role as an online teacher educator, I participated in sessions that utilized breakaway rooms to enable small-group discussions. While this approach allowed for additional personalised interactions and profound engagement, I also had to consider the potential that students might get distracted. In turn, this realisation underscored the need to set clear expectations for student participation and collaboration. As a result, I found it helpful to provide students with structured prompts and guidelines to support their group work. From the video recordings and discussion with fellow facilitators, it was clear that many of the students did not participate or contribute to the group discussions. This finding implies that I need to explore skills, techniques, technical tools, and applications further to support extensive student participation. Considering that Du Toit and Petersen (2023, p. 25) report that online educators in these excursions sometimes had to spend "more time sorting out and helping groups to form functional units than supporting the intended reflective learning and skills development", my need to further my professional development in this regard becomes even more critical. Research by Pynoo et al. (2011) emphasizes the importance of selecting appropriate tools based on the learning objectives and the needs of students. Through my experiences, I have found that being knowledgeable about the different online tools available and their potential benefits and limitations could help to create an effective and engaging learning environment. I should therefore always try to explore and experiment with new or unfamiliar tools before I use them with my students. Overall, my experience with providing technical support and using different technical tools has taught me that, while these are essential for online education, they should be accompanied by flexibility and adaptability to ensure a successful learning experience (Yu et al., 2019). I need to ensure that I continue my professional development to keep track of changes and updates in existing tools, but also to be informed about new tools and applications, which could enhance my technical role as an online educator.

6 Recommendations for Professional Development Goals to Strengthen My Contributions in Future WIL Excursions

Based on the findings and discussions presented, I have set the following professional development goals as recommendations for myself—and possibly other novice teacher educators—to enhance my (but also *our*) social, communication and technical roles in online education:

- **Develop interpersonal skills**: As an online teacher, it is important to establish a supportive and interactive learning community among students. Novice teacher educators therefore need to focus on building relationships with their students to facilitate a positive and productive learning environment. This can be achieved by developing rapport, demonstrating empathy, and managing own emotions well when difficult situations emerge.
- **Enhance communication skills**: Effective communication is critical for successful online teaching and learning. Novice teacher educators should work on improving their active listening and messaging skills to ensure that students can understand and engage with the material effectively. Developing—and continuing to develop—academic vocabulary would be useful to support this goal. Additionally, teacher educators should encourage communication and provide constructive feedback to help create a positive and engaging learning environment.
- **Understand the online learning environment**: Novice teacher educators need to have a deep understanding of the online learning environment and the needs of the students. This requires a combination of technical, pedagogical, and interpersonal skills.
- **Improve teaching skills continuously**: Novice teacher educators should continually seek opportunities to improve their teaching skills for in-person as well as online contexts. This can be achieved by attending professional development workshops, engaging in peer mentoring programmes, and seeking feedback from students and colleagues. Staying informed and up to date with new technical developments and applications would contribute to this goal.

By setting these professional development goals, novice teacher educators could enhance their online teaching skills and provide students with a positive and engaging learning experience in the online this environment.

7 Conclusion

Case study provided valuable insights into some of the professional development needs of novice teacher educators in the context of online excursions. I used the S-STEP research design to investigate the challenges I faced as a novice teacher educator, and to explain how I overcame them. My experiences were reported in line with three key roles for online educators, namely social, communication, and technical facilitation roles (Baran et al., 2011; Grammens et al., 2022). The findings highlight the importance of ongoing reflection and continuous learning to overcome limitations and enhance strengths as a teacher educator. Overall, my communication skills can be seen as the area where I need professional development most. This is not surprising, as academics in tertiary environments guide and lead students by voicing their opinions and critical insights. I will therefore continue striving to improve this role. By reflecting on these strengths and areas for improvement, I was able to gain insight into additional avenues required for my professional development. Such insight could assist universities in designing opportunities for similar development for their novice teacher educators. Future research could focus on preparing novice teacher educators for optimal functioning in online environments to narrow the gap reported by McMillan and Gordon (2017) further. Ultimately, such research could contribute to the preparation of future super teachers who are equipped to thrive in a complex profession.

References

Baran, E., Correia, A. P., & Thompson, A. (2011). Transforming online teaching practice: Critical analysis of the literature on the roles and competencies of online teachers. *Distance Education, 32*(3), 421–439. https://doi.org/10.1080/01587919.2011.610293

Bathmaker, A. M., & Avis, J. (2007). 'How do I cope with that?' The challenge of 'schooling' cultures in further education for trainee FE lecturers. *British Educational Research Journal, 33*(4), 509–532.

Berry, M. (2010). Introduction from the S-STEP Chair. In L. B. Erickson, J. R. Young, & S. Pinnegar (Eds.), *Navigating the public and private: Negotiating the diverse landscape of teacher education* (pp. 1–29). Proceedings of the Eighth International Conference on Self-Study of Teacher Education Practices, Herstmonceux Castle, East Sussex.

Bunt, B. J., White, L., & Petersen, N. (2023). Students' experiences of game-based learning to foster self-directed learning. In N. Petersen, A. du Toit, E. Mentz, & R. J. Balfour (Eds.), *Innovative curriculum design: Bridging the theory–practice divide in work-integrated learning to foster self-directed learning* (pp. 77–95). AOSIS. https://doi.org/10.4102/aosis.2023.BK426.04

Burgueño, R., González-Cutre, D., Sicilia, A., Alcaraz-Ibáñez, M., & Medina-Casaubón, J. (2022). Is the instructional style of teacher educators related to the teaching intention of pre-service teachers? A self-determination theory perspective-based analysis. *Educational Review, 74*(7), 1282–1304. https://doi.org/10.1080/00131911.2021.1890695

Burke, K. (2020). Virtual praxis: Constraints, approaches, and innovations of online creative arts teacher educators. *Teaching and Teacher Education, 95*, 103143. https://doi.org/10.1016/j.tate.2020.103143

Burn, K., Ingram, J., Molway, L., & Mutton, T. (2022). Beyond reactive responses to enduring growth: The transformation of principles and practices within initial teacher education. *Journal of Education for Teaching, 48*(4), 441–458.

Chen, J., Zhang, J., & Luo, Y. (2015). Teacher-student relationships: A literature review. *Journal of Education and Practice, 6*(7), 109–114.

Conklin, H. G. (2020). The preparation of novice teacher educators for critical, justice-oriented teacher education: A longitudinal exploration of formal study in the pedagogy of teacher education. *Teachers and Teaching, 26*(7/8), 491–507.

Creswell, J. W., & Creswell, J. D. (2018). *Research design: Qualitative, quantitative & mixed methods approaches* (5th ed.). London: Sage.

De Beer, J., Petersen, N., & Conley, L. (2022). 'Withitness' in the virtual learning space: Reflections of student-teachers and teacher-educators. In J. de Beer, N. Petersen, E. Mentz, & R. Balfour (Eds.), *Self-directed learning in the era of the COVID-19 pandemic: Research on the affordances of online virtual excursions* (pp. 221–240). AOSIS.

De Beer, J., Petersen, N., Mentz, E., & Balfour, R. J. (Eds.). (2023). *Self-directed learning in the era of the COVID-19 pandemic*. AOSIS.

De Beer, J., Van der Walt, M., & Bunt, B. (2020). The affordances of case-based teaching that draws on drama in pre-service teacher education. In J. de Beer, N. Petersen, & H. J. van Vuuren (Eds.), *Becoming a teacher: Research on the work-integrated learning of student teachers* (pp. 189–214) (NWU Self-Directed Learning Series Vol. 4). AOSIS. https://doi.org/10.4102/aosis.2020.BK215.07

Dewey, J. (1933). *How we think: A restatement of the relation of reflective thinking to the educative process*. DC Health.

Dobbs, C. L., Leider, C. M., & Tigert, J. (2022). A space for culturally and linguistically diverse learners? Using S-STEP to examine world language teacher education. *International Multilingual Research Journal, 16*(3), 237–245.

Du Toit, A. (2023). Entrepreneurial learning as curriculum innovation toward bridging the theory–practice divide when preparing future "super teachers". In N. Petersen, A. du Toit, E. Mentz, & R. J. Balfour (Eds.), *Innovative curriculum design: Bridging the theory–practice divide in work-integrated learning to foster self-directed learning* (pp. 119–143) (NWU Self-Directed Learning Series Vol. 12). AOSIS.

Du Toit, A., & Petersen, N. (2023). Re-imagining work-integrated learning excursions to decrease the theory-practice divide. In N. Petersen, A. du Toit, E. Mentz, & R. Balfour (Eds.), *Innovative curriculum design: Bridging the theory-practice divide in work-integrated learning to foster self-directed learning* (pp. 1–30) (NWU Self-Directed Learning Series Vol. 12). AOSIS.

El-Hussein, M. O., & Cronje, J. C. (2019). The role of novice lecturers in the success of the higher education system. *Journal of Education and Practice, 10*(4), 54–59.

Gao, Y., & Gao, Q. (2021). An empirical study on the relationship between online presentation quality and user experience. *Journal of Ambient Intelligence and Humanized Computing, 12*(8), 8727–8736.

Grammens, M., Voet, M., Vanderlinde, R., Declercq, L., & De Wever, B. (2022). A systematic review of teacher roles and competences for teaching synchronously online through videoconferencing technology. *Educational Research Review, 7*, 100461. https://doi.org/10.1016/j.edurev.2022.100461

Ibrahim, A. B., Mohamad, F., Rom, K. B. M., & Shahrom, S. M. (2013). Identifying strategies adopted by novice lecturers in the initial years of teaching. *Procedia-Social and Behavioral Sciences, 90*, 3–12.

Johnson, D., & Johnson, F. (2013). *Joining together: Group theory and group skills* (11th ed.). Pearson.

Johnson, D. W., & Johnson, R. T. (2019). The impact of cooperative learning on self-directed learning. In J. de Beer & R. Bailey (Eds.), *Self-directed learning for the 21st century: Implications for higher education* (pp. 37–66) (NWU Self-Directed Learning Series Vol. 1). AOSIS.

Jonsén, E., & Fossland, T. (2021). Novice lecturers in higher education: Challenges and opportunities. *Teaching in Higher Education, 26*(1), 1–18.

Kabashi, S., Xhaferi, B., & Krasniqi, B. (2021). The role of professional development in shaping teacher effectiveness. *European Journal of Education Studies, 8*(1), 67–82.

Kember, D., & Leung, D. Y. P. (2020). Characterizing and assessing the development of novice teachers. In *Characterizing and assessing learning in engineering education research* (pp. 211–233). Springer.

Kruger, C. C. G., & Mdakane, M. (2023). Exploring strategies to foster first-year students' critical reflection towards social justice praxis in a work-integrated learning experience. In N. Petersen, A. du Toit, E. Mentz, & R. J. Balfour (Eds.), *Innovative curriculum design: Bridging the theory–practice divide in work-integrated learning to foster Self-Directed Learning* (pp. 97–118). AOSIS. https://doi.org/10.4102/aosis.2023.BK426.04

LaBoskey, V. K. (2010). Teacher education and models of teacher reflection. In *International encyclopedia of education* (3rd ed., pp. 629–634). Springer.

LaBoskey, V. K. (2015). Self-study for and by novice elementary classroom teachers with social justice aims and the implications for teacher education. *Studying Teacher Education, 11*(2), 97–102. https://doi.org/10.1080/17425964.2015.1045770

Loughran, J. (2005). *Developing a pedagogy of teacher education: Understanding teaching and learning about teaching*. Routledge. https://doi.org/10.4324/9780203019672

Martin, R. (2009). *The design of business: Why design thinking is the next competitive advantage*. Harvard Business Press.

McMillan, W., & Gordon, N. (2017). Being and becoming a university teacher. *Higher Education Research and Development, 36*(4), 777–790. https://doi.org/10.1080/07294360.2016.1236781

Nieuwenhuis, J. (2010). *First steps in research*. Van Schaik.

Ou, C., Ledoux, T., & Crooks, S. M. (2004). The effects of instructor presence on critical thinking in asynchronous online discussion. In C. Crawford, R. Carlsen, K. McFerrin, J. Price, R. Weber, & D. Williz (Eds.), *Proceedings of the Society for Information Technology and Teacher Education International Conference* (pp. 2989–2993). AACE.

Peercy, M. M., & Sharkey, J. (2020). Missing a S-STEP? How self-study of teacher education practice can support the language teacher education knowledge base. *Language Teaching Research, 24*(1), 105–115.

Pinnegar, S., Hamilton, M. L., & Fitzgerald, L. (2010). Guidance in being and becoming self-study of practice researchers. In L. B. Erickson, J. R. Young, & S. Pinnegar (Eds.), *Navigating the public and private: Negotiating the diverse landscape of teacher education* (pp. 203–206). Proceedings of the Eighth International Conference on Self-Study of Teacher Education Practices, Herstmonceux Castle, East Sussex.

Pynoo, B., Tondeur, J., Van Braak, J., Duyck, W., Sijnave, B., & Duyck, P. (2011). Teachers' acceptance and use of an educational portal. *Computers and Education, 56*(4), 835–852. https://doi.org/10.1016/j.compedu.2010.11.012

Republic of South Africa. (2011). National Qualifications Framework Act (67/2008): Policy on the Minimum Requirements for Teacher Education Qualifications. *Government Gazette, 34467*, Notice 583. Government Printer.

Rodgers, C. (2002). Defining reflection: Another look at John Dewey and reflective thinking. *Teachers College Record, 104*(4), 842–866.

Sadler, D. R., & Good, E. (2021). The impact of feedback frequency on learning outcomes in a blended learning environment. *Computers and Education, 175*, 104202. https://doi.org/10.1016/j.compedu.2021.104202

Sadler, E. (2021). A practical guide to updating beliefs from contradictory evidence. *Econometrica, 89*(1), 415–436.

Trumbull, D., & Cobb, A. (2000). Comments to students and their effects. In J. J. Loughran & T. L. Russell (Eds.), *Exploring myths and legends of teacher education* (pp. 243–246). Proceedings of the Third International Conference of the Self-Study of Teacher Education Practices, Herstmonceux Castle, East Sussex.

Uunona, G. N., & Goosen, L. (2023). Leveraging ethical standards in artificial intelligence technologies: A guideline for responsible teaching and learning applications. In *Handbook of research on instructional technologies in health education and allied disciplines* (pp. 310–330). IGI Global.

Vanassche, E., & Kelchtermans, G. (2015). The state of the art in self-study of teacher education practices: A systematic literature review. *Journal of Curriculum Studies, 47*(4), 508–528.

Venter, E. (2019). Challenges for meaningful interpersonal communication in a digital era. *HTS Theological Studies, 75*(1), 1–6.

Vygotsky, L. S., & Cole, M. (1978). *Mind in society: Development of higher psychological processes*. Harvard University Press.

Yu, A., Tian, Y., & Guo, Y. (2019). Strategies for effective online teaching: A narrative literature review. *Journal of Computing in Higher Education, 31*(2), 278–301. https://doi.org/10.1007/s12528-019-09201-3

Exploring Reflective Practice as a Supportive Professional Development Tool for Novice Teachers: A Narrative Inquiry

Cisca de Kock

Abstract As a novice teacher, I experienced many obstacles in my first two years of teaching in a South African school context. Before embarking on my teaching career in South Africa, I taught in Taiwan for six years. The South African context proved to be very different and any or all expectations I had, was disempowering as there were no support programs in place for novice teacher. It thus became my concern to ascertain the possibilities of exploring reflective practice as a supportive professional development tool. This study was a narrative inquiry of processes to encourage and maintain novice teachers' professional development. The data in this study comprised of journal entries and field notes, which were constructed from my conversations with colleagues and my observations of my own practice. Main ideas were developed within my narrative to analyze. The purpose of this study was to ascertain the possibilities of professional development through reflective practice; to highlight reflective practice as a strategy which might bring about change, however imperfect, and to consider the human agency in this. The initial process of novice teachers entering the teaching profession is often associated with the terms "sink or swim". This process can often lead to feeling vulnerable and confused. The aim of this chapter is thus to show that based on my personal experience as a novice teacher, a "swim" mentality is possible for novice teachers by using reflective practice as a supportive professional development tool.

Keywords Reflective practice · Novice teachers · Support programs · Teacher education · Teacher effectiveness · Narrative inquiry · Work-integrated learning

C. de Kock (✉)
Cape Peninsula University of Technology, Cape Town, South Africa
e-mail: dekockc@cput.ac.za

1 Context of the Study

Research indicates that the initial experiences of novice teachers play an imperative role in further career development (Farrell, 2020; Farrell & Kennedy, 2019; McGarr, 2021). Regardless of how confident novice teachers feel about their career choice and the skills they acquired during their WIL/practicum teaching experience, having a solid support system can be regarded as beneficial when they make the transition from student to teacher. This transition can be met with a lot of anxiety and feelings of insecurity. In recent years, a number of models have been developed to describe novice teachers' professional development once they have entered the school arena, but one common feature that stands out is the first stage, the survival stage (Smith & Lev-Ari, 2005). Lortie (1975) describes the transition from the teacher training institution to school classrooms as something that can be characterized by a type of reality shock, in which the ideals that were formed during initial teacher education are replaced by the reality of school life. Studies on support mechanisms have shown that reality shock may have a negative effect on initial teaching experiences for novice teachers (Dvir & Schatz-Oppenheimer, 2020; Jiang et al., 2021; Voss & Kunter, 2020).

According to Jiang et al., (2021, p. 11) due to the unavoidable reality shock, novice teachers' experiences in schools, are likely to change their initial identities that they developed during the pre-service stage. Arends and Phurutse (2009, p. 31) stress the importance of support for novice teachers as this has been found to be a major factor in determining whether teachers stay in the profession for any length of time. In the absence of support, a high number of novice teachers have difficulty managing the school environment and, as a result, develop burnout symptoms and choose to leave the system (Arends & Phurutse, 2009, p. 31). This notion is further explored by Karlberg and Bezzina (2022, p. 624), who aver that the quality of a teachers' experience in the initial years is fundamental to developing and applying the knowledge, competences, beliefs, and attributes acquired during initial teacher education (ITE).

Furthermore, novice teachers are confronted with the demands of the job directly and need to adapt and draw on personal resources in order to survive and progress. Calderhead and Shorrock (2003) indicate that the socialization into a new school setting is a demanding and powerful process which often results in novice teachers changing their beliefs about teaching in order to fit in with the school's values and practices. Professional socialization into teaching requires agency from teachers. Agency can be described as having the power to make one's own decisions. Baez (2000) uses the term "free will" to describe agency and contrast this with structure which refers to the recurrent patterned arrangements which seem to influence or limit, and also enable, the choices and opportunities individuals have. Different points of departure (perspectives) and assumptions shape the identity of the individual. The power the teacher has (agency) and the constraints (structure) that they find themselves working in often has an influence on their "performance". Kahn (2009) provides an interesting perspective on the interplay between context and agency in terms of Archer's (2007) realist social theory. The interplay as discussed in Kahn (2009) links deliberative reflections about contextual factors and how these might influence the practice of novice teachers. Agency therefore plays a role in the development of such practices and is affected by the social conditions and cultural factors at play in the context.

2 Research Methodology

Three major elements supported the construction of this study. One was to develop clear insight on the augmentation of my own reflective thinking as a novice teacher. The second was to investigate ways which were pertinent to address my own needs as a novice. The third element was to convey the impact of reflective practice and other factors on my own educational practice and professional development.

The central research question that explicated this research was:

To what extent did practicing reflexivity and reflections as self-support mechanisms combat challenges as a novice teacher?

3 Qualitative Research

This study falls under the broad idea of a qualitative research process within an interpretive paradigm. Slavin (2007) describes qualitative research as research that emphasizes elaborate descriptions of social or instructional settings. The intention of qualitative research is to explore a social phenomenon by placing the investigator in the situation and to produce information on and given setting in its full richness and complexity (Slavin, 2007). As both the researcher and the participant, I placed myself in the school setting and investigated reflective changes in my given context. The product of this qualitative study was a thick description of narrative accounts. My experiences and lived stories are depicted in a way that gives the reader a sense of understanding what my "lived" experiences were like.

4 Narrative Inquiry

Narrative inquiry was used in order to accurately capture the relevant information needed for this particular research. Narrative inquiry is increasingly used in studies of educational experiences because human beings are storytelling organisms who, individually and socially lead storied lives (Connelly & Clandinin, 1990). Coulter et al. (2007) define narrative inquiry as a phenomenon that is widely recognized as a viable approach to conducting qualitative research. It has long been perceived as a pedagogical tool that accurately captures the relevant information. Creswell (2015) asserts that this may help reduce a commonly held perception by practitioners in the field that research is distinct from practice and has little direct application. In addition to this, this narrative study gave a voice which is rarely heard to experiences such as mine. Narrative inquiry is able to capture the everyday normal form of data that is familiar to individuals (Creswell, 2015). Clandinin and Connelly (2004) have argued that it is through storytelling that novice teachers engage in transformative pedagogical work.

5 Data Collection and Analysis

The main form of data collection involved keeping journals. Daily and weekly journals captured the essence of my experiences. These journals contained my own reflective entries. An autobiographical writing style was used to construct my lived experiences. This type of writing style contributed by enriching the narrative and assisting me to understand past events and experiences that influenced my present experiences. In these journal entries, I described and recorded my daily classroom experiences and context; things that went well in my lessons and things I needed to change or adapt. I analyzed my journal entries by looking at themes and patterns of personal and professional growth and the role that reflection played in fostering such growth. Other forms of data collection included observation and field notes, which I drafted to document accounts related to socialisation. Creswell (2015) proposes that the advantage of observation is to record information as it occurs in the actual school setting, to study the behaviour of the school, as well as to study individuals who might have difficulty in verbalising their ideas.

6 Challenges as a Novice Teacher

I experienced a variety of emotions when I found out that I got a teaching post. I felt relatively confident, and I believed that I could be an effective novice teacher. Upon entering the school, I was told by colleagues not to have any pre-conceived ideas or expectations of what type of learner I would be teaching. In hindsight, I was quite naïve in thinking that it would be easy for me to adjust to my new surroundings. If I could adapt to the school climate and culture overseas, surely, I would be able to find my feet in this new context. I was faced with the following challenges in my first year of teaching.

7 Non-existent Induction/Mentoring Program

One of my expectations were that there would be a structured induction/mentoring program to support my entry as a novice teacher, but there was no such program for novice teachers at the school. At the beginning of the academic year, I requested to be provided with four sets of guidelines concerning, (a) what was expected of me in terms of teaching and facilitating my subject; (b) a practical guide on the school's policies and procedures; (c) discussion of curriculum content of the grades assigned to me and (d) guidelines on how to approach setting up assessments for learners. Despite numerous requests, I was left to "sink or swim" and had to navigate myself through an extremely difficult adjustment period. This left me anxious, and I began to doubt myself because I did not feel confident in my teaching. This was largely due to my perception of feeling inadequate with no support. These feelings were brought on because I was given no guidelines and it felt as if I was incompetent. The lack of support appeared to be grounded in the erroneous belief that I should have learned all I needed to know to be successful at the start of my tenure after my teacher training education. I felt that if I was not successful, it would be my own fault. I was not tough enough or not fit in some way for the rigors of teaching. I wanted to become more efficient, proficient and most of all to be regarded as an effective teacher. Without much support it was difficult to cope with the demands of teaching, managing, and maintaining control, finding adequate resources, planning lessons, setting up assessment tasks and dealing with the learning disabilities of some learners.

8 Managing Large Class Sizes

I was forced to soldier on with little assistance and was required to teach large classes that other teachers did not want to teach. At times I would have sixty-five learners in my class with only forty desks. This was a reality shock to me. It became challenging when I had to look at the teaching strategies I was using. What worked in one class did not work in another. It was very difficult to find a balance. I started feeling perplexed because my learners seemed to lack so many necessary underlying skills and prior knowledge. I had to scramble around to find material that was appropriate and suitable for their level. Having large classes also meant that disruptive behaviour was a constant battle. Learning and teaching became a constant battlefield, and I dreaded every period and every day of being at school. It was difficult to cope with the expectations I had for myself and the expectations the school had. The expectations I had involved that every lesson would be a success and I would make significant changes in the lives of my learners. I expected that I would be given guidance and some mentorship to lead me on this new path. The school's expectation was that I had to deal with disruptive problems on my own.

9 Time Management

I found it difficult to manage my time, organize my workload and keeping up with demands. The content that needed to be taught and assessed felt overwhelming at times. It felt as if I was teaching to test and teaching towards completing the next task or assessment. There was no time to do remedial work, and it was discouraging to know that you had to move on to the next task, even though you knew that your learners were not grasping the work. I soon realized that I was not only employed as a teacher, but that skills other than teaching skills were also required of me; being an administrator, athletics coordinator, social worker, acting as a parent (in locus parentis), mediator, disciplinarian, school counsellor and behaviour support teacher took over much of my time.

10 Motivating Learners

I found it very difficult to 'read' my learners. Some of them were not motivated or had no goals in their lives. Their only goal seemed to be to get to school in the morning and spend time with their friends. A misconception among these teens were that they only had to do the minimum to pass to move on to the next grade. Learners had no aspirations at all. I would often start my lessons with a motivational speech. It seemed that I could only capture their attention for a few minutes, and whatever I said was out of their thoughts a few minutes later. I would often tell learners my own story hoping that it would inspire some of them. My story touched a few, and I could see a change in some learners, but the others could not be bothered to think about what their future would entail.

11 Parental Involvement

I feel that parental involvement is crucial in a learner's education. To have parents involved actively could have been a valuable resource in my classroom management plan. I felt that it was each parent's responsibility to be involved in classroom or educational activities. Parental involvement can mean supervising homework, helping learners' study and monitoring progress. It was difficult to contact and get a hold of the parents of learners who had difficulties and who were difficult to manage. Often the learners' parents could not come to school for meetings. Some of them simply had no interest in their children and the mentality that they had was that they could not control their children at home, and if their children were at school, the problem became that of the teacher solely. These same parents of disruptive and poor performers also did not attend parental meetings and intervention meetings.

12 Engaging in Types of Reflection

Reflective practice (RP) played a very central role in my growth as a novice teacher. My understanding of what is possible and what is less possible arose from using the reflective process to critically question my practice. I was able to evaluate my practice by using my knowledge, as well as knowledge or advice gained by collaborating with colleagues to improve the teaching and learning process during my first year as a novice teacher. I define RP as a phenomenon that enables a teacher to perceive the 'bigger picture'; it enables one to step back and evaluate one's practice, to see what the needs of the learners are, and how you as a teacher can adapt or change your approaches. As novice teachers, we bring experiences of our previous schooling into our present schooling environment. According to Singh (1996, p. 350) RP has the potential to change teachers' self-understanding and even transform teachers' practices and work situations. These attributes show what kind of facilitation RP can bring and what transformative changes it can bring to a novice teacher's practice. RP can thus be seen as a mode that integrates or links thinking as well as action. As a reflective teacher I sought to find alternatives, keep an open mind and compare and contrast ideas and suggestions. Schön (1983) considered two kinds of knowledge that professionals use in practice: technical rationality and tacit knowledge. Technical rationality is used when we apply the theory that we have learned to solve practical day-to-day problems. I had to rely on my tacit/intuitive knowledge, thinking on my feet to solve problems. Reflection became the tool by which I was able to focus on my own lived experiences in ways that helped me to confront, understand and work towards resolutions. By doing this, I became more empowered to take more appropriate action in future situations. Reflective thought did not only occur when something went wrong, it also occurred when something was spectacularly right. Through RP, I was able to identify learning needs. Ghaye and Ghaye (1998, p. 6) assert that reflection-on-practice helps us make sense of teaching and learning, and making sense is also about becoming more aware of the interaction between ourselves and the context in which we teach. Research conducted by Reed et al., (2002, p. 133) found that those teachers who appeared more able to be reflective-in-action during lessons and reflective-on-action when planning their teaching or discussing their work do offer learners richer, more coherent, and more appropriate scaffold learning experiences than those who appeared less able to teach reflectively. Van Manen (1977) distinguished different levels of reflection namely, technical reflection, practical/problematic reflection, and critical reflection. These levels became more evident to me once I was able to identify them within my practice. Identifying the reflection levels simplified and clarified where I had to change and improve my pedagogy, not only to improve the learning process for my learners, but to improve the teaching process for myself.

13 Technical Reflection

During my first year of teaching, classroom management and classroom participation were among the many concerns that I had. I struggled immensely in the first two terms of year one. I was not used to teaching large classes whilst dealing with disruptions and outbursts from learners. The school curriculum was densely packed, and I felt that I was not teaching the learners the skills that they so desperately needed. I set high expectations for myself and for my learners and I wanted to meet them all, but it was difficult to try out new techniques. Resources like overhead projectors were limited at the school. I was fortunate enough that an overhead projector was donated to me by the university. Having this type of equipment transformed the learning process immediately. Discipline problems became fewer as I was now able to face the class when teaching them, instead of turning my back towards them. I was also able to use visual aids in my lessons, which made the lessons interesting for learners, and it gave them a better understanding of what they needed to grasp.

14 Practical/Problematic Reflection

I engaged in this type of reflection with the view of improving my practice. I noticed that there was a need for improvement in my practice when assessing the work of learners. I had to find a strategy to collect information and document classroom procedures and to look at classroom culture and dynamics more carefully. In my first year as a novice teacher, I was also studying towards an Honors degree in Education. Exposure to educational research projects and literature on educational processes enabled me to gain skill in resolving problems which occurred regularly. One example of this was using cooperative learning as a means of instruction. By using this type of technique, I could see that there was a visible improvement in how this specific class, who performed very poorly before this type of instruction was used, improved.

15 Critical Reflection

Ghaye and Ghaye (1998) argue that critical reflection is not a process of self-victimization, but about taking a questioning stance towards what teachers and schools do, and it questions the means and ends of education. Critical reflection led me to engage in reflection-on-practice on a deeper level. Throughout the two-year period I drew on all of these different types of reflections. I think I relied a little more on technical reflection and practical / problematic reflection in my first year of teaching. During my second year of teaching, I was more familiar with the reflective process and the different techniques. Previously, I would reflect after my lessons. After some time, reflecting occurred before, during and after my lessons. Through writing personal narratives, I discovered the intrinsic role that reflection plays in the daily experience of a teacher. Writing a personal narrative became a way to connect educational theory with classroom practice and experience. I was able to constructively reflect on my teaching experience, rethink, expand and enhance my beliefs. This allowed me to see first-hand growth and I was able to notice the change on a personal, professional, and social level.

I started thinking like a reflective teacher, continually examining, assessing, and re-shaping my teaching beliefs and practice. As I remembered some key moments in my life, I realized how each one of them affected me as a person and, most importantly, as a teacher. At first, I felt nervous about sharing my narratives, but as I continued to share, I found that an audience of colleagues supported and enhanced my writing. In a sense I perceived that my autobiographical writing would be less powerful and expressive if it was only written for myself. A primary concern was to develop a sense of own efficacy, a sense of agency in the social context of schooling. The problem of agency is critical in education. A sense of personal efficacy can be encouraged through emphasis on autobiography as a social endeavour. In becoming a teacher, I entered a career-long agreement to become responsible for the school lives of my learners, and accordingly, for the chances they will have in life once they leave my classroom. I realized very soon that the teaching profession in South Africa and everywhere else in the world, for that matter, has been placed under an immense amount of scrutiny. Society has formed greater expectations for what teachers should know and be able to accomplish with their learners. Despite the external pressures that teachers have to experience on a daily basis, the choices that they make individually have an impact on the learners that they teach and the quality of the learning that takes place.

16 Developing Ideas and Actions for Professional Development

Stage 1: Trying out new ideas

Formal education for teaching only represents a starting point for a lifetime of professional growth and development. I knew that if I wanted to excel in the teaching profession and challenge myself to higher levels of expertise, it was important to realize that teaching was a continual learning experience that would span over the entire course of my career. I was aware of not knowing everything, especially working with many different learners with many different needs that presented ongoing challenges. To meet these challenges, I had to learn to adapt and face these challenges head on. Continual professional development on my part aided me in trying out new ideas and activities to benefit my learners. According to Howe (2006, p. 287) tacit understandings and wisdom in the practice of teaching can be uncovered and better understood through personal reflection and collaboration with colleagues.

Stage 2: Development of ideas and classroom practice

My ideas about classroom practice certainly changed. The illusive ideas I formed about classroom practice changed dramatically. The thought of creating 'magic' in a short period of time, was quickly extinguished when the reality shock kicked in. I realized that it was impossible to change the learners and to develop and mold them into the type of learners that I had in mind, the type of learner that was motivated, goal orientated and driven towards achieving success. In order to make a success of each lesson, I had to develop ideas; in a sense, I had to re-invent myself, using the ideas that I developed. According to Bell and Gilbert (1994, p. 491) the teachers in their study were changing from being constructivist technicians to being constructivist teachers. For those teachers, being a constructivist teacher was becoming a way of thinking and behaving for the teachers, rather than the implementation of some new teaching activities. I critically reflected on my practice and opted to move away from an over-concern with my 'performance' and routine discipline problems, to consider more fundamental teaching and learning issues. I engaged with the following questions: how should I teach in order to provide richer learning experiences? how will I know whether the change has had any impact, beneficial or otherwise? If teaching is to develop as an evidence-based profession, novice teachers need to question such claims and make the classroom itself the site for their enquiry and their professional development.

17 Agency for Change

Agency manifested through my personal deliberations about my work setting and contextual environment. I engaged in what Archer (2007) calls autonomous reflections. These included making journal entries and personal reflection in and on action. Sometimes I reviewed my work critically by engaging in deeper thinking about the context. Most important and prevalent was the fact that I was not given any form of induction or mentorship. Furthermore, the conditions of work and attitudes of learners did not fit into what I, as a novice teacher, valued as important ways of doing. This prompted me to engage with the social context in my reflexive deliberations in the development of and exercising of my agency. I feel that my actions seem to fit the description Archer (2007) provides for progressive specification of action based on reflexive deliberation. She argues that it is through progressive specification of action in social contexts that the agency of the individual emerges. I was constantly reflecting autonomously and prioritizing my performativity in relation to my practice. The changes I made and approaches I adopted as a result of my considerations and reflection on my work were the result of exercising my agency. As discussed by Archer (2007), I began to prioritize my concerns and this guided my conduct in my teaching and in relation to my responsibilities, with a view to improving my practice. This seems to be similar to the experiences of novice teachers as described in Kahn (2009). In Kahn's (2009) study, teachers engaged in reflexive deliberation that involved imagining, reliving, planning, and deciding on practical action, much of which I also engaged in. Like those teachers, my reflexive work was focused on new teaching responsibilities and finding ways to deal with these immediate concerns in my practice, hence my subjectivity influenced my agency and exercising of my agency. My changes in practice, particularly in the second year of teaching, involved strong exercising of agency. In my opinion, this also indicated professional growth. This is all linked to my expression and continual development of my agency through reflexive deliberations. My own agency gave me the power to make my own informed decisions. Structural influence like the school I was employed at should have had the power to enable choices and opportunities, but that was rarely the case. The power the teacher has (agency), and the constraints (structure) often have an influence on the teachers' performance. The more I used my own agency, the more I reflected and the more I grew professionally. If I had been exposed to a structured induction/mentoring program, my professional development as a novice teacher could have developed so much more. My agency was expressed through taking control of my situation. I viewed my teaching practice in a critical manner, and I made the choice to change my situation.

18 Findings

My study revolved on using RP as a self-support mechanism to develop professionally. In my experience this was indeed possible. From my experience of using reflection, I believe it to be a useful self-support mechanism. It can lead to the fostering of personal and professional growth and enable novice teachers to become more effective practitioners. Reflection can be difficult to integrate into the daily teaching routine in a substantial and meaningful way, but in order for novice teachers to reflect, they must be provided with a wide range of ongoing opportunities to think and talk about their teaching experience. We need to cultivate the art of reflection and develop a culture of reflective thought. It may be difficult for novice teachers to think and talk about their practice, because no one wants to be embarrassed or feel incompetent when asking for advice or help. It can also be difficult for novice teachers to think and talk openly about their work in meaningful ways. Novice teachers, for the most part, focus on the isolation of their classrooms and have little opportunity or encouragement to engage in any type of reflective activity with other teachers. When opportunities to reflect on practice are presented, many novice teachers have little understanding of what reflection really means and how it is accomplished.

Collaboration, RP and a shared vision for professional growth are essential guiding principles that afford scaffolding for professional development. In order to perform well as a novice teacher, it was a necessity to explore my inner terrain. I found that if I did not do this on my own, I would lose myself, practicing in self-delusion and running the risk of self-serving. I was in desperate need of the guidance that a community of collegial discourse should have provided, in order to sustain me through the trials of teaching. It became evident that it is important for novice teachers to work together as collaborators and colleagues to gain a better understanding of both their own school experience as well as that of their learners. Another finding was that there is a lack of structured induction/mentoring programs.

I expected a structured type of induction/mentoring program to be offered at the school where I was employed. Although I felt confident with what I had learnt from my experience and training overseas, I was not familiar with teaching in a different context, and that made me feel anxious. I had a lot of concerns that I did not know how to deal with at first. Lack of support created a very big problem. There was no supportive management staff that showed interest in my work. There was also no active support and receptiveness for my ideas. Knowing that I had some sort of support would have created the feeling that I could rely on solid, unwavering support, which would have instilled a sense of trust. This indicates a need for induction/mentoring programs to help ease the adaptation from being a student teacher to being a novice teacher.

19 Concluding Thoughts and Reflections

Through writing personal narratives, I discovered the intrinsic role that reflection can play in the daily experience of a teacher. Writing personal narrative became a means of connecting educational theory with classroom practice and experience. I was able to constructively reflect on my teaching experience. This narrative study allowed me to see first-hand growth. I was able to modify and enhance my beliefs as a result of my own experiences. The aim of my narratives was to strongly suggest that perhaps all novice teachers need a place to share their stories about public education in order to identify what their common experiences say about teaching and education. This research enhanced my life by bringing about positive changes and providing me with new understandings. The study reported personal change or growth; explaining how I have learned from mistakes made during planning and teaching by proposing adaptations to my instruction as a result of initial problems.

We should move away from the thought that novice teachers must mimic more experienced teachers. The emphasis should be on becoming more reflective thinkers who explore their own individual teaching styles. There is a need for reflective classroom experience early in ITE programs. It is important to link theory and practice through working closely with schools early in a pre-service teacher's career. In this way, they may be enabled to relate 'what' the practice of teaching is to the 'why' captured in the theories underlying the practice, to better comprehend why a particular practice does or does not work in a class. I learned that I should never doubt my abilities and that with structure and some guidance anything is possible. At the beginning of this study, I often felt that teaching was not my vocation, as I had thought during my international career. Emergent from this study was a teacher with confidence and a love for teaching. A combination of good induction/mentoring programs, reflection, and possibilities for agency in my opinion are essential for development and professional growth. I believe that the practice of reflection led to professional development in my case and provided the insights that I was able to use, to develop a better understanding of my practice and the conditions in which it occurred. I also developed a broader teaching repertoire, which increased possibilities and confidence, and this gave me more options to exercise agency.

References

Archer, M. S. (2007). *Making our way through the world: Human reflexivity and social mobility.* Cambridge University Press.
Arends, F., & Phurutse, M. (2009). *Beginner teachers in South Africa: School readiness, knowledge and skills.* HSRC Press.
Baez, B. (2000). Agency, structure, and power: An inquiry into racism and resistance for education. *Studies in Philosophy and Education, 19*(4), 329–348.
Bell, B., & Gilbert, J. (1994). Teacher development as professional, personal and social development. *Teaching and Teacher Education, 10*(5), 483–497.
Calderhead, J., & Shorrock, S. B. (2003). *Understanding teacher education: Case studies in the professional development of beginning teachers.* Routledge.
Clandinin, D. J., & Connelly, F. M. (2004). *Narrative inquiry: Experience and story in qualitative research.* Wiley.
Connelly, F. M., & Clandinin, D. J. (1990). Stories of experience and narrative inquiry. *Educational Researcher, 19*(5), 2–14.
Coulter, C., Michael, C., & Poynor, L. (2007). Storytelling as pedagogy: An unexpected outcome of narrative inquiry. *Curriculum Inquiry, 37*(2), 103–122.
Creswell, J. W. (2015). *Educational research: Planning, conducting, and evaluating quantitative and qualitative research.* Pearson.
Dvir, N., & Schatz-Oppenheimer, O. (2020). Novice teachers in a changing reality. *European Journal of Teacher Education, 43*(4), 639–656.
Farrell, T. S., & Kennedy, B. (2019). Reflective practice framework for TESOL teachers: One teacher's reflective journey. *Reflective Practice, 20*(1), 1–12.
Farrell, T. S. (2020). Professional development through reflective practice for English-medium instruction (EMI) teachers. *International Journal of Bilingual Education and Bilingualism, 23*(3), 277–286.
Ghaye, A., & Ghaye, K. (1998). *Teaching and learning through critical reflective practice.* David Fulton.
Howe, E. R. (2006). Exemplary teacher induction: An international review. *Educational Philosophy and Theory, 38*(3), 287–297.
Jiang, L., Yuan, K., & Yu, S. (2021). Transitioning from pre-service to novice: A study on Macau EFL teachers' identity change. *The Asia-Pacific Education Researcher, 30*, 11–21.
Kahn, P. (2009). Contexts for teaching and the exercise of agency in early-career academics: Perspectives from realist social theory. *International Journal for Academic Development, 14*(3), 197–207.
Karlberg, M., & Bezzina, C. (2022). The professional development needs of beginning and experienced teachers in four municipalities in Sweden. *Professional Development in Education, 48*(4), 624–641.
Lortie, D. C. (1975). *Schoolteacher* (2nd ed.). The University of Chicago Press.
McGarr, O. (2021). The use of virtual simulations in teacher education to develop pre-service teachers' behaviour and classroom management skills: Implications for reflective practice. *Journal of Education for Teaching, 47*(2), 274–286.

Reed, Y., Davis, H., & Nyabanyaba, T. (2002). Investigating teachers' 'take-up' of reflective practice from an In-service professional development teacher education programme in South Africa. *Educational Action Research, 10*(2), 253–274.

Schön, D. (1983). *The reflective practitioner*. Temple Smith.

Singh, M. (1996). Reflective teaching practice. In R. Gilbert (Ed.), *Studying: Society and environment: A handbook for teachers* (pp. 349–361). McMillan Education Australia.

Slavin, R. E. (2007). *Educational research in an age of accountability*. Allyn & Bacon.

Smith, K., & Lev-Ari, L. (2005). The place of the practicum in pre-service teacher education: The voice of the students. *Asia-Pacific Journal of Teacher Education, 33*(3), 289–302.

Van Manen, M. (1977). Linking ways of knowing with ways of being practical. *Curriculum Inquiry, 6*(3), 205–228.

Voss, T., & Kunter, M. (2020). "Reality shock" of beginning teachers? Changes in teacher candidates' emotional exhaustion and constructivist-oriented beliefs. *Journal of Teacher Education, 71*(3), 292–306.

A Self-study from the Work Integrated Learning Trenches: The Achilles Heel Stories

Zelda Barends and Carisma Nel

Abstract In response to the critical discourse surrounding teacher quality and effectiveness, especially in the context of South Africa, we explore the challenges faced by teacher educators during work integrated learning (WIL) within teacher education programs. Focusing on language preparation, the study delves into the lived experiences of teacher educators through collaborative self-study. Grounded in Wenger's Community of Practice framework, we examine the dialogues and reflections between teacher educators from different provinces in South Africa, revealing key challenges such as policy adherence, numerical pressures, the impact of COVID-19, and the inadequacies in language preparation. The study emphasizes the crucial role of language in achieving quality education and highlights the gaps in understanding its significance in global educational initiatives. By narrating our experiences as teacher educators, we extend our insights for policymakers, faculty leaders, and curriculum designers, contributing to informed decisions regarding the enhancement of work integrated learning within teacher education programs. In this chapter, we share immersed cases of work integrated learning in diverse contexts, fostering a deeper understanding of the challenges faced by teacher educators and preservice teachers alike.

Keywords Work-integrated learning · Reading literacy · Language of learning and teaching · Pre-service teachers · Self-study

Z. Barends (✉)
Stellenbosch University, Stellenbosch, South Africa
e-mail: zbarends@sun.ac.za

C. Nel
North-West University, Potchefstroom, South Africa
e-mail: carisma.nel@nwu.ac.za

1 Introduction

Why can't our children learn to read well? This is a question being asked by parents, the media, and various other educational stakeholders. If the statement by Anita Archer is correct that "The quality of *teaching* is the single most important factor in the educational system" (Archer, 2017) then it seems as if the current scrutiny of initial teacher education practices may be justified. Is the work-integrated learning component indeed "the spine of the teacher education programmes" (Liu et al., 2017, p. 175)? In this chapter, our aim is to respond to the scrutiny by telling our work integrated learning stories as we experienced and continue to experience it in the trenches as teacher educators in South Africa, as researchers, and as parents. In describing our lived experiences through a collaborative self-study, we reveal our critical reflections on our own practices and the current state of work integrated learning as we experience it within our institutions, with a specific focus on how to prepare our preservice teachers to teach reading, especially those specialising in the Foundation Phase (Grade R to Grade 3) as well as use the language of learning and teaching (LoLT) in the classroom, usually from Grade 4 (i.e., intermediate phase) onwards when English becomes the medium of instruction. In this study, we respond to the need highlighted by the South African National Planning Commission (2012, p. 306) "to improve the quality of teacher training" as well as the statement made by Spaull (2022, p. 4), based on the South African PIRLS 2016 and 2021 reading results, "It is now clear that, on the whole, faculties of education are not preparing incoming teachers to teach reading in the home language". The following research questions guided our collaborative exploration, namely (1) what challenges do we as teacher educators, researchers and parents experience when working in the work-integrated learning trenches? and (2) what did our stories reveal about the Achilles heel of work-integrated learning? To conclude, we provide recommendations, based on the findings of this study, for policy makers, initial teacher education institutions, schools as well as parents.

2 Theoretical Framework

This study is situated within Wenger's Community of Practice (CoP) theoretical framework (Wenger, 1998). Wenger and Wenger-Trayner (2015, p. 2) define communities of practice as "groups of people who share a concern or a passion for something they do and learn how to do it better as they interact regularly". Lave and Wenger (1991, p. 54) initially developed the concept to describe the social dynamics of learning. When individuals form part of a CoP there is almost always negotiation of meaning among the participants and this happens via two processes, namely participation and reification. Smith et al., (2017, p. 212) state that, "Participation involves acting and interacting, and reification involves producing artefacts, such as tools, words, symbols, rules, documents, concepts, theories, and so on, around which the negotiation of meaning is organized". Participation and reification are complementary processes in that each has the capacity to make up for the limitations of the other. For example, when viewing a webinar on explicit reading instruction participants may ask questions to obtain clarification or it may be modeled by the teacher educator, in this way, supporting the participants' understanding (i.e., a form of participation). Similarly, writing out a lesson plan (i.e., a form of reification) with a focus on explicit instruction may enhance the participants' understanding more than a mere explanation would.

3 Pre-service Teacher Preparedness to Teach: Work-Integrated Learning in the Spotlight

Internationally and in South Africa, teacher quality and effectiveness are under constant scrutiny (Bahr & Mellor, 2016; Deacon, 2016; Gravett, 2020; Taylor & Mawoyo, 2022). The media and research conducted during the COVID-19 pandemic play a consistent role in shaping this discourse (Macupe, 2018; Reimers, 2022), frequently questioning the quality of teachers and the preparation they receive at initial teacher education institutions. Critiques of teacher education are particularly prominent following the publication of results from international assessments such as PIRLS 2021 and 2016 and studies conducted during the pandemic focussing on learners' reading literacy achievements (Howie et al., 2017; Kotze et al., 2022). Similarly, increased participation in the initial teacher educator sector in South Africa brings with it challenges regarding access to, and success in this sector (Davids & Waghid, 2020). Questions of access to, and success in initial teacher education, specifically those specialising in language (e.g., Intermediate and Senior and FET Phases) and structured reading literacy (e.g., Foundation Phase) as well as those who have to use English as language of learning and teaching (LoLT), become really important when it is realised that many students now seeking participation in the sector do not necessarily come from backgrounds that have adequately prepared them for this participation (Nel & Adam, 2014). A study commissioned by the South African Department of Basic Education (2014) indicates that the problem is particularly acute where English is used as the LoLT (i.e., from Grade 4 onwards). According to the Centre for Educational Testing for Access and Placement (2020), in South Africa, students applying to education faculties are among the academically weakest, based on completion of the National Benchmark Test, applicants to any faculty. In the Minimum Requirements for Teacher Education Qualifications policy document, it is stated that:

> All teachers who complete an initial professional qualification should be proficient in the use of at least one official South African language as a language of learning and teaching (LoLT), and partially proficient (i.e., sufficient for purposes of conversation) in *at least one* other official African language, or in South African Sign Language, as language of conversational competence (LoCC) (Department of Higher Education and Training, 2015, p. 13).

A study conducted by Hurst (2016) indicates that 39% of the students at a university in South Africa identified English language competence as one of the areas that they would need support with. Findings from the Initial Teacher Education Research Project indicated that selected initial teacher education programmes were not preparing student teachers adequately to teach using English as the LoLT (Reed, 2014) or for effectively coping with learners who have multiple home languages in the classroom (Deacon, 2016). Research also indicates that student teachers at a university in South Africa start their higher education journeys with low proficiency in English (Nel & Adam, 2014), while Wildsmith-Cromarty and Balfour (2019, p. 310) state that, "teachers are starting their careers with a weak knowledge base of their subject, and limited proficiency in the LoLT (English)". Since language is the medium of learning in all subjects, all teachers need to be proficient in language. Clearly there is a large gap in the language skills of students entering ITE and what teachers need if they are to be effective in schools. These types of studies generate public concern about learner outcomes as well as pre-service teacher outcomes and raise questions of teacher quality that cannot be dismissed out of hand, given that there is widespread international agreement on the critical importance of teacher quality, with research evidence indicating a strong link between teacher effectiveness and learner learning outcomes (Barber & Mourshed, 2007; Hattie, 2009; World Bank, 2012).

In the Integrated Strategic Planning Framework for Teacher Education and Development in South Africa, 2011–2025 (DoBE & DHET, 2011, p.3), it is stated that universities have the responsibility for ensuring that the programmes being offered are of high quality and lead to meaningful development for teachers. In South Africa, the HEQC review in 2007 of BEd programmes found that "the greatest problems in programme design result from institutions' incapacity to meet minimum standards of internal coherence, alignment with purpose and intellectual credibility in terms of the relationship between theoretical, practical and experiential knowledge" (CHE, 2010, p 95). Many researchers note the prevalent view that teacher education does not prepare student teachers well for "life in schools and classrooms" (Flores & Day, 2006, p.189) because teacher education programmes are too theoretical, with insufficient links to practice (Darling-Hammond & Baratz-Snowden, 2005; Darling-Hammond et al., 2005; Risan, 2020). As a part of the Initial Teacher Education Research Project (ITERP), a project designed to examine the extent to which initial teacher education programmes offered by universities are adequately preparing pre-service teachers to teach in South African schools, JET undertook a large-scale survey of final year B.Ed. students in 2013. The results indicated that work-integrated learning was inadequate, characterized by limited and skewed exposure to prevailing school practices and conditions, insufficient and inexpert supervision and inconsistencies in the amount and quality of feedback and assessment. ITERP findings suggest that universities and schools need to work together in a much more planned and coordinated manner with regard to providing pre-service teachers with authentic school and classroom learning experiences (Deacon, 2015). Instead of criticizing teachers, the realization that they require more adequate training to effectively use language for instruction and teach children to read should spur action.

This highlights the ongoing disparity between what teachers require and what they have been provided with during their ITE. Initial teacher education (ITE) graduates in South Africa should have the capability to teach using the language of learning and teaching (LoLT) as well as teach children to read successfully in today's diverse environments as well as have the skills to adapt to meet the needs of teaching in the future (Barends & Nel, 2017).

4 Research Methodology

In this study, we used self-study as a methodology for studying our professional practice settings (LaBoskey, 2004). Our research was focused on collaborative inquiry into our experiences of work integrated learning in the trenches at our respective institutions and aimed at improving our practice as teacher educators, our research agenda and our awareness as parents. Self-study is important for enhancing professional skills, broadening professional knowledge, and participating in discussions aimed at improving teacher education for the benefit of society (Samaras & Feese, 2009). Through interaction, the methodology facilitates a thorough comprehension of professional practice by encouraging reflection, critical analysis, and evaluation.

5 Data Sources

This research is based on learning conversations, also understood as semi-structured interviews (Roulston, 2010), conducted via Zoom, between two teacher educators. The two teacher educators come from two different provinces in South Africa, namely the Western Cape Province and the Northwest Province. Informed by practitioner inquiry (Cochran-Smith & Lytle, 2009) and self-study of practice (Pinnegar & Hamilton, 2009), we understand the interview as a dialogic and reflective space in which meaning is co-constructed. As co-researchers, our stories and experiences became enmeshed within the rich conversations that emerged. Our research involved iterative cycles of data collection and analysis, which began with our own experiences as teacher educators, as researchers with specialisation in language education, and also as parents with children who are affected by the teacher candidates we deliver. We engaged in a series of conversations based on the criticism levelled against the preparation of teachers, specifically during work-integrated learning. Our data also included WhatsApp messages and voice notes. We then articulated the major themes stemming from our conversations and reflective journals. Jasper (2005, p. 250) noted that "the purpose of reflective writing is learning which will precipitate some form of action or change in behaviour… is to facilitate the researcher's discovery and provide a verifiable audit-trail of the research process." All conversations and journal entries were recorded, transcribed, and coded (Saldaña, 2021) based on in vivo codes (phrases that held energy), as well as using a metaphor to highlight the themes we identified.

6 Data Analysis

Thematic analysis guided the process of inductive coding and identification of themes (Braun & Clarke, 2006). Each author read each reflective journals individually to identify general impressions and preliminary codes for analysis (Dann et al., 2019). We first identified themes according to the questions and then moved to overarching themes. We then collectively analyzed and discussed the data and inductively explored themes related to recognizing experienced uncertainty and identification of support strategies. Later, we applied deductive coding (Hsieh & Shannon, 2005) when appropriate by drawing on our respective theoretical bases for explanation and interpretation. We ensured quality by critical engagement and in-depth exploration as we discussed, disagreed and refined our thinking during analysis. The idea is to collaboratively explore and interpret data to gain new insights that we would not have obtained on our own, based on our varying levels of expertise and insights.

7 Our Stories

[Z] is a teacher educator who is partially responsible for the preparation of language preservice teachers within a foundation phase initial teacher education programme. Teacher education is situated within university faculty. Within the South African context, teacher education resonates within Faculties of Education. Working in academia whilst positioned in such faculties demands that one fulfils various roles. The first role is focused on teaching and learning, another role is that of researcher and the last role refers to how you and your academic endeavours impact communities. The teaching and learning role give an opportunity to work at grass roots level with pre-service teachers as you have the responsibility to facilitate learning so that these pre-service teachers can enter teaching spaces as confident graduates ready to teach. Put simply, you should contribute to meaningful learning experiences for pre-service teachers as learning to teach is a complex activity (Hoban, 2002, p. 41) that is premised upon the acquisition, integration, and application of different types of knowledge practices (DHET, 2015, p. 10) to develop and supply skilled instructional practitioners or in this case, language, and literacy pre-service teachers. Work-integrated learning within initial teacher education programmes has been a research interest of mine. I have been a working member for the cross-cutting working group: work-integrated learning within the PrimTED programme funded by the European Union and the South African Department of Higher Education and Training.

I [C] have been a teacher educator for more than 30 years, preparing preservice teachers to teach English as Home Language and as First Additional Language across all school phases. My research has focused on English as the language of learning and teaching as well as reading literacy across various educational sectors and more recently on preparing pre-service teachers to teach reading, with a specific focus on the work-integrated learning component of the BEd programme. I am also a parent who had and still has children within the Senior and FET Phase. As the project leader for the cross-cutting working group: work-integrated learning, within the Primary Teacher Education Project, supported by the European Union and managed by the Chief-Directorate for Teaching and Learning Development in the Department of Higher Education and Training, I became increasingly aware of the need to critically reflect on my own teaching practice and experiences as a teacher educator within a higher education institution responsible for preparing pre-service teachers, specifically the students specializing in language and where they have to learn how to teach children to read during the WIL component of their programme in order to determine whether the widely voiced criticism is justified. I also realized that I would have to reflect using multiple hats; firstly, as teacher educator responsible for preparing pre-service teachers, secondly, as a researcher who is interested in research on the topic of work-integrated learning (i.e., teaching practice), specifically as it relates to preparing pre-service teachers to teach language and reading literacy, and thirdly, as a parent whose children are often taught by pre-service teachers during WIL or by beginner teachers.

8 Our Stories About Challenges Faced Within Work-Integrated Learning

As researchers, teacher educators and parents we faced and continue to face the following challenges within the trenches:

Centrality of Learners
Kriewaldt et al., (2017, p. 154) state that "The student and their learning needs are pivotal to all decision-making about what, when and how to teach". When I [C] think about what the focus is when we are at schools observing and assessing our fourth-year students, I realise that the above-mentioned statement is not representative of our practice. The focus is very much on what the pre-service teacher is doing or not doing and how he/she plans and prepares. On the summative assessment form, we use when assessing the students we are required to comment on aspects related to lesson planning, the lesson introduction, the formulation of lesson objectives, the teaching phase, learner activities, assessment, resources, consolidation phase, classroom management and ability to communicate. No information on the learners is required and whether they learnt something or how instruction takes their learning needs into consideration. It was also interesting to note that the pre-service teachers tended to have "go-to" learners when they asked questions to check comprehension; it seemed to be the same learners every time. My interactions with the students after their lessons indicated that the students were unable to answer questions such as, "What did you do in your lesson today to ensure that all your learners were able to engage with the content? Which learners do you think did not achieve the

objectives of the lesson?" Most of their responses turned to behavioral or classroom management issues.

Conversations with my children seem to corroborate my observations:

[C]: How was your day?

[A1]: Exhausting! The teacher kept asking questions, but nobody wanted to answer, so I spent the day answering - in nearly all our subjects.

[C]: What did you learn in English today?

[A1]: Nothing! I am not really sure what the purpose of the lesson was. We were told to guess the meaning of words from the reading passage or try to figure it out.

[C]: Did the teacher explain any vocabulary to you?

[A1]: No, we just have to use a dictionary.

[C]: What did you do in the lesson with the student teacher?

[A2]: Well, I don't know. We were supposed to do something about electric circuits, but I didn't get what he was trying to explain. His English was so confusing that I really didn't understand. I will have to ask our teacher to explain again, although he also has difficulty explaining. I will try and see if there aren't videos on YouTube.

After analyzing the planning and presentation of pre-service teachers, it appears evidence that they rarely, if ever, consider the learners' characteristics, circumstances, prior experiences, and background when making decisions about how to teach and where to begin.

9 Foundational Issues: Partnerships, Mentoring, Support and Context

Darling-Hammond (2006) emphasizes three critical features of effective teacher preparation, namely (1) right integration among courses, and between coursework and practical work in schools; (2) extensive and intensively supervised and mentored practical work integrated with coursework; and (3) close, proactive relationships with schools that serve diverse learners effectively and develop and model good teaching (Darling-Hammond, 2006). Putting these three critical features under the spotlight led us to question our partnerships with schools, mentoring, support that was provided to all involved during work-integrated learning as well as the contexts we were preparing our pre-service teachers for and placing them in.

Over the past 30 years, my interaction [C] with school principals and mentor teachers has indicated a lack of trust and a disconnect between universities and schools. Comments such as the following were and are frequently made during our conversations:

It feels as if you are using us. We babysit your students, look at lesson plans and let them disrupt our teaching schedules. We don't get any guidelines, just an email stating you will receive 10 students for the teaching practicum and here is an attached list of names.

We get students from three, sometimes four different universities and each one requires something different. Why? Aren't you supposed to be on the same page?

> It feels like entertainment. We keep them busy until you [teacher educators] pitch up and assess them. They try fancy stuff such as playing songs, letting the children dance, or they use technology, which seldom works smoothly, but as soon as you go everything goes back to the usual. We tell the learners to behave and do as they're told because the students are being assessed.

Similarly, my reflections [Z] highlight the lack of explicit roles and responsibilities of the teacher educators and the mentor teachers. I am reminded of a comment made by a school lead teacher who manages the student placement within a school setting:

> We realize that these are student teachers but they really aren't ready for classroom teaching. We do not have the time to teach them the nitty gritty of teaching. In schools they work with real learners so they need to be able to teach proper lessons. If they aren't able to do this our teachers have to reteach the lessons once students leave. This is such a waste of our time. We aren't here to teach the students, that is your job. Our role is to create spaces for students to practice their skills.

This contrasts with a statement made by Darling-Hammond et al. (2005, pp. 392–393), namely that teacher learning should be situated in contexts that allow for the development of expert practice. Should these perceptions, as listed in my reflection exist, this type of learning may be hindered.

Our engagement with the research indicates that while mentoring during the teaching practicum can be beneficial for pre-service teachers, there are some criticisms that have been raised regarding its effectiveness (Li et al., 2021; Taghreed & Mohd, 2017). My conversations [Z] with students highlighted how their presence at schools during the teaching practice period often resulted in mentor teachers being absent or leaving the pre-service teachers alone in a classroom full of learners to fend for themselves. I am reminded of comments I often hear from students upon their return from school-based placement:

> I could not fulfil my teaching practice obligations as I had to look after a class for a week,
>
> alone as the teacher was absent. The headmaster thought I could keep the class busy in the
>
> teacher's absence.

When reflecting on my interaction [C] with the mentor teachers during the past number of years I realized that the biggest challenge was communication, or rather the lack thereof. Pre-service teachers are placed at the schools, and they are allocated to a mentor teacher by the principal, or a staff member delegated to take responsibility for the pre-service teachers. They seldom if ever get any guidelines in terms of what is expected of them other than that which the students tell them they must do. Very often mentor teachers regard the teaching practicum as a time to complete administrative tasks that they need to catch up on; some leave the students to take over the teaching for the entire placement period. There was very little, if any, communication between teacher educators and the mentor teachers—the only time we exchanged words was when I was required to summatively assess a fourth-year student at the end of the teaching practicum period. My informal conversations with many pre-service teachers and mentor teachers indicated that very little collaborative discussion about teaching in general or subject-specific discussions were taking place. One comment from a mentor teacher I will never forget was:

> The students sit at the back of my class observing my teaching. When I asked them what they noticed they usually reply with – "What an excellent lesson. I liked the introduction." Nothing about the content, whether it was relevant; whether I reached my objectives or in what way I might have deviated from my lesson plan or how and if I differentiated my lesson for the various learners.

This made me realize that without providing structured guidance and support to the students they were at a total loss as to what to "notice" about teaching. An additional concern was that this practice remained the same from first year through the fourth year; there does not seem to be any growth or progression in their teaching. However, I did also see pockets of excellence where mentor teachers really understood their task and the growth in the pre-service teachers was noticeable; especially in the depth of their reflections and ability to link theory and practice. I tend to concur with the statement made by Simmons Zuilkowski et al. (2021, p. 3) that "Pre-service teachers should have a mentor teacher as well as supervision by a teacher educator from their PSTE program". Our observations of the pre-service teachers are usually once-off visits in their final year when it is far too late for collaborative reflection and dialogic engagement on their pedagogical practice. Our pre-service teachers are also very seldom assessed by the same teacher educator which means that the students hardly ever receive actionable feedback that they must respond to or show that their practice has improved. We tend to race from pre-service teacher to pre-service teacher due to time constraints, the number of students that need to be assessed and the distances we must travel. Give a mark and comply with university regulations and then you have done your job.

When reflecting on my [Z] interaction with mentor teachers over the years, I realize that one of the biggest challenges is that of the misconception of mentor teacher and how he/she understands how teacher education is organized. Mentor teachers often resort to comments about students' classroom knowledge of practice and teaching expectations. This is one aspect of the mentoring relationship that may influence the student experience as well as learning. One clear example came up in an informal conversation with a mentor teacher:

> It is really difficult to support your students, you are not teaching them what we learnt at teacher training colleges. They don't come to teaching practice with knowledge of apparatus and the practicalities of teaching. So, I have to teach them about apparatus for lessons first. The students don't learn what we learnt back in the training college days so we have to teach them all of this first before we can allow them to teach the children.

This perception and understanding of the mentor teacher contrast the debates around teacher knowledge. In fact, it perpetuates the weakness in the dichotomy between content knowledge and teaching knowledge (methods) as raised by Shulman (1986, p. 5).

The structure, timing and length of the practicum varies across countries and even among universities in a country (Akyeampong et al., 2013; Deacon, 2016). When I [C] think back, before 2018, placement of students for the school-based component was seen as an administrative matter. Students were asked where they wanted to go for teaching practice, and they would more often than not be placed there. Students often choose schools close to their home, for financial reasons, or schools where family members taught. When placing students very little consideration was and is given to the language of learning and teaching or home language specialization issues. For example, students were placed in a school where the home language offered at the school was IsiZulu, but the language the student was majoring in was SeTswana or the student majored in Afrikaans and was placed at a school where the medium of instruction was English, and English was offered as home language. My informal conversations with students after the practicum also made me realize that the length of time, they spend at school was too short for them to get to know the learners and see how they develop and learn. It does sometimes feel as if they are "play teaching" (Mutemeri & Chetty, 2011). Students who were placed in rural schools with sometimes up to 80 learners in a class would phone the work-integrated learning office and asked to be placed somewhere else because they did not know how to cope with the classroom context, and they did not know how to teach reading to the diverse learners with different needs in these classes. Many students do not want to be placed in rural and disadvantaged schools for various reasons, such as safety, lack of access to basic amenities and even electricity. We even get parents of pre-service teachers phoning the work-integrated learning office to complain about their placements and often demand that they be placed elsewhere. It seems clear that if the teaching practicum is to fulfil the pivotal role it is supposed to play in initial teacher education, the foundational issues will need to be addressed in a collaborative manner and with far more emphasis on the crucial role this component plays in preparing quality teachers. This may be an area where policy guidelines should be more explicit.

10 Curriculum Issues: Knowledge Base, Pedagogies of Teacher Education and Reflection

Research indicates that in low- and middle-income countries the curricular focus seems to be primarily focused on content knowledge rather than pedagogical content knowledge or pedagogical knowledge (Akyeampong et al., 2013; Barnes et al., 2019), and more on theory than practice, specifically practice-based learning opportunities (Nel & Marais, 2021).

My observations [C] of pre-service teachers' planning and instruction during the teaching practice sessions and the comments made in my reflective journal indicate the following red flags when it comes to students' reading content knowledge and their pedagogical content knowledge:

1. **Word Recognition**
    - The students tend to focus on 3-cueing systems such as the use of picture or context cues as well as emphasizing the first letter of a word as a cue.

- The learners are encouraged to memorize whole words, including high frequency words, by sight without focusing on sound/symbol correspondence.

2. **Phonics and Phonic Decoding**
   - Key words for letter/sound correspondence are not aligned with the pure phoneme being taught, for example using the word earth for /e/.
   - All sounds for one letter are often taught at the same time.
   - Blending is not explicitly taught nor practised.
   - Texts used in Grades 1 and 2 are primarily predictable.
   - There is often no advanced word study which includes instruction in multi-syllabic word decoding strategies and/or using morphology to support word recognition.

3. **Fluency**
   - Word-level fluency is not practiced to automaticity.
   - Fluency assessment allows acceptance of incorrectly decoded words if they are close in meaning to the target word; this was especially obvious in classrooms with diverse learners with various home languages.

4. **Background knowledge**
   - Opportunities to bridge existing knowledge to new knowledge is not apparent in their instruction.

5. **Vocabulary**
   - Learners are not exposed to rich vocabulary and complex syntax in reading.
   - Explicit instruction in morphology is not a feature of their instruction.
   - Instruction focuses on memorization of isolated words and definitions out of context.

6. **Language Structures**
   - Instruction does not include pre-service teacher modeling.
   - Learners are asked to memorize parts of speech as a list without learning in context and with application.

7. **Verbal Reasoning**
   - Inferencing strategies are not taught explicitly or may be based on textual clues.
   - Learners are not taught how to interpret inferential language.

8. **Literacy Knowledge**
   - Genre-specific text structures and corresponding signal words (i.e., connectives) are not explicitly taught or practiced.

9. **Reading Comprehension**

- Learners are asked to independently apply reading comprehension strategies primarily in short, disconnected readings at the expense of engaging in knowledge-building text sets.
- Learners are not taught methods to monitor their comprehension while reading.

10. **Spelling**
    - Spelling lists are based on content or frequency of word use and not connected to decoding/phonics lessons.
    - Learners practice spelling by memorization only, such as repeated writing.
    - Spelling patterns are taught haphazardly.

11. **Assessment**
    - Decoding skills are assessed using real words only.
    - Oral reading fluency assessments are seldom, if ever, used.
    - Assessments, specifically from Grade 4, measure comprehension only without additional assessment measures to determine what is leading to comprehension weaknesses.
    - Assessment data is not used to differentiate instruction based on learners' progress.

Overall, the main format of teaching the learners remains "lecturing". When I specifically asked about the approach they used, most students can quote their university prescribed textbooks to me; they don't know what it means to teach explicitly. Some responses included:

> Mam, the CAPS curriculum says we need to use a balanced approach.
>
> I don't know what modelling is? We just teach them the sounds and then ask to see if they can remember them and then the next day, we do other sounds or just test to see if they know the sounds.
>
> Mam, we never get any opportunity to practice what we learn before we go out on teaching practice. Some lecturers do microteaching, but I think it is so fake, because our peers think it is a joke and they can't respond like real learners do.

Some of my children's responses seem to support my observations:

> Mom, will you please just explain the root word to me and how I can figure out what it means. This teacher can't explain!
>
> Why do you keep telling me to prepare for my English exams when the teacher says you don't have to prepare. It is a reading comprehension – you can do it or you can't.

The lack of knowledge and implementation of explicit, systematic instruction made we critically reflect on my own practice and the extent to which I was modeling the practice I was discussing and also treating "the practical work of teaching as work that entails complex thought, professional judgment, and continual reflection" (Grossman, 2018, p. 2). Reflection is a crucial aspect of the teaching practicum, as it provides pre-service teachers with the opportunity to critically evaluate their own teaching practice and identify areas for improvement.

My [C] conversations with [Z] would focus on things that were puzzling me:

Can your students critically reflect on their lessons? What comments would they make? I am worried because in my analysis of their critical reflective journals I tend to get comments like: I think my introduction was not catchy enough. I need to work on my discipline skills. My lesson was too long, I didn't get to the ending. There reflections were very superficial and did not indicate a link between theory and practice. They cannot justify their choice of examples or why they do certain things. The most common comment is: My lecturer said so or the mentor told me to do it this way.

Our conversations [C & Z] made me consider the reflection sessions I would have in my lecturers post teaching practice. Students could articulate and describe experiences very well. Their thinking and reflections during these sessions were often rather at a superficial level, as the reflective thoughts were often simply descriptions of what happened in the teaching and learning situation. The purpose, educational value and theoretical connection were left unexplored (Van Manen, 1977, p. 225). The reflection is restricted to classroom management and the personal experience thereof and this is what Reddy and Menkveld (2000, p. 178) refer to as technical reflection as students never examined or explored the pedagogical reasoning for their choices.

11 What Our Stories Reveal About the Achilles Heel of Work-Integrated Learning

In this section, we would like to discuss what our stories seem to reveal about the Achilles Heel of work-integrated learning by presenting our experience and reflections in the form of a visual conceptual bridge linking theory (i.e., universities) and practice (i.e., schools) (cf. Fig. 1). Our experience and reflections seem to indicate that trying to link theory and practice may be a bridge too far if teachers' (i.e., teacher educator, pre-service teacher, and mentor teacher) teaching practices are not centred on enhancing learners' learning and development, the pivot point within our visual architecture. Kriewaldt et al., (2017, p. 155) state that "the centrality of the client is fundamental to all clinical practice." This implies that learners' learning should be the focus of pre-service teacher observation, assessment, and feedback and not what the pre-service teacher is doing (e.g., your introduction should be catchier; you need to take control of the classroom). Teaching should be focussed on enabling "meaningful learning" (Pellegrino, 2017). However, this does not mean that teachers should rely only on test scores and other performance measures but should also take cognizance of the competences learners require to function successfully in the twenty-first century (Center for Curriculum Redesign, 2022). As teachers, we should aim to understand and support the development of the whole learner, considering factors such as learners' ability to drive their own meaning, their persistence in the face of setbacks, and the ability to work effectively in a team. In this way, the learner is placed at the centre of learning and development, with a recognition of the physical, cognitive and social and emotional factors that contribute to it.

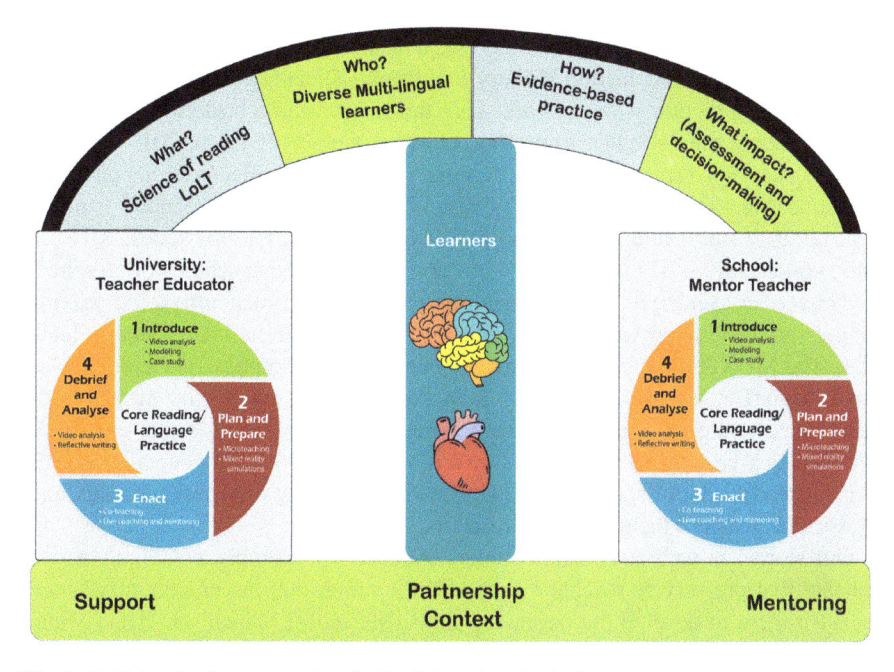

Fig. 1 Bridging the theory–practice divide. Original to the Authors

Secondly, our stories indicate that for work-integrated learning to be successful, certain foundational issues need to be addressed, namely partnerships, mentoring, support and context. Nationally and internationally research continues to emphasise the crucial role university-school partnerships play in effective work-integrated learning experiences (TEMAG, 2014). According to Darling-Hammond (2014, p. 548), one of the core features of effective initial teacher education programmes is "strong relationships, common knowledge, and shared beliefs among school- and university-based faculty jointly engaged in transforming teaching, schooling, and teacher education". Our stories seem to indicate that there is very limited joint engagement in terms of supporting and developing pre-service teachers' teaching practice. It seems clear that if universities and schools are seen as being extractive (Martin et al., 2011; Mutemeri & Chetty, 2011) rather than having a supportive relationship than resembles a community of learning and has clear benefits, roles and responsibilities for all stakeholders (Whatman & MacDonald, 2017), the practicum seems doomed. Similarly, such engagements are dependent on mentors.

In our stories, we experienced first-hand how the quality of mentoring varied with mentor's experience and expertise, as well as the amount of time and effort they are willing to invest in the process (Phillips-Jones, 2003). Mentoring can also have a limited scope; mentoring during the teaching practicum typically focuses on classroom management and lesson planning but may not address broader issues such as the challenges of working with diverse learners who have very different language and reading needs (Kimmel et al., 2021). Mentors may not be representative of the diverse populations of pre-service teachers, which can limit the effectiveness of the mentoring relationship (Military Leadership Diversity Commission, 2010). For example, a mentor who does not share the same cultural background as a pre-service teacher may struggle to provide effective support (Eguara, 2019). Mentor teachers may not receive sufficient training or support to effectively mentor pre-service teachers and teacher educators' observation of pre-service teachers is negligible (Hadi & Rudiyanto, 2017; Mutemeri & Chetty, 2011; Phillips-Jones, 2010). A study conducted by Wohlfahrt (2018) in Cameroon found that schools often scheduled in-service training for the teachers during the teaching practicum period, leaving the pre-service teachers to teach and cope on their own without supervision or feedback. The MUSTER project in Malawi, Ghana, Lesotho, South Africa and Trinidad and Tobago (Lewin, 2004, p. 7) reported that teacher educators' visits "tended to be badly timed, rushed, irregular, and mostly orientated to assessment. Sustained formative feedback geared to the student's own development does not generally occur." This can lead to a lack of consistency in the mentoring process and a failure to address the specific needs of the pre-service teachers.

Our stories as well as research studies conducted in Zambia and South Africa indicate that pre-service teachers were of the opinion that the practicum was too short for them to develop the necessary skills (Masaiti & Manchishi, 2011; Mutemeri & Chetty, 2011). Research also indicates that ITE institutions very often present teaching as a standardized process without consideration of the social, economic and cultural contexts of schools (Akyeampong et al., 2013; Pryor et al., 2012). Studies in South Africa indicate the ITE programmes do not prepare pre-service teachers well to teach in rural schools (Heeralal, 2014; Mukeredzi, 2016). This can impact their ability to work effectively with diverse groups of learners in the future.

12 Work-Integrated Learning: A Vehicle to Link Theory and Practice

Our stories seem to indicate that work-integrated learning should play a major role in linking theory and practice. Although there is no commonly recognized initial teacher education curriculum, pre-service teachers should possess subject content knowledge, pedagogical content knowledge, and general pedagogical knowledge (Shulman, 1986). Our stories indicate that despite attention to content knowledge focused on reading and academic language, it seems that many pre-service teachers still fail to achieve appropriate levels of content mastery. Moats (2020, p. 3) states that, "Teaching reading really is rocket science. Academic English is complex". Moats (2020, p. 4) continues that "Unfortunately, much of this research is not yet included in teacher preparation programs, widely used curricula, or professional development, so it should come as no surprise that typical classroom practices often deviate substantially from what is recommended by our most credible sources". This statement is supported within the South African context by Taylor and Mawoyo (2022, p. 165) who state that, "the overall quality of the L&L components of many BEd curricula remains far below where it needs to be if newly qualified teachers are to be effective in teaching children to read proficiently". The question is, therefore, what content should be taught? Research seems to be converging around the "science of reading" (Reading League, 2022). In order to comprehend the development of a learner's reading ability we refer to two theoretical frameworks that are supported by scientific research. The Simple View of Reading indicates that reading comprehension is a product of two components, namely word recognition and language comprehension rather than their sum, and that a weakness in either component can lead to a decline in reading comprehension (Tunmer & Hoover, 2019). This means that no amount of skill in one component can compensate for a lack of skill in the other. Although the Simple View of Reading offers a simplified view of the developmental process, skilled reading development is not simplistic (Moats, 2020; Reading League, 2022). In order to get a deeper understanding of the subcomponents of word recognition and language comprehension, Scarborough's (2001) Reading Rope adds value. The word recognition strand encompasses subcomponents including phonological awareness, decoding, and sight recognition. The language comprehension strand comprises subcomponents such as vocabulary, background knowledge, language structures, verbal reasoning and literacy knowledge. Both the Simple View of Reading and Scarborough's Rope also emphasize the importance of fluency which helps integrate word recognition and language comprehension skills.

13 Pedagogical Content Knowledge for Literacy Teachers

According to Shulman (1986), content knowledge is a necessary but not sufficient condition for effective teaching. In other words, having expertise in the subject matter (i.e., science of reading) alone does not guarantee that one can effectively teach it to others. The question as to how reading should be taught should focus on evidence-based reading practices. Pedagogical content knowledge refers to the intersection between content knowledge and pedagogical knowledge. This knowledge involves an understanding of how to teach specific subject matter concepts, and how to address common misconceptions or difficulties that learners may encounter when learning those concepts (Chen & Chen, 2021). Moats (2020, p. 5) states that "reading and language arts instruction must include deliberate, systematic, and explicit teaching of word recognition and must develop students' subject-matter knowledge, vocabulary, sentence comprehension, and familiarity with the language in written texts". Research clearly indicates that direct instruction in the alphabetic code enhances learning to read (Rastle et al., 2021); this is especially true for disadvantaged children (Tunmer et al., 2013). Pretorius et al., (2022, p. 150) state that, "Given the high levels of poverty in South Africa and the role that socio-economic factors play in education (Spaull, 2019), an evidence-based reading method that can help to reduce the achievement gap in a deeply unequal society needs to be taken seriously".

According to Anstrom et al., (2010, p. iv), academic language refers to "the language used in school to help students acquire knowledge" which is regarded as the backbone of most linguistic demands needed for teaching and learning for both written and spoken academic performance (Schleppegrell, 2012). This is also what Uccelli et al. (2019, p. 8) emphasizes - because children not only learn language but "learn how to learn through a language." Schleppegrell (2012, p. 409) states that:

> As children progress through the years of schooling, at each new level and in each new subject area they encounter expectation for how language should be used to accomplish the activities they engage in. Every subject is taught and learned through language, and teachers, without good knowledge about how language makes meaning in the subjects they teach, cannot provide all children in their classrooms with robust opportunities to learn.

Bailey (2007) explains that when student teachers are well prepared in a particular language of instruction and are confident users of academic language, they are likely to model this type of discourse behaviour when they teach learners. Research is clear about the need to teach academic language to enable teachers to teach it intentionally and explicitly (Bailey et al., 2008; Chamot & O'Malley, 1994; Schleppegrell, 2012; Snow & Uccelli, 2009; Uccelli et al., 2013, 2015). These authors suggest that, for teachers to invoke AL in their teaching, they themselves need knowledge of AL and its features, how it is taught, and how it is used by teachers and learners across disciplines and in different age-groups as a component of their pedagogical content knowledge (PCK) as conceptualized by Shulman (1986).

Pedagogical knowledge, on the other hand, refers to a teacher's knowledge about how to teach. This knowledge includes an understanding of the principles, strategies, and techniques that are effective in helping learners learn (Grossman et al., 1989). Pedagogical knowledge also includes the use of assessment to determine learners' progress and adjust instruction accordingly (Shulman, 1986). Pedagogical knowledge is essential for teachers to be able to translate their content knowledge into meaningful learning experiences for their learners. One of the primary issues with assessment during the teaching practicum is the lack of consistency in assessment criteria (Darling-Hammond et al., 2005). Different mentor teachers or teacher educators may have varying expectations and standards for their student teachers, which can lead to disparities in assessments. This can be particularly challenging for pre-service teachers who may receive conflicting feedback from different mentor teachers or teacher educators, making it difficult for them to know what they need to improve upon (Aspden, 2014). Another issue with assessment during the teaching practicum is the limited amount of time that pre-service teachers spend in the classroom. Depending on the length of the practicum, it may be challenging to assess a student teacher's ability to manage a classroom, build relationships with students, and effectively deliver instruction. The limited time frame may also prevent the student teacher from receiving feedback on all aspects of their teaching, which can hinder their growth as a teacher (Onyefulu et al., 2019). Lastly, assessment during the teaching practicum may not adequately measure a student teacher's ability to meet the diverse needs of their students. As classrooms become increasingly diverse, it is essential for teachers to possess culturally responsive teaching skills. However, these skills may not be explicitly assessed during the teaching practicum, leaving student teachers unprepared to effectively teach diverse groups of students.

We realised that what was needed was a learning cycle highlighting pedagogies for teacher education that could be used by teacher educators as well as mentor teachers to ensure a more integrated approach to theory and practice. The learning cycle is aligned with Wenger's (1998) communities of practice that sees learning as a collective activity between the teacher educators, mentor teachers and pre-service teachers during the teaching practicum. During stage one, the pre-service teachers are introduced to a core reading practice (e.g., modeling explicit instruction of blending a word) (University of Michigan, 2020). Teacher educators (i.e., lecturers) can introduce the core practice by allowing the pre-service teachers to analyze a video representation of the core practice while mentor teachers may model the practice. During the planning and preparation stage the teacher educators and mentor teachers can prepare the pre-service teachers to engage with the practice by providing them with practice-based opportunities such as mixed reality simulations where teacher educators, mentor teachers and pre-service teachers can be in the same mixed reality simulation environment to provide coaching and feedback to the pre-service teacher within a safe and risk-free environment. During the enactment stage, pre-service teachers can enact the lessons they had planned, prepared and rehearsed during the previous stage. During this stage the pre-service teachers receive mentoring or co-teach with the mentor teacher. During the debriefing and analysis stage, pre-service teachers revisit and learn from their enactments, making sense of the core practice and how it was delivered. This stage can be facilitated by video analysis of recorded mixed reality simulation sessions and also by reflecting on the lessons enacted during their school-based placement. Research has consistently shown that reflection plays a significant role in enhancing pre-service teachers' learning and professional growth during their practicum experience (Cavanagh et al., 2019). Loughran (2002) argues that it is not only the ability of pre-service teachers to recognize and understand key issues and concerns in their teaching, but to respond to them in a way that informs forward practice. Reflection enables pre-service teachers to assess the impact of their teaching practices on learners' learning. By reflecting on their teaching practices and their learners' responses, pre-service teachers can make adjustments to their teaching strategies to better meet the needs of their learners (Boud et al., 2013). Reflection promotes critical thinking skills as pre-service teachers analyze their teaching practices, evaluate their effectiveness, and identify areas for improvement. This can enhance their problem-solving skills and their ability to make informed decisions about their teaching practices. Hiebert et al., (2007: 49) state that, "a consequence of focusing on analytic skills is that the centre of teaching expertise shifts from on-the-fly performance in the classroom to preparation and reflection outside the classroom".

14 Recommendations for Policy Makers, Teacher Education Institutions, Schools and Parents

Based on our stories from the trenches, our discussion, and calls from across the basic and higher education sectors to increase the quality of teacher preparation and pay explicit attention to how pre-service teachers are taught to teach reading (cf. South African National Planning Commission, 2012; Spaull, 2022) we would like to make the following recommendations for policy makers:

- Require intentional school-based teaching practice placements in collaboration with partnership schools.
- Require a minimum practicum duration.
- Require placements in diverse and challenging environments, but where mentoring can be provided effectively.
- Require the inclusion of Knowledge and Practice Standards for Literacy to be compulsory in ITE curriculum.

Based on our stories from the trenches and our discussion we would like to make the following recommendations for initial teacher education institutions (teacher educators) and schools (mentor teachers):

- Utilize an aligned learning cycle with a focus on practice-based pedagogies.
- Ensure actionable feedback, specifically in terms of reading and LoLT CK, PK and PCK.
- Ensure that the educational partners align in terms of the science of reading, LoLT and evidence-based instructional practices.
- Emphasize reflective practice.

Based on our stories from the trenches and our discussion we recommend that parents become more involved in their child's reading journey.

15 Conclusion

This chapter places a lens on the lived experiences of teacher educators immersed in the trenches of work integrated learning within teacher education programmes. We narrate our own stories and critical reflections on our practices and the current state of work integrated learning as we experience it within our institutions, with a specific focus on the language preparation of our preservice teachers. Aspects related to the critical role of partnerships, mentoring, and reflective practice to enhance work integrated learning experiences for pre-service teachers in South Africa are put in the spotlight. We do this by analysing the challenges we experience as well as problematizing the weaknesses and vulnerabilities (i.e., the Achilles heel) of work integrated learning within teacher education programmes. In understanding this, we are able to present "immersed cases of work integrated learning within diverse contexts" (Barends & Nel, 2017) through the use of a collaborative self-study.

The broader implications of the findings include the need to address policy adherence to ensure quality teacher preparation, the importance of adapting work integrated learning practices in response to external factors such as the impact of COVID-19, the significance of enhancing language preparation for pre-service teachers, the critical role of effective mentoring and support in teacher development, and the necessity of fostering strong partnerships between universities and schools to create a collaborative and supportive learning environment. These implications highlight the importance of continuous improvement and innovation in teacher education programs to better prepare educators for the diverse and evolving needs of students in the twenty-first century.

These cases should contribute to the debate on the professional development of preservice teachers as well as help policymakers, faculty leadership and curriculum designers of teacher education programmes to make informed decisions affecting the work integrated learning of teacher education programmes.

References

Akyeampong, K., Lussier, K., Pryor, J., & Westbrook, J. (2013). Improving teaching and learning of basic maths and reading in Africa: Does teacher preparation count? *International Journal of Educational Development, 33*, 272–282. https://doi.org/10.1016/j.ijedudev.2012.09.006

Anstrom, K., DiCerbo, P., Butler, F., Katz, A., Millet, J., & River, C. (2010). *A review of the literature on academic English: Implications for K-12 English language learners.* The George Washington University Centre for Equity and Excellence in Education.

Archer, A. (2017). *The magic is in the instruction.* Paper presented at the DIBELS Super Institute in Las Vegas, USA. Retrieved from: https://acadiencelearning.org/wp-content/uploads/2020/07/Handout_Keynote_by_Anita_Archer_2017_DIBELS_Super_Institute.pdf

Aspden, K. M. (2014). *Illuminating the assessment of practicum in New Zealand early childhood initial teacher education* (Doctoral dissertation, Massey University). Retrieved from http://mro.massey.ac.nz/handle/10179/6473

Bahr, N., & Mellor, S. (2016). *Building quality in teaching and teacher education.* Camberwell, Victoria: Australian Council for Educational Research.

Bailey, A. (2007). Teaching and assessing students learning in English in school. In A. Bailey (Ed.), *The language demands of school: Putting academic English to the test* (pp. 1–21). Yale University Press.

Bailey, F., Burkett, B., & Freeman, D. (2008). The mediating role of language in teaching and learning: A classroom perspective. In B. Spolsky & F. Hult (Eds.), *The handbook of educational linguistics* (pp. 383–395). Blackwell.

Barber, M., & Mourshed, M. (2007). *How the world's best education systems come out on top.* McKinsey.

Barends, Z., & Nel, C. (2017). Work-integrated learning within the reading literacy component of foundation phase teacher preparation programmes. *South African Journal of Childhood Education, 7*(1). https://doi.org/10.4102/sajce.v7i1.435

Barnes, A. E., Boyle, H., Simmons Zuilkowski, S., & Bello, Z. M. (2019). Reforming teacher education in Nigeria: Laying a foundation for the future. *Teaching and Teacher Education, 79*, 153–163. https://doi.org/10.1016/j.tate.2018.12.017

Boud, D., Keogh, R., & Walker, D. (2013). *Reflection: Turning experience into learning.* Routledge.

Braun, V., & Clarke, V. (2006). Using thematic analysis in psychology. *Qualitative Research in Psychology, 3*(2), 77–101. https://doi.org/10.1191/1478088706qp063oa

Cavanagh, M., Barr, J., Moloney, R., Lane, R., Hay, I., & Chu, H. (2019). Pre-service teachers' impact on student learning: Planning, teaching, and assessing during professional practice. *Australian Journal of Teacher Education, 44*(2). Retrieved from: https://ro.ecu.edu.au/ajte/vol44/iss2/5

Center for Curriculum Redesign. (2022). *4D education framework.* Retrieved from: https://4dedu.org/wp-content/uploads/2022/10/4D-Education-Framework-Center-for-Education-Redesign.pdf

Chen, J., & Chen, M. (2021). Developing the pedagogical content knowledge of teacher candidates for integrating computational thinking into mathematics instruction: A case study of a teacher education program in Taiwan. *Journal of Educational Computing Research, 59*(1), 3–25.

Centre for Educational Testing for Access and Placement (CTAP). (2020). *The national benchmark tests. National report: 2019 intake cycle.* Centre for Educational Testing for Access and Placement, University of Cape Town. Retrieved from: https://nbt.uct.ac.za/sites/default/files/NBT%20National%20Report%202019.pdf

Chamot, A. U., & O'Malley, J. M. (1994). *The CALLA handbook: Implementing the cognitive academic language learning approach.* Addison-Wesley.

Cochran-Smith, M., & Lytle, S. L. (2009). *Inquiry as stance: Practitioner research for the next generation.* Teachers College Press.

Council on Higher Education. (2010). *Report on the national review of academic and professional programmes in education. HE Monitor No. 11.* Council on Higher Education.

Dann, D., Basford, J., Booth, C., O'Sullivan, R., Scanlon, J., Woodfine, C., & Wright, P. (2019). The impact of doctoral study on university lecturers' construction of self within a changing higher education policy context. *Studies in Higher Education, 44*(7), 1166–1182. https://doi.org/10.1080/03075079.2017.1421155

Darling-Hammond, L. (2006). Constructing twenty-first century teacher education. *Journal of Teacher Education, 57,* 300–314. https://doi.org/10.1177/0022487105285962

Darling-Hammond, L. (2014). Strengthening clinical preparation: The holy grail of teacher education. *Peabody Journal of Education, 89,* 547–561. https://doi.org/10.1080/0161956X.2014.939009

Darling-Hammond, L., & Baratz-Snowden, J. (2005). *A good teacher in every classroom: Preparing the highly qualified teachers our children deserve.* John Wiley & Sons.

Darling-Hammond, L., Hammerness, K., Grossman, P., Rust, F., & Shulman, L. (2005). The design of teacher education programs. In L. Darling-Hammond & J. Bransford (Eds.), *Preparing teachers for a changing world: What teachers should learn and be able to do* (pp. 390–441). Jossey-Bass.

Davids, N., & Waghid, Y. (2020). Tracking five years of teacher education enrolment at a South African university: Implications for teacher education. *South African Journal of Higher Education, 34*(2), 1–16. http://hdl.handle.net/10019.1/108620

Deacon, R. (2015). *Report on the 2013 survey of final year initial teacher education students.* JET Education Services.

Deacon, R. (2016). *The initial teacher education research project: Final report.* JET Education Services.

Department of Basic Education (DBE) & Department of Higher Education and Training (DHET). (2011). *Integrated strategic planning framework for teacher education: 2011–2025.* Government Printing Works.

Department of Basic Education. (2014). *Ministerial task team report on the National Senior Certificate (NSC).* Department of Basic Education.

Department of Higher Education and Training. (2015). *Revised policy on the minimum requirements for teacher education qualifications.* Government Printers.

Eguara, O. (2019). Cultural competence in the mentoring, recruitment and retention of black teachers in the UK. In *Proceedings of ICERI conference*, 11–13th November, Seville Spain.

Flores, M. A., & Day, C. (2006). Contexts which shape and reshape new teachers' identities: A multi-perspective study. *Teaching and Teacher Education, 22*, 219–232. https://doi.org/10.1016/j.tate.2005.09.002

Gravett, S. (2020). *Initial teacher education must be prioritised*. https://www.uj.ac.za/newandevents/Pages/Initial-teacher-education-must-be-prioritised-says-Prof-Sarah-Gravett.aspx.

Grossman, P. (Ed.). (2018). *Teaching core practices in teacher education*. Harvard Education Press.

Grossman, P. L., Wilson, S. M., & Shulman, L. S. (Eds.). (1989). Teachers of substance: Subject matter knowledge for teaching. In M. C. Reynolds (Ed.), *Knowledge base for the beginning teacher* (pp. 23–36). Pergamon.

Hadi, M. J., & Rudiyanto, M. (2017). *Significance of mentor-mentee relationship and training for effective mentoring outcomes*. Paper presented at the Annual International Conference on Islamic Education, 26

Hattie, J. (2009). *Visible learning: A synthesis of over 800 meta-analyses relating to achievement*. Routledge.

Heeralal, P. J. H. (2014). Preparing pre-service teachers to teach in rural schools. *Mediterranean Journal of Social Sciences, 5*(20), 1795–1799. https://doi.org/10.5901/mjss.2014.v5n20p1795

Hiebert, J., Morris, A. K., Berk, D., & Jansen, A. (2007). Preparing teachers to learn from teaching. *Journal of Teacher Education, 58*(1), 47–61. https://doi.org/10.1177/0022487106295726

Hoban, G. F. (2002). *Teacher learning for educational change*. Open University Press.

Howie, S. J., Combrinck, C., Roux, K., Tshele, M., Mokoena, G. M., & McLeod Palane, N. (2017). *PIRLS literacy 2016 progress in international reading literacy study 2016: South African children's reading literacy achievement*. Centre for Evaluation and Assessment.

Hsieh, H.-F., & Shannon, S. E. (2005). Three approaches to qualitative content analysis. *Qualitative Health Research, 15*(9), 1277–1288. https://doi.org/10.1177/1049732305276687

Hurst, E. (2016). Navigating language: Strategies, transitions, and the 'colonial wound' in South African education. *Language and Education, 30*(3), 219–234. https://doi.org/10.1080/09500782.2015.1102274

Jasper, M. A. (2005). Using reflective writing within research. *Journal of Research in Nursing, 10*(3), 247–260. https://doi.org/10.1177/174498710501000303

Kimmel, L., Lachlan, L., & Guiden, A. (2021). *The power of teacher diversity: Fostering inclusive conversations through mentoring*. American Institutes for Research.

Kotze, J., Wills, G., Ardington, C., Taylor, S., Mohohlwane, N., & Deliwe, C.-N. (2022). Learning losses due to the Covid-pandemic. Advisory note for the reading panel 2022. In N. Spaull (Ed.), *2022 Background report for the 2030 reading panel* (pp. 1–20). Reading Panel.

Kriewaldt, J., McLean Davies, L., Rice, S., Rickards, F., & Acquaro, D. (2017). Clinical practice in education: Towards a conceptual framework. In M. A. Peters, B. Cowie, & I. Menter (Eds.), *A companion to research in teacher education* (pp. 1025–1040). Springer.

LaBoskey, V. L. (2004). The methodology of self-study and its theoretical underpinnings. In J. J. Loughran, M. L. Hamilton, V. K. LaBoskey, & T. Russell (Eds.), *International handbook of self-study of teaching and teacher education practices* (pp. 817–869). Kluwer Academic Publishers.

Lave, J. & Wenger, E. (1991). *Situated learning: Legitimate peripheral participation*. Cambridge University Press.

Lewin, K. M. (2004). *The pre-service training of teachers: Does it meet its objectives and how can it be improved?* UNESCO.

Li, P. B., Sani, B. B., & Azmin, N. A. B. (2021). Identifying mentor teachers' roles and perceptions in pre-service teachers' teaching practicum: The use of a mentoring model. *International Journal of Education and Practice, 9*(2), 365–378. https://doi.org/10.18488/journal.61.2021.92.365.378

Liu, W., Koh, C., & Chua, B. (2017). Developing Thinking Teachers Through Learning Portfolios. In O. Tan, W. Liu, & E. Low (Eds.), *Teacher education in the 21st century: Singapore's evolution and innovation* (pp. 69–83). Springer.

Loughran, J. J. (2002). Effective reflective practice: In search of meaning in learning about teaching. *Journal of Teacher Education, 53*(1), 33–43. https://doi.org/10.1177/0022487102053001004

Macupe, B. (2018, January 26). Varsity doesn't prepare us to teach in rural areas. *Mail and Guardian.* https://mg.co.za/article/2018-01-26-00-varsity-doesnt-prepare-us-to-teach-in-rural-areas/

Martin, S. D., Snow, J. L., & Franklin Torrez, C. A. (2011). Navigating the terrain of third space: Tensions with/in relationships in school-university partnerships. *Journal of Teacher Education, 62*(3), 299–311. https://doi.org/10.1177/0022487110396096

Masaiti, G., & Manchishi, P. C. (2011). The University of Zambia pre-service teacher education programme: Is it responsive to schools and communities' aspirations? *European Journal of Educational Studies, 3*(2), 310–324.

Military Leadership Diversity Commission. (2010). *Mentoring relationships and demographic diversity* (Issue Paper #25). Retrieved from: https://diversity.defense.gov/Portals/51/Documents/Resources/Commission/docs/Issue%20Papers/Paper%2025%20-%20Mentoring%20Relationships%20and%20Demographic%20Diversity.pdf

Moats, L. C. (2020). *Teaching reading is rocket science: What expert teachers of reading should know and be able to do.* American Federation of Teachers.

Mukeredzi, T. G. (2016). The 'Journey to Becoming': Pre-service teachers' experiences and understandings of rural school practicum in a South African context. *Global Education Review, 3*(1), 88–107.

Mutemeri, J., & Chetty, R. (2011). An examination of university-school partnerships in South Africa. *South African Journal of Education, 31*, 505–517.

National Planning Commission. (2012). *National Development Plan 2030. Our future—Make it work.* The Presidency.

Nel, C., & Adam, A. (2014). The reading literacy profiles of first-year B.Ed. foundation phase students. *South African Journal of Childhood Education, 4*(3), 52–70. https://doi.org/10.4102/sajce.v4i3.226

Nel, C., & Marais, L. M. (2021). Assessing the wicked problem of feedback during the teaching practicum. *Perspectives in Education, 39*(1), 410–426. https://doi.org/10.18820/2519593X/pie.v39.i1.25

Onyefulu, C., Hughes, G., & Samuels, R. (2019). Assessing the performance of student teachers in a Bachelor of Education programme at the University of Technology, Jamaica. *Open Access Library Journal, 6*, e5449. https://doi.org/10.4236/oalib.1105449

Pellegrino, J. W. (2017). Teaching, learning and assessing 21st century skills. In S. Guerriero (Ed.), *Educational research and innovation. Pedagogical knowledge and the changing nature of the teaching profession* (pp. 33–47). OECD.

Phillips-Jones, L. (2003). *Skills for successful mentoring: Competencies of outstanding mentors and mentees.* Retrieved from https://web.archive.org. https://web.archive.org/web/20201112125542/. https://my.lerner.udel.edu/wp-content/uploads/Skills_for_Sucessful_Mentoring.pdf

Phillips-Jones, L. (2010). *First, do no harm.* https://www.ndi.org/sites/default/files/The%20Mentoring%20Group_First%20Do%20No%20Harm.pdf

Pinnegar, S., & Hamilton, M. L. (2009). *Self-study of practice as a genre of qualitative research: Theory, methodology, and practice.* Springer.

Pretorius, E., Rastle, K., & Mtsatse, N. (2022). A curriculum review of South African CAPS Grades R to 3. In N. Spaull & E. Pretorius (Eds.), *Early grade reading in South Africa* (pp. 15–37). Oxford University Press.

Pryor, J., Akyeampong, K., Westbrook, J., & Lussier, K. (2012). Rethinking teacher preparation and professional development in Africa: An analysis of the curriculum of teacher education in the teaching of early reading and mathematics. *Curriculum Journal, 23*(4), 409–502. https://doi.org/10.1080/09585176.2012.747725

Rastle, K., Lally, C., Davis, M. H., & Taylor, J. S. H. (2021). The dramatic impact of explicit instruction on learning to read in a new writing system. *Psychological Science, 32*(4), 471–484. https://doi.org/10.1177/0956797620968790

Reading League. (2022). *Science of reading: Defining guide*. Retrieved from https://www.therea dingleague.org/what-is-thescience-of-reading/
Reddy, C., & Menkveld, H. (2000). Teaching students to reflect: An exploratory study on the introduction of reflective practice in a pre-service teacher education course in a university environment. *South African Journal of Higher Education, 12*(3), 117–185.
Reed, Y. (2014). *Report on English courses for Intermediate Phase student teachers at five universities*. Jet Education Services.
Reimers, F. M. (Ed.). (2022). *Primary and secondary education during Covid-19*. Springer.
Risan, M. (2020). Creating theory-practice linkages in teacher education: Tracing the use of practice-based artefacts. *International Journal of Educational Research, 104*, 1–10. https://doi.org/10.1016/j.ijer.2020.101670
Roulston, K. (2010). Considering quality in qualitative interviewing. *Qualitative Research, 10*(2), 199–228. https://doi.org/10.1177/1468794109356739
Saldana, J. (2021). *The coding manual for qualitative researchers* (4th ed.). Sage.
Samaras, A. P., & Freese, A. R. (2009). Looking back and looking forward: An historical overview of the self-study school. In C. A. Lassonde, S. Galman, & C. Kosnik (Eds.), *Self-study research methodologies for teacher educators* (pp. 3–19). Sense Publishers.
Scarborough, H. S. (2001). Connecting early language and literacy to later reading (dis)abilities: Evidence, theory, and practice. In S. Neuman & D. Dickinson (Eds.), *Handbook for research in early literacy* (pp. 97–110). Guilford Press.
Schleppegrell, M. J. (2012). Academic language in teaching and learning. *The Elementary School Journal, 112*(3), 409–418.
Shulman, L. S. (1986). Those who understand: knowledge growth in teaching. *Educational researcher, 15*(2):4–14. https://doi.org/10.3102/0013189X015002004
Simmons Zuilkowski, S., Sowa, P., Ralaingita, W., & Piper, B. (2021). *Literature review on pre-service teacher education for primary-grade literacy and numeracy*. Retrieved from: https://scienceofteaching.site/pre-service-teacher-training/
Smith, S. U., Hayes, S., & Shea, P. (2017). A critical review of the use of Wenger's community of practice (CoP) theoretical framework in online and blended learning research. *Online Learning, 21*(1), 209–237. https://doi.org/10.24059/olj.v21i1.963
Snow, C. E., & Uccelli, P. (2009). The challenge of academic language. In D. R. Olson & N. Torrance (Eds.), *The Cambridge handbook of literacy* (pp. 112–133). Cambridge University Press.
Spaull, N. (2019). Equity: A price too high to pay? In N. Spaull & J. D. Jansen (Eds.), *South African schooling: The enigma of inequality* (pp. 1–24). Springer.
Spaull, N. (2022). *2022 Background report for the 2030 reading panel*. Reading Panel.
Taghreed, E. M., & Mohd, R. M. S. (2017). Complexities and tensions ESL Malaysian student teachers face during their field practice. *The English Teacher, 46*(1), 1–16.
Taylor, N., & Mawoyo, M. (2022). Professionalising teaching: The case of language and literacy. In N. Spaull & E. Pretorius (Eds.), *Early grade reading in South Africa* (pp. 179–195). Oxford University Press.
Teacher Education Ministerial Advisory Group. (2014). *Action now: Classroom ready teachers*. Retrieved from: https://www.aitsl.edu.au/docs/default-source/default-document-library/action_now_classroom_ready_teachers_accessible-(1)da178891b1e86477b58fff00006709da.pdf?sfvrsn=9bffec3c_0
Tunmer, N., Chapman, J. W., Greany, K. T., Prochnow, J. E., & Arrow, A. W. (2013). *Why the New Zealand national literacy strategy has failed and what can be done about it: Evidence from the progress in international reading literacy study (PIRLS) 2011 and reading recovery monitoring report*. Massey University Institute of Education.
Tunmer, W. E., & Hoover, W. A. (2019). The cognitive foundations of learning to read: A framework for preventing and remediating reading difficulties. *Australian Journal of Learning Difficulties, 24*(1), 75–93. https://doi.org/10.1080/19404158.2019.1614081

Uccelli, P., Dobbs, C. L., & Scott, J. (2013). Mastering academic language: Organization and stance in the persuasive writing of high school students. *Written Communication, 30*(1), 36–62. https://doi.org/10.1177/0741088312469013

Uccelli, P., Barr, C. D., Dobbs, C. L., Galloway, E. P., Meneses, A., & Sanchez, E. (2015). Core academic language skills: An expanded operational construct and a novel instrument to chart school-relevant language proficiency in pre-adolescent and adolescent learners. *Applied Psycholinguistics, 36*(5), 1077–1109. https://doi.org/10.1017/S014271641400006X

University of Michigan. (2020). *High leverage practices.* Retrieved from: https://soe.umich.edu/academics-admissions/degrees/bachelors-certification/undergraduate-elementary-teacher-education/high-leverage-practices. Accessed October 24, 2020.

Van Manen, M. (1977). Linking ways of knowing with ways of being practical. *Curriculum Inquiry, 6*(3), 205–228; Van Manen, M. (1977). Linking ways of knowing with ways of being practical. *Curriculum Inquiry, 6*(3), 205–228.

Wenger, E. (1998). *Communities of practice: Learning, meaning and identity.* Cambridge University Press.

Wenger, E., & Wenger-Trayner, B. (2015). *Communities of practice: A brief introduction.* Retrieved from: https://scholarsbank.uoregon.edu/xmlui/bitstream/handle/1794/11736/A%20brief%20introduction%20to%20CoP.pdf. Accessed May 27, 2020.

Whatman, J., & MacDonald, J. (2017). *High quality practica and the integration of theory and practice in initial teacher education: A literature review prepared for the Education Council.* NZCER. Retrieved from: https://educationcouncil.org.nz/sites/default/files/Practica_Review_Full_Report.pdf

Wildsmith-Cromarty, R., & Balfour, R. J. (2019). Language learning and teaching in South African primary schools. *Language Teaching, 52,* 296–317. https://doi.org/10.1017/S0261444819000181

Wohlfahrt, M. U. (2018). Primary teacher education in rural Cameroon: Can informal learning compensate for the deficiencies in formal training? *Africa Education Review, 15*(3), 1–20. https://doi.org/10.1080/18146627.2016.1224586

World Bank. (2012). *System approach for better education results (SABER): What matters most in teacher policies? A framework for building a more effective teaching profession.* World Bank.

Children's Participation in Work Integrated Learning in Early Childhood Education

Naseema Shaik and Andile Mji

Abstract Work integrated learning (WIL) forms a pivotal component contributing to pre-service teacher development. Whilst research highlights the advantages and challenges pre-service teachers experience during work integrated learning, there is a dearth of research that focuses on how children participate in WIL which adopts an adult perspective. In this theoretical chapter, we provide an overview of why children's participation as to how they experienced the lesson is required through a child centered perspective for work integrated learning. We conclude by offering potentialities for policy makers, public and private higher education institutions to reimagine and reconceptualize the role of young children and older children's participation in work integrated learning. Considerations are also presented for empirical studies to be carried out to explore the impact of children's participation in the form of feedback to how children experienced the lesson for both pre-service and in-service teachers teaching.

Keywords Children's participation · Work integrated learning · Early childhood education

1 Introduction

In South Africa, very few children have access to quality early childhood education (ECE), which is possibly due to several factors such as financial constraints or not knowing the critical role ECE plays in a child's lifelong educational accomplishments (Venter, 2022). Regarding financial constraints, in a media release, Statistics South Africa (2018) reports that about half (46%) of children in ECE "… were living in households belonging to the lower household income quintiles". The benefits of early

N. Shaik (✉) · A. Mji
Cape Peninsula University of Technology, Cape Town, South Africa
e-mail: shaikn@cput.ac.za

A. Mji
e-mail: MJIA@cput.ac.za

© The Author(s), under exclusive license to Springer Nature Switzerland AG 2024
I. C. Chahine and L. Reddy (eds.), *Educators' Work Integrated Learning Experiences*,
https://doi.org/10.1007/978-3-031-65964-5_7

childhood education are numerous, children who are healthy and prepared when they enter kindergarten do better in school and are more likely to graduate and enroll in higher education. Well-educated adults are more prepared for the job opportunities of a global marketplace and to contribute to the strength of their communities United Nations Children's Fund (UNICEF, 2017). In fact, Heckman (2012) points out that early childhood development is a vehicle that drives success in school life. In this regard, this author argues that for any country's economic future to be sustainable, an efficient way is to focus on early childhood education (Heckman, 2012). Whilst it is important that quality ECE contributes to a country's economic status and can reduce poverty and hunger achieving universal primary education, as well as reducing children mortality through achieving Millenium Goals (2023), little is known about the role that young children play as participants in work integrated learning. In this chapter, we argue for work integrated learning to also incorporate a child centered perspective and not only adopt an adult centered perspective.

2 Work Integrated Learning in the Foundation Phase

Work integrated learning forms an important component of teachers' professional practice and in turn prepares them for the world of teaching. In the Foundation Phase, which focuses on teaching children from Grade R (Reception Year), Grade 1, 2 and 3, work integrated learning (WIL) supports preservice teachers to strengthen their teaching approaches in subjects such as mathematics, the languages, and life skills. In addition, WIL is an essential component of learning and teaching that provides guidance in becoming a professional teacher. Preservice teachers registered for the Bachelor of Education degree with specialization in the Foundation Phase, are required to engage in WIL during all four years of the degree program. WIL exposes preservice teachers through several experiences that prepare them for future teaching. For example, in the first year, preservice teachers focus on practice teaching learners in Grade R also known as the Reception Year. In the second year, the preservice teachers gain experience in practice teaching Grade 1 learners, then Grade 2 and Grade 3 respectively in their final two years of study. One of the important components of WIL is evaluation. Evaluation is undertaken by the mentor (hosting) teacher and an evaluator from the Faculty of Education. Evaluators from the faculty of education are permanent staff from the department and also include evaluators who are external. External evaluators are also experienced former teachers who have a qualification in the Bachelor of Education Foundation Phase or a similar qualification with experience and specialization in the Foundation Phase.

A huge gap in the evaluation of pre-service teachers is the voice of the children being taught during WIL. It is important to note that all children who are in early childhood education that includes children from birth to nine years or even older spanning to secondary education are never included in the evaluation of preservice teachers, yet they witness and engage the pre-service teachers teaching during the four weeks that the pre-service teachers spend in their classrooms. Our focus is particularly concerned with how young children in early childhood education participate in WIL as providing feedback to their pre-service teachers regarding their lessons. This theoretical chapter will provide an overview of work integrated learning, child participation and considerations for the possibilities of developing a child-centered WIL framework whereby children can also participate in the evaluation of their pre-service teachers. This chapter has the potential to contribute to policies on WIL and how these policies need to include the voices of children, this study also has the potential to contribute to pre-service and mentor teachers understandings of including children's voice as feedback for their own teaching, practice and research.

There is a proliferation of research that focuses on the importance of appropriately trained teachers to teach children in early childhood education, which forms part of the Foundation Phase (Grade R to 3). Currently in South Africa, there is a shortage of appropriately qualified teachers (Bouwer et al., 2021) in the Foundation phase and therefore it is imperative that they gain appropriate training, which includes WIL. The Minimum Requirements for Teacher Education Qualifications (MRTEQ) policy (Department of Higher Education and Training (DHET), 2015, p. 11) stipulates that initial teacher education curricula must engage pre-service teachers in a variety of learning opportunities, which includes disciplinary, foundational, practical, pedagogic and situational learning. MRTEQ conceptualizes WIL as providing students with opportunities to enhance their practical and situational knowledge through experiencing practice teaching at schools for a stipulated number of weeks, which should align with the credits of the module. WIL forms part of the professional practice module and allocates towards a 50% weighting of the subject, which is a considerable proportion. If students fail WIL, not only do they have to repeat WIL, but they cannot matriculate into the following years of the subjects of mathematics and language even if they passed these subjects.

There are many benefits to WIL (MRTEQ, 2015). Firstly, preservice teachers experience concrete classroom experience and get the opportunity to engage in practical learning, which is regarded as an important condition for the development of tacit knowledge, which is an important contributor of learning to teach. Secondly, preservice teachers should accumulate this knowledge by engaging in observation and reflecting on lessons taught by both the mentor teacher and themselves. Thirdly, and very importantly, "WIL contributes to students situational learning as it exposes students to varied and contrasting contexts of schooling in South Africa" (p.18). In experiencing contrasting contexts, pre-service teachers need to practice teaching in contexts that are both advantaged and disadvantaged in terms of quintile schools.

There have been many studies exploring students' experiences of WIL both nationally and internationally. Nationally, Bouwer et al. (2021) explored Gr R presevice teachers' experiences of WIL and their ability to transfer their knowledge into practice. The study found that student teachers experienced both positive and negative aspects and these were related to the need for remodeling the WIL experience by moving from the periphery to full participation in classrooms. Abongdia et al. (2015) explored the challenges student teachers experience during WIL. Findings showed that a conducive environment, exploration of experiential knowledge, student centeredness and teaching language as a social practice are the essential teaching philosophies. Relatedly, Arosamwan and Mashiya (2021) investigated the experiences of pre-service foundation phase teachers of life skills during WIL. Findings indicated that pre-service teachers experience of support from mentor teachers was positive. However, there were several challenges including struggle with implementation of the Foundation Phase curriculum, realities of classroom interaction, inefficient language of interaction for the FP classroom, and lack of awareness of the important role that life skills as a subject played in the curriculum. Whilst there have been many studies focusing on varying aspects related to WIL and undertaken both nationally and internationally (Kanjee & Mthembu, 2015; Meiring, 2019; Steyn & Adendorff, 2020) as far as we searched, there have been no studies that focus on young children's participation in WIL opportunities.

During WIL, much emphasis is placed on evaluation, which is undertaken from an adult centered perspective whereby the evaluation takes place between mentor teachers and evaluators. Pre-service teachers are placed in classrooms such as Gr R, Gr 1, Gr 2 or Gr 3 where children are between the ages of 5–9 years. The student teachers are expected to complete their practice teaching during WIL for four weeks where they are expected to observe and teach a prescribed number of lessons from different learning areas, namely language, mathematics and life skills including art, music and movement. Preservice teachers are mentored by the mentor teacher receiving feedback and guidance regarding the teaching of their lessons. Whilst the students are on WIL, either an internal evaluator who is an academic from the institution or an external evaluator appointed by the institution visits the student to evaluate a lesson that the student teaches and finally a joint evaluation is completed between the evaluator and the mentor teacher. Whilst it is important that both the mentor teacher and evaluator jointly complete a final evaluation of the pre-service teachers for WIL, this evaluation emanates from an adult perspective and fails to seek the child-centered perspective, which can also inform preservice teachers of their strengths and weaknesses. Children's participation in the evaluation of the pre-service teachers is pivotal as their voices should also be considered as the pre-service teacher can use their feedback to reflect and improve the lessons. One might assume that offering children an opportunity to express themselves about how they experienced the pre-service or in-service teachers' lesson might be problematic and could result in teachers punishing children in different ways. However the United Nations Convention on the Rights of the Child (UNCRC, 1989) clearly highlights that children have a right to express themselves and make decisions regarding their learning as was articulated in articles 12 and 13 of the UNCRC and South Africa was one of the countries that ratified the UNCRC. The joint evaluation focuses on the overall learning environment and preservice teacher's professionalism, planning, preparation and delivery of lessons, which is pivotal for preservice teachers to reflect upon. Furthermore, pre-service teachers need to reflect after every lesson, and this is documented in their WIL portfolios. Each of these areas have specific criteria that the student teacher should show competence in, which is important as it contributes to the development of pre-service teachers' development as a teacher. However, there is only one criterion that refers to learners' active participation, which is very broad but no criterion focuses on how children's genuine participation is considered in the pre-service teacher's teaching.

3 Children's Participation

The United Nations Convention on the Rights of the Child (UNCRC, 1989) highlights through article 12 and 13 that children must be listened to, and their views taken seriously in accordance with their age and maturity. Children have the right to be active individuals in society to freely express their views, assembling, forming an association and asking for their views to be considered in all matters concerning them (Landsdown, 2011). Young children are considered competent persons who are experienced in their own ways, who have knowledge and understanding of their world and have the right to a voice in a wide range of contexts (Sommer et al., 2013). It is therefore pivotal that opportunities be afforded for children to express their views in all matters affecting them and to have them considered and be given due weight in the diverse contexts they attend or live in (United Nations Assembly, 1989; Percy-Smith & Thomas, 2010).

The right to participate in the Convention on the Rights of the Child (Article 12) states that in every matter affecting the child, children have the right to be present consciously and willingly and to directly or indirectly express their opinions freely and ensure that these views are considered (United Nations Committee on the Rights of the Child [UNCRC], 2005, 2009). The participation right emphasizes that all children should express their views on issues that concern them and that these opinions should be taken seriously. Considering this, WIL concerns children as they are the children receiving a lesson so it is pivotal that they should be provided with the opportunity to provide feedback to pre-service teachers regarding how they experienced the lesson.

Children has the right to be present consciously and to directly or indirectly express their opinions freely and to ensure that their views are considered (United Nations Committee on the Rights of the Child (UNCRC, 2005, 2009). The European Commission (2021) in line with the European Union (EU) Strategy on the Rights of the Child has been committed to promoting events with children as participants to strengthen expertise and practice on child participation. The European Union Strategy on the Rights of the Child has aimed to promote the rights of children in all aspects of their life and developing actions to empower children to be active citizens and members of democratic societies (Correia et al., 2022). In South Africa, children's participation in all arenas whether it is school, society or policy is well exemplified through the South African Constitution, the African Charter on the Rights and Welfare of the Child, the National Programme of Action and is included in other legislation and national policies. Whilst the importance for child participation to be supported is included in both national and international policies, children's participation is not included in WIL policies.

Participation focuses on information sharing and dialogue between children and adults, which is based on mutual respect wherein children can learn how their views and those of adults can be considered and can shape an outcome (Ruiz-Casares et al., 2017). When children are given an opportunity to provide feedback on a pre-service teacher's lesson, the pre-service teacher can use this feedback to improve their future lessons. This calls for purposeful listening wherein a listening culture and an ethics of listening to children is developed (Clark et al., 2005). Participation is understood as a complex process ingrained in cultural, social, and relational contexts (Lansdown, 2005). Children can participate in the family, school, health care, local community or at the political level (Correia et al., 2021) and most importantly children's participation can be supported in early childhood education, which is described as fundamental microsystems for children's development (Sylva et al., 2010). Children should be able to express their views, preferences, and choices regarding where, when or with whom to play (Correia et al., 2019) and we would add that children should also be able to provide feedback on how they experienced the lesson/s of the pre-service teacher. Children's participation is highly contributory to children's learning processes, quality learning outcomes, enhancement of school commitment and development of democratic values (Davies et al., 2006; Osler & Starkey, 2005). Participation is also contributory to children being participative citizens who can shape democratic practices (Pascal & Bertram, 2009). In South Africa, especially children from disadvantaged communities may find themselves unable to interact with their parents and we would argue participate meaningfully. This may be due to several factors, one of which for instance, relates to parents who may be in jobs, that by their nature, hinder participation in their children's education (Jensen, 2009). It is in situations like these that the involvement of early childhood educators is critical. Literature shows that early childhood educators who allow children to express themselves, invariably encourage language development, help improve children's cognitive development, as well as allow them to develop their social skills and emotional maturity (Test et al., 2010) In fact, these authors (Test et al., 2010, p. 12) suggest that early childhood educators should have

> … conversations for the sheer pleasure of it. Use positive, rich, and empathic language (rather than commands or negative statements). Be curious and ask thought-provoking questions. Give children time to respond, listen to what they say, and then respond to their ideas.

These findings have important implications for how pre-service and in-service teachers also need to ascertain from children how they experienced their lessons.

Children's participation is not a concept that occurs on its own (Koran & Avci, 2017) but needs to be supported by teachers. Participation needs to take place in a space where children feel safe and feel included (Lundy, 2007) to express their views and are aware that their needs are considered (Venninen & Leinonen, 2013).

Teachers play a pivotal role in guiding children to realizing their rights through practice and thus need to provide children with opportunities and support to exercise their rights and evolving capacities by sharing power and involving them in negotiation and decision making (Lansdown, 2010; UNCRC Article 5). Shier's model of participation emphasizes the importance of adults actively encouraging children's involvement by asking reflective questions. These questions help teachers assess and plan their work around creating openings, opportunities, and fulfilling obligations for children's participation. Whilst it is well researched that adults play an important role in supporting children's participation, implementation in practice is hugely challenging. Lundy (2007) asserts that child participation can cause challenges for some teachers as they may feel that by allowing children to participate, their power may be relinquished. It is therefore important that teachers rethink their roles as bearers of power, and they need to encourage children's participation in a non-conflicting environment (Kanyal & Gibbs, 2014). Shaik (2021) in a recent study also found that some teachers are also ingrained in transmissive pedagogies and unwilling to learn pedagogies that invite children's participation. The findings also indicated that student teachers needed additional training to effectively listen to children's voices, as they tended to focus on hearing the "correct" answers. Most teachers are also challenged to support children's participation due to heavy workloads, large classes (Correia et al., 2021) and a curriculum that is packed with prescribed outcomes that forces teachers to not to teach for surprises (Moss, 2011).

4 Why Should Children Participate in WIL?

States Parties shall assure to the child who is capable of forming his or her own views the right to express those views freely in all matters affecting the child, the views of the child being given due weight in accordance with the age and maturity of the child. For this purpose, the child shall in particular be provided the opportunity to be heard in any judicial and administrative proceedings affecting the child, either directly, or through a representative or an appropriate body, in a manner consistent with the procedural rules of national law (Article 12, UNCRC).

Children's right to form their views is considered to be a crucial provision and the cornerstone of the convention (Freeman, 2007 as cited in Lundy & Sainz, 2018). This right is considered as a passport to the realization of other rights. Lundy and Sainz (2018) warn us that if we ignore children's views on education, we undermine the realization of other rights in school (Lundy, 2007; Osler, 2010a, 2010b).

Whilst older children may have the opportunities to participate in collective participation in decision making, this is not always a reality. Very often young children's participation in decision making in early childhood is not considered and as a result decisions are often made on behalf of children daily without the input of children. Children are ignored and excluded in clear breach of their international human rights (Harris, 2009). Decisions are often made for children such as the schools they should attend, the subjects they should study, the educational provision they receive. During

WIL it is only the mentor teachers and evaluators who provide the feedback to the pre-service teacher and yet it is the children who experience the lesson, yet their voices are not considered as to how they felt about the lesson. The situation regarding young children's participation is even more concerning as one might argue that younger children are far too immature and in need of protection. They are therefore unlikely to participate meaningfully in WIL of the pre-service teachers. However, the sociology of childhood reminds us that young children are social actors, who participate and construct their own lives but also influence the lives of those around them and the societies in which they live and therefore contribute to learning as agents (James et al., 1998). Children have voice and agency, and they must be listened to (James et al., 1998). Young children can tell us more than we can really understand about how they perceive their environments and what happens there. It is therefore imperative that children's decisions regarding their input about their pre-service teachers teaching be taken seriously.

Interestingly, children have the capacity of expressing themselves through a variety of modalities such as crying, babbling, smiling, pointing, touching, gazing and uses of material (Murray, 2019). Research also informs us that group conversations encourage children to talk and assist one another (Gruae & Walsh, 1998). They are also child-friendly ways of obtaining children's feedback. Young children form part of the schooling environment within which preservice teachers practice teaching, yet they have no voice in the evaluation of their preservice teachers. It is the children who are exposed to the preservice teachers teaching so they need to have a voice and must be listened to. Listening pedagogy (Rinaldi, 2001) truly involves meaningfully listening to children so that children can also make a difference. If education is to be transformed everyone involved in it must have a voice for the realization of transformation. Freire (1970) postulates that teachers should not be depositors of knowledge through banking education into children who in this case are passive recipients. Children should therefore be active participants who can evaluate and contribute to the strengthening of pre-service teachers' work integrated learning. As indicated earlier, it is often the adults who make the decisions and thus have influence. Lundy (2007) developed the Lundy's model of participation where she describes the elements of voice, space, audience and influence for teachers to enable participation. Of the elements described in this model, influence is the most difficult element to be realized in practice. The argument encapsulated for influence is that children's views must be acted upon. It is worthless if children are listened to but nothing is done with the views that children have shared. The Lundy model highlights that the challenge is to find ways of ensuring that adults not only listen to children but that they take children's views seriously. While this cannot be universally guaranteed, one incentive/safeguard is to ensure that children are told how their views were considered. Often children are asked for their views and then not told what became of them; that is, whether they had any influence or not (Lundy, 2007, p. 938).

It is incumbent on adults to empower children so that they can participate in decision making processes. Children's influence should be planned by responsive adults who show children that they take children's decisions seriously and children can discuss their plans and ideas with teachers (Welty & Lundy, 2013). The idea is to act upon children's views regarding whether children would like new play items, planning a new activity, what type of playground they would like or even influencing the wider community (Clark, 2005; Council of Europe, 2020 as cited in Correia et al.). Similarly with WIL if children have the opportunity to share their views regarding the pre-service teachers' lesson and if the children's thoughts are considered, this will provide children with a sense of belonging and they will feel that they do have influence (Lundy, 2007).

Influence is a fundamental human right that holds significant value, not only in terms of children's learning and socialization or as preparation for the future, but also as something that is actively occurring in the present moment, here and now (Emilson, 2007). Influence is the right for everyone to be heard, seen and respected (UNCRC). Internationally, influence is an important contributor to democracy, and it is the teachers' task to ensure that this takes place. Influence is also a pre-requisite for children's learning because if children have influence over their learning their learning becomes more meaningful to them. If children do not have the opportunity to influence anything in the early childhood contest, then their participation is not realized. Influence is a condition for genuine participation to be realized (Emilson & Folkesson, 2006). However, studies show that children's influence is rarely realized in early childhood education and is dependent on teachers' attitudes (Emilson & Folkesson, 2006; Sheridan, 2001). In early childhood education contexts, which is characterized by strong teacher control and emphasis is placed on rules, norms and obedience and also partly by no control depicting a laisser-faire mentality, then quality of learning and teaching is low (Sheridan, 2001). In early childhood settings where teachers intentionally listen to children, attune to their needs, and encourage their participation, these environments foster high-quality learning and teaching. A recent study in South Africa (Mkhize-Mthembu, 2022) demonstrates how teachers enhanced their teaching practices by listening to and valuing children's voices. Lessons were audio-recorded and photographed as part of the teacher's teaching portfolio. By adopting a socio-cultural theoretical perspective, the teacher explored the principles of social justice and worked collaboratively with children to understand both collective and individual experiences of students and teachers. The findings underscore the importance of recognizing young children's perspectives, as they are significant contributors to and beneficiaries of the educational process.

From the above discussion it can be argued that children need to be supported to influence what happens in early childhood contexts. We argue that for genuine participation to be a reality during WIL children need to also have influence over how they have experienced their pre-service teachers' practice teaching.

5 Conclusion

This chapter provided a theoretical overview of why children's participation is so important in pre-service teachers' work integrated learning. The chapter unpacked work integrated learning and how work integrated adopts an adult perspective. We argued that an adult perspective is not sufficient as it silences the child's perspective when it is children who experience the practice teaching of the pre-service teacher for the larger duration of teaching practice. We also showed how evaluation forms for the pre-service teachers' performance show that most criteria focus on the adult perspective and no input from the children. We also unpacked the meaning of child participation and showed how from a policy perspective both nationally and internationally child participation should be realized. We supported this by arguing that children are social actors in the here and now and they can add valuable input into pre-service teachers' work integrated learning. The absence of verbal abilities in children to express their experiences with pre-service teachers should not be a barrier to their participation. Children can communicate their experiences through various modalities, such as laughing, crying, babbling, or pointing, providing valuable insights into how they perceive the teaching. It must be noted that children in Grade R might not have the capacity to provide a written account of how they experienced the lesson, but they have the verbal capacity to express themselves, which must be supported. This could be done through children's drawing, group conversations using puppets and persona dolls. Getting feedback from children does not prevent them from advancing on their academic development, in fact it is an opportunity to also develop them as critical thinkers. The children's feedback has the potential to help the pre-service teachers to reflect and improve their lessons. Rather than just asking children whether they enjoyed the lesson or not, pre-service teachers need to ask the why questions and what in particular the children enjoyed or not and provide reasons. We do believe that this theoretical overview will open more opportunities for empirical research to be carried out on children's participation in WIL. We also believe that such an overview is important for policy makers, public and private higher education institutions to reimagine and reconceptualize the role of young children and older children's participation in WIL.

Acknowledgements The main author would like to sincerely thank the Cape Peninsula University of Technology Research and Innovation Fund for Teaching and Learning (RIFTAL) for funding this study.

References

Abongdia, J. (2015, October 8). Pre-service teachers' challenges during teaching practice in one University in the Eastern Cape, South Africa. *International Journal Of Educational Sciences*, *11*(01). https://doi.org/10.31901/24566322.2015/11.01.06

Akyol, T., & Erdem, H. (2021). Children's participation from the perspectives of teachers. *Journal of Pedagogical Research*, 188–202.

Arasomwan, D. A., & Mashiya, N. (2021, March 11). Foundation phase pre-service teachers' experiences of teaching life skills during teaching practice. *South African Journal of Childhood Education, 11*(1). https://doi.org/10.4102/sajce.v11i1.700

Bouwer, M., Venketsamy, R., & Bipath, K. (2021, September). Remodelling work-integrated learning experiences of Grade R student teachers. *South African Journal of Higher Education, 35*(4). https://doi.org/10.20853/36-3-4331

Clark, A. (2005, August). Listening to and involving young children: A review of research and practice. *Early Child Development and Care, 175*(6), 489–505. https://doi.org/10.1080/03004430500131288

Clark, A., Kjørholt, A. T., & Moss, P. (2005). *Beyond listening: Children's perspectives on early childhood services.* The Policy Press University of Bristol.

Correia, N., Aguiar, C., & Amaro, F. (2021). Children's participation in early childhood education: A theoretical overview. *Contemporary Issues in Early Childhood*, 146394912098178. https://doi.org/10.1177/1463949120981789

Correia, N., Aguiar, C., & The participa Consortium. (2022, June 6). Children's right to participate: The Lundy model applied to early childhood education and care. *The International Journal of Children's Rights, 30*(2), 378–405. https://doi.org/10.1163/15718182-30020010

Correia, N., Camilo, C., Aguiar, C., & Amaro, F. (2019). May. Children's right to participate in early childhood education settings: A systematic review. *Children and Youth Services Review, 100*, 76–88. https://doi.org/10.1016/j.childyouth.2019.02.031

Council of Europe, (2020). *Listen-Act-Change: Council of Europe handbook on children's participation. For professionals working for and with children.* Available at https://rm.coe.int/publication-handbook-on-children-s-participation-eng/1680a14539

Davies, M., Williams, C., Yamashita, H., & Ko Man-Hing, A. (2006). *Impact and outcomes: Taking up the challenge of pupil participation.* Carnegie Foundation.

Department of Higher Education and Training. (2015). *Revised policy on the minimum requirements for teacher education qualifications.* Government Printer.

Emilson, A., & Folkesson, A. (2006, May). Children's participation and teacher control. *Early Child Development and Care, 176*(3–4), 219–238. https://doi.org/10.1080/03004430500039846

Emilson, A. (2007, June). Young children's influence in preschool. *International Journal of Early Childhood, 39*(1), 11–38. https://doi.org/10.1007/bf03165946

European Commission. (2021). *The EU strategy on the rights of the child and the European child guarantee.* Communication from the Commission to the European Parliament, the Council, the European Economic and Social Committee and the Committee of the Regions. Available at https://eur-lex.europa.eu/legal-content/en/TEXT/uri=CELEX%3A52021DC0142

First Things First. (2023). *Investing in early childhood.* Retrieved from https://www.firstthingsfirst.org/early-childhood-matters/investing-in-early-childhood/

Freeman, M. (2007). Why it remains important to take children's rights seriously. *International Journal of Children's Rights, 15*(1), 5–24.

Freire, P. (1970). *Pedagogy of the oppressed.* The Continuum Publishing Company.

Graue, M. E., & Walsh, D. J. (1998). *Studying children in context: Theories, methods, and ethics.* Sage.

Harris, N. (2009, August 6). Playing catch-up in the schoolyard? Children and young.

Heckman, J. J. (2012). The Heckman equation. In *Invest in early childhood development: Reduce deficits, strengthen the economy.* https://heckmanequation.org/

James, A., Jenks, C., & Prout, A. (1998). *Theorizing childhood.* Polity Press.

Jensen, E. (2009). *Teaching with poverty in mind: What being poor does to kids brains and what schools can do about it.* Association for Supervision and Curriculum Development.

Kanjee, A., & Mthembu, J. (2015). Assessment literacy of foundation phase teachers: An exploratory study. *South African Journal of Childhood Education, 5*(1), 142–168. https://doi.org/10.4102/sajce.v5i1.354

Kanyal, M., & Gibbs, J. (2014). Participation: Why and how? In M. Kanyal (Ed.), *Children's Rights 0–8. Promoting participation in education and care* (pp. 45–62). Routledge.

Koran, N., & Avci, N. (2017). Perceptions of prospective pre-school teachers regarding children's right to participate in classroom activities. *Educational Sciences: Theory & Practice.* https://doi.org/10.12738/estp.2017.3.0325

Lansdown, G. (2005). *Can you hear me? The right of young children to participate in decisions affecting them (Working papers in early childhood development No. 36).* Bernard van Leer Foundation.

Lansdown, G. (2010). The realisation of children's participation rights: Critical reflections. In B. Percy-Smith & N. Thomas (Eds.), *A handbook of children and young people participation* (pp. 33–45). New York, NY: Routledge.

Landsdown, G. (2011). *Everychild's right to be heard: A resource guide on the UN Committee on the rights of the child general comment no 12.* Save the Children and UNICEF.

Lundy, L., & Martínez Sainz, G. (2018, September 17). The role of law and legal knowledge for a transformative human rights education: Addressing violations of children's rights in formal education. *Human Rights Education Review, 1*(2), 04–24. https://doi.org/10.7577/hrer.2560

Lundy, L. (2007). Voice is not enough conceptualizing Article 12 of the United Nations convention on the rights of the child. *British Educational Research Journal, 33*(6), 927–942. https://doi.org/10.1080/01411920701657033

Meiring, L. F. (2019). Foundation phase science teacher identity: Exploring evolutionary module development to promote science teaching self-efficacy. *South African Journal of Childhood Education, 9*(1), 1–11. https://doi.org/10.4102/sajce.v9i1.603

Mkhize-Mthembu, N. S. (2022). Finding myself by involving children in self-study research methodology: A gentle reminder to live freely. *South African Journal of Childhood Education, 12*(1), a1043. https://doi.org/10.4102/sajce.v12i1.1043

Moss, P. (2011). *Democracy as first practice in early childhood education and care.* Encyclopaedia on Early Childhood Development. http://www.childencyclopedia.com/sites/default/files/textes-experts/en/857/democracy-as-first-practice-in-early-childhood-education-and-care.pdf

Murray, J. (2019). Hearing young children's voices. *International Journal of Early Years Education, 27*(1), 1–5. https://doi.org/10.1080/09669760.2018.1563352

Osler, A., & Starkey, H. (2005). *Changing citizenship: Democracy and inclusion in education.* Open University Press.

Osler, A. (2010a). *Students' perspectives on schooling.* McGraw-Hill Education (UK).

Osler, A. (2010b). *Students' perspectives on schooling.* Open University Press.

Pascal, C., & Bertram, T. (2009). Listening to young citizens: The struggle to make real a participatory paradigm in research with young children. *European Early Childhood Education Research Journal, 17*(2), 249–262.

People's "voice" and education rights in the UK. *International Journal of Law, Policy and the Family, 23*(3), 331–366. https://doi.org/10.1093/lawfam/ebp007

Percy-Smith, B., & Thomas, N. (2010). *A handbook of children and young people's participation: Perspectives from theory and practice.* Routledge.

Pramling, S., Sommer, D., & Hundeide, K. (2013). Early childhood care and education: A child perspective paradigm. *European Early Child Education Research Journal, 21,* 459–475.

Republic of South Africa. (1996a). *Constitution of the Republic of South Africa, Act 108 of 1996.* Government Printer.

Republic of South Africa. (1996b). *The constitution of the Republic of South Africa. Bill of Rights paragraph, 27.* Government Printer.

Rinaldi, C. (2001). The pedagogy of listening: The listening perspective from Reggio Emilia. *Innovations in early education: The International Reggio Emilia Exchange, 8*(4), 1–4. Retrieved from https://static1.squarespace.com/static/526fe9aee4b0c53fa3c845e0/t/540fce31e4b00c94d884e002/1410321969279/Pedagody+of+Listening+-+Rinaldi+-Fall+2001.pdf

Ruiz-Casares, M., Collins, T. M., Tisdall, E. K., & Grover, S. (2017). Children's rights to participation and protection in international development and humanitarian interventions: Nurturing a dialogue. *The International Journal of Human Rights, 21*(1), 1–13. https://doi.org/10.1080/13642987.2016.1262520

Shaik, N. (2021). "Supporting student teachers for a participatory pedagogy through Shier's model of participation in Grade R (Reception Year) South Africa". *Journal of Early Childhood Teacher Education.* https://doi.org/10.1080/10901027.2021.1881663.

Sheridan, S. (2001). *Pedagogical quality in preschool: An issue of perspectives.* Acta Universitatis Gothoburgensis.

Sheridan, S., & Samuelsson, I. P. (2001). Children's conceptions of participation and influence in pre-school: A perspective on pedagogical quality. *Contemporary Issues in Early Childhood, 2*(2), 169–194.

Sommer, D., Samuelsson, I. P., & Hundeide, K. (2013). Early childhood care and education: A child perspective paradigm. *European Early Childhood Education Research Journal, 21*(4), 459–475. https://doi.org/10.1080/1350293X.2013.845436

Statistics South Africa. (2018). *Media release—Education series volume IV: Early childhood development in South Africa.* Retrieved from https://www.statssa.gov.za/?p=10957

Steyn, G., & Adendorff, S. A. (2020). Questioning techniques used by foundation phase education students teaching mathematical problem-solving. *South African Journal of Childhood Education, 10*(1), 1–9. https://doi.org/10.4102/sajce.v10i1.564

Sylva, K., Melhuish, E., Sammons, P., Siraj-Blatchford, I., & Taggart, B. (Eds.). (2010). *Early childhood matters: Evidence from the effective pre-school and primary education project* (1st ed.). Routledge. https://doi.org/10.4324/9780203862063

Test, J. E., Cunningham, D. D., & Lee, A. C. (2010). Talking with young children: How teachers encourage learning. *Dimensions of Early Childhood, 38*(3), 3–14.

United Nations. (2005). Plan of Action for the first phase (2005–2009) of the World Programme for Human Rights Education. (New York, United Nations).

United Nations Convention on the Rights of the Child [UNCRC]. (1989). Retrieved from http://www.unicef.org/crc/crc.htm

United Nations General Assembly. (1989). *The United Nations convention on the rights of the child.* United Nations.

United Nations, UN Committee on the Rights of the Child. (2001). *General comment no. 1 on the aims of education.* CRC/GC/2001/1.

United Nations, UN Committee on the Rights of the Child. (2017). Consideration of reports submitted by States parties under article 44 of the Convention:

United Nations. (2023). *We can end poverty.* https://www.un.org/millenniumgoals/

Venninen, T., & Leinonen, J. (2013). Developing children's participation through research and reflective practices. *Asia-Pacific Journal of Research in Early Childhood Education, 7*(1), 31–49.

Venter, L. (2022). A systems perspective on early childhood development education in South Africa. *ICEP, 16,* 7. https://doi.org/10.1186/s40723-022-00100-5

Welty, E., & Lundy, L. (2013). A children's rights-based approach to involving children in decision making. *Journal of Science Communication, 12*(3), C02. https://doi.org/10.22323/2.12030302

Unveiling First-Year Student Teachers' Experiences: An Excursion Programme Rooted in Playful Learning for Active and Critical Learning

Neal T Petersen

Abstract This chapter investigates the role of virtual Work Integrated Learning (WIL) excursions in preparing future teachers to navigate the multifaceted challenges of a complex teaching profession. It addresses the persistent issues of novice teacher attrition stemming from the *'theory–practice divide'* and the *'apprenticeship of observation'* in teacher education. This study, introduced at a university in South Africa, is underpinned by social constructivism, and playful learning pedagogies. Employing interpretive qualitative methods and design-based research, it examines the experiences of first-year student teachers in a virtual WIL excursion, aiming to involve them in active and critical learning experiences. The excursion aims to engage first-year student teachers in active and critical learning experiences, fostering their self-directedness and cultural responsiveness. By engaging in authentic learning experiences and reflective discussions, the findings reveal that virtual excursions can contribute to promoting active and critical learning among student teachers, nurturing empathy, cultural responsiveness, and self-directedness. Through collaborative problem-solving activities and discussions on social justice issues, the student teachers develop a deeper understanding of diverse perspectives and cultivate empathy. Findings highlight the significance of the UBUNTU aspect, emphasizing collective inquiry and collaboration among student teachers. The chapter concludes by emphasizing the importance of integrating playful pedagogies and the UBUNTU philosophy into teacher education to bridge the *'theory–practice divide'* and sensitize them to overcome the *'apprenticeship of observation'*. The chapter underscores the need for ongoing research and innovative approaches in preparing agentic and culturally competent teachers for the diverse and evolving demands of the complex teaching profession.

Keywords Work integrated learning · Excursion · Pedagogy of playful learning · Teacher agency · UBUNTU

N. T. Petersen (✉)
Research Unit for Self-Directed Learning, North-West University, Potchefstroom, South Africa
e-mail: neal.petersen@nwu.ac.za

1 Introduction

Shulman (2004, p. 504) describes classroom teaching as "perhaps the most complex, most challenging, and most demanding, subtle, nuanced, and frightening activity our species has ever invented". Esau and Maarman (2021) advocate for robust teacher preparation programs to address this complexity. However, despite efforts, many teachers quit due to insufficient preparation and, lack the agency to navigate the profession (Sang, 2020). Rose (2020) defines agentic teachers as possessing self-efficacy, self-reflection, reflexivity, and intentionality—all qualities indicating their levels of self-directedness. Novice teacher attrition is a global concern, stemming from issues like the *'theory–practice divide'* and the *'apprenticeship of observation'* (García & Weiss, 2019; Hugo, 2018).

The *'theory–practice divide'* is one of the major causes of novice teacher attrition (Gravett, 2012). Mavhunga and van der Merwe (2020) explain that central to the dilemma of the theory–practice divide is " the recognition of the dissonance between the preparation to teach [*theory*] and the actual act of teaching [*practice*]" (p. 65). Teacher training often emphasizes theory over practical skills leading to a naïve understanding of teaching (Petersen et al., 2022). WIL aims to bridge this gap by exposing student teachers to real classroom practises (DHET, 2015).

According to the *Minimum Requirements for Teacher Qualifications in South Africa* (DHET, 2015), WIL is structured around two main components: learning *FROM* practice and learning *IN* practice. Learning *IN* practice involves direct teaching in authentic classroom settings, while learning *FROM* practice is the study of practice, using discursive resources to analyze different practices across a variety of contexts, including scaffolds such as case studies, games, and videos (DHET, 2015). This approach immerses student teachers in authentic classroom scenarios, providing them with a deeper understanding of teaching practices. During WIL and their subsequent teaching careers, student teachers must be equipped to implement the school curriculum, emphasizing "active and critical learning" (Department of Basic Education [DBE], 2011, p. 4). This necessitates teachers having the skills and agency to interpret and apply the curriculum effectively, encouraging active and critical learning instead of rote learning (DBE, 2011, p. 5). Future student teachers thus must be exposed to and participate in active learning while their higher-order thinking skills such as problem-solving, critical thinking, and being innovative can be developed.

Various definitions of critical thinking exist, with Facione (2020) describing it as a "pervasive and purposeful human phenomenon" (p. 9), involving both dispositions and cognitive skills. These skills encompass interpretation, analysis, evaluation, inference, explanation, and self-regulation. Critical thinkers also exhibit traits such as inquisitiveness, a sharp mind, dedication to reason, and eagerness for reliable information. Facione emphasizes the relevance of critical thinking across everyday life and professional domains, and highlights that it is a skill that can be learned. In Mardell et al.'s (2016) study, a teacher emphasized fostering critical thinking by encouraging students to be discerning consumers of information using familiar artefacts.

In South Africa, du Toit-Brits (2019) observes that most student teachers lack self-directed and lifelong learning skills because of the predominant teacher-centred approaches in schools and higher education institutions. This perpetuates what Lortie (1975) termed the '*apprenticeship of observation*', where novice teachers imitate the practices of their former schoolteachers, which hampers their preparedness for university and teaching roles. The exposure to predominant teacher-centred methods during their school years, shapes their skewed perceptions of what teaching entails. This underscores the necessity of nurturing proactive educators capable of navigating the complexities inherent in teaching.

To tackle these issues, the Faculty of Education at North-West University introduced educational excursions from 2016 to 2023 as part of the WIL experience for first-year Bachelor of Education (BEd) students. Grounded in a pedagogy of playful learning, these excursions aim to engage student teachers in active and critical learning by addressing authentic teaching challenges. This study evaluates the effectiveness of the excursion program in fostering active and critical learning among first-year student teachers, addressing two research questions based on the 2022 data: (1) How does the pedagogy of playful learning promote active learning? (2), and how does it foster critical learning? The subsequent sections will delve into the theoretical and conceptual frameworks guiding this research study.

2 Theoretical Framework

Social constructivism, rooted in Vygotsky's work (1978), serves as the theoretical framework for this study. Vygotsky emphasizes the significance of experience and social interaction in learning. In the context of this research, social constructivism is pertinent as student teachers engage in cooperative learning (CL) activities during the excursion, guided by a playful learning pedagogy within the zone of proximal development (ZPD). The ZPD, as defined by Vygotsky (1978), represents the gap between a learner's current developmental level and their potential level achievable with assistance. Playful learning, drawing from socio-constructivist theories, facilitates higher-order thinking through experiential and reflective activities in social settings. Vygotsky (1978) illustrates the connection between play and the ZPD, highlighting how play propels children beyond their typical behaviour, fostering holistic development. The term '*proximal*' denotes learners in '*close*' proximity to acquiring specific skills, with Vygotsky advocating for knowledgeable others to facilitate skill acquisition within the ZPD. Teachers are encouraged to focus on key elements supporting learning to guide learners through the ZPD, as demonstrated in Table 1 during the excursion's playful activities.

Figure 1 depicts how scaffolding, within the ZPD, took place during the playful learning activities. The figure also depicts how the students' higher-order thinking

Table 1 Crucial elements needed in the ZPD, and its presence during the excursion

Crucial elements that should be present in the ZPD (McLeod, 2024)	Actual elements present during the playful activities in the excursion
The presence of a *knowledgeable other* or other person whose knowledge and abilities exceed those of the learner	Lecturers and post-graduate students as facilitators and peers in the small groups
Social interactions in small groups with a knowledgeable other such as a teacher as a facilitator or a peer	Activities were done in cooperative small groups where interaction took place between group members (peers) and the facilitators
Guided support or *scaffolding* provided by the facilitator through the learners ZPD	Cooperative small group activities were guided by the initial video diary as a form of problem-based learning, with probing by the facilitators and interactive feedback sessions

Original to the author

skills like problem-solving and critical thinking may be developed while they engage in playful activities.

The paragraphs that follow explicate the conceptual framework constituting the following concepts: play; playfulness; playful learning; pedagogies of play; and UBUNTU.

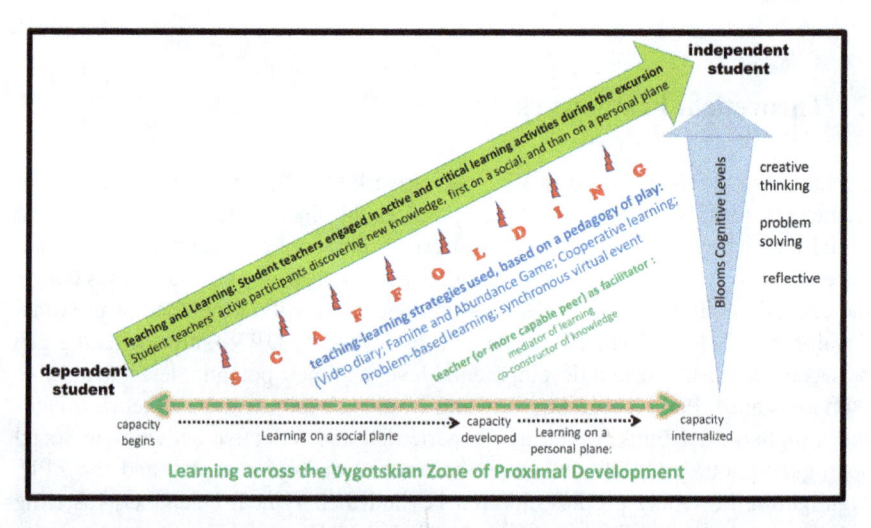

Fig. 1 Scaffolding within the ZPD during the excursion while engaging in playful learning activities (Adapted from Petersen, 2018, p. 1126)

3 Conceptual Framework

Mardell and et al. (2016. p. 3) define **play** as "typically considered a pleasurable, spontaneous, non-goal directed activity that can include anticipation, flow and surprise". They assert that "play is both objective and subjective, comprising qualities of observable behaviour as well as qualities of felt experience". Expanding on their definition, Mardell et al. (2023) describe play as chosen and directed by participants, involving imagination, active engagement, social interaction, and often enjoyment despite potential challenges. Fleet and Kemenyvary (2019), averred that play supports learning through meaningful, social, and active participation. Play is an activity with a particular mindset or a way of thinking in mind (Mardell et al., 2023). The authors explained, "**Playfulness** can be seen as the disposition (mindset) to frame or reframe a situation to include possibilities for enjoyment, exploration and choice" (p. 3). Playful learning environments can enhance problem-solving and divergent thinking skills. Through play, students develop self-efficacy and understand their strengths and weaknesses in a secure context (Robb, 2016). However, cultural differences can influence perceptions of play, emphasizing the importance of a 'playful mindset' in transforming tasks into enjoyable experiences (Mardell et al., 2023).

Mardell et al. (2023) emphasize that learning is fundamentally linked to thought processes, involving resolving conflicts or creating culturally valued outcomes. Playful learning, according to Mardell et al. (2016), is a method teachers use to enhance students' cognitive, social, emotional, and physical abilities, aligning adult learning goals with students' interests and curiosities. The particular language used to describe these emotions and behaviours can vary depending on the cultural context (Mardell et al., 2023). In a similar vein, Robb (2016) suggests that playful learning fosters creativity, serving as a motivator for students. Robb (2016) outlines ten motivators for playful learning, including choice, collaboration, meaningful discussion, problem-solving, inquiry, risk-taking, empathy, negotiation, and taking healthy breaks in between lessons.

Nonetheless, Playful learning does not entail playing without any rules—on the contrary, clear boundaries of engagement are 'in play'. The International School of Billund in Denmark (ISB) led a research project in Denmark, South Africa (SA), the United States (U.S.) and Colombia. During the research project, the researchers developed six theoretical principles of why a pedagogy of playful learning is needed. The six principles are (Mardell et al., 2023, p. 16): "play supports learning; playful learning in school involves play with a purpose; paradoxes between play and school add complexity to teaching and learning; playful learning is universal yet shaped by culture; playful mindsets are central to playful learning and supportive school cultures enable playful learning to thrive."

With a focus on the concepts of play, playfulness, and playful learning, Mardell et al. (2023, p. 48) aim to explore the essence of playful learning in schools by asking: "What does playful learning in schools entail?" They identify key markers of playful learning, termed 'cross-cultural indicators of playful learning,' namely:

- "Leading learning—exercising choice, ownership, empowerment, and autonomy regarding their learning
- Exploring the unknown—experiencing wonder, curiosity, and learning that is meaningful.
- Finding joy—experiencing feelings of delight and enjoyment" (p. 49).

These indicators are illustrated in Fig. 2 as part of the 'Indicators of the Playful Learning Model,' incorporating choice, wonder, and delight (Mardell et al., 2016). These authors argue that when all three indicators are present in a learning experience, it is indicative of playful learning.

To enable playful learning within educational settings, facilitators must employ appropriate teaching and learning strategies, termed 'pedagogies of play' in this context (Mardell et al., 2016). These pedagogies of play encompass systematic approaches to integrating playful learning and teaching, founded on principles of educational purposefulness, learner autonomy, experiencing choice, wonder and delight, and reflecting on playful experiences (Mardell et al.).

In a collaborative project with the IBS, a South African university explored how playful learning "looks and feels like" in South African schools (Solis et al., 2019, p. 1). In an African context, Ubuntu, with a strong focus on the collective, plays an important role in society and therefore also in education. Mbiti (1969), quoted in Solis

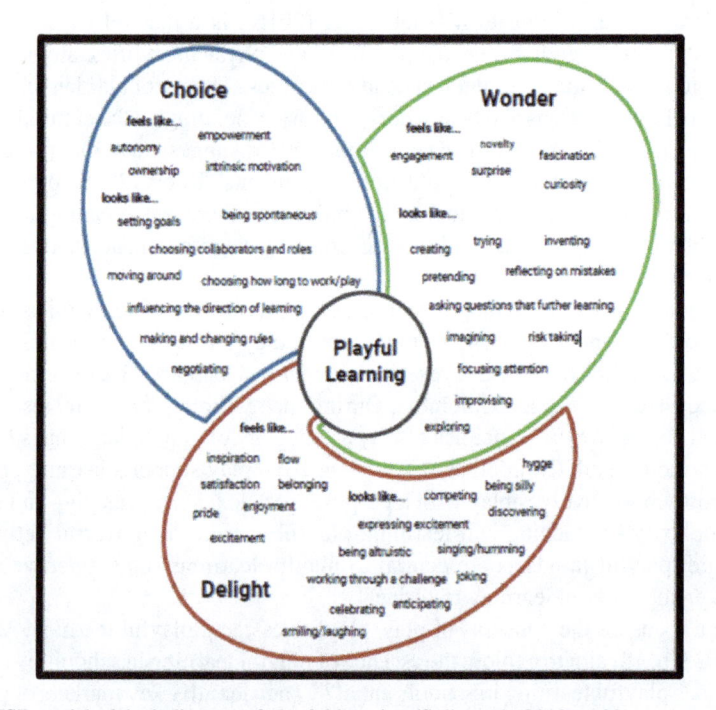

Fig. 2 ISB model of the indicators of playful learning (Solis et al., 2019, p. 33)

et al. (2019, p. 24), defines Ubuntu as "I am, because we are; and since we are, therefore I am—denoting social interdependence, community, and a sense of compassion and respect". Almost thirty years after the end of apartheid, references to Ubuntu are still frequently heard in South Africa. The term comes from the Nguni languages of Zulu and Xhosa, and its English definition is fairly broad. It describes "a quality that includes the essential human virtues of compassion and humanity" (Thompson, 2020, n.p.n). Ubuntu is the foundation of the African way of life and has an impact on almost all facets of people's well-being and societal life in African contexts and forges bonds within the African community (Lefa, 2015). Nelson Mandela describes Ubuntu as "a philosophy constituting a universal way of life, which underpins an open society" (Chinhanu & Adebayo, 2020, n.p.n.). Given the hybridity of identities and their effects on culture Chinhanu and Adebayo (2020), highlight the importance of recognizing and affirming the human dignity of all members within a learning community.

Creating inclusive learning environments aligns with UNESCO's call for achieving Sustainable Development Goal 4, emphasizing lifelong learning and equitable quality education for all by 2030 (UNESCO, 2018). Ubuntu's wisdom underscores the necessity of safeguarding human dignity to build healthy learning environments fostering respect, harmony, and a sharing community (Chinhanu & Adebayo, 2020). The same authors argue that when in a relationship with others, students are given the space to negotiate their own identities allowing them to belong in a better way. During the excursion students worked cooperatively in small diverse groups, learning from each other, and reflecting on their own cultural practices and their influence on who they are, and their identities.

Solis et al. (2019) adapted the IBS model within an Ubuntu perspective, asserting that playful learning in South African schools revolves around indicators of **ownership** (choice), **curiosity** (wonder) and **enjoyment** (delight), in which **Ubuntu** plays a foundational role (see Fig. 3). In Fig. 3, Ubuntu is written outside the figure, but the enactment of Ubuntu of the three indicators is written in the outer layer of the figure.

I will use the South African model of playful learning to indicate how the synchronous virtual excursion programme was structured around these indicators (Fig. 3) and will use this as an analytical tool to analyze the experiences of the student teachers.

4 The Excursion Programme

The virtual synchronous excursion programme, stretching over two sessions over two consecutive days, was based on cooperative learning (CL) and problem-based learning (PBL) principles. Each session started with a plenary session where a specific problem was presented to the student teachers by the facilitators (university teachers). After this, there were cooperative small group discussions followed by another

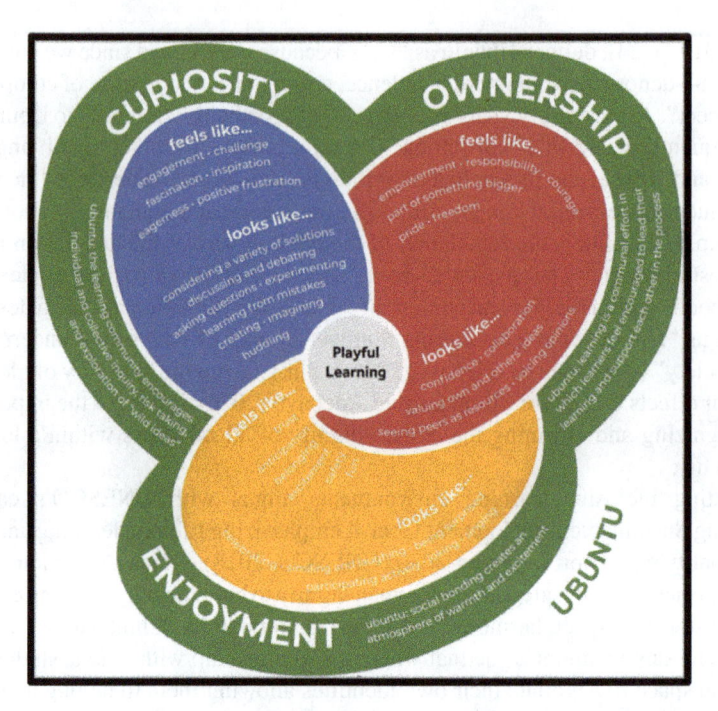

Fig. 3 South African model of the indicators of playful learning (Mardell et al., 2023: 215)

plenary session with feedback. Real-time engagement and feedback discussions took place between student teachers and facilitators.

De Beer and Petersen (2022, pp. 48–50) describe the design principles of the virtual excursion which are listed below:

- A pedagogy of playful learning should be used.
- It should be based on PBL, which depicts real-world classroom challenges.
- It should be held in a CL setting, where students collaborate in small, diverse groups of five.
- CL and PBL should be scaffolded in such a way to create opportunities for students to set individualised learning goals for themselves, fostering their self-directedness.
- It had to be a synchronous virtual event to maintain a sense of personal engagement and in real-time connection.
- It had to be structured to ensure the presence of the three core elements in an online learning environment, namely: cognitive presence, social presence, and teaching presence.
- Reflective sessions should offer answers to the issues shown in the video diary and be part of the assessment.
- An environment must be created that is both safe and disruptive in order to encourage social interaction and social learning.

Since 2016, as key contributors to the development of the excursion programme, we have made two significant adaptations for virtual excursions. Our first adjustment was informed by our prior involvement in face-to-face excursions, where we recognized the necessity of establishing a unifying theme (golden thread) to connect all activities. Leveraging our extensive experience as educators, we crafted a screenplay for a video diary featuring a fictional distressed principal. This diary authentically depicts common classroom challenges encountered in the South African educational context, providing a problem-based framework that was previously lacking. In face-to-face excursions, students were exposed to real-life instances of diversity and were sensitized to social justice issues such as inequality. To achieve this in the virtual realm, we utilized the famine and abundance game, a potent tool for prompting students to reflect on their own privileges. As designers of the excursion program, we understood the importance of scaffolding the virtual experience to ensure exposure to these critical aspects of social justice. The second modification entailed transforming the face-to-face engagement of the famine and abundance game into a real-time interactive activity. While virtual excursions may not replicate the same level of immersion, data suggests that they effectively sensitize students to become inclusive practitioners in their future roles as teachers (De Beer & Petersen, 2022).

Table 2 provides an overview of the two activities (relevant to this paper) and how they address two of the three indicators of playful learning (**ownership and curiosity**). The third indicator, **enjoyment**, will be elaborated on later in the discussion (see Table 3).

4.1 Creating an Environment for a Pedagogy of Playful Learning

A safe, trusted, and structured environment is necessary to encourage playful learning through different pedagogies of play. This will enable students and teachers to ask questions and take risks freely (Mardell et al., 2023). To create a safe environment where such playful learning can take place unhindered, Mardell et al. (2023, pp. 66–67) identify five key practices to foster playful learning, namely: "empower learners to lead their own learning, build a culture of collaborative learning, promote experimentation and risk-taking, encourage imaginative thinking and welcome all emotions generated through play". Table 3 shows practices and implementation strategies in its first two columns, while the third column illustrates how NWU's excursion programme was designed to promote enjoyable learning and implement these practices.

As someone who has designed and presented excursion programmes before, I know that creating a safe environment during the excursion is of utmost importance. This is because the student teachers are taken out of their comfort zones and are exposed to diverse groups, different cultures, and a different language. They are also confronted with controversial and emotional topics such as equality (the 'haves' and

Table 2 Playful learning activities during the virtual excursion

Name of learning activity	Short description of the activity	The rationale behind the activity in terms of the indicators of playful learning
Interrogation of ill-structured problem (video diary/simulation as a form of PBL as a pedagogy of play)	It was expected from student teachers to discuss the challenges (from their perspectives) in the video, and suggest possible solutions	Ownership: open-ended questions discussed from their own perspectives Curiosity: the diverse students listen to each others' opinions from other backgrounds
The Famine and Abundance game (gamification as a pedagogy of play)	A teacher must teach in diverse classrooms. A virtual passport of a country is randomly provided to each student. Student teachers also received virtual money, based on the Human Development Index of the country. This money can be used to purchase food in the virtual excursion shop. The outcome is that students from 'rich' countries can buy whatever they want, whereas students from 'poor' countries can hardly afford anything	Ownership: students are sensitised on being inclusive practitioners Curiosity: putting them in the shoes of others lets them wonder how it must feel to be poor or rich and how to act as future teachers to treat all learners equally

Original to the Author

'have-nots'), diversity and social justice matters in an educational context. During the excursion, the students worked in small cooperative learning groups and were able to reflect both individually and together, realizing their own biases towards others. The excursion also satisfies the Ubuntu requirement of the 'indicators of playful learning' as it encourages collaborative learning, where students take initiative and support one another, and where the learning community supports both individual and group inquiry.

5 Research Methodology

The qualitative study reported in this chapter is grounded in interpretivism. Pervin and Mokhtar (2022) describe interpretive research as focusing on understanding human behaviors within socio-cultural contexts, emphasizing the shaping of social reality through human experiences and are typically employed to explore experiences, meanings, and perspectives.

This study is part of an ongoing design-based research (DBR) initiative on WIL excursions since 2016, aimed at sensitizing student teachers to the complexities of

Table 3 Practices and strategies for playful learning and its implementation during the excursion programme [Adapted from Mardell et al. (2023:67)]

Practices (Mardell et al., 2023, p. 67)	Strategies (Mardell et al., 2023, p. 67)	Executed in excursion programme at NWU
Empower learners to lead their own learning	Get to know your learners Involve learners in decision-making Reflect on learning with learners	The excursion programme consisted of alternating plenary and group sessions. In the first plenary session presenters introduced themselves to the groups. When students provided feedback presenters also expected them to first introduce themselves When students worked in small cooperative learning groups to solve a problem, they had to manage themselves and decide on the processes they would use to come up with solutions Reflective discussions between the presenters and students took place during the plenary session, following the small group discussions
Build a culture of collaborative learning	Use play to build relationships Facilitate purposeful conversations to build knowledge Foster a culture of feedback	Students worked in small cooperative groups for the entire excursion where they began to know each other and to learn from each other All small group discussions were guided by a problem question to answer, based on the video diary of the principal They also had to alternate the group roles to provide feedback during the plenary sessions
Promote experimentation and risk-taking	Design open-ended investigations Encourage risk-taking as a strategy for learning	All the activities were based on open-ended questions that started with an ill-structured problem. Students had to decide on the strategies to execute the goal Working in diverse groups (in South Africa with an apartheid background and current racial polarization) put them out of their comfort zones and in the process also realize that they might be biased towards race, homophobia or have certain stereotypes of others. This realization might lead to them developing their own developmental learning needs

(continued)

Table 3 (continued)

Practices (Mardell et al., 2023, p. 67)	Strategies (Mardell et al., 2023, p. 67)	Executed in excursion programme at NWU
Encourage imaginative thinking	Share stories to engage and enhance learning and use role-play and pretend scenarios Provide materials and experiences that engage the senses and the body and ask questions that invite curiosity and imaginative thinking	The video diary depicted various authentic ill-structured problems with which many students can identify. Watching the video and reflecting on and sharing their experiences with group members makes the learning authentic, real and interesting The Famine and Abundance game expects them to put themselves in the shoes of others (the 'haves' or 'have-nots'), realizing that they had to be inclusive practitioners and think of possible solutions when they will be confronted with similar issues when teaching one day
Welcome all emotions generated through play	Design for joy Use play to explore complex issues Support learners in working through frustration	The video diary depicts issues like poor work ethics and lack of resources. Talking about these issues, with 'relatively easy' solutions may not be so challenging. However, they were also confronted with more difficult topics, such as social justice, equity and diversity issues. These are complex issues with no easy answers (most of which they will not have control over) This does, however, provide an opportunity to sensitize them about these matters and make them aware that they have to be inclusive practitioners. Issues like these also create the opportunity in which the students could realize their own shortcomings and convert them into their own learning needs

Columns 1 and 2—direct quotes from Mardell et al. (2023: 67); last column original to the author

the teaching profession while fostering their self-directedness. DBR involves an iterative process, where researchers continuously refine interventions based on analysis, design, and evaluation (Armstrong et al., 2020). Since 2016, iterative cycles of the excursion program have been conducted, with each cycle informing refinements to the program design. As part of the design team, I contributed to refining the programme based on core DBR processes: analysis and exploration, design and construction, and evaluation and reflection (McKenny & Reeves, 2019).

Figure 4 illustrates the iterative cycles of the excursions since 2016, with researchers serving as both theorists and curriculum designers (Barab & Squire, 2004). The 2022 virtual excursion, which is the focus of this chapter, aligns to use of playful learning to promote active and critical learning among students.

Unveiling First-Year Student Teachers' Experiences: An Excursion … 153

While this chapter specifically addresses the 2022 cycle, the overarching aim remains to sensitize students to the complexities of teaching while enhancing their self-directedness.

According to Sandoval (2014) in Scott et al. (2020), DBR is informed by several 'epistemic commitments', which they define as "engaging in certain practices that generate knowledge in an agreed-upon way" (p. 2). Two of these commitments are listed in Table 4 and the second column indicates how the excursion program adheres to the epistemic commitments.

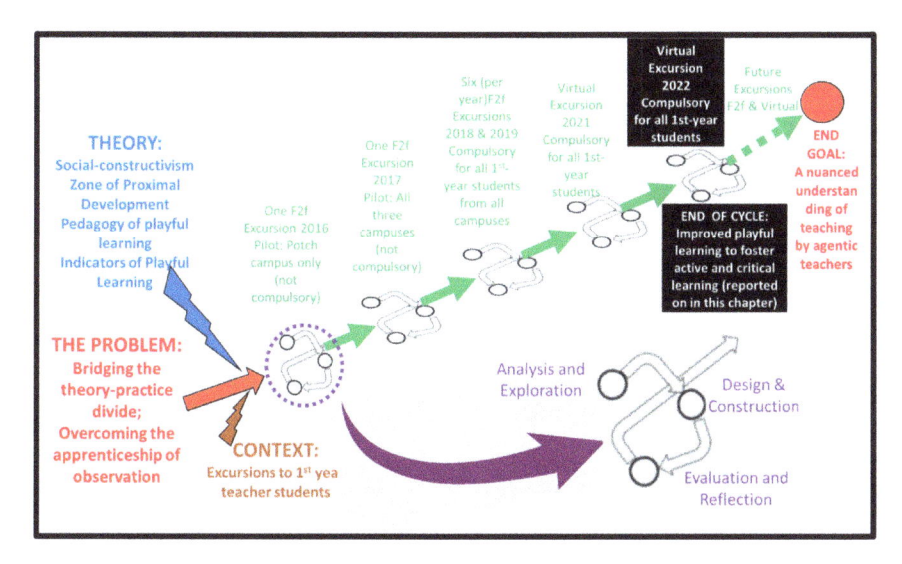

Fig. 4 The iterative process of DBR: WIL excursions 2016–2022. *Source* Adapted from Armstrong et al. (2020, p. 43)

Table 4 Epistemic commitments and adherence of the excursion programme

Epistemic commitments informing DBR Sandoval (2014) in (Scott et al., 2020, p. 2)	Adherence of the excursion programme to epistemic commitments
Theories of learning, such as constructivism, should be the foundation of design-based research	The entire excursion programme is embedded in social constructivist principles
Design principles that direct the creation and use of upcoming educational materials should be produced based on design-based research	The purpose of the video diary and the famine and abundance game aims that the student teachers are sensitised about the complexities of teaching is that they should be inclusive practitioners. The activities might lead them to a realisation of biases towards others

Column 1—direct quotes from Sandoval (2014) in (Scott et al., 2020, p. 2); last last column original to the author

6 The Study Sample

The NWU was established on 1st Jan 2004, merging the University of North-West, Potchefstroom University for Christian Higher Education, and the Sebokeng Campus of Vista University. The merger symbolized reconciliation and was successful. The NWU has three campuses: Mahikeng (MC), Potchefstroom (PC), and Vanderbijlpark (VC) with unique characteristics influenced by their pre-merger demography and history (Petersen et al., 2022, p. 82).

In 2022, there were 2237 first-year BEd students registered, consisting of 1966 contact students and 271 distance students (Table 5). All first-year BEd students were required to participate in a synchronous virtual excursion, resulting in a total population of 2237. Among these, 2200 students took part in one of 12 excursions, with 1424 students consenting to their data being used, forming the study sample.

Each of the three campuses, focuses on one or two of the 11 official languages. English and Afrikaans are used predominantly on the PC campus, English and Setswana at the VC campus, and English and Sesotho at the MC campus. Afrikaans and English are used for instruction on the PC campus, while English is used on the other campuses and for distance students.

7 Data Collection Methods

Qualitative data was collected through an open-ended questionnaire post-excursion and polling questions during the excursion to gauge student experiences with playful learning. The questionnaire, comprising 12 questions, assessed various aspects such as enjoyment level and teaching method experience.

Polling during activities prompted reflection. For example, after the Feminine and Abundance game, students were asked to express their emotions in a single word and justify the importance of considering socio-economic factors for teachers. You can find the resulting word cloud in Fig. 7.

Table 6 summarizes the data collection tools used during the excursion, with responses ranging from 148 to 1652. Notably, responses of pol one exceeded consented participants (N = 1652) due to attendance of 2 200. chapter. The data highlighted in grey in Table 6 (Polls 1, 5 and 8 and the open-ended questionnaire) is the information that was used and reported in this chapter.

Table 5 The 2022 Faculty of Education BEd First-year undergraduate numbers and demographics

Campus and phase	Contact					Distance				
Demo-graphics	African	Coloured	Indian/Asian	White	Total	African	Coloured	Indian/Asian	White	Total
Mahikeng	**629**	**1**	**3**	**1**	**634**					
SP AND FET	470		3	1	474					
FP	159	1			160					
Potchefstroom	**496**	**97**	**9**	**225**	**827**	**88**	**22**	**8**	**153**	**271**
IP	79	29	1	42	151	9	2		25	36
SP AND FET	312	40	7	106	465	25	11	5	57	98
FP	105	28	1	77	211	54	9	3	71	137
Vanderbijlpark	**469**	**5**	**2**	**29**	**505**					
IP	69	3		4	76					
SP AND FET	343	2	0	18	363					
FP	57		2	7	66					
Grand total	1594	103	14	255	1966	88	22	8	153	271

School phases in SA: Foundation Phase [FP]—grades R-3 (or lower primary education); Intermediate Phase [IP]—grades 4–6 (or primary education); Senior Phase [SP]—grades 7–9 (or lower secondary education); and Further Education and Training Phase [FET] (or upper secondary education)
Original to the author; statistics provided by the 2023 university system nwu.ac.za
The rows in bold, represent the sum of the numbers in the 2 or 3 rows that follows

Table 6 An overview of qualitative data collected during the WIL excursion in 2022

	Core excursion activities	Data collection instruments	Purpose	No. of students who completed the instrument
Day 1	Introduction and welcome	Poll 1: preparedness to teach	To explore students' apprenticeship of observation	1632
	Principal's digital diary	Poll 2: problems identified in dramatisation	To reflect on the issues in the video but also their own experiences of their own school days	667
	Engaging pedagogies	Poll 3: student experiences on EP	To expose them to active teaching learning strategies (breaking the 'chalk-and-talk' cycle) and Shoestring/frugal approaches	1286
Day 2	Super-powers	Poll 4 super-powers	To reflect on their own strong points (superpowers) as a future teacher	975
	The famine and abundance game	Poll 5 F&A game	To gauge the emotions of students (empathy) and the importance of social justice issues for teaching practice	1652
	Entrepreneurial learning	Poll 6 Poll 7	Determining students' perceptions and understanding of entrepreneurial learning and its value	1512 1368
	End of the excursion rating	Poll 8	Students rated the excursion and mentioned highlights and problems experienced during the excursion	1175

(continued)

Table 6 (continued)

	Core excursion activities	Data collection instruments	Purpose	No. of students who completed the instrument
2 weeks after the last excursion	Assessment of learning	Multi-modal assessments submitted (video, animation)	To determine the reflection abilities by assessing the assignment product (artefact)	440
	Overall experience of students	A post-excursion reflective open-ended questionnaire	To listen to their voices and experiences of the various aspects discussed/reflected during the excursion	148

Table from Du Toit and Petersen (2023, p. 18); last column original to the author

8 Ethical Matters and Data Analysis

Before data collection, requirements with regard to ethical considerations were adhered to and ethical clearance was obtained with the following ethics numbers: NWU-01013-21-A2 and the gatekeeper permission number: NWU-GK-21-065. An independent person was used to invite all students to take part in the sampling process.

The qualitative data was analyzed using a thematic approach based on Saldaña's (2009) process of coding to identify emerging themes using thick descriptions. Younas et al. (2023) argue that "*[T]*hick description of qualitative findings is critical to improving the transferability of qualitative research findings as it allows researchers to assess their applicability to other contexts and settings". The thick descriptions can provide academics involved in the excursion with valuable in-depth insight for redesigning excursions as part of DBR. The findings and discussion following this paragraph will be presented by answering the two research questions guiding this research.

9 Findings and Discussion

This chapter aims to address the following research questions: How did the pedagogy of playful learning promote active learning, and how did it foster critical learning? According to poll 8 (refer to Table 6), a total of 1188 student teachers rated the virtual excursion on its final day using a scale of 1–10, where 1 represents poor and 10 excellent. Among them, the majority (499) gave a perfect score of 10, while 235 students rated it as 9, 238 as 8, and 117 as 7. These results indicate that an overwhelming majority of students (91.6%) rated the virtual excursion as "good

**Question at the end of excursion:
How would you rate the excursion?**

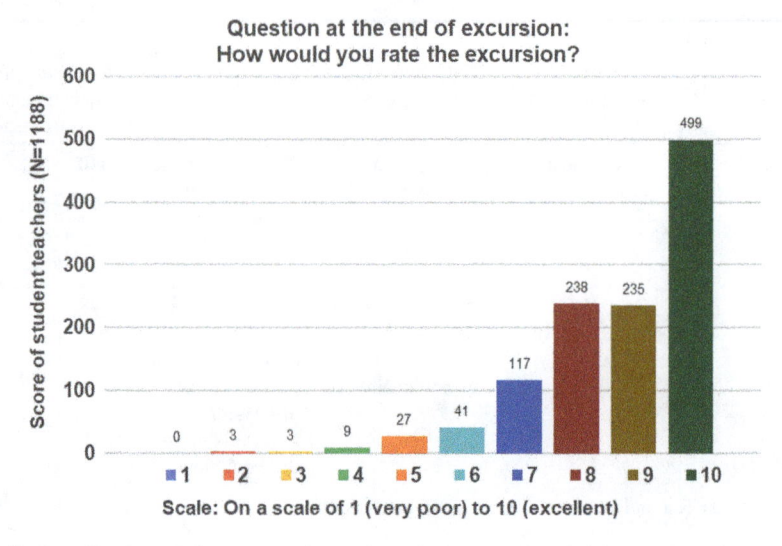

[Bar chart showing Score of student teachers (N=1188) on scale 1-10:
1: 0, 2: 3, 3: 3, 4: 9, 5: 27, 6: 41, 7: 117, 8: 238, 9: 235, 10: 499
Scale: On a scale of 1 (very poor) to 10 (excellent)]

Fig. 5 Overall rating of virtual excursion at the end of the last day. Original to the author

to excellent." This finding underscores the overall success of the virtual excursion, which was entirely based on playful active learning strategies. The bar graph in Fig. 5 illustrates the responses of the participants (N = 1188 [out of a sample of 2200]). These positive experiences are consistent with previous excursions conducted by the same university (De Beer, 2019; De Beer et al., 2020, 2022; Petersen et al., 2023).

The rest of the findings will be described under the two research questions mentioned above.

10 How Did the Pedagogy of Playful Learning Foster Active Learning?

The two findings that emerged under this research question are described below and were based on data from the end of the excursion poll and questions 5 and 6 of the open-ended questionnaire.

During the virtual excursion, the students participated in playful learning activities and seemed to enjoy themselves. After the excursion, an online open-ended questionnaire was completed by 148 students. One of the questions asked was: "Which aspects of the virtual excursion did you most enjoy? Motivate your answer". Out of 148 student teachers, 139 responded to this question indicated that they had fun and found the excursion program to be joyful. Figure 6 breaks down the number of students who enjoyed each activity. Two students commented on their experience, further supporting the finding that the students enjoyed the excursion:

It was a fun experience, I enjoyed it. It was interesting and insightful. It was captivating and fun to learn how we will be addressing situations in our future one day.

Well I gained a lot, what stereotyping is and how to not judge others, I also gained confidence because as we were given tasks in to discuss in our groups at first, I was scared but eventually started participating.

This finding corresponds with the high scores of the student teachers' overall rating of the excursion (Fig. 5).

A second finding from the first research question showed that participating student teachers believe playful learning can enhance active learning. At the end of the excursion poll 8 in Table 6, the following question was posed: "What were the

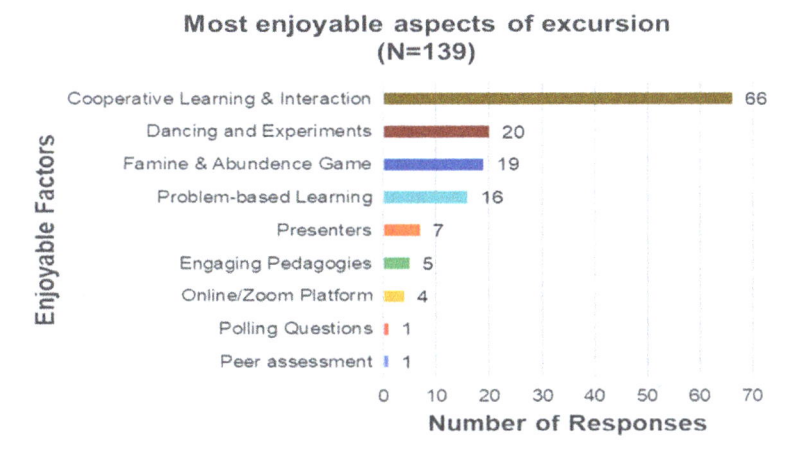

Fig. 6 First-year students overall rating of the activities they enjoyed most. Original to the author

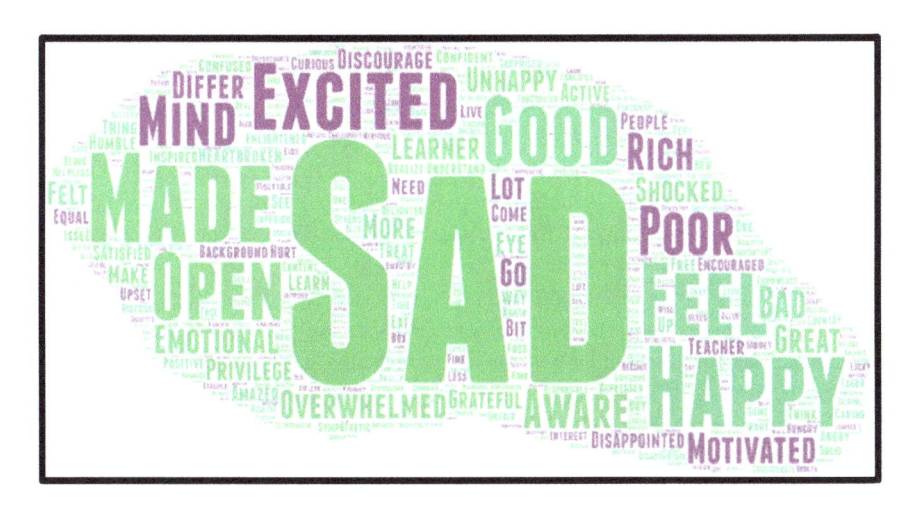

Fig. 7 Word cloud describing the emotions of student teachers after playing the famine and abundance game. Original to the author

highlight(s)/aspects that you enjoyed/appreciated **the most**, and why"? For this poll 1 172 answered the question. If the responses of the students are searched with the following keywords: "group work", "cooperative" [learning]; "engaging" [with others], "together" [with others] and "break" [out sessions/rooms] the search delivers 221 results- referring to the students who experienced the group sessions a highlight, referring to the fact that they really enjoyed CL. Some responses of students provide evidence for this finding: *"Us being in breakout rooms to discuss what we understand over what Doc and Prof were saying"*; another student said *"Group work, we were able to share our ideas";* and yet another one insightfully said

> It [group work] made me aware that teaching is not about what the curriculum or CAPS documents wants a teacher to deliver to the learner, but it is about creating an exciting learning environment for learners and making them know their abilities and potentials that will help them change the world. Working as a group improved my confidence even when the group work wasn't a face-to-face thing, but I got to learn how to work with people especially those who you do not really know.

In an online questionnaire after the excursion, 92% of 128 students reported a positive experience with working in CL groups. 47% of the 139 respondents identified CL as their most enjoyable experience, as shown in Fig. 6.

Studies by the unit of self-directed learning at a South African university found that many student teachers and learners had negative experiences working in CL groups (Mentz et al., 2019; Petersen et al., 2019). This trend is not exclusive to South Africa as researchers in France (Bächtold et al., 2023) and the US (Owens et al., 2020) have also observed that students resist active learning strategies like CL. This study revealed that CL facilitated active learning among student teachers and that group members worked together to co-construct knowledge and find solutions to discussions and posed problems during breakaway sessions.

Since peer participation served as a useful scaffold to support learning, students were able to actively engage and learn in their ZPD without becoming overwhelmed by information. In response to the overall experiences of participating in the virtual, online excursion, one student teacher explained, *"During the virtual excursion, I got exposed to teamwork and how to manage my time effectively. I got very participative group members which made everything so easy for everyone because they were engaging and keeping the communication going".* In terms of the South African model of the Indicators of Playful Learning, namely ownership, curiosity, and enjoyment, in which Ubuntu plays a foundational role (see Fig. 3), the students value each other's contribution to their own development. There is thus a trust relation to one another, relying to support each other as sources to complete a common task together. This cooperative engagement refers strongly to the Ubuntu aspect of the model. According to the Ubuntu ideology, learning is a group activity (a social construct according to Vygotsky, 1978) in which students are encouraged to take the lead and assist one another (Mardell et al., 2023, p. 215).

To summarize, and with regards to fostering active learning during a pedagogy of playful learning, two aspects emerged: overall, teachers found the experience joyful, but more importantly, it creates a space for individual and group learning and reflections. Table 7 provides some quotes as evidence for the findings regarding joyful experiences and fostering active learning, but also looks at each quote and how these can be interpreted through the South African Indicators of Playful Learning (Fig. 3).

In accordance with Mardell et al. (2016), playful learning is most likely to have occurred when all three indicators are present in a learning experience. Based on the interpretation depicted in Table 7, as well as the preceding discussions of the two findings, it seems evident that a pedagogy of playful learning, anchored in the South African indicators, can contribute to students enjoying the learning process and indeed foster active learning.

Table 7 Direct quotes through the lens of the South African indicators of playful learning

Examples of direct quotes (end of the excursion polling question 2)	Indicators of playful learning: author's interpretation based on direct quotes of students' experiences of the virtual excursion (how playful learning in SA 'looks like' and 'feels like')		
	Curiosity	Ownership	Enjoyment
"Being able to participate in group work meeting new people and learning about how I can solve certain challenges I face"	Active engagement working in CL groups; face challenges while solving problems	Be part of something bigger through active participation; courage to participate in diverse groups not knowing each other, in the process of finding solutions to the challenges posed by them (taking responsibility)	Students experience a sense of belonging while working cooperatively; There is a feeling of anticipation to learn new things about others
"I loved how we were divided into groups and I found it very interesting how everyone had a different point of view and how we were able to learn from each other"	Active engagement working in CL groups Inspired by listening to new ideas, and an Eagerness to know more	Be part of something bigger through active participation; There is a form of taking responsibility and pride in learning new things resulting in their own empowerment from an inclusive practitioner	Students experience a sense of belonging while working cooperatively Excitement to work in small CL groups
"The breakup rooms, it was fun meeting new people and listening to their views on certain things and I learned new things from them"	Active engagement working in CL groups; Students are fascinated by learning new things	Be part of something bigger through active participation In their discussions, they value their own and others' ideas	Students experience a sense of belonging while working cooperatively There is a feeling of anticipation and trust in learning new things from others in the group, and experiencing it as fun

Original to the author

11 How Did the Pedagogy of Playful Learning Foster Critical Learning?

Although the entire excursion programme embraced playful learning, the data from the 'famine and abundance' game [*enjoyment*: participating actively; being surprised] was scrutinised to gauge its impact on student teachers' critical learning. Through this game, student teachers grappled with challenging social justice issues like equality and diversity, prevalent in South African classrooms. The game allowed them to empathise with different socioeconomic backgrounds, fostering a deeper understanding of privilege and poverty [*ownership*: valuing other's ideas; realization to be part of something bigger]. Initially playing individually [*curiosity*: engagement; fascination], students then engaged in small group discussions, reflecting on their own socioeconomic backgrounds of being more or less privileged [*ownership*: empowerment; voicing opinions]. The plenary session provided further opportunities for collective reflection. This approach aligns with the Ubuntu aspect of the South African model of playful learning, encouraging both "individual and collective inquiry" (Mardell et al., 2023, p. 215).

Following group discussion, student teachers were asked to express their feelings about the game in one word during the plenary session. Out of 1653 responses, the majority leaned towards negative descriptors like "sad," contrasting with fewer positive words such as "privileged." This exercise prompted cognitive processes, including self-evaluation of their socioeconomic status in relation to the country's, and contemplation of its potential impact on their future teaching roles. Additionally, it fostered empathy and curiosity, encouraging students to consider diverse perspectives. Summarising emotions in a single word encouraged critical reflection, aligning with Facione (2020) and Bora's (2020) notion of a critical person. These word choices are visualised in a word cloud in Fig. 7.

In the same poll (5) during the famine and abundance game, student teachers were asked whether it's important for a teacher to take note of socioeconomic factors. Of the participants, 1.5% (25) answered "NO" while 98.5% (1628) responded "YES," [one student did not answer]. It is possible that the students who responded NO may have attended schools with monocultural environments, may come from more privileged backgrounds, or may have not been exposed to socioeconomic issues related to equality, diversity and social justice matters (which was the focus of the game). Conversely, students who affirmed (YES) the importance of considering socioeconomic factors likely have firsthand experiences with these issues and recognize their significance in shaping teaching practices. Table 8 presents sample quotes from students who answered "NO" or "YES," along with interpretations by the author to assess critical learning elements. The table also evaluates these comments against South African indicators of playful learning, determining their alignment with key indicators.

Recent trends in research on teacher development indicate a shift away from simply studying what teachers learn to studying how they learn, how they enhance their learning, and how they put their skills and knowledge into practice to provide

Table 8 Direct quotes, critical learning skills and indicators of play

Direct quotes from students	Critical learning skills	Indicators of playful learning
Some of the quotes of students who felt YES "*I think that teachers should take note so that they can ensure that their learners are handled in the same manner as everyone else. No one should discriminate. Teachers should know when a student is experiencing poverty* etc. *so that they can help them*"	Interpretation Evaluation Explanation A zealous dedication to reason Regard for others' perspectives Impartiality	Ownership: feels like courage (a need to help) and looks like valuing other ideas Enjoyment: feels like fun playing the game and looks like active participation in the activities. This assists in fulfilling the UBUNTU indicator where they work together in a safe and warm environment Curiosity: feels like engaging and challenging to put you in the shoes of others; and looks like listening to others considering various solutions (collective enquiry = UBUNTU)
"*We as teachers need to understand the huge gap in the learner's socio-economic backgrounds so we can mend our lesson plans to accommodate the different levels of literacy*"	A probing inquisitiveness A zealous dedication to reason Impartiality The inclination to look for reason Adaptability Regard for others' perspectives	
"*Because it affects the way the students learn because students with hard backgrounds find it harder than those with better backgrounds. Thus it could also be harder for the teacher to teach learners who find it hard to learn and teachers should also understand these differences*"	Interpretation Evaluation Explanation Inference The inclination to look for reason	
"*As a teacher, you should know that everyone has a different story! They should never judge or look down upon someone that isn't as privileged! So a teacher should notice everyone and ask if someone is looking down so that they can help*"	Interpretation Evaluation Inference Impartiality Regard for others' perspectives Receptiveness (approachability)	

(continued)

Table 8 (continued)

Direct quotes from students	Critical learning skills	Indicators of playful learning
Some of the quotes of students who said NO *"Because it is not for the teachers to know how socio-economic factors strongly influence the future education levels, social status, and housing, etc."*	Interpretation Analysis Evaluation Inference	Though it is evident that these students did think about social-justice matters and how it may influence them, their answers indicate that the famine and abundance game did not sensitize them sufficiently to realize the importance of equality and diversity issues and how to handle it one day. A possible conclusion may be that the students who made these comments come mostly from mono-cultural schools. It almost seems as if the indicators of playful learning are not at play at these students
"Because focusing on other socio-economic is not important"		
"Because they have nothing to do with teaching"		
"Teachers should rather focus on teaching"		

Original to the author

their own students with a better educational experience (Wittmann & Olivier, 2021). From 2016 to 2019, the NWU offered face-to-face excursions, and in 2021 and 2022, they offered virtual excursions. These excursions were designed to provide student teachers with practical experience and a better understanding of the teaching profession. Through these excursions, student teachers were exposed to real-life teaching problems to help prepare them for their future careers (De Beer et al., 2020, 2022; Petersen et al., 2023).

During the excursion, student teachers were scaffolded using various strategies to promote playful learning (Mardell et al., 2023). Initially, they viewed a video diary of a principal illustrating authentic challenges in South African classrooms, serving as a catalyst for discussions throughout the excursion. Then, they collaborated in small groups, taking responsibility for group dynamics. They also had ample time for problem-solving discussions, reflecting on their perspectives and those of their peers to generate solutions. Finally, they shared their findings in a plenary session to assess their progress and personal insights. These strategies may have empowered them, built a culture of collaboration and UBUNTU, ignited imaginative thinking, and encouraged them to wrestle with their own emotions and possible biases and stereotypes. This may led to them realized that these stereotype/biases could become areas of personal professional development. I believe that the evidence from the participant quotes and discussions above supports this argument.

During the excursion, the activities were structured across the students' ZPD (Vygotsky, 1978). The student teachers were guided by knowledgeable presenters and peers, which created a safe and supportive environment for small group discussions and feedback during plenary sessions. This fostered social interaction and a sense of community, which is referred to as UBUNTU (Solis et al., 2019; Thompson, 2020). As per Vygotsky's theory, student teachers were first scaffolded to learn socially (inter-personally) and then internalized the content on a personal level (intra-personally). This helped them move from a point of dependence on others to independence, while also developing critical thinking skills. "Using play as a strategy to explore complex topics can lead to new insights or ways to think critically about issues" (Mardell et al., 2023, p. 81).

One of the activities during the excursion, the famine and abundance game, focused on difficult topics like social justice issues such as equality (or inequality) and diversity. In most South African classrooms, diversity and inequality are part of the daily aspects that a teacher is confronted with. In conclusion, the evidence indicates that the virtual excursions, based on a pedagogy of playful learning, were effective and contributed to fostering the students' active and critical learning.

12 Conclusion

WIL remains a vital aspect of teacher training. The Minimum Requirements for Teacher Training in SA, stress the importance of learning both *FROM* and *IN* practice to equip student teachers with the agency to handle the numerous obstacles that they would encounter as inexperienced teachers. Common challenges faced by novice teachers, such as the 'theory–practice divide' and the 'apprenticeship of observation,' are deeply rooted in the South African education system, requiring ongoing research to resolve them. This chapter proposes that employing various playful learning pedagogies can help bridge the gap between policy, research, and practice. This study explains how active participation in learning that is perceived as pleasant, meaningful, socially engaged, engaging and iterative can help student teachers develop their cognitive, social, emotional, creative and physical skills (Parker et al., 2022). The findings of this study show that carefully scaffolded virtual excursions can sensitize student teachers to the complexities of the teaching profession, potentially shaping their perceptions and attitudes toward teaching. Real-world case studies during these excursions offer opportunities for learning *FROM* practice through playful pedagogies. Despite the best intentions, virtual excursions cannot fully replicate the learning experiences offered during face-to-face interactions. In the excursion programme mentioned above, it was noted that a virtual excursion can never provide the same experiences in terms of social justice issues. As future teachers, students must recognize and address their biases, preconceptions, and stereotypes. Although small CL groups can tackle challenging topics like diversity and inequality, the primary limitations of virtual excursions lie in the absence of physical interaction (embodiment) with individuals from diverse backgrounds, such as race, ethnicity, gender, and religion. Nonetheless, engagement in virtual activities can also push students out of their comfort zones, allowing them to confront discomfort and develop personal growth goals to address it effectively. Although virtual excursions lack immersion and authenticity, they provide better access, are much more cost-effective in terms of transportation and accommodation, and are also a safer alternative. Despite these limitations, embracing playful learning pedagogies and the UBUNTU philosophy can create an environment conducive to active and critical learning among student teachers. This approach may empower them to navigate both theoretical concepts and the various engaging pedagogies encountered during excursions, ultimately enhancing their preparedness for the teaching profession.

References

Armstrong, M., Dopp, C., & Welsh, J. (2020). Design-based research. In R. Kimmons & S. Caskurlu (Eds.), *Students' guide to learning design and research* (pp. 40–45). EdTechBooks.

Bächtold, M., Roca, R., & Checchi, D. (2023). Students' beliefs and attitudes towards cooperative learning, and their relationship to motivation and approach to learning. *Studies in Higher Education, 48*(1), 100–112. https://doi.org/10.1080/03075079.2022.2112028

Barab, S., & Squire, K. (2004). Design-based research: Putting a stake in the ground. *Journal of the Learning Sciences, 13*(1), 1–14. https://doi.org/10.1207/s15327809jls1301_1

Chinhanu, C. A., & Adebayo, S. B. (2020, July 8). *Ubuntu in education: Towards equitable teaching and learning for all in the era of SDG 4*. Norrag Global Education Centre. Retrieved June 20, 2023, from https://www.norrag.org/ubuntu-in-education-towards-equitable-teaching-and-learning-for-all-in-the-era-of-sdg-4-by-chiedza-a-chinhanu-and-seun-b-adebayo/

Bora, A. (2020). Critical thinking and creative thinking as the focus on mathematics education. *International Journal of Scientific Development and Research, 5*(3), 235–241. https://www.researchgate.net/publication/340102954

De Beer, J. (2019). The importance of context for self-directed learning. In E. Mentz, J. De Beer, & R. Bailey (Eds.), *Self-directed learning for the 21st century: Implications for higher education* (pp. 103–131). AOSIS.

De Beer, J., & Petersen, N. (2022). The affordances of face-to-face student excursions and implications for migration to virtual excursions. In J. de Beer, N. Petersen, E. Mentz, & R. J. Balfour (Eds.), *Self-directed learning in the era of the COVID-19 pandemic: Research on the affordances of online virtual excursions* (pp. 39–54). AOSIS.

De Beer, J., Petersen, N., Mentz, E., & Balfour, R. J. (Eds.). (2022). *Self-directed learning in the era of the COVID-19 pandemic: Research on the affordances of online virtual excursions*. AOSIS.

De Beer, J., Petersen, N., & Van Vuuren, H. J. (Eds.). (2020). *Becoming a teacher: Research on the work-integrated learning of student teachers*. AOSIS.

Department of Basic Education (South Africa). (2011). *Curriculum and assessment policy statement: Life sciences*. Government Printing Works.

Department of Higher Education. (South Africa). (2015). *Minimum requirements for teacher education qualifications*. Department of Higher Education and Training.

Du Toit, A., & Petersen, N. (2023). Reimagining work-integrated learning excursions to decrease the theory-practice divide. In N. Petersen, A. du Toit, E. Mentz, & R. J. Balfour (Eds.), *Innovative curriculum design: Bridging the theory-practice divide in work-integrated learning to foster self-directed learning* (pp. 1–30). AOSIS.

Du Toit-Brits, C. (2019). A focus on self-directed learning: The role that educators' expectations play in the enhancement of students' self-directedness. *South African Journal of Education, 39*(2), 1–11. https://doi.org/10.15700/saje.v39n2a1645

Esau, D. E., & Maarman, R. (2021). Re-imaging support for beginner teachers in relation to initial teacher education policy in South Africa. *South African Journal of Education, 41*(4), 1–8. https://files.eric.ed.gov/fulltext/EJ1333100.pdf

Facione, P. A. (2020). *Critical thinking: What it is and why it counts*. Advancing Thinking Worldwide. Retrieved from https://www.etsu.edu/teaching/documents/whatwhy.pdf

Fleet, A., & Kemenyvary, M. (2019). Growing playful pedagogies: A case study of educational change. In S. Alcock & N. Stobbs (Eds.), *Rethinking play as pedagogy* (pp. 69–86). Routledge.

García, E., & Weiss, E. (2019, July). *U.S. schools struggle to hire and retain teachers*. Economic Policy Institute. https://files.epi.org/pdf/164773.pdf

Gravett, S. (2012). Crossing the "theory-practice divide": Learning to be(come) a teacher. *South African Journal of Childhood Education, 2*(2), 1–14. https://doi.org/10.4102/sajce.v2i2.9

Hugo, J. P. (2018). *The development and implementation of an effective mentoring programme to improve job satisfaction among beginner teachers at primary schools in the Mpumalanga Province of South Africa* (Doctoral thesis). Available from SciELO 15 (SciELO document ID 15 2519-5670). http://hdl.handle.net/10500/24842

Lefa, B. (2015). The African philosophy of Ubuntu in South African education. *Studies in Philosophy and Education, 1*(1), 1–15. https://www.researchgate.net/publication/274374017

Lortie, D. (1975). *Schoolteacher: A sociological study*. University of Chicago Press.

Mardell, B., Wilson, D., Ryan, J., Ertel, K., Krechevsky, M., & Baker, M. (2016). *Towards a pedagogy of play: A project zero working paper*. International School of Billund.

Mardell, B., Ryan, J., Krechevsky, M., Baker, M., Schulz, T. S., & Liu-Constant, Y. (2023). *A pedagogy of play: Supporting playful learning in classrooms and schools*. Project Zero.

Mavhunga, E., & van der Merwe, D. (2020). Bridging science education's theory-practice divide: A perspective from teacher rducation through topic-specific PCK. *African Journal of Research in Mathematics, Science and Technology Education, 24*(1), 65–80. https://doi.org/10.1080/181 17295.2020.1716496

Mbiti, J. S. (1969). *African religions and philosophy*. Heinemann.

McKenny, S., & Reeves, T. C. (2019). *Conducting educational design research*. Routledge.

McLeod, S. (2024, February 1). Vygotsky's zone of proximal development and scaffolding. *SimplyPsychology*. Retrieved from https://www.simplypsychology.org/zone-of-proximal-development.html

Mentz, E., De Beer, J., & Bailey, R. (Eds.). (2019). *Self-directed learning for the 21st century: Implications for higher education* (pp. i–436). AOSIS.

Owens, D., Sadler, T., Barlow, A., & Smith-Walters, C. (2020). Student motivation from and resistance to active learning rooted in essential science practices. *Research in Science Education, 50*(1), 253–277. https://doi.org/10.1007/s11165-017-9688-1

Parker, R., Thomsen, B. S., & Berry, A. (2022). Learning through play at school: A framework for policy and practice. *Frontiers in Education, 7*. https://doi.org/10.3389/feduc.2022.751801

Petersen, N., Du Toit, A., Mentz., E., & Balfour, R. J. (Eds.). (2023). *Innovative curriculum design: Bridging the theory-practice divide in work-integrated learning to foster Self-Directed Learning*. AOSIS.

Pervin, N., & Mokhtar, M. (2022). The interpretivist research paradigm: A subjective notion of a social context. *International Journal of Academic Research in Progressive Education and Development, 11*(2), 419–428. https://doi.org/10.6007/IJARPED/v11-i2/12938

Petersen, N., Mentz, E., & De Beer, J. (2022). First-year students' conceptions of the complexity of the profession, sense of belonging, and self-directed learning. In J. de Beer, N. Petersen, E. Mentz, & R. J. Balfour (Eds.), *Self-directed learning in the era of the COVID-19 pandemic: Research on the affordances of online virtual excursions* (pp. 77–100). AOSIS.

Petersen, N. (2018). Selfgerigte leer: Die ervarings en menings van lewenswetenskappe-onderwysstudente tydens die gebruik van werkkaarte in 'n koöperatiewe onderrig-leer-omgewing. *LitNet Akademies, 15*(3), 1119–1142. https://www.litnet.co.za/wp-content/uploads/2018/12/LitNet_Akademies_15-3_Petersen_1119-1142.pdf

Petersen, N., Golightly, A., & Dudu, W. T. (2019). Engaging pedagogies to facilitate the border-crossing between the natural sciences and indigenous knowledge: Implications for science teacher education. In J. De Beer (Ed.), *The decolonisation of the curriculum project: The affordances of indigenous knowledge for self-directed learning* (pp. 143–180). AOSIS.

Robb, E. (2016, April 6). *10 motivators to promote learning*. Retrieved July 10, 2023, from https://therobbreviewblog.com/uncategorized/10-motivators-to-promote-learning/

Rose, K. L. (2020). Taking control: Self-directed professional development and teacher agency. *Teacher Learning and Professional Development,* 5(1), 62–78. file:///C:/Users/11115068/Desktop/pkpadmin,+Rose_Final.pdf

Saldaña, J. (2009). *The coding manual for qualitative researchers.* Sage.

Sandoval, W. (2014). Conjecture mapping: An approach to systematic educational design research. *Journal of the Learning Sciences, 23*(1), 18–36. https://doi.org/10.1080/10508406.2013.778204

Sang, G. (2020). Teacher agency. In M. Peters (Ed.), *Encyclopedia of teacher education* (pp. 1–5). Springer.

Scott, E. E., Wenderoth, M. P., & Doherty, J. H. (2020). Design-based research: A methodology to extend and enrich biology education research. *CBE Life Science Education, 19*(11), 1–12. https://doi.org/10.1187/cbe.19-11-0245

Shulman, L. S. (2004). *The wisdom of practice. Essays on teaching, learning and learning to teach.* Jossey-Bass.

Solis, L., Khumalo, K., Nowack, S., Blythe-Davidson, E., & Mardell, B. (2019). Towards a South African pedagogy of play. A pedagogy of play working paper. http://www.pz.harvard.edu/sites/default/files/Pedagogy%20of%20Play%20South%20Africa_Working%20Paper%20Final_Mar%207.pdf

Thompson, A. (2020, June 11). *Understanding the meaning of Ubuntu: A proudly South African philosophy.* Retrieved from https://theculturetrip.com/africa/south-africa/articles/understanding-the-meaning-of-ubuntu-a-proudly-south-african-philosophy

UNESCO. (2018). *Global education monitoring report: Migration, displacement and education—Building bridges, not walls.* UNESCO.

Wittmann, G., & Olivier, J. (2021). Blended learning as an approach to foster self-directed learning in teacher professional development programmes. *The Independent Journal of Teaching and Learning, 16*(2). https://hdl.handle.net/10520/ejc-jitl1-v16-n2-a7

Vygotsky, L. S. (1978). *Mind in society: The development of higher psychological processes.* Harvard University Press.

Younas, A., Fabregues, S., Durante, A., Escalante, E. L., Inayat, S., & Ali, P. (2023). Proposing the "MIRACLE" narrative framework for providing thick description in qualitative research. *International Journal of Qualitative Methods, 22,* 1–13. https://doi.org/10.1177/16094069221147162

Examining Collaborative Mentoring to Improve the Professional Learning of a Pre-service Teacher During Work Integrated Learning Practicum Experience: A Case Study of Practice

Cisca de Kock

Abstract This chapter focusses on the lived experience of a pre-service teacher (PST) enrolled in a four-year Bachelor of Education Degree. This study cross examines the theoretical understandings of the ways in which a PST acquires professional learning (PL) during the work integrated (WIL) practicum period. This was done with the implementation of collaborative mentoring between the PST and the university lecturer. Mentoring in the WIL practicum period is vital, as this is the space where PSTs experience real life teaching situations. The role of the university lecturer in fostering teaching and learning is often not well understood and little research has been undertaken to examine how university lecturers envision and construct the pedagogical relationship between their interns and themselves. This research employed an interpretive case study design using a multiple method approach. Firstly, findings of this research study provide a deeper understanding of the dynamics between the mentor and mentee relationship within a WIL practicum environment. Secondly, findings that emerged from this study indicated that aspects of initial teacher education (ITE) programs that are related to the disjuncture between university and schools, require much needed attention. PSTs often find it difficult to navigate the alignment of both university and school contexts. It is anticipated that the transition from the PST to novice teacher phenomenon as a central component for PL could be better understood through this research study.

Keywords Collaborative mentoring · Actor network theory · Networks · Collaborating · Mentoring · Pre-service teacher · Case studies · Professional learning · Work integrated learning

---

C. de Kock (✉)
Cape Peninsula University of Technology, Cape Town, South Africa
e-mail: dekockc@cput.ac.za

1 Context of the Study

The qualifications structure for teacher education is subject to the minister's policy on qualifications in terms of the Higher Education Act, 1997. The primary purpose of all ITE qualifications is to certify that the holder has specialized as a beginner teacher in a specific phase and or subject (MRTEQ, 2015, p. 18). One of the recognized initial teaching qualifications is the Bachelor of Education (B.Ed.) degree. The program is spread over the course of four years, within the respective learning area/subject phase in which the PST wishes to specialize in. During the four-year program, PSTs are expected to develop subject matter knowledge, develop an understanding of barriers to learning and matters relating to diversity and inclusivity within schools. PSTs must also develop knowledge of their own teaching philosophies and pedagogy and engage in the formation of teacher/professional identity and agency. The Department of Higher Education and Training (DHET) (2011, p. 18) in South Africa require that the programs leading to ITE qualifications, take cognisance of the need for PSTs to engage in WIL. This should be structured appropriately, accompanied by structured supervision, mentoring and assessments. According to the Council on Higher Education (CHE) (2011, p. 4), the integration of theory and practice in student learning can occur through a range of WIL practicum approaches. The CHE (2011, p. 4) uses the analogy of WIL as an umbrella term that describes curricular, pedagogic and assessment practices across a range of academic disciplines that integrate formal learning and workplace concerns. ITE programs that include WIL offer opportunities for PSTs to prepare for, and learn from, the workplace to transfer discipline-based theory and a wide variety of skills learned in their formal education to an authentic context as a colleague and employee, with all the responsibilities and expectations such a role entails (CHE, 2011, p. 6). PSTs feel that there is a growing gap between what they are taught in theory at university and what they experience in the WIL practicum period. In South Africa, this further highlights the issue of preparedness of PSTs. According to the South African Higher Education Qualifications Framework, all ITE programs are the responsibility of Higher Education institutions.

2 Research Methodology

This study employed a case study research design within an interpretive paradigm. The interpretive paradigm is concerned with the individual as a social actor. Presenting a case study provided a unique example of real people in real situations. This also enables readers to understand ideas more clearly than simply presenting them with abstract theories or principles. Noted by Rule and John (2011), a case study researcher is interested in the data that can be generated by the sample, that would allow for a full and transparent account. Case studies are described as comprehensive depictions and inquiries into a bounded system and unique depictions of, for example people in authentic situations that affords the reader a clearer and richer presentation.

The bounded systems in this study are the WIL practicum experience and collaborative mentoring. The types of data methods that were used included, multiple semi-structured interviews between the PST and researcher (university lecturer), observations of lessons taught by the PST and reflective journals. The central research question to explicate this research was:

2.1 Can Collaborative Mentoring Improve the Professional Learning of a Pre-Service Teacher During the WIL Practicum Experience?

By means of analyzing the collected data, the argument that will be made is that it is important for all PSTs to be provided with PL opportunities by means of collaborative mentoring during the WIL practicum so that they can acquire the habit of PL in order to answer the demands in their careers for constant renewal. PSTs will, when becoming in-service teachers, need to undergo continuous PL in their subjects of specialization as well as in any other area of professional need.

3 Learning to Teach Within the WIL Practicum Experience in a South African Context

In South Africa the WIL practicum experience is the time spent at schools where PSTs are faced with the true realities of teaching. In some cases, it can be described as the make or break of a PSTs' perception of and ideologies around teaching as a profession. The WIL practicum period also gives PSTs some insight into how to work as part of a team and interact with learners and teachers in a school environment. Rusznyak and Bertram (2021) assert that much of South African research suggests that WIL practicum experiences of PSTs are uneven. This means that there is a need to provide PSTs with explicit, structured professional learning opportunities to consider how the teachers they observe enact their teaching and why. Rusznyak and Bertram (2021) recommend that a structured WIL practicum experience should be a space in which to recognize and engage in forms of pedagogic reasoning. The WIL practicum sessions usually range from eight weeks to six months. Since 2015, however, the Department of Higher Education determine how long PSTs must attend WIL practicum sessions at schools. According to the current policy documents (MRTEQ, 2015) PSTs must spend a minimum of twenty weeks and a maximum of 32 weeks in schools for a B.Ed. qualification over a period of four years.

4 Conceptualising Collaborative Mentoring as a Space for Professional Learning

Mentoring is considered to be a guide towards pedagogical decision making within the quality of instruction, which is further linked to the PL of PSTs. In most educational literature, mentoring is referred to as a hierarchical relationship between an experienced teacher and a PST (Orland-Barak & Yinon, 2007; See, 2014). However, Brondyk and Searby (2013) argue that, although research is slowly emerging that identifies specific knowledge, skills, and dispositions that contribute to mentor effectiveness, the educational field has yet to develop research-based universally agreed upon "best practices" in mentoring. This disparity could be due to the complexity of mentoring as a practice. In ITE programs, lecturers act as mentors for PSTs and are expected to provide guidance on a continual basis throughout the four years. This is done to develop everyday routines and to connect university coursework with the realities of teaching. The focus is mainly on lesson preparation and teaching processes, managing classroom discipline, evaluation, and assessment, implementing the curriculum correctly, creating and implementing intervention plans and administrative tasks and school involvement. Van Velzen et al., (2012, p. 230) agree that mentoring provides guided participation and may offer opportunities not only for the intentional structuring of participation in workplace activities and interactions at school, but also for constructing shared knowledge conceptions based on collaboration and critical reflection. In promoting a culture of collaborative mentoring, it eliminates the practice of PSTs and university lecturers working in isolation. The collaborative mentoring approach (Fig. 1) that Van Velzen et al., (2012) introduced encompasses the combination of modelling practical knowledge with a focus on learning needs.

This is helpful to address any needs that the PST might require. Pre-lesson conversations are important in discussing the preparation of lessons and exchanging ideas.

Fig. 1 The mentoring process model adapted from Van Velzen et al. (2012). Author's Depiction

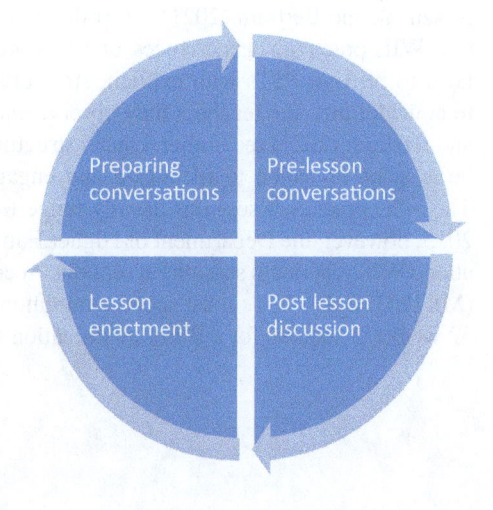

Lesson enactment is closely linked to teaching collaboratively. Post lesson discussion relies on discussing teaching experiences and critical reflections.

5 Conceptual Framework

This study is framed in terms of Actor Network Theory (ANT). ANT is a collection of theoretical and methodological principles derived out of science and technological studies and foremost accredited to Latour (1987), Callon (1984) and Law (1992). ANT is often explored to look at a series of analytical approaches to and considerations about knowledge, subjectivity, the real and the social world. Latour described an actor as a human or non-human entity that can exert force. An actor as a human or non-human entity can also change and be changed within a constantly fluent and associative network of other actors. Furthermore, Latour (1999) contends that actors are in constant motion and interactions between human and non-human actors. Therefore, they are never fixed territories, but always changing. Thus, exploring the experiences of the actors and developing themselves in the WIL practicum as a PL space, a collaborative mentoring theoretical framework with both human and non-human links was used to analyze the data. ANT provides the ability to trace networks between human and non-human actors to find the relationships and alliances between them. The more allies and interactions, the stronger and more powerful the networks become. Fenwick and Edwards (2010: 2) define ANT as a theory that examines the interconnectedness of human and nonhuman entities based on an anti-foundationalist approach in which nothing exists prior to its performance or enactment. In the field of education, knowledge is not an isolated set of rules accessed only when necessary, but is an entity that is distributed among individuals, contexts, activities, and other forms of interaction that take place Fenwick and Edwards (2010) are of the opinion that the language of ANT can open new questions and its approaches can sense phenomena in rich ways that discern the difficult ambivalences, multiplicities and contradictions that are embedded in so many educational issues. ANT can use paradigms to investigate and execute educational change in highly diverse indicators. When a PST enters a school community, they form part of this community and this interaction should enable them to share and negotiate their knowledge with other "actors" in this process, to enable stronger PL. Fenwick and Edwards (2010) posit that the objective of ANT is to understand how human intentions and interactions come together and manage to hold together to assemble collectives or "networks" that produce force and other effects: knowledge, identities, routines, behaviours, policies, curricula, innovations, oppressions and reforms. According to Fenwick and Edwards (2011), ANT traces how different human and non-human entities come to be assembled to associate and exercise force; and to persist or decline. ANT is a framework that is gaining tremendous popularity among educational researchers, because it conceptualizes individuals and their environments as a holistic unit of analysis. Figure 2 represents the elements of ANT within this study.

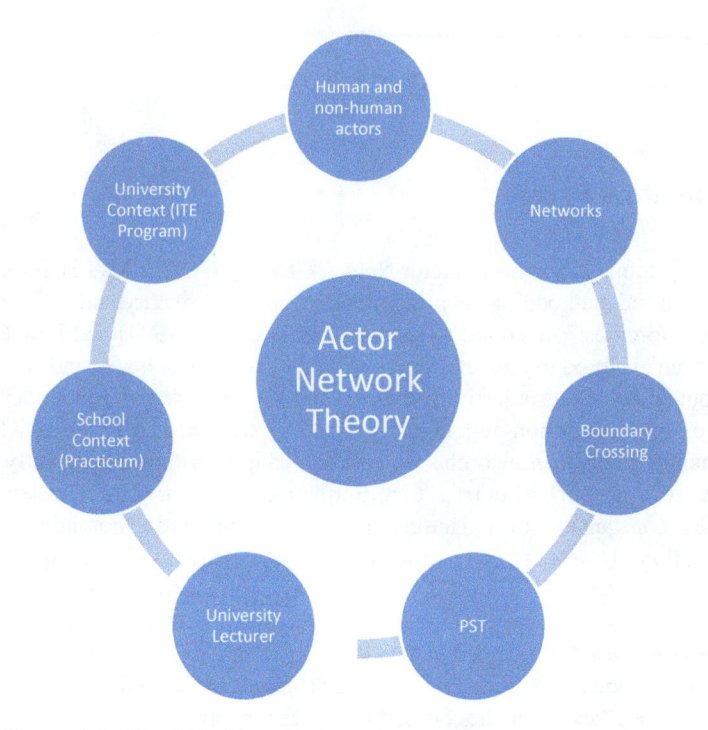

Fig. 2 Elements of ANT within this study. Author's Depiction

ANT can be used to find possible alliances and agreements that are formed with the PST, university lecturer, the WIL practicum, the ITE program and the key factors that contribute to it. Learning to become a teacher is viewed as an active and complex process rather than an event. Within this process, learning is a personal, social and context bound activity. Therefore, viewing PL through a flexible lens such as ANT will allow for understanding the connectedness between collaborative mentoring, PST and the WIL practicum. Using ANT enabled the researcher to ask questions about the connections and associations between actors and networks. In this study the actors were the PST, university lecturer and the networks were Higher Education Institutions and the National Education Department. ANT provided insights into the kind of qualities that different networks produce through connections and the type of outputs these networks can create for it, as well as for the actors involved in this process. Fenwick and Edwards (2010: 2) assert that things may connect with other things in ways that lock them into a particular collective, or they may pretend to connect, partially connect, or feel disconnected and excluded even when they are connected. For this study, the PST engaged in two different networks Higher Education Institution (Initial Teacher Education program) and Basic Education Department (School management, mentor teachers, learners,) each working with a particular set of required activities. Each group forms a bounded system engaged in a particular activity and is seen to be operating within a boundary for that activity. By exposing the participant to crossing boundaries the PST is able to revisit and rethink their practices, share ideas, and develop new ideas for renewed practices. Knowledge is not an isolated set of rules accessed only, when necessary, but is a shared entity that is distributed among individuals, their contexts, activity, and artefacts. To provide an in-depth understanding of PL there is a need to gain insight into the interplay between actors and conditions within the WIL practicum period.

6 Participants and Researcher's Role

Non-probability sampling was applied as it was purposive and convenient in this study. The participant was chosen based on the criteria for obtaining rich information which would be relevant to the inquiries of this study and purposive sampling enabled this. Purposive sampling is a non-representative subset of some larger population and is constructed to serve a very specific need or purpose (Rai & Thapa, 2015, p. 6). It is important to note that gender, race, and religious background were not factors for consideration. By using convenient sampling, the researcher was able to save on costs and this enabled the researcher to meet regularly with the participant on a systemic basis. Jason[1] was the PST that took part in this study during his 3rd year of studying towards qualifying for the degree B.Ed. (Intermediate and Senior Phase). It was acknowledged that as a participant I could present a certain degree of bias. Thus, within this context, my preconceived ideas were considered, and appropriate research ethics were applied to avoid influencing observations. I had been one of Jason's lecturers and thus had established a relationship of trust before the commencement of this study. As a lecturer at the institution in question, I always endeavoured to avoid comments, tone or non-verbal behaviour, which might cause bias in my responses. Therefore, I always remained neutral. I ensured the confidentiality and anonymity of the participant and continued to maintain the highest level of professionalism. Lastly, I was objective about how I went about obtaining knowledge, to not allow my own values and attitude to affect my research study. Thus, exploring the experiences of the actors and developing themselves in WIL as a PL space, a collaborative mentoring theoretical framework with both human and non-human links is used to analyse the data. I started working with Jason during his 3rd year of studies. It was important to get a sense of what his experience was during his 1st and 2nd year and to focus on the challenges he experienced. Overall, the context and learning by observation within a collaborative atmosphere created a sense of belonging for Jason. The data showed that the WIL practicum experience influenced Jason's PL constructively, cumulatively, intentional and goal orientated. Dreyer (2015) asserted that experiencing WIL is a time-honoured way to assist in the preparation of PSTs before they start their careers. This shows the critical role that the WIL practicum plays in the PSTs learning. According to the DHET (2011:8) learning in practice involves teaching in authentic and stimulated classroom environments. This research also showed that the practicum

---

[1] Jason is a pseudonym for the purposes of this study.

is a period in which a PST develops personally as well. It was important for the PST to know that learning to teach is very complex. This is in agreement with Menon et al. (2007) who conceded that the development of a teacher's professional knowledge develops over time through the successes acquired in the classroom, which result in new experiential insights.

7 Theme 1: Work-Integrated Learning is Constructive

Jason's first practicum experience was the WIL practicum workshop that he attended in his first year before he had to do his practicum later that year. Although some of the topics discussed were useful, it did not cover all the aspects that a PST could encounter during the WILL practicum periods. Jason had to learn everything once he entered his first practicum session. This is where he learned constructive learning that involved cognitive processing and active thinking.

"As Jason explained...".

> The school was one of the top performing schools and I believed that the school would provide me with a positive practicum experience. The school was well resourced with interactive white boards, big classrooms and resources. I firmly believe that my previous experience in the hospitality industry and the opportunity I had working with people would influence the way I approached the school management, staff and learners. Although the school was quite big, there was generally a pleasant atmosphere in the school and amongst the staff members. I felt like this part of the practicum allowed me to see how roles can be shifted and how adaptable one must be in the teaching profession.

8 Theme 2: Work-Integrated Learning is Cumulative

While one of the topics in the WIL practicum workshop covered was lesson planning, Jason felt that there were other topics that should have been covered as well to make the transition to teaching in front of learners easier and more adaptable. The learning that took place in the WIL practicum workshops were cumulative as new knowledge was constructed based on prior knowledge. Jason learned that a well-developed lesson plan was very important, but through his reflective journal entries he revealed that the WIL practicum workshop did not aid in his PL in terms of feeling competent and self-sufficient. It became clear from the data that Jason's PL was intentional. He not only attempted to understand his interactions within each of the schools, but also compared his PL in each of the contexts.

"As Jason explained,"

> Subjects are great, just teach us more how to implement the work so that it will be a fun learning experience for our learners. We do not know how to compile the learners' portfolios or how to handle parents. We have no idea how to do admin at school level. The ITE program is great as it is but needs more focus on life skills and ethics that PSTs need to have when they are in a classroom situation. One frustration, though, was the process of lesson preparation and assessment. He feels that there must be further discussion at university.

It became clear from the data that Jason's PL was intentional through a comparison of his experiences in past WIL practicums. He not only attempted to understand his interactions within each of the schools, but also compared his PL in each of the contexts. His comparisons were based on his prior working experience in the hospitality industry. Extending such tacit workplace knowledge made him aware of the influence of management and subsequent development of an employee. Within the context he was working he found moments that allowed him to stimulate his creative side of teaching as he experimented with different teaching strategies.

"As Jason explained.."

> When you think of the bigger picture then yes, the university is preparing me for the teaching world. It provides you with the necessary "book" knowledge to handle and approach certain situations you may encounter as a teacher. On the other hand, the university is lacking in the way the lectures are conveying the work/content to the students. I, as a student teacher, was not taught how to teach learners the work that is being taught to us, in the classroom settings at school.

9 Theme 3: Work-Integrated Learning is Intentional, and Goal Orientated

WIL can be intentional, and goal orientated, where PL can occur incidentally or by accident, but it is more likely to occur if the PST intends to learn. Jason's learning was thus intentional, and goal orientated driven. Jason's intentions were to learn and to complete any tasks successfully. As stated earlier, WIL practicum period offered opportunities for situated learning. During our semi-structured interviews, Jason stated that he thinks subject content knowledge and PL should go hand in hand. It is his belief that a teacher with subject content knowledge must firstly be willing to learn new things daily. Jason sometimes struggled with classroom management and managing his time, and these were the things he wanted to improve on. Jason's strengths lied in his ability to plan lessons for effective learning to take place. His learning was intentional, and goal orientated. I observed Jason six times in his 3rd year at two different schools. Three observations in the first WIL practicum and three observations in the second WIL practicum of his 3rd year of studies. After each lesson observation, we had a feedback session. I always started this session off by asking Jason what he thought worked well in the lesson and what he thought he could improve on. After my first observation, I explained to Jason, that we learn to improve our teaching through feedback and reflecting on our lessons. I felt that he could have created a more effective learning situation, by making the lesson more stimulating and interesting for the learners. He needed to include teaching material that would be accessible to learners and applicable to the learning situation. During his second and third observation, he made use of technology and instantly had the learners' attention. The learners were also able to relate to the content. We discussed the fact that he had to ensure that he makes provision for diversity. For example, different learning styles and to have a more learner centred approach than teacher centred approach. During observation four, five and six he was more cognisant of his actions and how he interacted with the learners. When it came to his interpersonal relationships, he was a little nervous and at times became flustered. Jason also told me that he was too scared to do a cooperative learning activity with the learners, because he was afraid that it might be chaotic. We spent quite some time on this criterion, and we discussed ways of how he could create a more effective learning situation by promoting social skills. We discussed solutions for possible problems and how to be prepared for every possible contingency. During the last observation, he was much more confident, and I could see his classroom management had a lot to do with how he confidently gave instructions to the learners and how they interacted with the content of the lesson. Jason had prepared a very detailed lesson plan for a history lesson to a grade 6 class. Jason's goals were clearly defined in his lesson plan, but he struggled to bring it across in the lesson. I too experienced growth in my own PL. From our semi structured interviews, it occurred to me that what happens in these WIL practicum sessions, has a great impact on the quality of the PSTs that are trained. I started reflecting on my own practice as a university lecturer. I asked myself what my own expectations were of PSTs; what their expectations were of me. I reflected on my own subject courses which were English First Additional Language and English First Additional Communication. The mode of lecture delivery that I used for my English First Additional Language course was mostly a top-down approach, and for English First Additional Communication, an interactive approach. Even though my English First Additional Language course was not based on the methodology of teaching English as a First Additional Language, I lacked exposing my PSTs to what was happening at schools. From the analysis of the data, it was clear that as lecturers we ourselves must become more reflective practitioners. As lecturers we need to promote critical thinking more, because once PSTs are emerged in the WIL practicum process and unless PSTs were exposed to interactive approaches and critical thinking, they will not be able to become change agents that form part of the ongoing changes in education. As university lecturers we become the model or ideal teacher for the PST, and very often they try to emulate the approaches that they themselves have been exposed to. One of the expectations we have as lectures when doing lesson evaluations during the WIL practicum period is that PSTs present interactive and stimulating lessons to their learners, thus we ourselves must practice what we preach. We need to expose them to different teaching strategies and approaches, so that they are not limited when they are teaching during the WIL practicum process. Jason felt that some lecturers were not adequately addressing his needs as some of them lacked the knowledge or experience to the new curriculum taught at schools. As a lecturer at a HEI, it is important to me that there is a clear focus on both the content as well as the way the content is being taught, and that we need to evolve with the changes as well.

I based my conversations with the PST on teacher enquiry and reflection, emphasising that these two factors were key to developing teaching theory. As the researcher I also took a closer look at the ITE program we offered. I found that the ITE program focussed largely on the theory and failed to include much of the practicalities of teaching. I started evaluating my own content and could see that there was a need for much improvement. I found that my own PL improved as I changed my outcomes to my courses to focus more on how to link theory to practice in more contextualised and concrete ways. It is important that the PST is afforded opportunities to apply what is being learned and in his or her own way refine it. Findings show the value of a PST developing within a collaborative mentoring frame. However, there is a need specifically in the final year WIL practicum session to allow for more PL opportunities to shift to becoming more self-reliant. This type of practice can allow a shift from the theory–practice gap to ensure a connected teaching and learning approach. Using collaborative mentoring as a frame offered an open and protective space for PL that is underpinned by conditions of trust, professional learning communities and openness to reflect. Structured support, attentiveness to the PST, and aligned expectations from each person with clear communication ensured a smooth collaborative process. The collaborative process comprised of joint interactions between mentor and mentee. In this study, Jason had the opportunity to work with his university lecturer who observed him during his WIL practicum, six times. The time was sufficient as both parties knew how to approach the WIL practicum period. Furthermore, findings also included that there appears to be an urgent need for a shift to occur from teaching in isolation to a school and university-wide collaboration and conversation. Meaningful collaboration is not something that can only be the product of a suggestion made by someone, nor a one-shot venture, but rather a series of continuous collaborative activities.

10 Recognizing the Actors

Fenwick and Edward (2010) note that representations of networks are themselves concrete, implying the realities to be far more stable and durable than imminent, precarious shifting relations ever can be. The clearly defined actors articulated within the analysis of this network was the PST, the university lecturer, the school, the learners, the university, the DHE, and the Western Cape Education Department. Pendleton-Jullian and Brown (2018) noted that the agents within a system are so interdependent and interconnected that all actions taken affect the system which changes the context and changing the context changes the problem, recreating the context anew. In this light, notions of curriculum, pedagogy and assessment can be added to the Actor Network which constitutes with both human and non-human actors in this research study. The research findings showed the following:

- PL in an Actor Network opened up space for speaking out within the bounds of the network to create opportunities for development and critical thinking.
- PL in an Actor Network encouraged learning through failure and belief in one's own self-efficacy (to achieve things), encourage perseverance and a willingness to try and find what worked in the participants contexts.
- PL in an Actor Network employed mechanisms and techniques for self-regulated learning that allowed the PST to experiment with uncertainty and develop.

- The technique or mechanism of PL as an actant in a network was defined. This is an issue of granularity of looking inside the actant of PL and examining how it achieves the change at an operational level.
- Mechanisms are often processes or techniques that operate at the tactical or operational level. While a human actor uses a mechanism, ANT bestowed agency to the actant (PST) because its presence has an effect on other actors.
- The idea of mechanism, and how it works, allowed that the workings of the actant (PST) were made visible and self-regulated learning was unpacked.

The system is influenced by external factors and relationships that are unique to them, but all also share common interests and perspectives. They are all contributing key practice factors that shape professional learning of PSTs. In this method the network is already extant and all that we need to do is draw a line around the areas that we are interested in. Conversely, the boundaries of an Actor Network are created by the actors and actants who are invested in the 'problem or goal' through the act of translation which is the act of recruiting new actors into a new or reformed network and through that, establishing its boundary. Findings of this study revealed that PL in an Actor Network scaffold and encourages the participation of all actors involved. Within an Actor Network, data revealed that planning and goal setting afforded by PL also scaffolded motivation and the data revealed that ways of thinking were also purported to have changed. The data revealed that using PL in an Actor Network developed teamwork and collaboration and brought PL opportunities for developing skills in conflict resolution and mutual support. New insights were gained into working collaboratively in a network and the PST realized that he was able to take on any challenges because of mutual support. Increased participation was a key aspect of the actant's pedagogy switch. The PST in this research while engaged in an Actor Network, claimed that he was thinking differently rather akin to Gee's (2005) conceptualization of authentic professionalism, where experiences transform individuals into becoming teachers. Data revealed that PL creates a context where learning is negotiated, and hierarchy is less important. By using an ANT approach in this research study, the PST stopped being a passive receptor and became an actor and mediator in broader networks. As the university lecturer, I noticed this release of agency within Jason and myself. Within this research ANT looked at conditions and possibilities for a new approach to develop PL of PSTs. By using an ANT approach for this research, even more issues emerged when considering non-humans and proliferation networks. The uptake of an ANT approach was particularly beneficial in looking at innovation and implementation of new frameworks that are at play to influence the PL of PSTs.

11 Closing Thoughts

There is a definite need for systemic improvement and a design in South Africa's ITE programs that will foster implementation and engagement that is coupled with a collaborative mentoring system. An early exposure of PL for PSTs could possibly ensure that PSTs do not only survive and excel during the WIL practicum, but also become competent and effective in their profession/career and stay in the profession. This study shared how to create opportunities to promote the transformation of teaching and PL for all actors involved in the WIL practicum process as well as the ITE program as a unit. Given the paradigm shifts in ITE programs it is crucial for all stakeholders involved to attend to the PL needs of all teachers, but most importantly PSTs. If we continue to persist in the use of traditional PL models in the WIL practicum period, where environments of non-collaboration with limited communication and co-ordination are promoted, we will be perpetuating the system where there will continuously be a separation between theory and practice. The partnership between schools and universities is fundamental, in that universities provide the development of teaching skills and schools need to provide PL opportunities for PSTs to implement and reflect on these skills in the form of learning by teaching, learning by reflecting and learning by collaborating. Unless this is seriously considered, WIL practicum will become a practice of trial and error, which in turn will leave PSTs to chance. In conclusion, well-formulated policies that will promote the development of collaborative partnerships and augment the PL of high-quality PSTs enabling their readiness to enter the world of teaching is recommended.

Reference lists

Brondyk, S., & Searby, L. (2013). Best practices in mentoring: Complexities and possibilities. *International Journal of Mentoring and Coaching in Education, 2*(3), 189–203.

Callon, M. (1984). Some elements of a sociology of translation: domestication of the scallops and the fishermen of St Brieuc Bay. *The Sociological Review, 32*(1_suppl), 196–233.

Council on Higher Education. (2011). Work-integrated learning: Good practice guide. *HE Monitor, 12*.

Department of Basic and Higher Education and Training. (2011). *Integrated strategic planning framework for teacher education and development in South Africa.* 2011–2025. Government Printer.

Department of Education. (2006). The national policy framework for teacher education and development in South Africa. In *More teachers; Better teachers*.

DHET (2015). Policy on Minimum Requirements for Teacher Education Qualifications. Pretoria: Department of Higher Education and Training

Dreyer, J. (2015). A positive and enriching teaching practice experience. *Teaching practice, perspectives and frameworks*, 3–10.

Fenwick, T., & Edwards, R. (2010). *Actor-network theory in education.* Routledge.

Fenwick, T., & Edwards, R. (2011). Introduction: Reclaiming and renewing actor network theory for educational research. *Educational Philosophy and Theory, 43* (sup1): 1–14.

Gee, J. P. (2005). Learning by design: Good video games as learning machines. *E-Learning and Digital Media, 2*(1), 5–16.

Latour, B. (1987). *Science in action: How to follow scientists and engineers through society.* Harvard University Press.

Latour, B. (1999). On recalling ANT. *The sociological review, 47*(1_suppl), 15–25.

Law, J. (1992). Notes on the theory of the actor-network: Ordering, strategy, and heterogeneity. *Systems Practice, 5*, 379–393.

Menon, M., Rama, K., Lakshmi, T. K. S., & Bhat, V. D. (2007). *Quality indicators for teacher education.* Retrieved from: http://www.col.org/SiteCollectionDocuments/PUB_QITE.pdf

Orland-Barak, L., & Yinon, H. (2007). When theory meets practice: What student teachers learn from guided reflection on their own classroom discourse. *Teaching and Teacher Education, 23*(6), 957–969.

Pendleton-Jullian, A. M., & Brown, J. S. (2018). *Design unbound: Designing for emergence in a white water world, volume 2: Ecologies of change* (Vol. 2). MIT Press.

Rai, N., & Thapa, B. (2015). *A study on purposive sampling method in research* (p. 5). Kathmandu School of Law.

Rusznyak, L., & Bertram, C. (2021). Conceptualising work-integrated learning to support pre-service teachers' pedagogic reasoning. *Journal of Education (University of KwaZulu-Natal), 83*, 34–53.

Rule, P., & John, V. (2011). *Your guide to case study research.* van Schaik.

See, N. L. M. (2014). Mentoring and developing pedagogical content knowledge in beginning teachers. *Procedia-Social and Behavioral Sciences, 123*, 53–62.

Sharma, G. (2017). Pros and cons of different sampling techniques. *International Journal of Applied Research, 3*(7), 749–752.

South Africa. (2011b). Department of basic education and department of higher education and training. In *Integrated strategic planning framework for teacher education and development in South Africa 2011–2025.* Government Printer.

Van Velzen, C., Volman, M., Brekelmans, M., & White, S. (2012). Guided work-based learning: Sharing practical teaching knowledge with student teachers. *Teaching and Teacher Education, 28*(2), 229–239.

Variations in South African Novice Mathematics Teachers' Lived Experiences and Reflections on Multiple Solutions Problem-Solving: Implications for Work-Integrated Learning

Sfiso Cebolenkosi Mahlaba and Iman C. Chahine

Abstract This study investigates the under-researched area of South African novice teachers' experiences with multiple solution tasks (MSTs) problem-solving in Euclidean geometry. While evidence from prior research reveals difficulties with geometry problem-solving among South African teachers, a gap exists regarding their lived experiences of MST problem-solving and the implications for work-integrated learning (WIL). In contributing towards this gap, this study used a qualitative approach grounded in interpretive phenomenology to explore the variations of four novice teachers' lived experiences after engaging in individual MST problem-solving. Novice teachers' responses to the MSTs and semi-structured interviews following MST problem-solving were used to collect data. Thematic analysis revealed that while novice teachers struggled with MST problem-solving due to their lack of geometry knowledge, limited experience with MST problem-solving and poor teacher training they acknowledge the importance of MST problem-solving for educators and students. These results hold significance for teacher training and WIL which are discussed in this chapter.

Keywords Multiple solution tasks · Problem-solving · Euclidean geometry · Work integrated learning

---

S. C. Mahlaba (✉)
University of Johannesburg, Johannesburg, South Africa
e-mail: msfiso@uj.ac.za

I. C. Chahine
University of Massachusetts, Lowell, USA
e-mail: Iman_Chahine@uml.edu

© The Author(s), under exclusive license to Springer Nature Switzerland AG 2024
I. C. Chahine and L. Reddy (eds.), *Educators' Work Integrated Learning Experiences*, https://doi.org/10.1007/978-3-031-65964-5_10

1 Introduction

Problem-solving is a core aspect of mathematics education, evidenced by its extensive research focus and position as the highest level of learning (Gagné, 1965) and highest level of assessment in the curriculum and assessment policy statement (CAPS) (DBE, 2011). Paul Halmos argues that problem-solving is central to learning mathematics because the subject itself revolves around problems, and effective teaching should focus on engaging students in solving them (Halmos, 1980). However, despite its importance, problem-solving is considered one of the most difficult processes to teach and learn. Pioneering work by Polya (1973) established a foundation for problem-solving with his four-step heuristic, but the field continues to evolve with diverse perspectives from scholars like Kilpatrick (1969) and Schoenfeld (1985). This chapter emphasizes the importance of teacher proficiency in problem-solving alongside a strong conceptual understanding of problem-solving as a pedagogical approach. While we advocate for developing teachers' problem-solving abilities, our focus here is on their reflections on lived experiences following a one-month long individual experience with multiple solution task (MST) problem-solving. This study's findings not only shed light on novice teachers' experiences with MST problem-solving and their views on its efficacy as a pedagogical strategy, but also discusses implications for work-integrated learning (WIL). Building upon research by Silver et al. (2005), which documented a shift in teachers' perceptions of MST problem-solving and its classroom implementation due to a year-long professional development (PD) program, this study investigates the lived experiences of novice mathematics teachers following a one-month immersion in MST problem-solving. This study defined novice teachers as those with less than five years of experience teaching mathematics in Grade 12. The research aims to answer the following questions:

1. What are novice teachers' lived experiences and reflections after immersion in MST problem-solving?
2. What are the WIL implications for these lived experiences and reflections?

2 Study Significance

This study was motivated by research findings indicating that experienced mathematics teachers struggle with non-routine problem-solving (Bansilal et al., 2014) and that pre-service teachers (PSTs) struggle with solving problems of a higher cognitive demand (Bansilal & Ubah, 2019). Therefore, the findings of our study sheds light on some of the challenges related to teacher struggles with non-routine problem-solving that requires a high cognitive demand. A recent study also concluded that final-year PSTs are not well prepared to teach mathematics (Taylor, 2021), while most PSTs graduate with poor knowledge of solving Euclidean geometry (henceforth geometry) problems and teaching geometry (Tachie, 2020). Our findings inform teacher training institutions on approaches to improve well-prepared mathematics teachers. Furthermore, by examining novice teachers' perspectives on MST problem-solving as an unorthodox teaching method compared to common traditional methods like 'chalk-and-talk,' the study contributes to the ongoing conversation about fostering a wider range of pedagogical approaches in mathematics education.

Mhlolo (2017) identified a concerning trend where teachers often disregard non-traditional student solutions. This means potentially gifted students who may produce non-traditional solutions are not supported to develop to their full potential (Kokot, 2005). Our investigation sheds light on potential reasons behind such practice among novice teachers. Lastly, the focus on MST problem-solving is particularly relevant as it equips teachers with the specialized content knowledge required to judge the "mathematical soundness of different solution strategies" (Copur-Gencturk et al., 2019, p. 488) produced by students. This knowledge is crucial for fostering a classroom environment that supports students' various mathematical abilities and promotes deep mathematical understanding. Ultimately, the study's significance extends to informing WIL practices within South African mathematics teacher training programs.

3 Brief Literature Review

3.1 Problems and Problem-Solving

Schoenfeld (1992) differentiates between routine and non-routine problems, arguing that true problem-solving occurs when encountering a non-routine problem. These problems do not require applying a single, fixed procedure like routine problems, instead, they demand a combination of previously learned and newly devised strategies. However, even routine problems can be transformed into non-routine ones by explicitly requiring multiple solutions (Leikin, 2014). This elevates the cognitive demand of the original problem. Furthermore, mathematical problems can be deliberately designed as MSTs for educational purposes (Schoenfeld, 1991). Importantly, a problem's 'routineness' depends on the individual's experience in the domain it addresses. The same task can be routine for *person A*, who can solve it with existing procedures, but non-routine for *person B*, who lacks the necessary routines or prior experience. In this case, *person B* would be engaged in genuine problem-solving, needing to develop new strategies to find a solution, potentially with assistance from others (Schoenfeld, 1992). This highlights that teachers' views of problem-solving, whether as routine or non-routine, have significant implications for their practice.

We define problem-solving in the context of non-routine problems, emphasizing the value of approaching mathematical tasks from multiple perspectives. To effectively engage students in 'doing mathematics,' teachers need to design or select tasks that stimulate mathematical thinking (Schoenfeld, 1994). Doing mathematics involves equipping students with the skills to devise various solution strategies and choose the most appropriate one during problem-solving. Thus, teacher training should, therefore, equip PSTs with the skills to guide students through a 'productive struggle' of doing mathematics to develop problem-solving skills. Engaging students in MST problem-solving can be a powerful tool for introducing them to this 'productive struggle' and ultimately developing mathematical thinking and problem-solving (Levav-Waynberg & Leikin, 2009; Stupel & Ben-Chaim, 2017).

3.2 Multiple Solution Tasks and Problem-Solving

Mathematical tasks encompass the day-to-day problems students encounter, either from textbooks or teacher design, that stimulate mathematical thinking and application (Tekkumru-Kisa et al., 2020). These tasks vary in complexity, demanding different levels of cognitive ability from problem-solvers (Stein & Smith, 1998). Low cognitive demand tasks typically involve applying memorized procedures, while high cognitive demand tasks engage students in a deeper understanding of 'doing mathematics' (Tekkumru-Kisa et al., 2020). Our focus here is on MSTs—"tasks that contain explicit requirements for solving a problem in multiple ways" (Guberman & Leikin, 2013, p. 36) or tasks with the potential for multiple solution approaches (Mahlaba 2020). While MSTs include three solution spaces: expert, group, and individual (Levav-Waynberg & Leikin, 2012), we focus on individual solution spaces. MSTs do not have readily applicable procedures necessitating that the solver actively design all or part of the solution method (Lampert, 1990), positioning MSTs as highly cognitively demanding tasks (Tekkumru-Kisa et al., 2020). However, while cognitive activation is a recognized element of effective teaching (Jacob et al., 2017), some teachers remain hesitant to engage students in highly cognitively demanding tasks (Baier et al., 2019). They are concerned these tasks have the potential to confuse students (Silver et al., 2005). If experienced teachers struggle to engage students in high cognitive demand tasks like MSTs and lack the ability to solve them themselves, it is pertinent to explore how novice teachers experience and view MST problem-solving.

3.3 Work Integrated Learning and Problem-Solving

WIL is a learning approach that merges theoretical learning with practical experience. WIL provides students with the opportunity to apply classroom knowledge to real-world problems (Stirling et al., 2016). For PSTs, WIL offers a valuable component for not only understanding professional conduct but also for developing problem-solving skills applicable to classrooms, equip them with essential competencies, including critical thinking, creativity, collaboration, communication, decision-making, information literacy, and technology skills (Jackson et al., 2022; Petersen et al., 2023; Stirling et al., 2016). Ultimately, WIL ensures teachers are well-prepared for their professional journeys and future careers. In this chapter, we conceptualize WIL as a concept linked to the self-directed learning (SDL) process, where learning continues beyond the initial training period for PSTs. This ongoing WIL can manifest in various ways, such as PSTs pursuing postgraduate degrees or engaging in professional development programs to further refine their teaching skills.

Equipping teachers with proficiency in problem-solving pedagogy ensures their ability to effectively teach students with diverse mathematical abilities. A comprehensive repertoire of problem-solving pedagogy strategies allows teachers to explain mathematical problems in multiple ways, catering to different learning styles and fostering deeper understanding (Mahlaba, 2021). The real-world nature of WIL makes it an ideal complement to problem-solving pedagogy. Integrating WIL with problem-solving pedagogy can provide teachers with a more profound grasp of mathematics and a heightened awareness of its practical applications in daily life. Engaging in MST problem-solving within WIL experiences can offer additional benefits for PSTs and novice teachers. It can foster a sense of ownership over their learning and develop resilience and perseverance when tackling challenging mathematical problems (Mahlaba, 2021). Furthermore, WIL experiences that incorporate MST problem-solving can contribute to developing a growth mindset that emphasizes the belief that skills and abilities can be improved through dedicated training, effort, and practice (Boaler et al., 2022; Dweck, 2015) amongst PSTs and novice teachers.

3.4 *Teacher Knowledge in Mathematics and Problem-Solving*

School mathematics presents distinct challenges compared to academic mathematics. Teachers must effectively cater to students with diverse learning paces and abilities (Dreher et al., 2018). As Shulman (1986) posits, effective mathematics teachers draw from a multitude of knowledge domains, with content knowledge (CK) remaining the central pillar (Taylor, 2019). In this context, rich problem-solving knowledge is a critical determinant of teacher effectiveness (Baier et al., 2019). For a strong CK, teachers should be able to solve mathematical problems using various approaches. In practice, this translates to engaging students in activities that encourage exploring diverse solutions to the same problem, allowing them to choose the approach that resonates most (Semanišinová, 2021). Furthermore, teachers need the ability to provide timely and appropriate feedback on these different approaches—a crucial element of Mathematical Knowledge for Teaching (MKT) (Semanišinová, 2021). Examining teachers' experiences and reflections on MST problem-solving cannot only benefit students' mathematical thinking development but also broaden teachers' understanding of mathematics pedagogy. However, this is contingent on teachers' own ability to solve problems using multiple strategies and valuing the integration of MSTs within their classrooms. If teachers themselves struggle with diverse solutions or see no value in MSTs, demonstrating these approaches to students becomes nearly impossible.

Research suggests that prospective teachers often lack awareness of the benefits of problem-solving and struggle with non-routine problems due to limited experience and content knowledge (Doğan-Temur, 2012). This limited perspective is exemplified by a participant in Chapman's (1999) study who stated, '*math is different because you always have to know the right method or formula to get the answer*' (p. 130). This perception positions problem-solving as a non-exploratory endeavour, where problem-solving is solely about applying the correct formula or algorithm. Consequently, some teachers resort to directly showing students how to solve problems, while others offer limited control, only allowing students to recognize familiar patterns (Chapman, 1999; Chirinda & Barmby, 2018). These teacher behaviors are often attributed to contextual factors, such as overcrowded classrooms leading to disruptive noise levels (Chapman, 1999; Chirinda & Barmby, 2018). However, this may also indicate an underlying belief that students lack the capacity for independent problem-solving ownership—a situation potentially exacerbated with MSTs. Overall, the prevailing view among many teachers appears to be that problem-solving is simply the application of algorithms and procedures (Ford, 1994; Son & Lee, 2021).

3.5 Why is the South African Context an Interesting One?

The South African context for mathematics education presents a unique set of challenges and opportunities, making it a valuable area for research. One of the key concerns is the consistently low performance of South African students in mathematics assessments. This underachievement persists despite the national curriculum, the CAPS, emphasizing critical and creative thinking skills through problem-solving. Studies like Chirinda (2021) have shown, however, that CAPS graduates struggle to apply these concepts to solve problems, highlighting a gap between curriculum goals and student outcomes. This situation underscores the need for developing PSTs who can effectively integrate problem-solving into their teaching. Here, the concept of MSTs emerges as a promising approach.

MSTs encourage students to explore different approaches to reach a solution, fostering creativity and critical thinking (Leikin, 2011; Levav-Waynberg & Leikin, 2012). However, the current mathematics instruction in South Africa relies heavily on tasks with predetermined, single solutions (Chirinda & Barmby, 2017, 2018). This not only limits student exposure to diverse problem-solving strategies but also reflects potential misconceptions among some teachers regarding MSTs (Chirinda & Barmby, 2018; Mhlolo, 2017). Furthermore, research suggests limited opportunities for problem-solving activities within the implemented curriculum (Jagals & Van der Walt, 2016) because teachers themselves often lack clarity on how to incorporate problem-solving effectively (Chirinda & Barmby, 2018).

Beyond these instructional limitations, the South African educational system faces additional complexities. Issues like class size, resource limitations, and time constraints create barriers to achieving educational equity (Spaull & Jansen, 2019). Overcrowded classrooms can hinder student interaction and discourse, crucial elements for collaborative problem-solving (Chirinda & Barmby, 2018). Additionally, English as the primary language of instruction can present challenges for some students (Planas & Setati-Phakeng, 2014; Sibanda & Graven, 2018). Despite these obstacles, research consistently highlights the importance of engaging students with challenging problems and fostering communication skills to express mathematical ideas effectively (Juta & Van Wyk, 2020). These calls continue for incorporating exploration and challenging problems into mathematics instruction (De Villiers & Heideman, 2014).

In this context, exploring how novice teachers reflect on their experiences with MST problem-solving can be particularly insightful. This study aims to illuminate their readiness to integrate MSTs into their classrooms (Chirinda & Barmby, 2018), identify challenges and needs related to problem-solving instruction, and ultimately inform improvements in PST training programs. By investigating the potential of MSTs and WIL within the South African context, this research has the potential to contribute significantly to improved mathematics education for all students.

3.6 Empirical Investigation

3.6.1 Methods and Methodology

This study used a qualitative approach with an interpretive phenomenological design (Frechette et al., 2020). This design aimed to gain a deeper understanding of the lived experiences of novice teachers in generating multiple solutions to geometry problems. Furthermore, this design facilitates thematic analysis of the data, allowing for the identification of the core essence and meaning within participants' lived experiences (Miles et al., 2014). The research process involved two stages. First, participants received a task sheet containing five purposefully chosen geometry problems. They were given one month to complete and submit their written responses to the researcher. Second, individual semi-structured interviews were conducted with each participant.

3.6.2 Participants

This study involved four novice mathematics teachers in their first year of teaching within the Further Education and Training (FET) phase at four different public schools in South African rural areas. These teachers were purposefully selected based on the following three criteria: (i) they had less than five years' experience of teaching, (ii) they were teaching mathematics in in the FET phase in rural schools, and (iii) they willingly agreed to participate in the study by signing an informed consent form.

3.6.3 The Instruments

The instruments used in this study include a multiple solution written task and a semi-structured interview which are explained in more detail below.

Multiple *solution written task*

The first author deliberately selected five geometry problems (see Appendix) designed to challenge novice teachers to employ different solution strategies. Participants were instructed to submit all their attempts, including solutions they considered both correct and incorrect. This comprehensive approach aimed to gain a deeper understanding of their experiences with MST problem-solving. For example, while solutions 1 and 2 might appear similar, solution 2 demonstrates a more sophisticated approach due to its conciseness. The problems were chosen based on the following criteria: firstly, the problems are standard within the South African curriculum and require a combination of knowledge from different stages of the participants' prior geometry learning. This ensured that novice teachers would be equipped to approach the problems using at least one (or more) methods.

Secondly, the problems centered on Euclidean geometry, a topic recognized as challenging for both students and teachers in South African mathematics education, aligning with the study's focus. Lastly, each problem was designed to allow for multiple solution approaches. In other words, there was more than one valid strategy that could be used to arrive at a solution. Figure 1 illustrates an example of an MST with two distinct solution approaches.

The semi-structured interviews

In addition to the task sheet, semi-structured interviews were conducted with the four novice teachers to delve deeper into their experiences while solving the MST

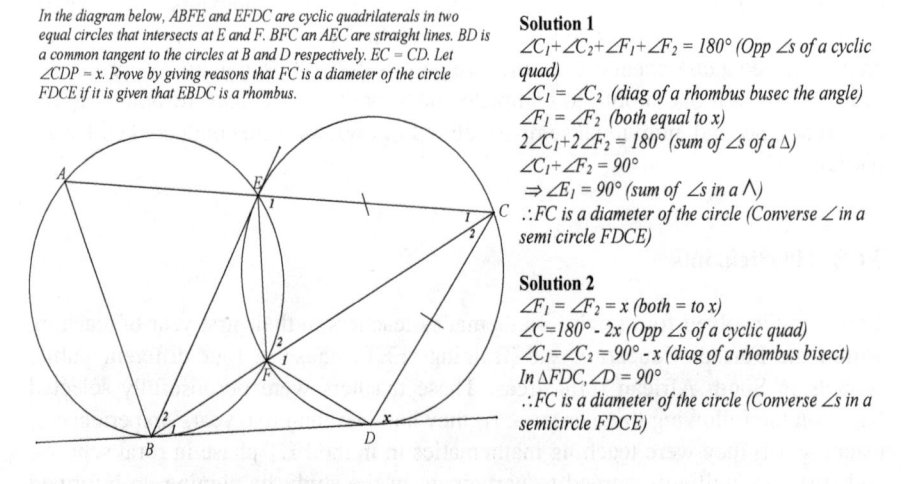

In the diagram below, ABFE and EFDC are cyclic quadrilaterals in two equal circles that intersects at E and F. BFC an AEC are straight lines. BD is a common tangent to the circles at B and D respectively. EC = CD. Let $\angle CDP = x$. Prove by giving reasons that FC is a diameter of the circle FDCE if it is given that EBDC is a rhombus.

Solution 1
$\angle C_1 + \angle C_2 + \angle F_1 + \angle F_2 = 180°$ (Opp $\angle$s of a cyclic quad)
$\angle C_1 = \angle C_2$ (diag of a rhombus busec the angle)
$\angle F_1 = \angle F_2$ (both equal to x)
$2\angle C_1 + 2\angle F_2 = 180°$ (sum of $\angle$s of a $\triangle$)
$\angle C_1 + \angle F_2 = 90°$
$\Rightarrow \angle E_1 = 90°$ (sum of $\angle$s in a $\triangle$)
$\therefore$ FC is a diameter of the circle (Converse $\angle$ in a semi circle FDCE)

Solution 2
$\angle F_1 = \angle F_2 = x$ (both = to x)
$\angle C = 180° - 2x$ (Opp $\angle$s of a cyclic quad)
$\angle C_1 = \angle C_2 = 90° - x$ (diag of a rhombus bisect)
In $\triangle FDC, \angle D = 90°$
$\therefore$ FC is a diameter of the circle (Converse $\angle$s in a semicircle FDCE)

Fig. 1 An example of an MST in the task sheet provided to teachers

problems. These interviews were audio-recorded and transcribed by the first author. The semi-structured format offered several advantages: it facilitated the collection of rich data through open-ended questions (Cohen et al., 2018), while also allowing for flexibility in the interview process to explore emerging themes or probe participants' responses beyond the predetermined questions. This flexibility, combined with the use of prompts, facilitated the gathering of in-depth data. Furthermore, triangulation was employed by cross-referencing the interview data with the task sheet responses. This tool triangulation served to enhance the reliability and trustworthiness of the findings by establishing corroborating evidence from multiple sources.

3.6.4 Data Analysis

This study employed a two-step coding process based on Saldaňa's (2009) framework to analyze data from both the task sheet responses and interview transcripts. The first step involved open coding, where transcribed interviews were segmented into initial codes reflecting keywords that described the nature of teachers' lived experiences while engaged in solving MSTs. The second step utilized axial coding, in which these initial codes were further examined and reorganized into broader concepts. This process continued until theoretical saturation was achieved, indicating no emergence of new themes. Finally, connections were established between the four major themes identified within the data. Data from the semi-structured interviews underwent thematic analysis. The resulting themes were then used to address the research question posed at the outset of the study. Task sheet data served to substantiate and enrich participants' interview responses. Solutions from each participant, for each problem, were compared and analyzed for their flexibility and level of methodological sophistication. The data analysis culminated in a set of categories describing variations in teachers' experiences with MSTs. Furthermore, it yielded a structure, termed the outcome space (Marton, 1986; Åkerlind, 2012), that visually represents the relationships between these categories.

4 Findings

This study revealed that three out of the four novice teachers encountered difficulties in generating multiple solutions for the Euclidean geometry problems. While the remaining participant achieved multiple solutions for all problems, some exhibited inconsistencies due to the lack of logical reasoning, incorrect geometrical statements, or missing elements necessary for complete proofs. Through their reflections, the novice teachers identified various factors contributing to their struggles with MSTs. Limited geometry knowledge and past educational experiences were cited as key challenges. Interestingly, despite acknowledging the potential benefits of MST problem-solving in promoting mathematical learning and procedural fluency, these teachers also perceived MSTs as inherently difficult. Thematic analysis of the data yielded three main themes: one focused on novice teachers' solution strategies, while the remaining two explored their perceptions and lived experiences related to MST problem-solving.

4.1 Theme 1: Solving Mathematical Problems Using Analogous Strategies Based on Procedural Similarity of Tasks and Faulty Reasoning in Solution Approaches

The novice teachers primarily used different approaches and strategies when tackling the posed MSTs. However, some instances revealed analogous approaches between participants. For example, P2 and P4 (see Fig. 2) utilized a comparable method to solve problem 3.1. While this similarity suggests analogous experiences with MST problem-solving, the final steps of their solutions in Fig. 2 highlight the nuanced variations in their approaches. It is noteworthy that despite using similar initial approaches, neither P2 nor P4 identified additional solutions beyond the one presented in Fig. 2.

P4's solution for task in question 1 in Fig. 3 exemplifies a concise approach utilizing abbreviated reasoning, contrasting with P3's more extensive approach characterized by longer reasoning chains. These variations highlight how participants interpreted the task based on their existing knowledge, past experiences, and potentially other solution strategies within their repertoire. P3's extended approach can be viewed as an exploratory effort to identify a procedural solution suitable for the problem at hand. Similarly, for a task in question 2, P2 initially attempted a lengthy solution followed by a shorter second attempt. This second approach demonstrates the identification of a potentially successful strategy, but P3 ultimately failed to translate this strategy into the specific procedural steps required for the problem. Furthermore, P2's second, shorter solution contains an error in the second statement,

Fig. 2 Analogous solution approaches from P2 and P4

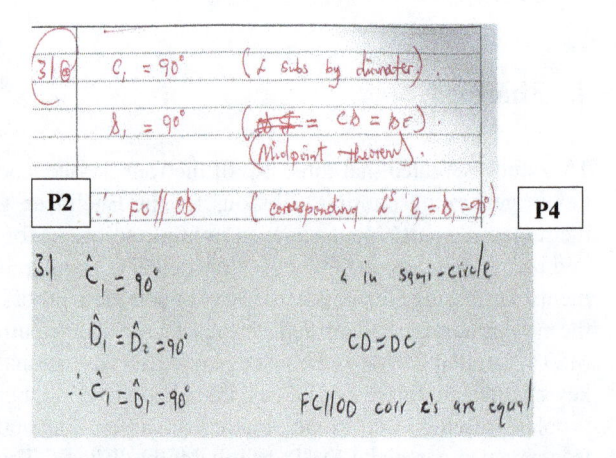

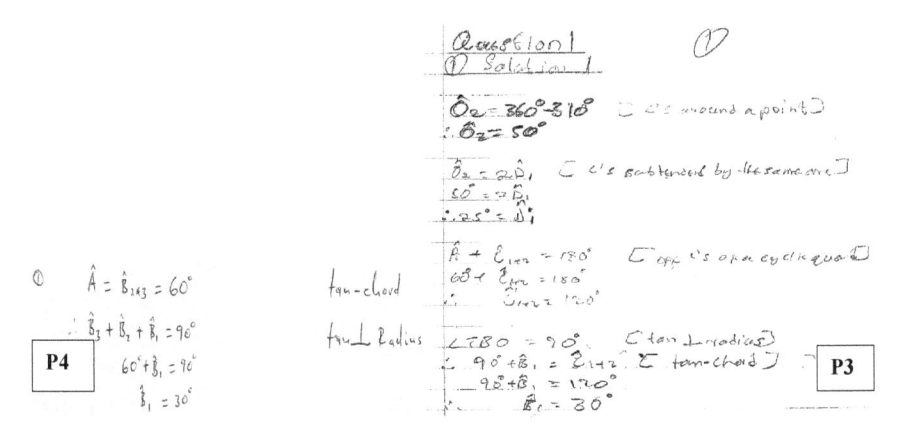

Fig. 3 An example of a similar approach used by novice teachers in solving question 1

incorrectly stating that $\angle E_1 = \angle D$ which is not true because chords EC and CD subtend angles $\angle F_1$ and $\angle F_2$ (see Appendix). This error, along with the general preference for analogous and procedural solutions observed in both P2 and P4, suggests a tendency to rely on algorithmic approaches to problem-solving, even when such approaches may not be optimal.

Similar to P2 in Fig. 7, P3 also identified a relevant theorem—the theorem for finding the sum of interior angles in a triangle. However, when applying this theorem to task 2 (see Fig. 4), P3 mistakenly included an angle that lies outside the designated triangle. As illustrated in Appendix, $\angle C_1$ is outside $\triangle CFD$, yet P3 incorporated this angle instead of $\angle C_2$. This discrepancy highlights how P3's solution strategy was built upon an erroneous initial statement, despite the chosen theorem being applicable to the problem.

P3's reasoning in their solution to task 3.1 (see Fig. 5) also exhibits an inconsistency. Their conclusion regarding the midpoint theorem is inaccurate because a crucial statement is missing from their proof which is $FO = OE(radii)$ which qualifies the midpoint theorem when combined with $CD = DE(given)$ in $\triangle FEC$. While P3 identified the relevant solution strategy, their execution was hampered by the omission of this essential element.

These examples from P3's solutions (Figs. 4 and 5) illustrate a tendency among novice teachers to rely heavily on algorithmic procedures. This reliance can obscure their understanding of the underlying solution approach needed for the specific

Fig. 4 P3's statement of solution 1 in question 2

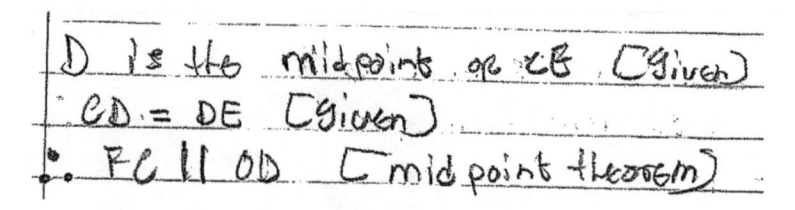

> D is the midpoint of CE (given)
> CD = DE (given)
> ∴ FC ∥ OD (midpoint theorem)

Fig. 5 P3's solution to question 3.1

problem. In contrast, P1 (Fig. 6) successfully identified and applied relevant information about triangles and angles with accurate reasoning.

However, P1 encountered difficulty in progressing towards a solution and ultimately wrote *"no way forward, wrong"* on the task sheet. During the interview, P1 explained, *"…I knew that I had to use the other second circle, but I don't know how. The way forward, maybe if I knew how to use the other circle, I would solve [the problem]."* This statement highlights the potential limitation of overreliance on procedures and how it can hinder the development of flexible problem-solving strategies.

These findings reveal that these novice teachers primarily relied on familiar solution approaches adapted from past experiences (finding analogous approaches). However, their solutions often contained faulty reasoning and a struggle to connect their chosen strategies to the specific problem requirements. These results suggest that pre-service teacher training should emphasize transferable knowledge applicable

Fig. 6 P1's attempt to answer question 2

> In △CEF and △CDF
> $C\hat{O}F = D\hat{F}C = x$ converse tan chord theorem
> $\hat{E}_1 = x$ ext ∠ = opp inter opp
> $\hat{F}_1 = \hat{F}_2 = x$ opp equal sides (EC = CD)
> ~~$E_1 = D$~~
> $D = 180° - x$ (opp cyclic quad)
>
> $\hat{F}_1 + \hat{C}_2 + \hat{D} = 180°$
> $x + C_2 + 180° - x = 180°$ No way forward
> $C_2 = 180 - 180$ wrong.

to novel contexts, strong reasoning skills, and the development of flexible problem-solving strategies with metacognitive awareness. By incorporating these elements into WIL experiences and PD programs, teacher education can better equip future teachers to guide students through MSTs effectively.

For PSTs still in training, WIL experiences can be designed to target problem-solving skills. During WIL placements, teacher trainers should encourage reflective practice and critical thinking in PSTs when encountering WIL-related problems. This involves analyzing solution approaches, identifying areas of flawed reasoning, and seeking feedback from trainers, mentors, and peers. These experiences mirror the ongoing self-assessment expected of professionals, fostering continuous improvement. Integrating WIL-based problem-solving, underpinned by MSTs, can equip PSTs with differentiated problem-solving abilities to benefit their future students. Additionally, applying knowledge and skills in real-world educational settings through WIL allows PSTs to address difficulties before entering the classroom independently.

Secondly, incorporating real classroom contexts, like WIL experiences, exposes PSTs to problem-solving scenarios that necessitate novel solution approaches, not just routine procedures. This emphasizes the importance of graduating PSTs with the ability to design new problem-solving strategies, a skill that can be honed through engaging with MTS. However, PSTs lacking this proficiency can be supported through PD programs where they collaborate with experienced educators on solving problems aligned with MTS. These PD programs allow PSTs to observe effective approaches in action and gain practical insights into tackling MTS-based problems. Finally, encouraging PSTs to connect their problem-solving strategies with specific WIL challenges can be fostered through structured reflection exercises, discussions with mentors, and collaborative problem-solving activities.

4.2 Theme 2: Novice Teachers' Explanations of Why They Faced Challenges in MST Problem-Solving

Analysis of novice teacher experiences revealed a variety of perspectives regarding engagement with MTS problem-solving. While some participants found advantages in this approach, others encountered challenges. Notably, a common difficulty reported in the interviews was finding multiple solutions. P2 stated, *"my experience was quite challenging in terms of figuring out more solutions per problem."* However, P2 also acknowledged the potential benefit of finding multiple solutions: *"it would be good because it would challenge me to learn more."* Despite describing MTS problem-solving as a *"good experience,"* P2 emphasized the difficulty of achieving this goal. A specific challenge P2 encountered when seeking multiple solutions was differentiating between solution structures as he mentioned:

Sometimes you can claim that we have two solutions, but rather you still have that same solution and you have written it in different ways. Because to have solutions, you might have rewritten it in different ways using the same theorems.

The importance of prior knowledge in finding multiple solutions emerged from comments by P2 and P3. P2 stated, "*...in most cases, there is always something I know about the problem. So, I start with what I know and take it from there*," highlighting his reliance on existing knowledge. Similarly, P3 mentioned, "*...[I] see if I can relate it [the problem] to anything that I have learned prior*," indicating the use of prior knowledge as a foundation for finding multiple solutions. While both P2 and P3 acknowledged the value of finding multiple solutions, they expressed differing perspectives regarding time constraints. P2 recognized the potential benefit of multiple solutions, stating, "*it would be good because it would challenge me to learn more.*" However, he emphasized the impracticality of finding multiple solutions under examination pressure, where time is limited and specific, efficient solutions are rewarded. P3, on the other hand, expressed a willingness to find multiple solutions when time allows. He viewed this as an opportunity to showcase the "*richness of mathematical problem-solving*" by demonstrating that a problem can have multiple approaches. This perspective aligns with a broader educational goal that values not only achieving correct answers but also fostering deep understanding and the ability to solve problems from various angles. In essence, these comments reveal a potential conflict between the desire to demonstrate understanding through multiple solutions and the practical limitations of time-bound assessments. Both teachers demonstrate an awareness of how context and specific assessment demands can influence their approach to teaching.

[P2] ... definitely. It shows understanding... but no, you cannot do that in an examination, the exam will give you specific marks for a problem so there is no need to give three solutions. Because the examination is about marks and time; [P3] Okay, in a context where I am not limited to time, I would do that, to show that this problem has more than one solution.

P2 and P3 attributed their difficulty in finding multiple solutions to a reliance on specific Euclidean geometry theorems. This suggests that a limited set of theorems restricts the available tools and strategies for tackling problems, hindering flexibility and creativity in their approach. These novice teachers' experiences highlight the challenges posed by curricular constraints in mathematics education, particularly in geometry. The emphasis on applying prescribed theorems implies a need for a more flexible and exploratory approach to problem-solving. This would allow students to engage with a broader range of mathematical tools and strategies, fostering a deeper understanding of concepts and promoting creative problem-solving skills.

[P4] I think one thing that was making the process a bit difficult is being restricted to using particular theorems that are used in Grade 11 or maybe in Grade 10 being restricted to the theorems that a prescribed in that grade. [P2] So, especially when you are doing Euclidean geometry mostly, it is limited to those theorems.

P4 attributed his difficulty in finding multiple solutions to a perceived lack of knowledge in Euclidean geometry. He expressed a belief that his teacher training courses did not adequately equip him with the flexibility required for different problem-solving approaches. In his view, the university curriculum did not sufficiently develop a strong foundation in Euclidean geometry for future teachers. He mentioned:

> [P4] I think it's because of limited knowledge. The teacher training courses we received are not sufficient to develop flexibility in problem-solving. The university courses do not expand teachers' knowledge, which is why our understanding of geometry is limited. This confines us to solving problems in a particular way. Unlike other topics where teacher training provides some education, geometry content seems to remain largely at the high school level.

This analysis emphasizes the importance of robust and comprehensive teacher training programs. Such programs should equip educators with the necessary knowledge and skills to effectively teach and engage students with mathematical concepts, particularly in advanced areas like Euclidean geometry. The need for stretching and enriching content in university courses aligns with the importance of continuous professional development (CPD) to enhance novice teachers' proficiency and flexibility in teaching mathematics. P1 exemplifies a pragmatic problem-solving approach, relying on trial and error. However, they acknowledge a limitation that may hinder his problem-solving and leads to giving up. P1's reliance on trial and error suggests a need for additional problem-solving strategies or a broader knowledge base. This, in turn, could help P1 overcome limitations that currently lead to abandoning problem-solving attempts.

> [P1] "I used trial and error to solve and if the information that I have is limited, then I cannot solve that problem."

P1's case exemplifies the potential negative impact of past educational experiences on future problem-solving approaches. He attributed his difficulty to a teaching style in his younger years that discouraged finding multiple solutions and rewarded only the first attempt. This instilled a fear of deviating from conventional methods, even when encountering problems conducive to multiple approaches. P1's experience emphasizes the influence of the educational approaches on students' problem-solving strategies and suggests the potential detrimental effects on creativity and exploration in mathematical problem-solving.

> [P1] We are discouraged from doing that [find multiple solutions]. At a young age, I used to attempt questions differently the teacher will say I will mark the first solution … so even if we are exposed to other questions, we are still afraid to do that [find multiple solutions].

P1's utterance raises important questions about how teacher training programs can prepare an environment that encourages experimentation, exploration of multiple solutions, and the use of varied problem-solving strategies. Such an environment would foster a more inclusive and creative learning atmosphere for PSTs. Furthermore, P1's experience exemplifies the potential drawbacks of an instructional approach that emphasizes applying fixed procedures in Euclidean geometry. According to P1, this approach hindered his ability to find multiple solutions to problems within the domain of MST problem-solving. This suggests a need for teacher training programs to move beyond a purely procedural approach to geometry, instead emphasizing the development of flexible problem-solving skills.

> [P1] I think, uh, it is the procedure that, eh, Euclidean geometry was introduced to us. That's the problem, eh, they only taught us to solve using the procedure and less application.

P4 also highlighted his own initial reluctance to change his established problem-solving methods. Reflecting on his experiences as a teacher, P4 observed a general tendency among educators to rely on previously successful methods for familiar problems. He attributed this reluctance to the comfort and efficiency associated with established approaches. However, P4 further noted that this familiarity can become restrictive, hindering teachers' exploration of new knowledge and approaches. This resistance to change may ultimately limit a teacher's professional growth and their ability to present different problem-solving strategies to their students.

> [P4] ... in my experience was that us as teachers sometimes we become reluctant in finding other ways of doing things or solving problems better to a particular problem. Most of the questions that were in the task were questions that I have seen before. So, because I have seen them before and found the solution in a particular way, I become restricted and only use that particular method to find the solution. So, I think that we become reluctant to equip ourselves and finding new knowledge in terms of how we can do things better. We become resistant to change because it has always been working.

This emphasizes the importance of developing a growth mindset among teachers, encouraging them to explore new methods and embrace change for the benefit of their own professional development and the enriched learning experiences of their students. Another challenge was that teachers lacked the initiation of collaborating with other teachers to look for better solution strategies.

> [P4] Also again, one more point is that we [teachers] tend to do things in isolation, we do not collaborate with other teachers to find out how they do things in their classroom, or which other methods do they use to solve geometry problems in their classrooms.

This study highlights valuable insights for both individual learning and instructional design in teacher training. The findings emphasize the importance of equipping PSTs with different problem-solving techniques to navigate a variety of problems. All novice teachers in this study indicated that a strong foundation in Euclidean geometry is crucial, as deficiencies in this area can hinder their ability to find multiple solutions.

4.3 Theme 3: Novice Teachers' Perspectives on the Benefits of MST Problem-Solving

This study investigated novice teachers' perspectives on the benefits of finding multiple solutions through MST problem-solving. The findings revealed that novice teachers considered MST problem-solving to be an important element of teacher knowledge for several reasons. P3 and P4 specifically highlighted the potential for

MST to promote student autonomy in choosing solution strategies. They viewed this approach as empowering students to move beyond relying on teacher-demonstrated or textbook methods. Furthermore, the novice teachers emphasized how MST problem-solving can portray problem-solving as a flexible and creative process, not merely the application of a fixed procedure.

> [P4] It does not mean that the teachers' way is the only way to solve a particular problem… It also gives learners confidence that there are different ways of responding to a question and not be restricted to one way of doing things [solving problems], [P3] …we explored about three to four methods of solving one problem so that learners could have options and the second reason was so that those who find a certain method difficult can find something else that they will be accustomed to.

P3 specifically emphasized the value of MST problem-solving in equipping students with a repertoire of problem-solving strategies. This allows students encountering difficulty with one approach to leverage a more understandable alternative strategy to solve the problem.

> [P4] … It triggers learners to be self-directed in their learning and allows them to look for information, that can help them find information on their own and devise strategies to solve problems that work for them in particular… It also opens a door for flexibility, the next person will know that mathematics is not for people that think in a certain way, but everyone can use their knowledge to find a solution to a problem.

This analysis highlights the potential of MST problem-solving to develop essential twenty-first-century skills in students. P4 specifically emphasized the value of MST in promoting autonomy, self-directed learning, and flexibility in problem-solving. These skills are increasingly important for success in today's digital world. Furthermore, P4 suggested that engaging in MST problem-solving can help to dispel the notion of mathematics as a subject accessible only to a select few. This can foster a more inclusive learning environment and broaden student perceptions of mathematics.

Multiple participants (P2, P3, and P4) emphasized the value of MST problem-solving in fostering a deeper understanding of mathematical connections between topics. P4 specifically noted that the ability to generate multiple solutions enhances a teacher's capacity to explain concepts effectively to others, P2 concurred. This highlights the pedagogical value of MST problem-solving, as it equips teachers to communicate mathematical ideas more effectively. Furthermore, P3 and P4 both observed that finding multiple solutions can help teachers identify relationships between mathematical topics, potentially even fostering connections across different subjects. This suggests that MST problem-solving can promote a broader understanding of how mathematical concepts interconnect, enriching the teacher's perspective and potentially fostering interdisciplinary learning.

> [P4] It develops conceptual understanding … I think I would really appreciate being able to produce multiple solutions to mathematical problems or geometry problems because I think it provides a high chance of conceptual understanding whether explaining to the next person or developing yourself as a teacher; [P2] definitely, it shows understanding … you are representing it in different ways and with valid reasons why it can be done this way and that

way. It shows deep understanding of the problem. [P4] ... for better conceptual understanding and also in linking relationships between topics or linking relationships between geometry and other fields or subjects; [P3] I'd have to look into other topics, meaning I'd move away from the domain of this topic and move into other topics and look at how they integrate or build a linkage with the current topic or problem.

Another benefit of MST problem-solving was observed when P4 emphasized the importance of keeping student learning at the forefront *"one should keep in mind that what we are doing here, it is actually for the benefit of the learners,"* suggesting that finding multiple solutions can positively impact students' learning outcomes. This aligns with broader educational philosophies that advocate for student-focused teaching practices designed to facilitate meaningful learning experiences and a deeper understanding of mathematical concepts. Furthermore, P3's experience exemplifies the intellectually stimulating and motivating potential of MST problem-solving. He highlighted not only a deeper understanding of specific theorems but also a rekindled and expanded knowledge of mathematics overall. For P3, engaging in MST problem-solving became a dynamic process of learning, application, and rediscovery, contributing to a more enriched and interconnected understanding of mathematical concepts.

[P3] It was a, how do I put it, it was a thrilling experience because it pushed me to get a much greater understanding of corollary theorems, I had to understand those because I was not that big on them, so it pushed me to learn more about them and how to use them, and also it became an eye-opener on a lot of things that I had actually forgotten, so it pushed me to learn more or re-learn some of the things that I have actually done because it has been actually a while since I have done riders before.

P4 emphasizes the importance of recognizing student diversity in learning. His statement, *"we must always remember we are teaching learners with different thinking capacities and different levels of knowledge and also that have different ways of thinking,"* emphasizes the need for an inclusive, adaptable, and student-centered approach in teaching. Recognizing and respecting the variations in students' thinking abilities, knowledge levels, and cognitive styles is crucial for creating a positive and effective learning environment that caters to all students.

[P2] The more you interact with such problems, [MSTs] the more you broaden your thinking, so now if an unfamiliar problem comes, you will have the experience of solving problems differently. It's like adding more spanners to your toolbox. [P1] I have looked not only to expand my knowledge and also to solve the problem. Maybe in future, if it comes again, I want to solve it; that's also part of expanding knowledge.

P2 emphasized the multifaceted benefits of engaging with MST problem-solving, extending beyond finding immediate solutions. This process fosters broader thinking, acquisition of diverse problem-solving strategies, knowledge expansion, and development of skills applicable to future problems. P2's metaphorical imagery aptly describes accruing a varied toolkit of problem-solving approaches through MST experiences. However, P4 highlighted the importance of efficiency in certain contexts. He noted that MST problem-solving can equip students with the ability to find the quickest solution, particularly valuable in time-constrained situations like formal assessments.

[P4] …I think that teachers should keep in mind that it is not about finding all the solutions but finding a quicker way to respond to the question.

The following section builds upon the study's findings by discussing their connection to existing literature and the implications for WIL programs related to mathematics teacher training.

5 Discussion

This study identified a lack of Euclidean geometry knowledge as a critical barrier to MST problem-solving among novice teachers. These findings align with previous research on experienced teachers struggling with cognitively demanding tasks (Bansilal et al., 2014). The participants attributed their difficulties to insufficient pre-service training in both MST problem-solving and Euclidean geometry, echoing concerns raised by van der Sandt and Nieuwoudt (2005) and Alex (2019). These studies suggest that limitations in university curricula may contribute to graduating PSTs' weak Euclidean geometry knowledge, hindering their problem-solving abilities. In response, teacher training institutions should consider revising mathematics PST curricula to equip future teachers with the necessary knowledge and skills. Revised curricula should integrate components that focus on MST problem-solving and higher-order mathematical tasks, while simultaneously bridging the gap between theoretical knowledge and practical application. Furthermore, WIL experiences should be incorporated to provide opportunities for deepening content knowledge, particularly in Euclidean geometry. Collaboration with experienced educators and mathematicians through workshops, seminars, and practical sessions can further enhance PSTs' mathematical proficiency. By implementing these revisions, teacher training programs can prepare graduates to effectively engage with MST problem-solving and foster deeper student learning in mathematics.

This analysis revealed a critical challenge that limited Euclidean geometry knowledge led most novice teachers to rely on analogous problem-solving strategies, evident in their task sheets. These teachers predominantly used "orthodox" approaches, often unsuccessful for MSTs problems which typically require "unorthodox" approaches (Leikin, 2011). This aligns with one teacher's interview, highlighting resistance to changing established methods as a barrier to MST problem-solving success. These findings suggest novice teachers' dependence on *crystallized expertise* rather than the *fluid expertise* needed for MSTs (Leikin, 2011), potentially reflecting the influence of epistemic emotions (Di Leo et al., 2019) and existing belief systems (Schoenfeld, 1985) on problem-solving. To address these challenges, WIL experiences should be designed to equip future educators with the necessary flexibility and adaptability. These experiences should promote *fluid expertise* by encouraging exploration of diverse solution strategies and adaptation to different contexts. Teacher trainers should also acknowledge that emotions, such as fear or discomfort with new approaches, can inhibit effective problem-solving. Therefore, WIL environments should be positive and supportive, encouraging PSTs to step outside their comfort zones and embrace new approaches without fear of failure. Furthermore, WIL experiences should develop a growth mindset among PSTs, helping them understand that problem-solving abilities can be developed and improved over time. By emphasizing that making mistakes and trying new approaches are essential steps in the learning process, WIL programs can prepare future educators to excel at MST problem-solving.

Despite challenges in finding multiple solutions, novice teachers' experiences highlighted the significance of MST problem-solving proficiency. They recognized its potential to enhance flexible thinking, aligning with findings by Silver (1997) and Guberman and Leikin (2013). Furthermore, they believed their ability to solve problems in various ways could improve student learning by demonstrating the existence of multiple approaches beyond textbook methods. As one teacher (P2) stated, it equips them with a broader *toolbox* of problem-solving strategies, mirroring the experiences of participants in Silver et al.'s (2005) study. Leikin (2011) further suggests that MST problem-solving can provide students with opportunities to learn new mathematical knowledge as the teachers in this study mentioned.

Novice teachers also saw the potential of MST problem-solving to enhance their teaching practice. They believed it could allow for differentiation of instruction to cater to diverse student needs, emphasizing the importance of context-specific solutions. Additionally, they felt MST problem-solving could equip them with the ability to tackle unfamiliar problems efficiently, broadening their skillset and preparing them for future challenges (Mahlaba, 2021). These skills would be particularly valuable during WIL experiences, allowing them to explain content using different methods. Finally, novice teachers perceived benefits for their own mathematical development, including increased flexibility in problem-solving, deeper conceptual understanding of Euclidean geometry, and broader thinking. These findings align with previous studies that engaged teachers in MST problem-solving (Guberman & Leikin, 2013; Silver, 1997; Silver et al., 2005).

Novice teachers recognized that MST problem-solving can bridge connections between different mathematical disciplines. They observed that problems in Euclidean geometry could potentially be solved using algebraic or trigonometric methods. This aligns with research by Guberman and Leikin (2013), Leikin (2011), Levav-Waynberg and Leikin (2009, 2012) demonstrating the application of knowledge and strategies from various mathematical domains through MSTs. Szabo et al. (2020) further emphasize the importance of viewing mathematics as interconnected, not isolated disciplines. This resonates with the WIL's goal of preparing future educators to collaborate effectively across disciplines, a common practice in professional settings. For instance, STEM education highlights the value of interdisciplinary collaboration (Martín-Páez et al., 2019). Thus, equipping PSTs with the ability to solve problems across domains through MSTs is crucial.

6 Closing Thoughts

Findings of this study revealed that novice teachers struggled with MST problem-solving due to various reasons. However, they held a conviction that MST problem-solving constitutes a fundamental competency indispensable for both teachers' execution of professional duties and personal cognitive benefits. This study identified several challenges faced by novice teachers in MST problem-solving. While they recognized the importance of MSTs for both professional practice and personal cognitive development, their solutions often relied heavily on analogous approaches based on procedural similarity. Additionally, faulty geometrical reasoning and limited content knowledge, potentially due to prior training deficiencies, further hampered their abilities to find multiple solutions. These factors suggest a lack of diverse problem-solving strategies. Despite these struggles, the teachers' lived experiences highlighted the potential benefits of MSTs, including fostering flexible thinking, enriching problem-solving repertoires, deepening geometrical understanding, and promoting broader thinking skills. Ultimately, MSTs can equip teachers to solve novel problems efficiently, broaden their skillsets, MST problem-solving can bridge connections between different mathematical disciplines, and prepare them for future problems, ultimately benefiting both teachers and students in their mathematical learning journeys. Novice teachers acknowledged the pedagogical value of MST problem-solving, perceiving it as a tool to enhance their teaching strategies and expose students to diverse problem-solving approaches beyond textbooks, fostering deeper learning. However, they expressed concerns regarding integration into daily lessons due to prescribed curriculum pacing and potential misalignment with assessments focused solely on achieving high grades.

Results from this study had several WIL implications for teacher training institutions. The observation that novice teachers struggled with MST problem-solving due to limited geometry content knowledge implies a need for targeted PD programs for novice teachers. However, for PSTs, WIL initiatives could play a role in providing opportunities to engage in MST problem-solving to enrich their geometry content knowledge. This would help them become more effective in handling MST problem-solving scenarios and aligning their classroom practices with the curriculum requirements. Thus, mathematics teacher training institutions should consider integrating MST problem-solving into their programs. This integration could enhance the readiness of future teachers to engage in effective mathematics teaching, equipping them with valuable problem-solving skills. WIL programs can provide a platform for such research and serve as a bridge between academic research and practical classroom application. Understanding the contextual nuances of MST problem-solving in South African educational settings can inform more tailored and effective teacher training strategies.

While MST problem-solving is acknowledged for its pedagogical and cognitive merits, it should not be seen as a standalone solution. WIL initiatives can emphasize the importance of integrating MST problem-solving with a range of other effective teaching and learning strategies. This balanced approach ensures that teachers are equipped with a diverse toolkit for improving both their content knowledge and problem-solving abilities. The study findings also emphasize that there should be an emphasis on reflective practice within WIL experiences. WIL experiences should encourage PSTs to reflect on their challenges during MST problem-solving and how their preservice training can be improved. These reflective experiences can also include regular reflection on their problem-solving processes, identifying areas where they may be resistant to change or where their prior knowledge is limiting them.

The study proposes recommendations for both research and teacher training. First, future research could involve a PD program where teachers enrich their geometry knowledge through MST problem-solving. Second, investigating how teachers integrate MSTs in South African classrooms would provide a contextual understanding of their implementation and related challenges. Finally, further research could explore teachers' experiences after incorporating MST problem-solving. Regarding teacher training, incorporating MST problem-solving into curricula would expose PSTs to diverse problem-solving strategies. We neither conclude that MST problem-solving is superior to other methods in improving teachers' geometry knowledge nor assume that it is more effective in improving teachers' problem-solving strategies and abilities. We rather recommend that MST problem-solving be integrated with a pool of other rich teaching and learning strategies proven to be effective in developing teachers' knowledge and problem-solving strategies.

Funding National Research Foundation Thuthuka Grant number: TTK2204113056.

Appendix

https://drive.google.com/file/d/1BcP8hdRNWB8prLJjy9ehF_frmA0dnV36/view?usp=sharing.

References

Åkerlind, G. S. (2012). Variation and commonality in phenomenographic research methods. *Higher Education Research & Development, 31*(1), 115–127. https://doi.org/10.1080/07294360.2011.642845

Alex, J. K. (2019). The preparation of secondary school mathematics teachers in South Africa: Prospective teachers' student level disciplinary content knowledge. *Eurasia Journal of Mathematics, Science and Technology Education, 15*(12).

Baier, F., Decker, A.-T., Voss, T., Kleickmann, T., Klusmann, U., & Kunter, M. (2019). What makes a good teacher? The relative importance of mathematics teachers' cognitive ability, personality, knowledge, beliefs, and motivation for instructional quality. *British Journal of Educational Psychology, 89*(4), 767–786.

Bansilal, S., Mkhwanazi, T., & Brijlall, D. (2014). An exploration of the common content knowledge of high school mathematics teachers. *Perspectives in Education, 32*(1), 34–50.

Bansilal, S., & Ubah, I. (2019). The use of semiotic representations in reasoning about similar triangles in Euclidean geometry. *Pythagoras, 40*(1), 1–10.

Boaler, J., Brown, K., LaMar, T., Leshin, M., & Selbach-Allen, M. (2022). Infusing mindset through mathematical problem-solving and collaboration: Studying the impact of a short college intervention. *Education Sciences, 12*(10), 694.

Chapman, O. (1999). Inservice teacher development in mathematical problem-solving. *Journal of Mathematics Teacher Education, 2*(2), 121–142.

Chirinda, B. (2021). Professional development for teachers' mathematical problem-solving pedagogy—What counts? *Pythagoras—Journal of the Association for Mathematics Education of South Africa, 42*(1). https://doi.org/10.4102/pythagoras.v42i1.532

Chirinda, B., & Barmby, P. (2017). The development of a professional development intervention for mathematical problem-solving pedagogy in a localised context. *Pythagoras, 38*(1), 1–11.

Chirinda, B., & Barmby, P. (2018). South African Grade 9 mathematics teachers' views on the teaching of problem-solving. *African Journal of Research in Mathematics, Science and Technology Education, 22*(1), 114–124.

Cohen, L., Manion, L., & Morrison, K. (2018). *Research methods in education.* Routledge.

Copur-Gencturk, Y., Tolar, T., Jacobson, E., & Fan, W. (2019). An empirical study of the dimensionality of the mathematical knowledge for teaching construct. *Journal of Teacher Education, 70*(5), 485–497.

Department of Basic Education (DBE). (2011). Curriculum and assessment policy statement: Mathematics Grade 10 - 12. Government Printers.

De Villiers, M., & Heideman, N. (2014). Conjecturing, refuting, and proving within the context of dynamic geometry. *Learning and Teaching Mathematics, 2014*(17), 20–26.

Di Leo, I., Muis, K. R., Singh, C. A., & Psaradellis, C. (2019). Curiosity… Confusion? Frustration! The role and sequencing of emotions during mathematics problem-solving. *Contemporary Educational Psychology, 58*, 121–137.

Doğan-Temur, Ö. (2012). Analysis of prospective classroom teachers' teaching of mathematical modeling and problem-solving. *Eurasia Journal of Mathematics, Science and Technology Education, 8*(2), 83–93.

Dreher, A., Lindmeier, A., Heinze, A., & Niemand, C. (2018). What kind of content knowledge do secondary mathematics teachers need? *Journal für Mathematik-Didaktik, 39*(2), 319–341.

Dweck, C. S. (2015). Growth. *British Journal of Educational Psychology, 85*(2), 242–245.

Ford, M. I. (1994). Teachers' beliefs about mathematical problem-solving in the elementary school. *School Science and Mathematics, 94*(6), 314–322.

Frechette, J., Bitzas, V., Aubry, M., Kilpatrick, K., & Lavoie-Tremblay, M. (2020). Capturing lived experience: Methodological considerations for interpretive phenomenological inquiry. *International Journal of Qualitative Methods, 19*, 1–12.

Gagné, R. M. (1965). *The conditions of learning.* Holt.

Guberman, R., & Leikin, R. (2013). Interesting and difficult mathematical problems: Changing teachers' views by employing multiple-solution tasks. *Journal of Mathematics Teacher Education, 16*(1), 33–56.

Halmos, P. R. (1980). The heart of mathematics. *The American Mathematical Monthly, 87*(7), 519–524.

Jackson, D., Shan, H., & Meek, S. (2022). Enhancing graduates' enterprise capabilities through work-integrated learning in co-working spaces. *Higher Education, 84*, 101–120.

Jacob, B., Frenzel, A. C., & Stephens, E. J. (2017). Good teaching feels good—But what is "good teaching"? Exploring teachers' definitions of teaching success in mathematics. *ZDM—Mathematics Education, 49*(3), 461–473.

Jagals, D., & Van der Walt, M. (2016). Enabling metacognitive skills for mathematics problem-solving: A collective case study of metacognitive reflection and awareness. *African Journal of Research in Mathematics, Science and Technology Education, 20*(2), 154–164.

Juta, A., & Van Wyk, C. (2020). Classroom management as a response to challenges in mathematics education: Experiences from a province in South Africa. *African Journal of Research in Mathematics, Science and Technology Education, 24*(1), 21–30.

Kilpatrick, J. (1969). Problem-solving and creative behavior in mathematics. In J. W. Wilson & L. R. Carey (Eds.), *Reviews of recent research in mathematics* (Vol. 19, pp. 153–187). School Mathematics Study Group.

Kokot, S. (2005). Addressing giftedness. In E. Landsberg, D. Kruger, & N. Nel (Eds.), *Addressing barriers to learning: A South African perspective* (pp. 469–484). Van Schaik Publishers.

Lampert, M. (1990). When the problem is not the question, and the solution is not the answer: Mathematical knowing and teaching. *American Educational Research Journal, 27*(1), 29–63.

Leikin, R. (2011). Multiple-solution tasks: from a teacher education course to teacher practice. *ZDM—Mathematics Education, 43*(6), 993–1006.

Leikin, R. (2014). Challenging mathematics with multiple solution tasks and mathematical investigations in geometry. In Y. Li, E. Silver, & S. Li (Eds.), *Transforming mathematics instruction*. Advances in mathematics education. Cham: Springer. https://doi.org/10.1007/978-3-319-049 93-9_5

Levav-Waynberg, A., & Leikin, R. (2009). Multiple solutions to a problem: A tool for assessment of mathematical thinking in geometry. Paper presented at the *Sixth Conference of the European Society for Research in Mathematics Education (CERME-6)*.

Levav-Waynberg, A., & Leikin, R. (2012). Using multiple solution tasks for the evaluation of students' problem-solving performance in geometry. *Canadian Journal of Science, Mathematics and Technology Education, 12*(4), 311–333.

Mahlaba, S. C. (2020). The state of South African mathematics education: Situating the hidden promise of multiple-solution tasks. *EURASIA Journal of Mathematics, Science and Technology Education, 16*(12), 1–12.

Mahlaba, S. C. (2021). Assessing pre-service mathematics teachers' problem-solving proficiency using multiple-solution tasks: An imperative for self-directed learning. In E. Mentz, D. Laubscher, & J. Olivier (Eds.), *Self-directed learning: An imperative for education in a complex society* (Vol. 6, pp. 211–242). AOSIS.

Martín-Páez, T., Aguilera, D., Perales-Palacios, F. J., & Vílchez-González, J. M. (2019). What are we talking about when we talk about STEM education? A review of literature. *Science Education, 103*(4), 799–822.

Marton, F. (1986). Phenomenography: A research approach investigating different understandings of reality. *Journal of Thought, 21*(3), 28–49.

Mhlolo, M. K. (2017). Regular classroom teachers' recognition and support of the creative potential of mildly gifted mathematics learners. *ZDM—Mathematics Education, 49*(1), 81–94.

Miles, M. B., Huberman, M., & Saldana, J. (2014). *Qualitative data analysis: A method sourcebook*. Sage.

Petersen, N., du Toit, A., Mentz, E., & Balfour, R. J. (Eds.). (2023). *Innovative curriculum design: Bridging the theory–practice divide in work-integrated learning to foster self-directed learning*. OASIS.

Planas, N., & Setati-Phakeng, M. (2014). On the process of gaining language as a resource in mathematics education. *ZDM—Mathematics Education, 46*(6), 883–893.

Polya, G. (1973). *How to solve it: A new aspect of mathematics method*. Princeton University Press.

Saldaňa, J. (2009). *The coding manual for qualitative researchers* (Vol. 3). Sage.

Schoenfeld, A. H. (1985). *Mathematical problem-solving*. Academic Press, Inc.

Schoenfeld, A. H. (1991). What's all the fuss about problem-solving. *Zentrallblatt für Didaktik der Mathematik, 91*(1), 4–8.

Schoenfeld, A. H. (1992). Learning to think mathematically: Problem-solving, metacognition, and sense making in mathematics. In D. Grouws (Ed.), *Handbook for research on mathematics teaching and learning* (pp. 334–370). Macmillan.

Schoenfeld, A. H. (1994). What do we know about mathematics curricula? *The Journal of Mathematical Behavior, 13*(1), 55–80.

Semanišinová, I. (2021). Multiple-solution tasks in pre-service teachers course on combinatorics. *Mathematics, 9*(18), 2286.

Shulman, L. S. (1986). Those who understand: Knowledge growth in teaching. *Educational Researcher, 15*(2), 4–14.

Sibanda, L., & Graven, M. (2018). Can mathematics assessments be considered valid if learners fail to access what is asked of them? *South African Journal of Childhood Education, 8*(1), 1–12.

Silver, E. A. (1997). Fostering creativity through instruction rich in mathematical problem-solving and problem posing. *ZDM—Mathematics Education, 29*(3), 75–80.

Silver, E. A., Ghousseini, H., Gosen, D., Charalambous, C., & Strawhun, B. T. F. (2005). Moving from rhetoric to praxis: Issues faced by teachers in having students consider multiple solutions for problems in the mathematics classroom. *The Journal of Mathematical Behavior, 24*(3), 287–301.

Son, J.-W., & Lee, M. Y. (2021). Exploring the relationship between preservice teachers' conceptions of problem-solving and their problem-solving performances. *International Journal of Science and Mathematics Education, 19*(1), 129–150.

Spaull, N., & Jansen, J. D. (2019). *South African schooling: The enigma of inequality*. Springer.

Stein, M. K., & Smith, M. (1998). Mathematical tasks as a framework for reflection: From research to practice. *Mathematics Teaching in the Middle School, 3*(4), 268–275.

Stirling, A., Kerr, G., Banwell, J., MacPherson, E., & Heron, A. (2016). *A practical guide for work-integrated learning: Effective practices to enhance the educational quality of structured work experiences offered through colleges and universities*. Higher Education Quality Council of Ontario.

Stupel, M., & Ben-Chaim, D. (2017). Using multiple solutions to mathematical problems to develop pedagogical and mathematical thinking: A case study in a teacher education program. *Investigations in Mathematics Learning, 9*(2), 86–108.

Szabo, Z. K., Körtesi, P., Guncaga, J., Szabo, D., & Neag, R. (2020). Examples of problem-solving strategies in mathematics education supporting the sustainability of 21st-century skills. *Sustainability, 12*(23), 10113.

Tachie, S. A. (2020). The challenges of South African teachers in teaching Euclidean geometry. *International Journal of Learning, Teaching and Educational Research, 19*(8), 297–312.

Taylor, N. (2019). Inequalities in teacher knowledge in South Africa. In N. Spaull & J. D. Jansen (Eds.), *South African schooling: The enigma of inequality: A study of the present situation and future possibilities* (pp. 263–282). Springer.

Taylor, N. (2021). The dream of Sisyphus: Mathematics education in South Africa. *South African Journal of Childhood Education, 11*(1), 1–12.

Tekkumru-Kisa, M., Stein, M. K., & Doyle, W. (2020). Theory and research on tasks revisited: Task as a context for students' thinking in the era of ambitious reforms in mathematics and science. *Educational Researcher, 49*(8), 606–617.

van der Sandt, S., & Nieuwoudt, H. D. (2005). Geometry content knowledge: Is pre-service training making a difference? *African Journal of Research in Mathematics, Science and Technology Education, 9*(2), 109–120.

Work Integrated Learning in the Forest: The Journey of a Science Educator

Tara M. Goodhue

Abstract This chapter outlines my journey as an educator as I immersed myself in the Harvard Forest's Schoolyard Ecology Long Term Ecological Research (LTER) Program. This program supports teachers and students in collecting authentic ecological field data right in their own schoolyards. I have been involved with three projects through the Harvard Forest since 2016: the "Our Changing Forests" project, which tracks forest composition over time, "Woolly Bully: The Hemlock Woolly Adelgid" which examines the relationship between tree growth and infestation of an invasive species, and "Buds, Leaves, and Global Warming," which tracks the growing season of trees on the school campus. I use a work-integrated learning (WIL) lens to gain a deeper understanding of my own experiences, practices, and perspectives within this specific context. A self-study design was used to determine how my self-perception as an educator shifted as a result of participation in this program, the insights I gained from this experience that helped to inform other, similar partnerships between scientists and my students, and also how the project helped to transform relationships I have with my students. Five main themes emerged through the analysis of qualitative data: membership in a sustained schoolyard science project increased my content knowledge, my confidence in designing transformational learning experiences for students increased through schoolyard science participation. standardized testing and other school calendar factors limit the amount of time spent on schoolyard science projects, working with authentic data sets gives students exposure to technical skills they do not have access to in regular high school curriculum, and experiential outdoor learning is joyful for both teachers and students.

Keywords STEM · Schoolyard science · Communities of practice · Work integrated learning · Science practices · Mentoring

T. M. Goodhue (✉)
University of Massachusetts, Lowell, MA, USA
e-mail: Tara_Goodhue@uml.edu

1 Introduction

This chapter follows my journey as I began a schoolyard excursion into science. My name is Tara, and I began teaching high school science in 2008. I have been passionate about the outdoors since I was a child, spending a large part of my childhood in the woods in back of the house where I grew up in northern Massachusetts. As an adult, I love to spend time hiking, gardening, and simply immersing myself in the outdoors observing animals and identifying plants. One of the main reasons why I chose to become a science teacher was to share my love of the outdoors with my students. I live in New England, where we enjoy four seasons and have a variety of ecosystems. Most students I have taught throughout my career come from Lowell, which is a richly diverse city that was the cradle of the Industrial Revolution in the United States. My students come to my class with a wide range of experiences with the outdoors, from students who regularly go on camping trips with their families to those who rarely spend time outdoors and have little access to green spaces. Lowell is made up of eight main neighborhoods which have considerable socioeconomic divides. The higher income neighborhoods have a lot of tree cover and access to parks, while the lower income neighborhoods have little access to parks and also little tree cover.

In 2016, my ninth-grade science students' scores on the state biology dropped to an all-time low. This was a significant issue, as a passing score on the state biology assessment is needed for students to achieve a high school diploma. Students need a minimum score to qualify for the Abigail Adams Scholarship, which waives tuition to all state-funded universities. Disenchanted with direct instruction and teacher-driven test-prep curriculum, I set out to find a way to engage my students and to make science come alive for them, which I believed would help my students to be more successful on the exam. Recalling that a former university professor had talked about citizen science, where students could collect authentic data and help to contribute to "real" scientific research, I decided to reach out to the Harvard Forest (Harvard University's 4000 acre experimental forest and research center) to get information about their Schoolyard Ecology program. This led me to engage with a rich community of educators, scientists, and environmental activists who were passionate about sharing their knowledge of science, data, and transformative learning experiences for students of all levels.

Faced with competing mandates and initiatives from the local, state, and federal level, schools struggle to find the time to offer content-specific professional development (PD) to their teachers. Local content -specific professional development is rare, and many schools are still in the nascent phases of offering time for professional learning communities to collaborate and engage in meaningful work. As a result, teachers are forced to seek content-specific professional development outside of their districts. Citizen science projects, also known as participatory science projects, bring teachers and scientists together, which creates the perfect foundation for science-specific PD. Additionally, teachers may be involved with these projects for years, which gives them a sustained, supportive network to develop as both teachers and as scientists.

In this chapter, I explore the schoolyard science projects offered by the Harvard Forest using a work-integrated learning lens in an effort to understand how my participation has shaped me as an educator. Next, I will discuss the affordances and barriers to the implementation of such projects. Lastly, I will discuss the power that schoolyard science has to transform relationships between teachers and students.

The following research questions will be addressed in this chapter:

1. How has my self-perception as a science educator shifted throughout my sustained engagement in this project?
2. What insights can be drawn from my experiences that might inform the future implementation of similar sustained schoolyard science initiatives?
3. In what ways has my relationship with my students evolved as a consequence of my deep involvement in the project?

2 School Context

Lowell is a mid-sized city situated on the Merrimack River in northern Massachusetts, which is a state in the northeast of the United States. Lowell experiences four distinct seasons: a beautiful autumn with incredible foliage, a (usually) cold and snowy winter, a rainy spring when flowers begin to bloom, and a hot and humid summer. Lowell was the first planned industrial city in the United States and is considered the cradle of the Industrial Revolution. Today, it is home to over 100,000 residents, 48% of whom are White, 9% Black, 22% Asian, 18% Hispanic, and 3% multi-race (United States Census Bureau, 2022). Long known for embracing immigrants, today Cambodian and Brazilians account for over a third of the more than 30,000 foreign-born residents (New American Economy, 2019).

I have spent my entire teaching career working with Lowell students. From 2008 to 2022, I taught science at Greater Lowell Technical High School (GLTHS), which is located in the suburban town of Tyngsboro. GLTHS is a public, regional technical high school that any student from Lowell or the surrounding communities of Dracut, Dunstable, and Tyngsboro may apply to. GLTHS gives students a rigorous academic education which prepares them for college, and a technical education in a shop or trade of the students' choice which prepares them for careers. This makes the school attractive for many students. Admission is competitive. At the time of the study, the student body was 45% White, 3% Black, 16% Asian, 32% Hispanic, and 4% Multi-Race. Sixty three percent of the student body was classified as high needs, which includes low-income students, English learners, and students with disabilities (DESE, 2023). GLTHS is situated on a seventy-acre campus that includes forests, fields, and a stream.

In 2022, I accepted a new position teaching science at Lowell High School in downtown Lowell, which is Lowell's mainstream public high school. Lowell High is also located by the Merrimack River but could not be more different despite the mere five-mile difference. Lowell High is located right in downtown Lowell and consists of four separate buildings. Between the "1980 building" and the "1920" building is a canal that once helped to power the city's textile mills. The canal is surrounded by Lucy Larcom Park, which is owned by the Lowell National Historical Park. The student body is richly diverse, with 21% White, 7.6% Black, 26.7% Asian, 39.6% Hispanic, and 4.1% Multi-Race at the time of the study. Eighty-three percent of students were identified as high needs, which is a stark contrast to 55% of students across the state in the same category.

3 Science Curriculum Frameworks in the United States

The Science, Technology, and Engineering curriculum frameworks for Massachusetts, released in 2016, are based on the Next Generation Science Standards (NGSS), which were first released in 2013. NGSS is a result of a multi-state effort across the United States to develop new education standards that are "rich in content and practice, arranged in a coherent manner across disciplines and grades to provide all students an internationally benchmarked science education" (NGSS Lead States, 2013). They include both content standards and science practices, which are "behaviors that scientists engage in as they investigate and build models and theories about the natural world and the key set of engineering practices that engineers use as they design and build models and systems" (NSTA, 2014).

4 Citizen Science

Citizen science is a collaboration between scientists and members of the public, where large quantities of data are collected across a variety of habitats over time and the results are used in scientific studies (Bonney et al., 2009). Ecological research requires large sets of data and is commonly associated with citizen science. It is an ideal vehicle for authentic scientific experiences in the classroom. Citizen science is a powerful tool to educate people of basic scientific processes and concepts in a society that is becoming increasingly technological (Brossard et al., 2005).

Although the term "citizen science" is widely used in the literature, it is slowly being phased out for more inclusive language (Ellwood et al., 2023). Since 2007, there has been a debate over the terms "citizen science" versus "community science" which reflected the extent to which scientific projects reflect the priorities of the community. Alternatives such as "collaborative science" and "participatory science" are becoming more common because these terms are inclusive of all people regardless of their citizenship status.

4.1 Schoolyard Ecology

Schoolyard ecology refers to citizen science projects that are conducted within the confines of a school's outdoor spaces. In schoolyard science, the schoolyard becomes the subject of science lessons and is rigorously studied by students in their science classes year after year, which can result in valuable long-term data sets that are maintained by students. Collecting long-term ecological datasets can be challenging. For one, field research is often conducted by graduate students, who often move to different projects and sites upon graduation. Trees do not grow quickly, so collecting data that paints a complete picture of their life cycles takes decades. It can be difficult to find people to collect these data consistently over time. Aiming to remedy this issue and to build environmental awareness was a key rationale behind the development of the Harvard Forest's Schoolyard Science program. Founded in 2004, this is part of a national network of sites that supports K-12 teachers and students in ecological research (Harvard Forest, 2021). These programs are supported by the National Science Foundation's Long Term Ecological Research (LTER) network, which includes 28 field sites that conduct decades-long ecological research studies.

The Harvard Forest's Schoolyard Ecology program has three main projects that schools can participate in. The *Buds, Leaves, and Global Warming* project invites students to study a particular branch on a tree in the spring to observe the specific date of "budburst" and the specific date of "leaf drop," which allows them to calculate the length of the growing season. Through project *Woolly Bully: The Invasive Pest, the Hemlock Woolly Adelgid,* students track the number of eggs the invasive insect, the Hemlock Woolly Adelgid, lays on hemlock tree branches and then measures how much the branch grows in a year. The *Our Changing Forest* project has teachers set up a forest plot on the schoolground. Trees are tagged in the plot, and then students go out to identify all of the trees in the plot and measure the diameter at breast height, which allows students to calculate the amount of carbon stored in the trees. Participating in these projects over time allows students to observe long-term trends and patterns and discover how they respond to ecological disturbances.

Teachers who participate in the Schoolyard Ecology program attend a summer institute where they are trained on the projects, a winter data analysis workshop, and a spring workshop where they share their projects with other teachers. Additional professional development and coaching opportunities are offered by the Harvard Forest throughout the school year.

5 Conceptual Model

I employed a conceptual model based on Billett's (2009) research on work-integrated learning and McRae and Johnston's (2016) proposed global work-integrated learning framework (Fig. 1). Four key characteristics of work integrated learning in the context of a schoolyard science project will be examined: meaningful connections to science

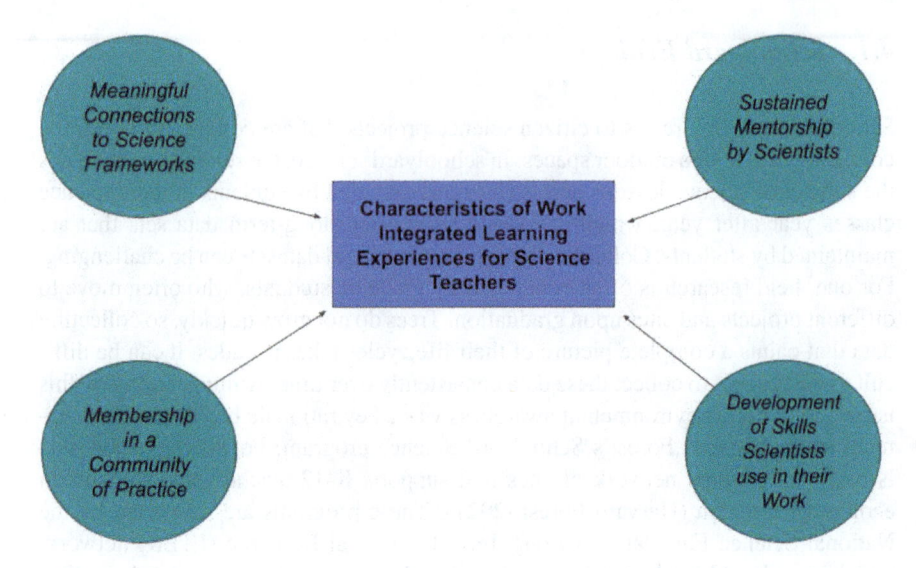

Fig. 1 Author's depiction of the conceptual model based on Work-Integrated Learning principles

frameworks, sustained mentorship by scientists, membership in a community of practice, and development of skills scientists use in their work. Being a part of the Harvard Forest's Schoolyard Science Program gave me, a science teacher, the invaluable opportunity to be mentored by professional scientists. It introduced me to a rich community of practice, where I was able to learn with and from other teachers and scientists. Immersing myself in the protocols for the schoolyard science projects allowed me to develop skills that the scientists employ in forestry research. All the content and skills addressed in these projects were connected to the Massachusetts Science, Technology, and Engineering Frameworks which guide the content I teach these students.

Experiential learning, proposed by Kolb (1984) underpins the work-integrated learning theoretical framework outlined by Stirling et al. (2016). Rooted in the work of Dewey, Levin, and Piaget, experiential learning theory stresses the central role of experience in the process of learning. Kolb (1984) describes experiential learning as a "holistic integrative perspective on learning that combines experience, perception, cognition, and behavior" (p. 21). As such, experiential learning is based on six principles:

1. Learning is a process rather than a set of outcomes.
2. All learning is relearning, and is "best facilitate by a process that draws out the students' beliefs and ideas about a topic so that they can be examined, tested, and integrated with new, more refined ideas" (p. 194)
3. Learning requires learners to move between the opposing modes of reflection, action, feeling, and thinking.
4. Learning is a holistic process of adaptation to the world and involves the total person- thinking, feeling, perceiving, and behaving.

5. Learning results when the learner interacts with the environment and assimilates new experiences into existing concepts.
6. Learning is the process of creating knowledge.

As the learner immerses themselves in new workspaces, they create new knowledge. Participating in science outside of the classroom beside professional scientists allowed me to assimilate new, authentic experiences into the existing concepts I teach, which allowed for the development of transformational learning experiences for my students.

6 Methodology

I employ a self-study design to study myself in action within my own setting to better understand myself and my work environment (Pithouse-Morgan, 2022). I explore in depth my journey while engaged in schoolyard science projects through the lens of work-integrated learning to gain a deeper understanding of my own experiences, practices, and perspectives within this specific context. The rationale for choosing this qualitative research approach is to focus on self-reflection, self-examination, and self-discovery.

6.1 Self-study Methodology

The self-study methodology is a powerful tool to take ownership over one's own professional development and growth (Woods, 2021). The following self-study guidelines put forth by Bullough and Pinnegar (2001) were used to ensure quality in my study:

- Self-studies should promote insight and interpretation (p. 16).
- Biographical and autobiographical self-studies in teacher education are about the problems and issues that make someone an educator (p. 17).
- The autobiographical self-study researcher has an ineluctable obligation to seek to improve the learning situation not only for the self but for the other (p. 17).
- Quality autobiographical self-studies offer fresh perspectives on established truths (p. 18).

The self-study methodology was chosen to examine my journey as an educator through the lens of work integrated learning with the hope of "improving the learning situation not only for the self but for the other" (Bullough & Pinnegar, 2001, p. 17), specifically for other science teachers who are seeking science content specific professional development.

7 Data Collection and Analysis

I collected multiple data sources, including artifacts (reflective journals, photographs of students working in the field, emails and course reviews from students), interviews, and observations to reflect critically on my own actions, decisions, and experiences consequently gain insights into my journey.

Artifacts collected included photographs that I took of teachers and students working in the field. I keep a notebook specifically for schoolyard science, where I take notes at workshops and jot down notes whenever my students go out into the field. I reflect on these experiences in the notebook after workshops and lessons. I was also able to draw from student course evaluations, emails, and notes from students that I have collected over the years.

Interviews were conducted informally with colleagues and students who participated in the projects. I took notes during conversations and then wrote analytic memos following the informal interviews to write down my reflections of the conversations and begin the process of coding the data.

The process of documentary analysis and researcher introspection was used to analyze the data using a coding scheme adopted from Saldaña (2021), who defines a code as "most often a word or short phrase that symbolically assigns a summative, salient, essence-capturing, and/or evocative attribute for a portion of language-based or visual data" (p. 3). Documentary analysis was employed, as the reflective journals represented my introspection as the researcher, which is defined as "an ongoing process of tracking, experiencing, and reflecting on one's own thoughts, mental images, feelings, sensations, and behaviors" (Gould, 1995, p. 719) The theoretical framework guiding the study was consulted as code schemes were developed.

8 Positionality of the Researcher

It is important to note that I am both the researcher and the subject of this study. Much of this study was derived from my own introspection, documents, and artifacts I generated, as well as from informal interviews with my colleagues. All the student work samples I examined through the data analysis were taken from students that have taken my courses in the past, I no longer have any power over their grades. I do not have a supervisory role over any of the colleagues I interviewed for this study and have protected their privacy by changing names. My position as a White female who loves the outdoors is a potential source of bias as I interpret and analyze data. I was privileged to grow up in a place with access to the outdoors: my mother would open our back door after breakfast, and we would not come back into the house until lunchtime. As I reflect on my journey, I must be sensitive to the fact that not everyone has had the same privileges that I have enjoyed. Not everyone has easy access to green space and views the outdoors in the same way that I do. I must continually examine my own assumptions and potential biases in order to broaden my perception and understanding of other people's experiences.

As a person who has grown up with a love of and complete comfort in the environment, I enjoy an insider status with regards to the environment. When I look at ads for outdoor gear or photographs of people enjoying nature, I see people who look like me. This puts me in the dominant group with regards to the environment. I must recognize that many people, including most of my students, may consider themselves outsiders when it comes to the environment. It is crucial that I examine this status and reach out to critical friends as I engage in this study to help check my assumptions and biases.

Self-study inherently includes bias as I am both the researcher and subject of this study. As such, I took several steps to increase the validity of this study. I collected data from multiple points in an attempt to triangulate, or cross-examine, findings at multiple points (Savin-Bader & Major, 2013). Member checking was also used to gain feedback for the interpretation of data.

9 Findings

Once initial coding was completed, initial codes were collapsed and organized into conceptual categories, which resulted in 36 axial codes. These axial codes were consolidated to five themes shown below in Table 1.

Five themes emerged: *membership in a sustained schoolyard science project increased my content knowledge, my confidence in designing transformational learning experiences for students increases through schoolyard science participation. and standardized testing and other school calendar factors limit the amount of time spent on schoolyard science projects, working with authentic data sets gives students exposure to technical skills they do not have access to in regular high school curriculum,* and *experiential outdoor learning is joyful for me and students.*

9.1 Theme 1: Participation in a Sustained Schoolyard Science Project Improves My Content Knowledge

Although I have always loved the outdoors, I did not have a lot of knowledge about environmental science before participating in the Harvard Forest's Schoolyard Science program. In college, I was on a pre-med track until I took Anatomy and Physiology and realized that studying the human body did not interest me nearly as much as it did my classmates, who cackled over naming all of the bones on the skeleton tuxedo t-shirts that they wore to class on Halloween. Instead, in college I found I

Table 1 Themes from data analysis

Theme	Axial code
1. Membership in a schoolyard science project increased my content knowledge through mentorship by professional scientists	Reading nonfiction books about the environment, learning about GIS, visualizing data, mentorship from Harvard scientists, conference workshop participation, tapping maple trees, trail camera study, student tapping a birch tree, real-world data that is relevant to our lives
2. My confidence in designing transformational learning experiences for students increases through schoolyard science participation	Taking risks to try new ideas, encouraging students to create and design own experiments, developing CERs, public easy-to-get data, presenting at conferences, joining professional networks, art-science connection, capstone guidance
3. Standardized testing and other school calendar factors limits the amount of time spent on schoolyard science projects	We don't have time for that, MCAS, depth over breadth, ecology is easy, pacing and coverage, concerns about substitutes
4. Working with authentic data sets gives students exposure to technical skills they do not have access to in regular high school curriculum	Calculators in statistics class, never used a spreadsheet before, learning about spreadsheets helps us for college, spreadsheets are not in frameworks, my students cannot use spreadsheets, I don't have time to teach students how to use spreadsheets, public, easy-to-get data
5. Experiential outdoor learning is joyful for me and my students	Students laughing and smiling, playing with sticks, pointing at a tree, asking to check the trail camera, I actually get to go outside in this class, nature isn't my thing but she made it fun

was drawn to studying molecular biology and biochemistry, wondering at the interactions between molecules and drawing endless benzenes and chair cyclohexanes in my notebooks.

As a child, I spent hours roaming around the small patch of woods in my backyard, building forts and raking paths for my bike. My mother and I would take walks around our neighborhood together after school. In the fall, she would peel the backs of maple helicopters (scientific term: *samara*) to reveal a sticky sap that she would use to stick these green whirligigs onto her nose, cackling like a witch. My mother was a keen observer of nature and taught me the importance of taking joy in small things. As I moved through college, I made like-minded friends who shared my love of nature. Two of my college roommates spent summers working for the Appalachian Mountain Club in New Hampshire. My eyes were opened to a whole new world of possibility when they introduced me to the White Mountains and took me on my first trips into the backcountry.

When I began my first teaching job at Greater Lowell Tech, I was excited to learn that they had an Outing Club which brought students on hikes and other outdoor adventures. The advisor, Deb Gustafson, was a veteran teacher and a fascinating person who had traveled the world scuba diving, sea kayaking, and camping. She took me under her wing as a co-advisor and quickly became a hugely influential mentor to me. Deb encouraged me to apply for an Earthwatch Fellowship, which became a major turning point for me as an educator.

Earthwatch is an environmental nonprofit organization whose mission is to connect "people with scientists worldwide to conduct environmental research and empowers them with the knowledge they need to conserve the planet" (Earthwatch, 2024). People can sign up for Earthwatch expeditions around the world where they can participate in field research and help scientists to collect data. They refer to this as "participatory science" rather than "citizen science" in an effort to use more inclusive language that does not come with the adverse connotation associated with citizenship. In 2014, I had the privilege of becoming an Earthwatch Fellow and went to Cosanga, Ecuador to participate in their "Climate Change and Caterpillars" expedition. I went into the cloud forest to collect caterpillars, learned how to pin butterflies to ship to museums, helped to set up experiments in the forest canopy, and attended lectures by the ecologists in the evenings. A photograph of the field station in Ecuador is shown below in Fig. 2. Both the field experience and cultural immersion aspect of this program impacted me so much that I went back to school determined to bring what I learned to my students.

I was not totally sure how to transition what I learned about field work to a high school biology classroom without taking time away from the content we needed to cover in the curriculum. In Massachusetts, students are mandated to pass a standardized test in biology (called the MCAS) to receive their high school diploma. This test covers a huge amount of content, from molecules to ecosystems. Balancing covering content with meaningful, rich inquiry experiences is difficult to do as a teacher. At the same time, our school wide MCAS biology scores were significantly below state average. The administration was becoming alarmed but was not totally sure how to respond.

Fig. 2 The Yanayacu Field Station in Cosanga, Ecuador, by the author

Fig. 3 From left to right: Bryanna, Kim, and I walking through light snow at the Harvard Forest. From *Harvard Forest Schoolyard Ecology Blog,* by Pamela Snow, 2017 (https://hfnatu restudents.blogspot.com/ 2017/03/late-winter.html)

Our curriculum director at the time, Mike, was brought in to help our team. A former Fulbright teacher scholar, he was a history teacher who was a strong proponent of project-based learning. Mike encouraged us to rethink our teaching practice and move away from didactic instruction and to move towards a project-based model. He told us that he was willing to support us in doing anything that got students engaged in their learning. I remembered hearing about citizen science back in one of my science teaching methods courses. I thought that citizen science would be the perfect vehicle for replicating my incredible experience in Ecuador with my students. It would give me the support and training I needed to help my students participate in "real" science. After doing some research, I found the Harvard Forest Schoolyard Ecology program and decided to reach out.

Pam Snow, the former director of education for the Schoolyard Science program, welcomed us with open arms. Three of us drove out to the Harvard Forest on a snowy day in early March to meet Pam and learn about the programs. A photo of our team is shown below in Fig. 3.

After walking through the fairy-like hemlock forest, I was hooked. My colleague, Bryanna, and I signed up for the summer institute and began to plan how to integrate this into the biology curriculum. We began the following fall with students participating in the *Our Changing Forests* program, where we set up a 10 by 10-m forest plot. Students identified all the trees in the plot, did a field site assessment, and measured the diameter at breast height (DBH) of all of the trees, which allowed them to calculate the amount of carbon sequestered in the plot.

Being part of the Schoolyard Science program did not end at the first summer institute. The Harvard Forest holds a winter data workshop annually, where you can bring in the data from your site and learn how to analyze the data directly from Harvard scientists. They are willing to teach you everything from how to set up a simple graph in Excel to more advanced topics, such as explaining how scientists figured out the formulas for calculating carbon sequestration from the DBH. Every spring, there is a workshop for teachers to come together to share out how they integrated the projects in their classroom. This is always an incredible time for inspiration and networking with educators from all grade levels around the state.

My participation in the Schoolyard Science program led me to many other wonderful opportunities. I had the privilege of participating in the Research Experience for Teachers program in the summer of 2020, where I worked in the Thompson lab, which studies broad-scale changes in forest ecosystems and investigates long-term patterns in land use. I worked closely with their GIS research assistant, Joshua Plisinski, to develop and write a "Data Nugget" based on a paper co-authored by the Thompson lab, which was an incredible learning experience. "Data Nuggets" are classroom activities that are co-created by scientists and teachers that engage students in authentic data sets and real research.

9.2 Theme 2: My Confidence in Designing Transformational Learning Experiences for Students Increased Through Schoolyard Science Participation

Being part of the community of practice that was offered through the schoolyard science program opened my eyes to a whole new world of data. Harnessing these publicly available datasets transformed my teaching, allowing me to design place-based learning experiences for students. One student reported that "one of the most useful aspects of this course was the way we were able to both collect, organize and interpret real-world data that is relevant to our lives." Another student commented that the projects we engaged in "showed me that even concepts perceived to be complex can be studied and better understood using public, easy-to-get data."

When I changed school districts, I was fortunate to be able to continue my work with the Harvard Forest. Being in downtown Lowell, we do not currently have direct access to a forest plot, so the *Our Changing Forests* project is on hold until we find a way to make that happen. We began a new project titled *Buds, Leaves, and Global Warming,* where students measure the length of the growing season by observing the date of "bud burst" of a particular tree in the spring and then "leaf drop" in the fall. This project was already happening at Lowell High under the direction of Massachusetts Audubon educator Sally Farrow, who had been following a red maple tree next to the Freshman Academy building for years. Because I already knew Sally through the Harvard Forest, we were able to pick right up on this project. She taught me how to collect the data and gave me support as I implemented this protocol on new trees with my students.

My experiences with the schoolyard science program paved the way for other meaningful opportunities for both me and my students. The program coordinator at the Harvard Forest recently connected me with a researcher at a local university who is studying transpiration in trees in urban settings. She wants to get students involved with her research, so we placed a sensor next to the high school, which will allow students to be involved in data collection and analysis. A photo of this

Fig. 4 A sensor placed in a tree at Lowell High School that will measure transpiration rates in the tree, by the author

sensor is displayed below in Fig. 4. Multiple environmental groups throughout the city have contacted us to find ways to support climate change education. Currently, I am working as the teacher partner in the "Parks for Every Classroom" program through the National Park Service. I am working with a ranger from the Lowell National Historical Park and a community partner from the local university to co-create place-based professional development on climate change for teachers. This opportunity has given me, as the teacher, an opportunity to become involved in yet another community of practice that will result in richer learning opportunities for my students. The agency that I gained through participation in the schoolyard science program opened the door for this experience.

9.3 Theme 3: Standardized Testing and Other School Calendar Factors Limit the Amount of Time Spent on Schoolyard Science Projects

Over the years, I have introduced four separate colleagues to the Harvard Forest by bringing them to workshops. I was so excited by what I learned that I could not wait to share. Unfortunately, this has been met with considerable resistance. Although people are generally excited about the idea of getting students involved, few follow through and implement the projects.

"I just don't have time for that. We have so much to cover for the MCAS, I can't spend the time going outside" is what many people say. In Massachusetts, students must pass a standardized test in science to receive their high school diploma. Most school districts choose biology as their testing subject. Although the frameworks were revised in 2016 in an effort to align with the national science standards (NGSS) and emphasize the practices of science, there is still a daunting amount of content to cover. The biology curriculum covers everything from micro—including the four main classes of organic compounds—to the macro- ecosystems and the process of evolution. Homeostasis in the major human body systems is thrown in for good measure. Not surprisingly, many teachers do not feel that they can justify taking students outside during their biology course to identify trees and measure their trunks.

Schoolyard science is a natural choice for elective courses such as environmental science. I argue that this is inequitable: only a small fraction of students choose to study environmental science as their elective, leaving only a small part of the school population having the opportunity to engage in these authentic, place-based science experiences where they immerse themselves in the role of a scientist.

9.4 Theme 4: Working with Authentic Data Sets Helps Students to Develop Valuable Mathematical and Technical Skills

When I first began to teach AP Environmental Science, I was shocked to learn that most of my students had no idea how to use a simple spreadsheet. These were top-ranked students who were enrolled in the most challenging mathematics and science courses the school offered. Inputting data, using formulas, and sorting data—all skills I believed were simple—were foreign to them. Most students struggled to create even a simple bar graph with a pre-filled spreadsheet. At the time, I thought this problem was endemic to my school district. I learned that this was not the case when I got a new job at a neighboring school district and began to talk to teachers in other schools. Students who knew how to use Google Sheets and Excel told me that they had to teach themselves how to use these programs, and that they rarely had exposure to them in their regular math and science courses. Upon further investigation, I learned that the Massachusetts Curriculum Frameworks does not specifically have any requirements for students to learn how to use spreadsheets. The closest framework I could find for this was the Science Practice standard of students being able to "Analyzing and interpreting data" (DESE, 2016). Math and science teachers I have had informal conversations with across the state report similar problems, which highlights a serious deficit in the Massachusetts curriculum frameworks.

Once my students realize how powerful and useful spreadsheets can be, they become determined to master them. Many students were inspired to watch tutorials on YouTube and to seek out older friends and siblings who were in college to learn how to do far more than what I was able to teach them. In a course evaluation, one student reported that they "found…whenever we did data analysis or worked with spreadsheets or graphs the most useful as it allowed us to use spreadsheets and other resources to view and analyze data, something that usually most high school courses don't do." This was echoed by a second student, who stated that "one of the most useful aspects of this course was the way we were able to both collect, organize and interpret real-world data that is relevant to our lives."

Students were always amazed by the fact that we were able to use real-world data that was "relevant to our lives." They revealed that this "showed me that even concepts perceived to be complex can be studied and better understood using public, easy-to-get data." Too often, science and math classes use sanitized data sets where the dirty work has already been done for them: the data is sorted, the outliers are removed, and the graph is already made with the goal of illustrating a predetermined concept or conclusion that the teacher or curriculum developer has decided the students *should* make.

9.5 Theme 5: Experiential Outdoor Learning is Joyful for Both Teachers and Students

I went through years of photographs to organize the visual data that informed this study. Photographs of students armed with clipboards and forestry tape abounded, showing off their sneakers covered with plastic bags from our local grocery store, Market Basket. One thing that all of the photos had in common was this: students were smiling. While some of the photos were obviously staged (I found a few where students were studiously pointing at their notebooks, which were visibly upside down), I took many candid photos, as well. Every year I would make an end-of-year slideshow set to music for students to enjoy before they left for the summer. There were photos of students rolling over dead logs, pointing to worms and centipedes. There was a photo of a student pushing over a dead tree next to our plot (to my protests!). One photograph showed a group of boys holding a stick that was about ten feet long. I can remember having a hard time convincing them to leave it outside. They compromised by breaking off a piece of the stick and proudly displaying it on our lab bench.

Something magical happens when you bring students outdoors. If you set the atmosphere right, if you are able to convince students to buy in, they are able to shed the burdens of the social norms thrust upon them by society and become kids again. I wrote the following as part of my personal teaching statement in 2022: "Students are reluctant to return to the building at the end of class, but the magic of the forest remains. They have an extra spring in their steps, their eyes are twinkling, and they are smiling."

I see this transformation across all age groups and types of learners: from the students who have significant disabilities and cannot be in mainstream classrooms all the way up to the undergraduates I teach at the local university. I recently asked a former university student to write a letter of recommendation for me. She wrote "One of the first big things we did in class was go on a nature walk at Hawk Valley Farm. While nature isn't really my thing, [Dr. Goodhue] made it super fun...Dr. Goodhue always emphasized that when we become teachers, that we can and should take our students outside."

I also experience joy from taking my classes outside. There is nothing that brings me greater satisfaction as a teacher than watching my students discover the world around them. When students come to me with photographs of different plants and animals in their neighborhood, or with reports of exciting animal sightings, I know that I have accomplished my mission.

10 Discussion of Findings

This study sought to understand how participating in the Harvard Forest's Schoolyard Science program influenced my journey as an educator, and, ultimately, resulted in rich classroom experiences for my students. The discussion of findings for the research question underpinning the study is presented below. Artifacts and interviews used in this study yielded valuable data to inform the research questions, allowing for triangulation of data.

11 The Affordances and Challenges of WIL in the Context of a Schoolyard Science Project

Work integrated learning (WIL) is a practice that integrates learning experiences from workplace settings with educational settings (Billett, 2009). By participating in the Schoolyard Science program, I realized that students are afforded opportunities to "become" scientists themselves. They learn how to "do science like scientists do" (Alcorn, 2020, p. 111). As my students participated in these projects, they were able to learn skills that professional scientists use and integrate this knowledge with mathematics, technology, and content knowledge that is covered in their regular science class. Themes which emerged from my journey that demonstrated the affordances of WIL were theme 1: *membership in a schoolyard science project increases my content knowledge through mentorship by professional scientists,* theme 2*: my confidence in designing transformational learning experiences for students increases through schoolyard science participation,* and theme 5: *Working with authentic data sets helps students to develop valuable mathematical and technical skills.*

Participation in a community of practice allows the learner to work alongside practicing experts (or 'old timer') in a social context, which allows the learner to experience new workplace norms and develop their identity (Lave, 1991). Being part of the schoolyard science network allowed me to learn how to "do science like scientists do" (Alcorn, 2020, p. 111). This allowed me, who had only "worked" in science as an undergraduate student, to understand the science subculture and understand what it meant to be a scientist (Zegwaard and Coll, 2011). The mentorship I gained through participation in the program developed my skills and increased my awareness of careers within the field of science.

Skill development was another important affordance I gained through participation in the schoolyard science network. Through the mentorship of scientists, my understanding of the research design process grew exponentially. I learned how to collect and analyze data in the field, and gained many important tools to help my students work with data using mathematics.

Time was found to be the main barrier for participation in this project. Teachers I spoke with had concerns about what content they would be missing if they took the time to integrate these projects into the regular biology curriculum. I feel pressure to fit in content amidst time constraints such as school cancellations due to extreme weather (generally snow in the Northeastern United States), and loss of time on learning due to other standardized tests and other school initiatives. My colleagues reported to be overwhelmed by the in-class preparation for these projects leading up to the experience, the time it takes to go outside to collect data in the field, and to then analyze the data and reflect on the learning. As such, this project has been relegated to elective courses and, possibly, to the category of "end-of-the-year, fun activities" (Alcorn, 2020) that students have described when asked to recall projects that they found to be engaging.

12 Reflections

I began my undergraduate studies on a pre-med track, which led me to focus on courses in organic chemistry, biochemistry, microbiology, molecular biology, and genetics. At the time, what really fascinated me was the micro: the fact that the tiny molecules composing our cells and organelles could have huge impacts on our entire systems when they were defective. Unfortunately, upon taking human anatomy, I discovered that I had no interest in memorizing the names of bones and muscles and was put off at the idea of becoming a physician. As a result, I graduated with little training in ecology and environmental science.

One of my college roommates, Elizabeth, worked in New Hampshire's White Mountains for a time after graduation. She was on the "croo" of one of the huts built for people hiking the Appalachian Trail. I remember being absolutely enchanted by the mountains and the forest when I visited her one weekend. Part of her job was to take people on nature walks and to teach them how to identify trees. This fascinated me and made me want to learn more about the forest. This is one of the major factors that influenced me to reach out to the Harvard Forest for the first time.

Engaging in the work-integrated learning that membership in the Schoolyard Ecology program entails allowed me to fill gaps from my academic studies. I became aware of a field of research that was entirely new to me. Some of the methods were relatively simple and I was able to adopt easily. One part that I struggled with in the beginning, however, was the management of all the data collected. Developing systems to organize the data the students collected, verify that they collected the data correctly, and to enter the data into the system took a while to master. My teacher colleagues in the Schoolyard Ecology had invaluable ideas for this. Additionally, the scientists were always happy to help troubleshoot problems. One year, several of the hemlock branches we were studying were cut down. Initially, I was worried that the whole study would need to be scrapped. Fortunately, we were able to tag other branches, document the disturbance, and move on.

My work-integrated learning journey led to significant personal growth and transformation. I became so intrigued by the impact of these projects on my students' learning that I decided to enroll in the University of Massachusetts, Lowell's doctoral program so that I could learn how to study this formally. This required me to step far out of my comfort zone and grow considerably as a professional. I have presented my research at several conferences and have been invited to teach science to elementary education majors at the university level. I have worked with several different scientists to find ways to make their research accessible to students.

Being part of a community of practice has been the most valuable aspect of my work-integrated learning journey. I have met incredible, passionate people through the Schoolyard Ecology program. When I began working at Lowell High School, I was delighted to bump into Sally Farrow in the hallway after school one day. Sally is a teacher-naturalist with the Massachusetts Audubon Society, a nonprofit organization that is dedicated to conservation and environmental education. Sally has been working in the Lowell Public schools for years and has been tracking a tree through the Schoolyard Ecology program on the Lowell High campus since 2011. Her enthusiasm for environmental education is infectious. After catching up, Sally and I, along with Tony from the Lowell Parks and Conservation Trust, decided to join forces and merge the Lowell High Environmental Club with the TREEs club that they had co-founded with students several years before. This club has been one of the highlights of my work at Lowell High School. Sally regularly brings in owls, kestrels, hawks, cockroaches, and other exciting animals for students to meet. Guest speakers, including Katharine from the Harvard Forest, come to talk to students about their research and environmental careers. The students participate in city clean-ups, they plant trees, and engage in other environmentally based activities. I feel incredibly supported in my work by Sally, Tony, and the entire staff at the Harvard Forest, and am continually inspired to find even more ways to engage my students in meaningful field experiences.

References

Alcorn, T. (2020). *Woolly bully: Exploring high school students' science identities and attitudes in the context of a citizen science project* (Order No. 27964360). Available from ProQuest Dissertations & Theses A&I; ProQuest Dissertations & Theses Global (2415457640). https://www.proquest.com/dissertations-theses/woolly-bully-exploring-high-school-students/docview/2415457640/se-2

Billett, S. (2009). Realising the educational worth of integrating work experiences in higher education. *Studies in Higher Education, 34*(7), 827–843. https://doi.org/10.1080/03075070802706561

Bonney, R., Cooper, C. B., Dickinson, J., Kelling, S., Phillips, T., Rosenberg, K. V., & Shirk, J. (2009). Citizen science: A developing tool for expanding science knowledge and scientific literacy. *BioScience, 59*(11), 977–984. https://doi.org/10.1525/bio.2009.59.11.9

Brossard, D., Lewenstein, B., & Bonney, R. (2005). Scientific knowledge and attitude change: The impact of a citizen science project. *International Journal of Science Education, 27*(9), 1099–1121. https://doi.org/10.1080/09500690500069483

Bullough, R. V., & Pinnegar, S. (2001). Guidelines for quality in autobiographical forms of self-study research. *Educational Researcher, 30*(3), 13–21. https://doi.org/10.3102/0013189X030003013

Earthwatch. (2024). Earthwatch. https://earthwatch.org/

Ellwood, E. R., Pauly, G. B., Ahn, J., Golembiewski, K., Higgins, L. M., Ordeñana, M. A., & Von Konrat, M. (2023). Citizen science needs a name change. *Trends in Ecology & Evolution, 38*(6), 485–489. https://doi.org/10.1016/j.tree.2023.03.003

Gould, S. J. (1995). Researcher introspection as a method in consumer research: Applications, issues, and implications. *Journal of Consumer Research, 21*(4), 719–722.

Harvard Forest. (2021). Schoolyard LTER program. Schoolyard LTER Program | Harvard Forest. https://harvardforest.fas.harvard.edu/schoolyard-lter-program

Kolb, D. A. (1984). *Experiential learning: Experience as the source of learning and development*. Pearson Education.

Lave, J. (1991). Situating learning in communities of practice. In L. B. Resnick, J. M. Levine, & S. D. Teasley (Eds.), Perspectives on socially shared cognition (pp. 63–82). American Psychological Association. https://doi.org/10.1037/10096-003

Massachusetts Department of Elementary and Secondary Education. (2016). *Professional development frequently asked questions*. Frequently Asked Questions—Professional Development. https://www.doe.mass.edu/pd/faq.html

Massachusetts Department of Elementary and Secondary Education (DESE). (2023). School and District Profiles. https://profiles.doe.mass.edu/general/general.aspx?topNavID=1&leftNavId=100&orgcode=01600000&orgtypecode=5

McRae, N., & Johnston, N. (2016). The development of a proposed global work-integrated learning framework. *Asia-Pacific Journal of Cooperative Education, 17*(4), 337–348.

New American Economy. (2019, July 8). New report shows immigrants in Lowell accounted for nearly 90 percent of recent population growth. New American Economy. https://www.newamericaneconomy.org/press-release/new-report-shows-immigrants-in-lowell-accounted-for-nearly-90-percent-of-recent-population-growth/

NGSS Lead States. (2013). *Next Generation Science Standards: For States, By States*. Washington, DC: The National Academies Press.

NSTA. (2014). *Science and engineering practices*. NGSS@NSTA. https://ngss.nsta.org/PracticesFull.aspx

Pithouse-Morgan, K. (2022). Self-study in teaching and teacher education: Characteristics and contributions. *Teaching and Teacher Education, 119*, 103880. https://doi.org/10.1016/j.tate.2022.103880

Savin-Baden, M., & Major, C. (2013) Qualitative research: The essential guide to theory and practice. Routledge, London.

Saldaña, J. (2021). *The Coding Manual for Qualitative Researchers.* SAGE Publications Ltd. http://digital.casalini.it/9781529755992

Stirling, A., Kerr, G., Banwell, J., MacPherson, E., & Heron, A. (2016). *A practical guide for work-integrated learning: Effective practices to enhance the educational quality of structured work experiences offered through colleges and universities.* Higher Education Quality Council of Ontario.

United States Census Bureau. (2022). Lowell, Massachusetts Profile. https://data.census.gov/profile/Lowell_city,_Massachusetts?g=160XX00US2537000#race-and-ethnicity

Woods, J. C. (2021). Self-study: A method for continuous professional learning and a methodology for knowledge transfer. *Quality Advancement in Nursing Education 7*(2), 7. https://doi.org/10.17483/2368-6669.1278

Zegwaard, K. E., & Coll, R. K. (2011). Using cooperative education and work-integrated education to provide career clarification. *Science Education International, 22*(4), 282–291.

Learning Through Teaching: A Year in an All-Girls Engineering Class

Mariel Kolker

Abstract This chapter narrates a work-integrated learning experience in which I navigate a year of teaching an all-girls high school engineering class with the aim of improving girls' engagement and success in STEM fields. My initial hypothesis was that teaching girls in engineering would be similar to teaching boys, but the experiential learning process led me to recognize the need for tailored pedagogical approaches. Through reflective inquiry and engagement with educational literature on gender bias, I came to identify three main pedagogical shifts to my practice as a result of the work-integrated learning experience. These are: (1) modifying my teaching practice to include additional structure and support for girls during engineering instruction, (2) holding conversations with girls about gender stereotypes and implicit gender bias which improved my teacher-student relationships and effectiveness as a teacher, and (3) developing a new confidence in modifying the curriculum to meet the specific needs of a student population. This study resulted in positive outcomes, with girls expressing increased interest in engineering and leaving the course with a sense of competence. Throughout the chapter I emphasize how hands-on problem solving and transformative inquiry-based learning, coupled with critical reflective thinking, have transformed my teaching approach, emphasizing the importance of adapting curriculum to meet the needs of diverse student populations.

Keywords Work-integrated learning · Self-study · Reflective inquiry · STEM · Girls · Gender bias

1 Introduction

As a second career teacher, most of my development and becoming as an educator has come exclusively in the form of experiential learning. Having begun this career as an in-service teacher with a decade of experience in industry and no understanding of pedagogy, I developed my knowledge of teaching largely through reflective inquiry

---

M. Kolker (✉)
Morristown High School, Morristown, NJ, USA
e-mail: mariel.kolker@msdk12.net

and work-integrated learning. This chapter details a case study of a specific teaching and learning experience which afforded me an opportunity to expand my knowledge and practice and to contribute to the broader base of knowledge about girls in pre-engineering domains.

My desire to understand and meet my students' educational needs drew me to embark on a year of self-study in which I applied reflective, analytical thinking to my own practice. This research became a transformative inquiry-based learning process for the purposes of my own professional development as well as possible long-term educational reform. My work-integrated learning culminated in a public presentation at a national educators' conference on how teachers can understand and meet girls' educational needs in engineering and STEM classes.

In examining my own practice through stages of experiential learning, I sought out the participation of my students as collaborators. I shared my learning journey with the girls and invited them to actively engage in the process by providing data for my reflection and sense making. By involving the students, my self-study became a back-and-forth activity in which students would express their opinions, I would help identify trends, make changes to my teaching practice, seek feedback, and iterate. My desire to understand the factors that made our class 'different' and 'special' became a secret, conspiratorial secondary curriculum. It fostered a productive relationship among us that helped promote my reflective practice (Dinkelman, 2003) throughout this experiential learning opportunity.

2 Context

This case study took place at Morristown High School, a mid-sized, public suburban secondary school in northern New Jersey. The high school housed 1880 students over 9th-12th grades. The student population was 51% White, 36% Latinx, 8% African American, and 5% Asian. The percentage of economically disadvantaged students was 26%, and English Language Learners (ELL) were 12% of the population. The high school had a graduation rate of 87%, of which 82.5% went on to a 2- or 4-year college (*NJ School Performance Report*, 2018–2019, n.d.).

As a former woman in STEM, I am acutely aware of the persistent dearth of women in STEM fields and felt proud to be a role model to high school girls as a professional female engineer from the heavily male-dominated electric power generation, transmission and distribution industry. When my high school began to offer the full-year elective Principles of Engineering (POE) from the national engineering curriculum company Project Lead The Way (PLTW) during the 2011–2012 school year, I was selected to teach it. The course enjoyed full enrollment and a waiting list, however a problem of practice soon emerged: a troubling decrease in the number of girls enrolling.

The first cohort of students included six girls out of 36 students, or 17%. The following year, I saw two girls out of 36 students, or 6%. During the third year only one girl enrolled in a class of 24 students, which was 4%. This trend did not go unnoticed by me.

In an initial effort to address this problem, I had proposed to administrators that we run an all-girls section of the course. This idea was rejected as impossible to justify or execute in a public school setting. Regardless, I conducted some action research to test my theories that girls need to be personally invited into an engineering class, and that an all-girls class might prove to be an incentive to enroll. During the midwinter months of 2014 I visited 35 science classes over the course of two days, introducing hundreds of underclassmen to some of our newer science electives, including POE. I visited each physics, biology and chemistry class, in which I spent approximately ten minutes explaining the new elective courses to students. I also mentioned, subversively, that we *might* be able to create an all-girls section of Principles of Engineering if enough girls enrolled. I had students indicate their interests on a form which I collected.

The timing of the visits preceded guidance scheduling sessions in which students chose their courses for the following school year. Weeks later I was pleased to discover that a total of 67 girls had selected Principles of Engineering as their first or second choice of elective. The school was able to create three sections of the engineering course, and I gained approval to make one an all-girl section. Using the data I collected, I worked with guidance to shuffle students among the three sections until one was all-girls, and the other two co-ed with four to six girls in each.

Having graduated with a degree in mechanical engineering, I understand the career possibilities and salary that an engineering degree brings. I knew girls were fully capable of meeting the requirements of an engineering program, and believed they simply needed to be exposed to it. The problem I thought I was addressing was a lack of exposure to engineering as a college major and career. By bringing more girls into the POE course, I could expose them to a new career path and possibly convince more of them to pursue engineering after high school. In preparing to teach the all-girl section, I was intentional about staying true to the PLTW curriculum and ensuring that the course was as rigorous as the other two sections. Same instruction, same pace, aiming to strike the same balance between direct instruction and hands-on activities.

Investigating the girls' experiences in my class through reflective inquiry, I came to understand fundamental differences in how these girls approached engineering as a subject. I learned quickly that I was, in fact, wrong about the girls and what they needed in order to see themselves as engineers. Just being in the engineering class was not enough. My teaching practices were not meeting the girls' needs in ways that had allowed boys to be successful in classes I had taught in past years.

Thus began my journey of experiential learning and self-study. I began to examine the girls' perspectives through classroom conversations and surveys. Reflecting-in-action (in the moment) and reflecting-on-action (afterward), I became a researcher in the practice context (Schön, 1983). I began to conduct research in educational literature around gender bias in science. As I started to make sense of what I was observing with the girls, I reflected on my own teaching practice and analyzed it through reflective inquiry, with the goal of making changes to better meet their academic needs. This became the core of my practice. Moving through all four of Kolb's stages of experiential learning (1984), I developed my teaching practice in three distinct ways over the course of that academic year.

3 Research Questions

The research questions for this self-study were developed as a natural reaction to this case study I had created. Being aware that single-sex classes have been found to exacerbate inequality in teaching and learning, I was determined to teach with the same consistency and rigor as I had taught boys in the past. The purpose of my self-study, therefore, was to confirm my hypothesis that teaching girls in engineering was no different than teaching boys. My research questions grew out of this assumption.

Research Question 1: To what extent is my teaching pedagogy in an all-girls engineering class as effective as in a mixed-gender class?

Research Question 2: How does my teaching pedagogy need to change to meet the educational needs of girls in an engineering or physics class?

4 Hypotheses

My initial hypothesis in the fall of 2014 was that my teaching would be equally effective irrespective of class gender composition. Indeed, I had succeeded in my own mechanical engineering undergraduate degree program that was 90% male. I believed that the girls in my class would succeed in the engineering tasks without exception, as I had. My secondary hypothesis was that my teaching practice would not need to change to meet the educational needs of the girls. Why would it?

5 Conceptual Framework

The framework of Kolb's (1984) theory of experiential learning and work-integrated learning serve as a foundation for this chapter. Work-integrated learning is a form of experiential learning in which the workplace provides an enriched educational experience for optimal learning (Stirling et al., 2016). Kolb's (1984) theory divides learning into four major modes:

1. *Concrete experience*, which emphasizes the learning that occurs during immersive engagement in the practice or work that is the focus of the learning.
2. *Reflective observation*, in which the learning occurs when there is reflection and analysis of experiences and outcomes.

3. *Abstract conceptualization*, which focuses on the learner's making sense of the experience by conceptualizing them and forming theories.
4. *Active experimentation*, in which the learner applies their theories or concepts in practice, in an attempt to test their understanding and to refine their skills.

In Kolb's (1984) view of optimal learning, the learner experiences all modes during the course of the work experience, although they may be at different times and not necessarily followed in a linear fashion. Throughout my year teaching the all-girls engineering class, I clearly inhabited all four modes as I constructed new understandings of effective teaching.

6 Methodology

This research employs self-study methodology as it allows ways of knowing and knowledge acquired as a result of narrative research into one's own practice. Self-study is not a recipe or a procedure, but rather a methodology for studying professional practice settings (Bullough & Pinnegar, 2001; Loughran, 2007). There is not one prescribed set of methods that applies to self-study; the researcher is granted the freedom to employ whatever methods will provide the needed evidence and context for understanding their practice. Research methodology of self-study favors narrative research. As such, this study employs a narrative form that promotes insight and interpretation and promotes the place of story in teachers' development and understanding of practice (Bullough & Pinnegar, 2001; Pithouse et al., 2009).

Schön (1983) recognized reflection-in-action and reflection-on-action to be rigorous forms of continuous learning necessary for growth. Educational literature recognizes many definitions of self-study and reflective practice. While these are related constructs with significant overlap, self-study is defined in this chapter as "intentional and systematic inquiry into one's own practice" (Dinkelman, 2003, p. 3), which "utilizes cycles of inquiry that rely upon and promote critical reflection" (LaBoskey, 2004, p. 838). Reflective inquiry as an activity is thereby a component of the process of self-study. LaBoskey (2004) posits that the aims of self-study are twofold: to study one's practice in order to improve it, and to produce public knowledge that can contribute to the practice of others, raising the stakes for this form of learning by suggesting that self-study methodology, "demands that we formalize our work and make it available to our professional community for deliberation... and judgment" (p. 860).

LaBoskey (2004) defines the practice of self-study as maintaining four critical characteristics. Firstly, the methodology of self-study looks for and requires evidence of the reframed thinking and transformed practice of the researcher, which are derived from an evaluation of the impact of those development efforts. Secondly, self-study methodology is interactive at one or more points during the research process. Those interactions with our colleagues, with students, with the educational literature, and with our own previous work help to confirm or challenge our developing understandings and require us to justify and interrogate our assumptions, assertions, and values. Thirdly, the methodology of self-study employs multiple, primarily qualitative methods, some that are commonly used in general educational research, and some that are innovative. Multiple methods provide us with opportunities to gain different and thus more comprehensive perspectives on the educational processes under investigation. Lastly, self-study methodology demands that we formalize our work and make it available to our professional community for deliberation, further testing, and judgment. We advance the field through the construction, testing, sharing, and re-testing of exemplars of teaching practice.

Self-study work focuses on the self with concern for the other, in this case the girls in my engineering class. During the course of this study, my own practice was the subject of my research, with respect to its efficacy and success with the girls. The self-study as described in this chapter is time-bounded, beginning at the start of September 2014 and continuing through June 2015.

6.1 Data Collection and Analysis

The data in this study were assembled through course evaluations and surveys, assignments and assessments from the course, narrative research as documented in a presentation I first gave in April 2015, and a personal blog I authored in 2015. Qualitative data were coded and analyzed in 2015 and again, according to Saldaña (2009), in 2023.

6.2 Validity

LaBoskey (2004) asserts that validation for self-study must be conceptualized differently than in traditional research. She correlates validity as trustworthiness in the researcher to accurately and competently represent the complexity and context of the situation. Toward the end of the academic year in question, in May 2015, I aimed to earn this trustworthiness from my community of practice when I presented the findings of my self-study to a convened group of educators at an NSTA (National Science Teaching Association) STEM EXPO Conference. Through articulating my observations, reflections and growth as an educator, my aim was to offer the knowledge I had gained for the benefit of this community of practice. According to LaBoskey, the goals of self-study include the production of public knowledge that can contribute to the improvement of the practice of others. By presenting my newfound understandings, I later came to appreciate that I was bringing empirical evidence to the practice of developing one's own pedagogical skill development and growth (Loughran, 2010).

6.3 Limitations

This self-study is limited to my development as an educator with regard to the education of high school girls in the science and engineering domains. This story stands as a lived experience in which I took an opportunity to identify gender-specific student needs that had previously gone unnoticed, and to consequently facilitate the personal development of new pedagogical approaches to address those needs. While my observations are limited to the education of high-school aged female students in science and engineering domains, I hope that the lessons learned, and skills developed will still benefit the reader.

7 Discussion of Findings

My time in the all-girl engineering classroom was a unique opportunity to develop my understanding of the ways in which girls experience science and engineering and how I can use that knowledge to calibrate my pedagogy to engage them in the most effective way possible. Girls have difficulty seeing themselves in engineering careers traditionally inhabited by men, and this can interfere with their engagement and skill-development while in classes meant to prepare them for these careers (Kolker, 2020; Morgan et al., 2013).

The focus of this data analysis is around pedagogical factors that impacted student success during the school year. Success in this study is defined both quantitatively, as measured by traditional assessments, and qualitatively through nodal moments informed by student feedback (Bullough & Pinnegar, 2001).

In reflecting on my journey through the lens of work-integrated learning, I came to recognize the presence of all four major modes of learning as outlined by Kolb (1984). It began with the *concrete experience* of teaching engineering to the girls, in which I intuited that student needs were going unmet. I proceeded to become a *reflective observer*, collecting data and reflecting on it as a way to understand the dynamic in the classroom. This was followed by a period of *abstract conceptualization* in which I dove into the educational literature on gender bias and began to apply the concepts I was researching to what I was experiencing. Lastly, I became an *active experimenter*, making changes to the course to better serve the needs of my students.

There are three themes that emerged during this year of experiential learning that came to inform my practice and skill development as an educator. These themes are: (1) My teaching practice evolved to include additional structure and support for girls during engineering instruction, (2) Conversations with girls about gender stereotypes and implicit gender bias improved my teacher-student relationships and my effectiveness as a teacher, and (3) I have developed a new confidence in modifying the curriculum to meet the specific needs of a student population.

Theme One: My teaching practice evolved to include additional structure and support for girls during engineering instruction.

Six weeks into teaching the course, in mid-October, I found myself in what I came to call *The Intervention*. The girls were assigned an engineering activity that involved construction of a series of metal structures using VEX kit parts. I had given few instructions, having observed that greater time spent in direct instruction caused frustration in male students and did not achieve the desired effect of clarifying questions or increasing understanding. The boys were simply not attending to the instruction and preferred to experiment and solve the challenge on their own. When I gave minimal instructions on an assignment for the third time, in mid-October, a group of them came to me and initiated a conversation in which they articulated their displeasure and frustration with the lack of direction. I composed a blog post in the fall of 2015 that detailed this interaction, excerpted here.

> I knew the all-girls Principles of Engineering class I had fought for and was now teaching at Morristown High School would be special because it was a first. I had no intention of teaching differently to the girls, why would I? Same quizzes, same content, same hands-on projects. Then came the day when they pushed back.
>
> *Mrs. Kolker, you really need to stop that.*
>
> Stop what, Melissa?
>
> *Stop throwing us into the building activities without any direction. Tell us what to do.*
>
> I was shocked. Tell them what to do? C'mon girls, get with the program! Lean In! But they weren't having it, and this was when it finally hit home, during what I later referred to as *The Intervention*. This was the conversation during which I was forced to accept what I had hitherto refused to believe: that engineering is different for girls. Rather, that girls have different needs when it comes to setting the stage for learning engineering, and that I was not addressing these needs adequately. And they made sure I knew it.

What I experienced in that instant was evidence of a gap in student learning; a problem of practice. In the moment, I listened to the girls' concerns and frustrations and made adjustments to my near-term lesson plans. It was only after I sat with the experience and allowed myself an opportunity to reflect on the interaction that I was able to recognize larger forces at play. I realized my unconscious hypothesis going into this course was that girls and boys had equal educational needs and experiences while in engineering and science spaces. These girls, however, had taught me a valuable lesson about my own assumptions.

Without being aware of it, I began a year of experiential, work-integrated learning. Through this genuine *concrete experience* (Kolb, 1984), I recognized a need in my classroom and was starting to challenge my previously held assumptions about the educational process. I identified an initial research question: *To what extent is my teaching pedagogy in an all-girls engineering class as effective as in a mixed-gender class?* I wondered if there were other aspects of the course's structure and my delivery of content that would pose additional challenges to the girls along our journey together.

Concrete experience, according to Kolb (1984), involves subjective feelings that are attached to the learner's present reality. For me, this manifested as my intuition that the girls were experiencing an elevated level of anxiety about inhabiting a role traditionally reserved for males. They demonstrated tremendous insecurity and self-doubt around engineering activities and resulted in reduced engagement and heightened grade anxiety. This experience was the effect they had on their academic performance and comfort level in the classroom. I dedicated the remainder of the year to learning about their situational needs and to developing strategies in the classroom to reduce these anxieties and increase engagement in the engineering curriculum.

Through early conversations with the girls during class, it became evident that they were bringing different prior experiences and manifesting different emotions than boys did around being in an engineering class. This was a true *concrete experience* in which I was unaware of the existence of a problem until I experienced it in my classroom. I began to consider collecting data, becoming a *reflective observer* (Kolb, 1984) by turning my attention to my students' perspectives and reflecting on the causes of the phenomenon I was witnessing. I decided to uncover what they needed and to adjust my pedagogy to meet their needs. This led to a second research question, *How does my teaching pedagogy need to change to meet the educational needs of girls in an engineering class?* As a self-study researcher I was intent upon examining my interactions with the girls and the impact of those interactions on myself and my teaching, as well as on them and their learning. As Bullough and Pinnegar suggest, "the aim of self-study research is to provoke, challenge, and illuminate rather than confirm or settle" (2001, p. 20). With this new information, I was willing to challenge my long-held assumptions and embrace evidence that would ultimately lead to my own professional development and growth as a teacher. My goal for the school year became to identify and implement the most effective teaching techniques for the girls in order to achieve maximum engagement in the engineering material.

As I began the *reflective observer* stage of learning (Kolb, 1984), I recognized the importance of asking questions and collecting data to bring understanding and clarity to the complexity of my new experience. Data collection for this self-study research took the form of class discussions, small group and individual conversations, and surveys. Figure 1 shows the results of a survey of the entire population of POE students (n = 70) during the 2014–2015 year, including both my girls and the boys and girls in the two mixed gender sections running concurrently. In this particular survey, the students were asked to agree or disagree with the following two prompts: (1) In POE, I would rather get my information from the slide decks at home, head straight for the toolbox in class and figure it out on my own, and (2) In POE, I would prefer my teacher to walk us through all the steps on how to build something before we get started.

As a *reflective observer*, I conducted this survey shortly after *The Intervention* in order to confirm what I was seeing and hearing as a phenomenon influenced by gender and not just a few students expressing their opinions. While the numbers of girls agreeing with each of the two opposing statements are roughly equal, the results indicate that there was indeed a significant difference between the educational needs of girls and those of boys. I subsequently conducted our first class meeting in which I

Fig. 1 How much guidance do you want? Survey results from three sections of POE students. Author unpublished raw data

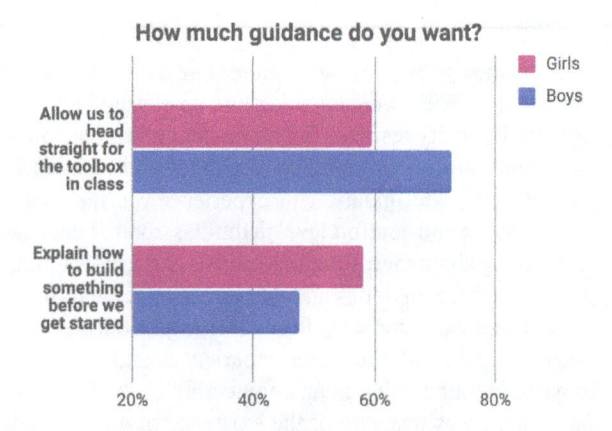

How much guidance do you want?

Category	Girls	Boys
Allow us to head straight for the toolbox in class	~60%	~75%
Explain how to build something before we get started	~60%	~45%

addressed the way in which the course content was delivered, rather than the content of the course itself.

While I had not yet developed an understanding of the motivation underlying the desire for scaffolding and support of our engineering activities, I promised the girls I would do better in meeting their needs. I began to give clear and scaffolded instructions for each hands-on building activity, including an introduction to each tool and its proper use. I provided more structure in delivering all technical content, making sure I explained each step and did not assume prior knowledge in anything engineering-related.

Transitioning into the *abstract conceptualization* phase of my experiential learning (Kolb, 1984), I began to research educational literature on girls' confidence in STEM fields. This led me to an understanding of the construct of self-efficacy as a proxy for confidence (Bandura, 1986). I discovered that girls' lack of self-efficacy in science and mathematics is thought to be one of the leading causes of the gender gap in STEM fields (Bandura, 1986; Colbeck et al., 2001; Dweck, 2006; Mann & DiPrete, 2013; Pajares, 2005; Pajares et al., 2007; Zeldin & Pajares, 2000). Self-efficacy is a better predictor of academic ability for girls than objective measures of ability such as tests and grades (Colbeck et al., 2001), meaning that what girls believe to be true about their capability can become reality.

In this engineering class, I came to realize that girls did not believe they could accomplish the engineering course assignments competently on their own. Lack of self-efficacy can lead to a lack of engagement in skill development, which can then lead to further lack of self-efficacy, becoming a self-fulfilling prophecy (Shumow & Schmidt, 2014).

I began to wonder how I could shift my pedagogy to address and overcome this challenge to engagement. The academic theories on anxiety on self-efficacy helped me to see the underlying factors leading to the girls' desire for structure and support. Understanding the reasons for their academic needs helped guide my thinking when reinterpreting my lesson plans and rethinking the course structure. I struggled to identify needs and to shift my pedagogy to meet them.

As I proceeded on my journey of experiential learning, I began to see my role as teacher less in the form of a facilitator and more as supporter and advocate. I became even more deliberate in my efforts to engage students, including the students in my five physics classes. I did everything I could to make science more approachable and worked to disarm anxieties, particularly for girls. I created more all-girl lab groups and made sure that no one girl found herself in a group with all boys. I began to explicitly compliment girls on their problem-solving skills. I recommended girls to take POE and spoke with parents about this recommendation during conferences. I noticed that the parents of my female students were often surprised, one saying "I didn't realize she was a candidate for engineering!" I noted that parents of my male students never reacted with surprise when I gave them the same recommendation. Without realizing it, I had begun to synthesize theoretical knowledge, personalize it and use it to inform my teaching practice (Kember et al., 2008). I had entered the abstract conceptualization stage of learning, in which I was applying concepts and theory to my experience (Kolb, 1984).

The problems faced by the girls, a historically underrepresented minority in the engineering profession, constituted a complex problem of practice. Having differentiated the academic needs of the girls, I was indeed open and eager to learn how best to use reflective inquiry to determine what they needed and how I could meet their needs through changing my own teaching practice (Kolb, 1984; Rogers, 2001).

The girls had answered my first research question, "To what extent is my teaching pedagogy in an all-girls engineering class as effective as in a mixed-gender class?" with sound recognition that my pedagogy was not, in fact, as effective as it had been with the boys. This moment became the driving force behind my year of experiential learning. Moreover, *The Intervention* opened the door to a conversation between the girls and myself around the different needs and experiences of girls and boys in an engineering domain. I provided the girls with more structure on novel, engineering-based activities which helped alleviate their anxieties. The girls recognized that I was an educational ally and began to open up to me about their concerns and their interests, giving me constructive feedback when I needed it. Furthermore, we began to share our experiences of gender bias in STEM domains.

Theme 2: Conversations with girls about gender stereotypes and implicit gender bias improved my teacher-student relationships and my effectiveness as a teacher.

Taking on the role of *reflective observer* (Kolb, 1984), I began to conduct deliberate conversations during class meetings that explicitly dealt with gender bias and the ways in which it impacted the classroom dynamics. Not fully understanding the effects of gender bias myself, I continued to collect survey data, both quantitative and qualitative. The girls unanimously articulated the significance of an all-girl space providing a lack of judgment and a boost in confidence.

As validated by the girls, I was purposeful in calibrating the classroom climate to be as collaborative, friendly and noncompetitive as possible. In one of my frequent surveys, I asked them to indicate the most important aspect of working on the mechanics unit capstone compound machine design (Table 1). They clearly indicated

Table 1 Survey results from the all-girls engineering class on priorities

What was the most important part of the compound machine design for you?	
Accomplishing something tangible	36.80%
Applying knowledge gained in the unit	36.80%
Working with my hands	15.80%
Getting a good grade	5.30%
Working with friends	5.30%
Competing for highest IMA	0%

their enjoyment in "accomplishing something tangible" and "applying knowledge gained in the unit." These are true indicators of engagement and skill-building in a classroom setting, something that was less likely to happen in an all-gender classroom but was happening before my eyes in this special situation.

I reflected on the data, noting that the girls were not interested in competing; they were there to accomplish something. I was learning what they needed, and the knowledge I was gaining helped me to reinforce what was important to them—relationships, collaboration—and to minimize that which was not.

Transitioning into the *abstract conceptualization* stage of work-integrated learning (Kolb, 1984), I was doing research into literature on gender bias and applying concepts and theories I was identifying to my classroom experience. In an open-ended, qualitative survey I gave the girls, my aim was to identify what about the class was meaningful to them. Extricating their feelings helped me better visualize the dynamics present in class and to align them with theories of gender bias and stereotype threat. The question I posed was: "What about this class makes it different from prior science classes, if anything?" I analyzed the data and translated my results into a presentation I was preparing for the 2015 NSTA STEM Expo (Fig. 2).

Recoding the data for this accounting according to Saldaña (2009), these themes re-emerged. Girls used a consistent set of vernacular to describe the class community we had created. Repeated phrases emerged, including: "more comfortable,"

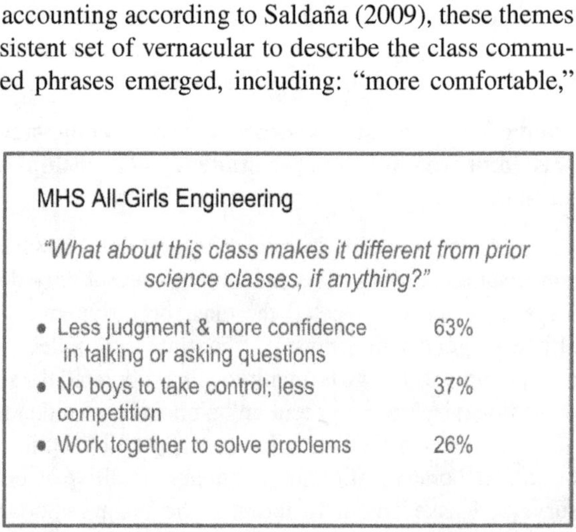

Fig. 2 MHS all-girls engineering, slide from presentation with data from all-girls class. Author unpublished raw data

MHS All-Girls Engineering

"What about this class makes it different from prior science classes, if anything?"

- Less judgment & more confidence in talking or asking questions — 63%
- No boys to take control; less competition — 37%
- Work together to solve problems — 26%

"relaxed," "laid back," with "more liberty" and "more freedom" to be themselves. They also said they felt "less judgment," "less pressure," and that the class was "less intimidating." They also mentioned how they didn't worry about "feeling inferior" or "looking stupid," and experienced a "lack of insecurity."

One anonymous response indicated that girls enjoyed the feeling of being free to be successful in engineering without being judged:

> Student 1: Unlike other science classes, I personally feel a lot more comfortable to show my knowledge. In this one, I am not as intimidated to be the "smart one."

Many other responses showed the impacts of gender stereotype threat they themselves were just becoming aware of.

> Student 2: I feel the difference is that the girls can be themselves and feel comfortable enough to answer questions without looking stupid.

> Student 3: I feel as though in this class my opinions are always heard and appreciated. In other class[es] regardless of this being the 21st century, I still often feel inferior to males in the class. Sometimes they act like they are better, smart etc. In this class my comfortability level is at an all-time high. The tone is also more relaxed. All of the girls work together to solve problems instead of competing against boys often do.

> Student 4: no insecurity in being wrong

> Student 5: Its [sic] also nice to feel like you can speak your mind without being judged like in some other classes where there are mostly boys or many, sometimes its [sic] more difficult to speak your mind.

Reflecting on the data within the context of theories on gender bias and self-efficacy, I was beginning to understand the fundamental forces at play in my classroom. I realized the feelings the girls were having were fully validated by the theories about girls in STEM in academic literature. I read that exposure to stereotypes about girls' abilities in STEM domains strongly thwarts the development of a sense of academic competence or self-efficacy in these domains (Brown & Leaper, 2010; Ertl et al., 2017). I also learned that stereotype threat contributes to anxiety and disengagement in both classroom and workplace (Corbett & Hill, 2015). Reading about stereotype threats in educational literature validated my observations and helped me develop a deeper understanding of the pressures experienced by the girls. The integration of theory and practice facilitated through the reflective inquiry I was doing propelled my learning (Billett, 2009; Cooper et al., 2010) and positioned me within the *abstract conceptualization* stage of my experiential learning journey (Kolb, 1984).

Throughout the year I shared my new theories and ideas with the girls, and we examined the concepts of stereotype threat and implicit gender bias together. As I accumulated relevant academic literature on these topics, I found ways to share what I had learned with the girls. We engaged in short impromptu discussions between activities, or at the start or end of class. I knew the climate I had created was significant to the learning process as the girls became more comfortable in space and began to flourish. Eliminating the competitive nature of the activities and focusing on collaboration and teamwork put the girls at ease and enabled them to better engage in the engineering content. When they experienced anxiety around testing, I encouraged them to believe in themselves and the skills they had developed, and I watched their confidence grow as they succeeded. The relationship we had built together transcended any I had developed in my teaching career. I came to see in a new light the profound impact that trust and a positive teacher-student relationship could have on student achievement (Lee, 2012).

Theme 3: I have developed a new confidence in modifying curriculum to meet the specific needs of a student population.

Out of my developing understanding of stereotype threat and the impacts of anxiety on academic performance in this class, I grew into the *active experimentation* phase of my work-integrated learning (Kolb, 1984). I structured activities and labs to be collaborative in nature. While attending all lessons as prescribed by the curriculum, I eliminated all references to competition, instead framing activities as opportunities for optimization.

Prior to the all-girls course, my goals for each school year were confined to helping my students master the approved curriculum. The POE girls would learn the topics covered in the PLTW engineering course, as had the boys. Once my self-study journey began, however, I started to see places where the POE curriculum fell flat in engaging the girls. I saw opportunities to make the course better, and even ways to bend the curriculum slightly, to make the course more relevant to the girls' lives. Yet, it felt heretical to me to change anything in the official PLTW curriculum that I had agreed to deliver with fidelity.

The first time I took a risk and went "off script" was small in retrospect, although it felt like a completely subversive and radical act. Wanting to fully embrace these moments of developing self-awareness we were all going through and to honor and encourage these conversations, I conducted a class book club in which we read a chapter of Mika Brzezinski's book *Know Your Value: Women, Money, and Getting What You're Worth*. I had read the book and was talking about it with the girls, and they suggested we all read a section together. I assigned a chapter to the girls and asked them to speak with women in their lives about it and to come back ready for a conversation. While I had assigned the chapter to be discussed "at some point," the girls demanded that we have the conversation shortly thereafter. The girls had collected a trove of stories from their female family members that they were eager to share. We held an hour-long discussion about knowing our own value in professional spaces. The girls were wholly engaged and enthusiastic about this topic. Everyone left that class feeling inspired and empowered, myself included. This unsanctioned addition to the course did not teach the girls about engineering, however it was exactly what they needed to help them in developing their nascent STEM identities. I felt emboldened by the feedback I had received from the girls, and the contribution this small act had on the climate in the room and the validation it gave us all as future (or former) women in STEM.

The second change I made was to a foundational project within the POE curriculum. The POE course was aligned with engineering taught in post-secondary programs; however, it was not resonating with the girls. Over the course of the year,

Learning Through Teaching: A Year in an All-Girls Engineering Class 245

it became clear to me that many of the girls, while succeeding in the engineering assignments, were still not seeing the relevance of engineering to their lives and aspirations. I was beginning to understand the importance of self-recognition to the career path of pre-college students, and I felt the need to do more to encourage girls to see themselves as future engineers.

In my research I had come across the Morgan et al. (2013) study Occupational Plans of Women in STEM Majors, in which College women interested in STEM are leaving to pursue other degrees in record numbers. The authors assert that women's occupational plans had been formed prior to college and warn that "much earlier interventions are warranted" (p. 1003). I came to realize that the girls weren't seeing themselves as engineers, computer scientists, technicians. It occurred to me that I was going to have to make a choice between strictly adhering to the curriculum as written and addressing the academic needs of the girls. I came to the realization that I would have to take the risk of changing the program to better serve their needs.

I had observed that the girls engaged more in activities they could connect with altruism and caring for others. I thereby made the decision to change the course's Career Report assignment, a required component of the POE curriculum, into a Humanitarian Engineering Report. My intent was to tap into the interests of the students and help them develop self-recognition in seeing themselves as future engineers. This option was embraced by more than half of the class.

The Career Report assignment is one in which each student chooses, research and reports on one of the many accredited engineering programs in the US. My modifications took the form of choices: the girls could follow the assignment as written or they could focus on the humanitarian aspect of engineering, whether through a company or organization, or through an entire field. Some girls chose the former, although many more chose to focus on the humanitarian aspect of engineering. The assignment I created read as follows:

> What is Humanitarian Engineering? It is research, design and development to directly improve the well-being of poor, marginalized, or under-served communities which often lack the means to address pressing problems. This is a philosophy, not a discipline. You cannot get a degree in HE. But you can find evidence of it everywhere, all over the world. People helping people.
>
> You will write a report on one aspect of Humanitarian Engineering, of your choosing. It may be a type of degree program, such as environmental or biomechanical engineering. It may be the work that is done by corporations or non-governmental organizations (NGOs) with engineers who build water systems or fortify electrical power systems in a country or build prosthetics for wounded veterans. Or it may be a project of a charity group such as Engineers for A Sustainable World or Engineers without Borders, professionals and students who take on projects all over the world.
>
> Reading the girls' essays, I recognized that I had indeed discovered a way to make engineering resonate with a majority of them.
>
> Student 1: "I am planning to pursue Prosthetics and Orthotics engineering… The curriculum is extremely difficult and fast paced but the payoff of being able to work one on one with people who have been through dramatic life events and being able to make them physically

whole again… truly fills me with pure joy and pride knowing that some say I will be able to do that with my life."

Student 2: "I chose this career field to do research on because it is so interesting, and there isn't a place that a civil engineer hasn't created something to improve our everyday life. I especially liked how they are the engineers who help the poor, I'd like to think, the most out of all other engineers. The best aspect of this career is definitely helping the less fortunate, and being able to make a difference in the world."

These small changes, while minor in scope, felt radical and subversive in the moment. To my mind, I had become a teacher wise enough to bend the curriculum to the needs of her students. This was beyond professional development, this *active experimentation* (Kolb, 1984) redefined my role in the classroom. My allegiance was to my students and their learning, the curriculum was solely the medium for the learning. Through self-study, my perspectives had been transformed by the girls and the learning experience they afforded me (Kember et al., 2008). By altering the course activities and environment, it became clear I was evolving as an educator.

8 Reflection

Through the year of this case study, I performed a reflective study of my teaching practices that resulted in transformative learning. The experiences in the all-girl classroom enabled me to develop improvements to my own teaching practice. In response to my second research question, "How does my teaching pedagogy need to change to meet the educational needs of girls in an engineering or physics class?" I have settled on three distinct changes to my pedagogy that are a direct result of this experience. I have learned (1) to provide girls with additional structure and support in navigating engineering activities, (2) to conduct explicit conversations about stereotypes, implicit bias and knowing one's worth with girls, and (3) to be confident in modifying curriculum to meet the particular needs of my students.

Was I effective in teaching the girls engineering? Did the changes to my teaching practice benefit them academically? Did the all-girls course make a difference? In one of the class surveys I collected, a student explicitly acknowledged my efforts and validated the effectiveness of the changes I had made to my teaching. When asked what she would change in order to improve the course for the following year, she responded,

Nothing really, although I would continue with the change we made towards the beginning of the year, where the concepts and how to do everything was explained to us first, and then we would go and try on our own. I also like when we do a practice problem before attempting a problem on our own.

I conducted one final survey at the end of the class to find out how they felt about taking the course, which produced the following response:

I am glad I took it because it persuaded me to go into engineering. I was unsure whether I wanted to continue it because I did not want to go to a college that I would end up disliking. This class showed me I have a talent for it and enjoy it.

Indeed, a mid-year poll had indicated she was not alone. I asked all POE students, boys and girls, about how the engineering course was having on their intent to take future engineering courses in college. I asked them to quantify their feelings at the start of the class on a Likert-type scale, and again at the time of the poll (midyear), and then I graphed the change in perceptions (Fig. 3). Approximately twenty percent of girls and twenty percent of boys realized, halfway through the school year, that they were not interested in pursuing engineering. On the other hand, when it came to experiencing a positive change in interest, 39% of girls expressed an increased interest in taking future engineering courses, which was nearly double the 22% of boys with a similar experience. The girls experienced more of an increase in interest than boys in engineering as a result of participation in the class. This gave me evidence to support the theory that taking an engineering course in high school has a significant impact on girls and indicated that my teaching practice positively affected the girls' experience in the class.

In the final course survey, more students anonymously validated that they were leaving the course with feelings of competence. For example,

Anonymous student 1: "I am glad i took it because it opened my eyes up to all the engineering possibilities and showed me just how much work and how difficult it is to do engineering, but I also feel like because I was able to complete the class and do well that I have more of an ability to do engineering that I previously thought."

Anonymous student 2: "I took physics my sophomore year, but since I was in a class full of juniors and seniors, I didn't feel that comfortable there and didn't enjoy it, but I did enjoy the physics in this class."

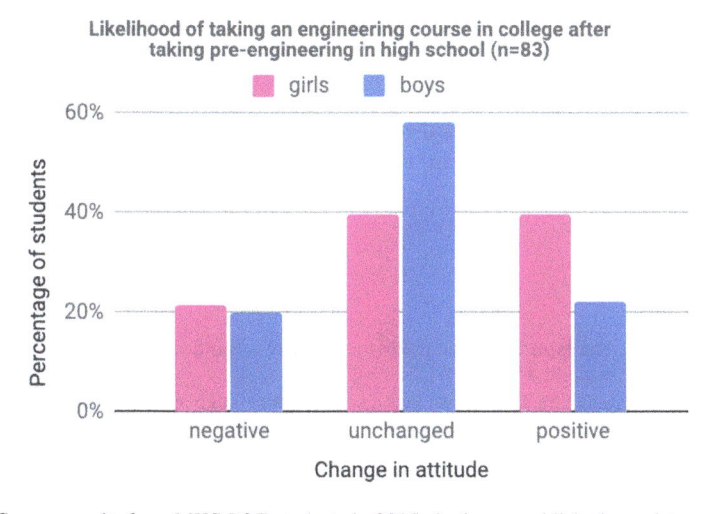

Fig. 3 Survey results from MHS POE students in 2015. Author unpublished raw data

Girls who leave engineering and physics classes with a sense of self-efficacy are more likely to persist in these domains. (Zeldin & Pajares, 2000). I had evidence that the changes I had made to my teaching practice had made a difference.

This experience of reflective inquiry enabled me to transform my teaching practice in fundamental and profound ways. I now view a curriculum as a medium for creating learning opportunities. I have made it my duty as an educator to help bend the curriculum toward the particular needs and skill sets of each new class of students. In this period of experiential learning, I aimed to improve the course and my teaching practices for the benefit of the girls, in order to encourage more to take up engineering in college. Marrying educational theory with situated inquiry enabled me to formalize my learning, demonstrating a knowledge of practice as I presented my learning to the professional community of science teachers (Loughran, 2007).

My work-integrated learning journey traversed all four of Kolb's stages. I began with an authentic *concrete classroom experience* which completely took me by surprise. I engaged in *reflective observation* in order to better understand the phenomenon at hand, then through *abstract conceptualization* I conducted research in order to apply logic, theory and new concepts to the experience. By the second semester of this year, I was compelled to engage in *active experimentation* as a means of improving outcomes for the students. Throughout this year of experiential learning, I became a more effective educator, tailoring my teaching to the needs of my students. I learned to provide additional support to girls in engineering and physics classes as a way to assuage their situational anxiety. I better understand the connection between teacher-student relationships and academic achievement, and I have become more authentic with my students in the classroom. Lastly, I am now confident that modifying the curriculum to better suit the needs and culture of the students improves learning.

The process of self-study was never something that I planned to undertake. I entered into it genuinely and naively as a means for improving the experience of my students. I did not expect my assumptions to be upended or for my teaching practice to be so profoundly changed. This case study was a transformative experience in my professional career. Self-study is now a part of my practice. I now look upon each class as an opportunity for situated learning, to deepen my teaching practice and move ever closer to the teacher I am becoming.

References

Bandura, A. (1986). The explanatory and predictive scope of self-efficacy theory. *Journal of Social and Clinical Psychology, 4*(3), 359–373.
Billett, S. (2009). Realizing the educational worth of integrating work experiences in higher Education. *Studies in Higher Education, 34*(7), 827–843.
Brzezinski, M. (2018). *Know your value: Women, money, and getting what you're worth*. Hachette Books.

Brown, C., & Leaper, C. (2010). Latina and European American girls' experiences with academic sexism and their self-concepts in mathematics and science during adolescence. *Sex Roles, 63*(11–12), 860–870.

Bullough, R. V., Jr., & Pinnegar, S. (2001). Guidelines for quality in autobiographical forms of self-study research. *Educational Researcher, 30*(3), 13–21.

Colbeck, C., Cabrera, A., & Terenzini, P. (2001). Learning professional confidence: Linking teaching practices, students' self-perceptions, and gender. *The Review of Higher Education, 24*(2), 173–191.

Cooper, L., Orrell, J., & Bowden, M. (2010). *Work integrated learning: A guide to effective practice.* Routledge.

Corbett, C., & Hill, C. (2015). *Solving the equation: The variables for women's success in engineering and computing.* American Association of University Women.

Dinkelman, T. (2003). Self-study in teacher education: A means and ends tool for promoting reflective teaching. *Journal of Teacher Education, 54*(1), 6–18.

Dweck, C. (2006). *Mindset: The new psychology of success.* Random House.

Ertl, B., Luttenberger, S., & Paechter, M. (2017). The impact of gender stereotypes on the self-concept of female students in STEM subjects with an under-representation of females. *Frontiers in Psychology, 8,* 703.

Kember, D., McKay, J., Sinclair, K., & Wong, F. K. Y. (2008). A four-category scheme for coding and assessing the level of reflection in written work. *Assessment & Evaluation in Higher Education, 33*(4), 369–379.

Kolb, D. A. (1984). *Experiential learning: Experience as the source of learning and development.* Prentice Hall.

Kolker, M. C. (2020). *Identifying factors contributing to positive STEM identity for high school girls* [Doctoral dissertation, University of Massachusetts Lowell].

LaBoskey, V. K. (2004). The methodology of self-study and its theoretical underpinnings. In *International handbook of self-study of teaching and teacher education practices* (pp. 817–869). Springer Netherlands.

Lee, J. S. (2012). The effects of the teacher–student relationship and academic press on student engagement and academic performance. *International Journal of Educational Research, 53,* 330–340.

Loughran, J. (2007). Researching teacher education practices: Responding to the challenges, demands, and expectations of self-study. *Journal of Teacher Education, 58*(1), 12–20.

Loughran, J. (2010). Seeking knowledge for teaching: Moving beyond stories. *Studying Teacher Education, 6*(3), 221–226.

Mann, A., & DiPrete, T. (2013). Trends in gender segregation in the choice of science and engineering majors. *Social Science Research, 42*(6), 1519–1541.

Morgan, S. L., Gelbgiser, D., & Weeden, K. A. (2013). Feeding the pipeline: Gender, occupational plans, and college major selection. *Social Science Research, 42*(4), 989–1005.

New Jersey Department of Education. (2018–2019). NJ school performance report. https://rc.doe.state.nj.us/report.aspx?type=summaryschool&lang=english&county=27&district=3385&school=050&schoolyear=2018-2019.

Pajares, F. (2005). Self-efficacy during childhood and adolescence: Implications for teachers and parents. In Urdan & Pajares (Eds.), *Self-efficacy beliefs of adolescents* (pp. 339–367). Information Age Publishing.

Pajares, F., Johnson, M. J., & Usher, E. L. (2007). Sources of writing self-efficacy beliefs of elementary, middle and high school students. *Research in the Teaching of English, 42*(1), 104–120.

Pithouse, K., Mitchell, C., & Weber, S. (2009). Self-study in teaching and teacher development: A call to action. *Educational Action Research, 17*(1), 43–62.

Rogers, R. R. (2001). Reflection in higher education: A concept analysis. *Innovative Higher Education, 26*(1), 37–57.

Saldaña, J. (2009). *The coding manual for qualitative researchers.* Sage Publications.

Schön, D. (1983). *The reflective practitioner: How professionals think in action.* Basic Books.

Shumow, L., & Schmidt, J. A. (2014). *Classroom insights from educational psychology. Enhancing adolescents' motivation for science: Research-based strategies for teaching male and female students.* Corwin Press.

Stirling, A., Kerr, G., Banwell, J., MacPherson, E., & Heron, A. (2016). *A practical guide for work-integrated learning: Effective practices to enhance the educational quality of structured work experiences offered through colleges and universities.* Higher Education Quality Council of Ontario.

Zeldin, A., & Pajares, F. (2000). Against the odds: Self-efficacy beliefs of women in mathematical, scientific, and technological careers. *American Educational Research Journal, 37*(1), 215–246.

Full Circle: A Personal Journey of Work-Integrated Learning and Self-Directed Discovery

Karin A. Loach

Abstract This chapter delves into my personal and professional journey through an unconventional route toward my chosen career in education. Departing from the traditional path, I share two pivotal narratives highlighting the transformative power of work-integrated learning (WIL) and my impact on future educators. Grounded within the theoretical frameworks of WIL, Embodied, Situated, and Distributed (ESD) cognition, and Self-Regulated Learning (SRL), this chapter underscores the importance of experiential learning across a diverse set of circumstances. Further, central to my journey lies the construct of self-directed learning (SDL), which allowed me agency and autonomy along my educational journey. This chapter serves as a testament to the transformative power of experiential learning and self-directed inquiry in shaping both my personal and professional growth within the realm of education.

Keywords Science, Technology, Engineering, Mathematics (STEM) · Teacher efficacy · Work integrated learning · Embodied situated distributed learning

1 Introduction

I was not a traditional student who entered my chosen career in my early twenties. Instead, my life experiences ignited a passion for education and learning, eventually leading me to my science classroom, leadership opportunities, doctoral studies, and beyond. In this chapter, I tell two stories. The first highlights my work-integrated learning experiences, which led to my emergence as a practitioner leader. The second describes my impact on those carrying the academic torch after me.

K. A. Loach (✉)
Worcester State University, Worcester, MA, USA
e-mail: kloach@worcester.edu

2 Thematic Relevance

Work Integrated Learning (WIL), Embodied, Situated, and Distributed (ESD) cognition, and Self-Regulated Learning (SRL) frameworks serve as a foundation for this chapter. WIL is a pedagogical practice that promotes experiential learning across educational and workplace settings (Billett, 2009, 2020). Grounded firmly within Herman Schneider's Cooperative Educational and Internship paradigm, where classroom studies were combined with practical work (Cooperative Education & Internship Association, Inc., 2022), WIL can include learning within the workplace and community or service learning. Tied to ESD learning, WIL asserts that knowledge acquisition is situated within a workplace or program (Cooper et al., 2010). Accessing WIL teacher education programs, whether for in-service teachers in the form of professional development or preservice teachers, courses are charged with fostering theoretical understandings of teaching and learning as well as pedagogical knowledge (Junqueira et al., 2011). ESD cognition theoretical framework examines how multisensory experiences within a learner's natural and cultural-historical worlds influence learning (Chahine, 2013). Although deeply rooted in cognitive science (Agostini & Francesconi, 2021), ESD can be tied to all facets of education. Grounded in Dewey's (1938) Experiential Learning Theory, learning intersects with meaningful environmental and cognitive processes. Referring to the experiential learning process, Kolb (1984) notes that learning is constructed and reconstructed through sets of experiences. Kolb (1984) further asserts that, "Learning involves transactions between the person and the environment." (p. 34) SRL, however, is a process by which learners set goals for learning, monitor their progress, and adjust strategies to achieve them. SRL includes metacognitive, behavioral, motivational, and emotional/affective aspects of learning (Panadero, 2017, p. 1).

WIL and SRL are situated in the constructivism learning theory, which suggests that learners construct knowledge through experiences and interactions. For example, Piaget (1972) proposed that learners must actively engage with their environments to build knowledge. He further asserted that learners move through cognitive stages of development as they interact with their environments to build increasingly complex mental structures. Similarly, Vygotsky (1978) emphasized the role of social interactions with others with a more significant knowledge base to help learners expand their understanding and build new cognitive concepts and ideas.

Research surrounding Self-directed learning (SDL) is akin to learner autonomy, where learners are more engaged in and take control over their learning process (Mercadal, 2021; Thornton, 2013). Further noted is that SDL is a cyclical process that involves four phases:

- Planning: In this phase, specific and achievable learning goals are set based on interest and need.
- Learners also identify resources and strategies they will employ to achieve said goals.
- Monitoring: Here, learners track their own progress toward learning goals.

- Regulation: In this phase, learners use self-selected strategies and resources to achieve learning goals.
- Reflection: Learners reflect and evaluate progress towards goals and readjust as necessary to meet goals.

The SDL cycle framework is flexible, can be applied to a myriad of learning situations, and is used by learners of all ages and abilities. As a result, users of the SLR cycle become more self-directed, motivated, and effective in their learning processes (Thornton, 2013).

Through a deep examination of the theoretical learning constructs mentioned above, the following text is a self-study of my personal and professional experiences that have shaped my expanding knowledge and evolving pedagogy.

3 Review of Significant Literature

There is a growing body of research on WIL and self-directed learning (SDL) related to preservice teachers and learners in general. Du Plessis (2010) noted a disconnect between coursework and practical teaching experiences in a mixed-methods study focused on preservice teachers participating in distance learning coursework. Du Plessis further asserted that effective WIL focuses on "the application of theory in an authentic, work-based context" (p. 62). Data showed that, for WIL to be successful, it must be purposeful, well-planned, and highly structured.

Also centered upon preservice teacher training, Rusznyak and Bertram (2021) found that WIL approaches are ineffective when they are seen as a logistical matter of simply placing preservice teachers in schools. The author further explained that mentor teachers are pivotal in WIL placement success as they engage in relevant conversations and set high expectations for preservice teachers.

4 Methodology

This study employs a study of self to reflect upon and understand my sense of self and the development of my pedagogical practice. Qualitative data were collected through self-narratives and autobiographical memories, which revealed influences upon my personal and professional identities. The following are pivotal moments in my journey that have profoundly impacted my sense of self.

5 Personal Work Integrated Learning Journey

To say that my life has been surrounded by science, technology, engineering, and mathematics (STEM) would be an understatement. My mother loves to tell stories of how I disassembled my leg braces and crib as a toddler or spent most of my time on merry-go-rounds looking at the gears to see how they worked. My father, a civil engineer, owned a construction company and taught my sisters and me how to read blueprints and use tools; as we got older, he took us to job sites to help with finish work on buildings. So, you could say I was into STEM subjects long before they became in vogue.

In early 2000, my husband, children, and I moved back to Massachusetts after my husband had served ten years in the United States Navy. We spent those years having wonderful adventures and living in diverse cities and towns across the United States. I held various jobs during these years, knowing that each was temporary. Hence, I was not invested in looking for a long-term career at the time. However, in November of that year, I accepted a special education instructional assistant position in a local school system. I was tasked to work with special education students in grades three through five. For three years, I enjoyed working with students and their diverse abilities, helping them reach their fullest academic potential. Realizing I had a knack for working with students with behavioral challenges, the superintendent transitioned me to our town's middle school as a one-to-one aide. This year was tough for me. My young student displayed many challenging behaviors I had not encountered before. Still, I persevered and learned to navigate her behavior while helping her with her class studies. As difficult as my student was then, I was open to learning how to motivate her to learn while managing her behaviors. During this time, I also fell in love with teaching and learning at the middle school level and yearned for my own classroom. With my husband's and principal's support, I left the school system at the end of the school year and enrolled at a local college pursuing a degree in Natural Science with a Middle School Education minor. I completed my degree and was quickly rehired at middle school to teach eighth-grade science. Working as an eighth-grade science teacher, I continually strive to help my students see how their disciplines of study are intertwined and that by understanding this interconnectedness, a deeper connection with content is created, leading to more significant knowledge acquisition. Within my first few years of teaching, I deeply desired to continue my education. Therefore, I began considering master's programs in my local area. After much research, I discovered an online program that met my needs as a busy wife, mother, and teacher. Working through the program, I dove into educational theory. I soaked in information on how to meet the needs of my diverse learners while learning the skills necessary to become an educational leader.

6 Becoming a Teacher-Leader: A Development of Self-Esteem

As the 2010–2011 school year ended and the science curriculum coordinator position became available, I was approached by my colleague, Diane. Diane was a friend and a veteran teacher, and when I was hired, she served as my mentor. It is common practice for districts to provide new teachers with mentor practitioners to help integrate the new educator into the culture of the school building and to provide WIL experiences in efforts to provide support, feedback, and encouragement as they navigate their first years of teaching. Furthermore, mentors, such as Diane, provide WIL experiences to help new educators to build professional networks within the school, district, and community. Additionally, mentors help new teachers make connections with colleagues, building resources, and provide opportunities for collaboration, ultimately supporting their professional growth and development.

Diane explained that the department ideals had become stale, and she and other veteran teachers thought they needed an infusion of new ideas. She explained to me that I would be the best candidate for the position of science curriculum coordinator as she saw my focus as a science teacher was not just to purvey science content but to help my students see how their disciplines of study are connected with one another and that through the understanding of the correlation, a deeper connection with content could form. In addition, Diane saw how dedicated I was to bring new ideas into my classroom and recognized that my dedication and positive energy were just what the department needed. I must admit that at this point, I was flattered and terrified at the same time. Would I have anything of substance to add not only to the department but to the school as a whole? Would veteran teachers from other departments take me seriously? These are some of the questions I grappled with as I considered applying for the position. With great trepidation, I applied for the position and was immediately relieved when my principal applauded my decision. As the next school year and department head meetings began, I decided to wait to introduce my ideas directly. At this time, I had low self-efficacy in my ability to bring about real change within the department. After all, I was still considered a "new teacher," what could I offer these veterans? As I listened to those veteran teachers' trials, tribulations, and laments on doing things "like we always have," I became convinced I could be a catalyst for positive change within the building. I was bursting with energy and fresh ideas about getting kids and educators excited to learn. During the school year, through WIL opportunities afforded to me in my new position, I became more confident and more vocal, asserting my ideas for bringing about positive change and building our school's professional learning community. I started a gardening club for staff and students, sought funds to bring in new (and much-needed) science supplies and equipment, and participated in new initiatives that celebrated student achievement.

7 A Challenge of a Different Kind: The Development of Self in Social Contexts

In the fall of 2011, I was called to my principal's office along with two of my colleagues, Erik, a fellow science teacher, and Bill, a technology engineering teacher at our school. The principal had learned about the Innovation Schools Planning Grant Initiative offered as a component of An Act Relative to the Achievement Gap (The 193rd General Court of the Commonwealth of Massachusetts, 2010), which was signed into law by Governor Duval Patrick in 2010 and was looking for a team of teachers to do research and compose the grant proposal. However, with only three weeks until the deadline for submission, Bill, Erik, and I were apprehensive. We all had little experience preparing grant requests, and it was a monumental task to research, plan, and generate the necessary documentation in three weeks.

In the days following, we sifted through the requirements of the grant and quickly realized that we had the power to create programs and garner funds to bring about real change for our school. The literature surrounding WIL suggests that learning can occur through systematic training or sustained work experiences (Bleakney, 2019). Navigating the uncharted waters of the grant writing process while attempting to meet the needs of various stakeholders and working under the guidance of our principal, we each took on leadership roles and responsibilities as we proposed programs with a focus on Science, Technology, Engineering, and Mathematics (STEM) education for the betterment of our students.

We set goals and expected outcomes for our writing using the SDL cycle. We first sought to enhance our Technology Education department by infusing it with much-needed, updated supplies and equipment. We believed revamping the old "wood shop" to a more advanced engineering space was necessary to strengthen the program. Also, as a Massachusetts Comprehensive Assessment System (MCAS) underperforming district, we looked to provide remediation instruction for students falling in the "warning and needs improvement" categories. As a direct result of this initiative, we created our school's Math II program, which worked in conjunction with traditional math classes and focused on building basic math skills. Further, as a science teacher and department head, I looked for ways to bring the science curriculum to life for my students. Much of the middle school curriculum is, by and large, unobservable within a middle school classroom. It was paramount for me to provide students with experiences that would enhance their understanding of challenging curriculum topics. Therefore, I proposed using Gizmos (Explore Learning, 2024), which is a learning platform composed of online interactive laboratory activities. With these lab activities, students can view atoms on subatomic levels or study how plate tectonics influence Earth's process. With the proposition and development of the aforementioned programs, the writing team was responsible for designing the curriculum and creating budgets and measurable goals. Finally, we created a STEM summer camp, of which I became camp counselor and director. The STEM camp utilizes a curriculum from the Boston Museum of Science to present campers with unique engineering challenges based on yearly themes. Whether stranded on a deserted island, trekking through the Amazon, or scaling Mt. Everest, we explore STEM curriculum at each step. I take great pride in providing our campers a fun and educational program each summer.

As the deadline for submission for the grant drew near, we were required to present our prospectus to the building's faculty, who would then vote to accept or reject our proposal. As major stakeholders, the faculty's motivation for our initiatives would significantly determine its success. We were surprised during our presentation by how many faculty members resisted the proposed programs, seeing them as more work placed upon them. Pažur Anicic and Divjak (2022) note that "stakeholders' motivation for participation in WIL has a substantial impact on successful outcomes" (p. 51). Collectively, the writing team clarified that the programs would supplement already great work within the building and create clubs and a summer camp for students interested in STEM subjects. After much discussion, the faculty responded with a vote of acceptance. Our next presentation was to the district's school committee, which immediately voted to accept the proposal.

As we submitted our grant to the Massachusetts Department of Elementary and Secondary Education (DESE), the writing team felt an overwhelming sense of accomplishment and pride that we had proposed programs that would benefit and support both our staff and students. In addition, through this WIL opportunity, we honed leadership skills in creating programs, policies, and budgets to get our programs off the ground with minimal increase in teacher workload.

We waited anxiously for a month until we got word that we would be awarded a $10,000 planning grant to develop our proposal further. Again, Bill, Erik, and I assembled and enhanced our original proposal to include a newly designed school schedule and purchasing PITSCO engineering products to further supplement the Math II and technology engineering program. Finally, with great satisfaction, we received word that our school had been awarded $25,000 to implement all our proposed programs.

The writing of the Innovation Schools Grant was a turning point for me as it allowed me to take a leadership role and work within a team to create and plan innovative programs for our school. Writing this prospectus changed my vision of leadership and curriculum development as I broadened my view to look outside my classroom and department and began to work on creating programs for the betterment of the school at large.

8 District Leadership Opportunity: Development of Self-identity

In the Spring of 2013, I was asked by our district's Assistant Superintendent to represent our district at the National Math + Science Initiative's (NMSI) Laying the Foundation PreAP science training. I was also asked if I would share gained knowledge with my department in the fall. Of course, I agreed, as I believe seeking out new strategies to increase student understanding and achievement is imperative.

The training was exceptional, and, at the end of the week, I was asked by NMSI to be our district's lead PreAP teacher with duties that included holding vertical department meetings with our high school, providing professional development to the vertical team, keeping logs of the sessions, and providing summaries of the meetings. Vertical team meetings involve educators from differing grade levels coming together to collaborate on curriculum and strategies to enhance student learning. Smith and Ferns (2018) note that WIL opportunities, such as vertical team meetings, benefit teachers by providing deep understanding of pedagogy and an improved ability to apply theoretical knowledge in real-world settings. Therefore, I eagerly accepted the opportunity to share my new knowledge with teachers in my district.

With excitement, I planned the first meeting. What I did not expect was the resistance I experienced from secondary school teachers. How could I, a teacher for only six years and only a middle school general science teacher, have anything to teach them? This attitude was evident as, although these teachers attended the meeting as mandated, they clearly did not find the meeting of any value. Some teachers ignored me entirely, busying themselves with other work. My colleague's behavior and disrespect floored me. Knowing I had to hold three more of these meetings over the school year, I needed to figure out how I could make the high school teachers see me as a curriculum leader and not just a middle school general science teacher.

With only one month until our next meeting, I planned a presentation on PreAP laboratory activity on global climate change. Wanting to engage all the educators, as part of the presentation, I had all participants complete portions of the activity, which I had differentiated to meet the needs of each grade level represented. At first, the high school teachers rolled their eyes and looked exasperated. However, after some firm prompting, they participated in the activity and seemed to enjoy themselves. Much to my relief, many (not all) of the secondary school teachers spoke to me much more respectfully by the end of the meeting.

As the school year went on and we held the rest of our vertical team meetings, the atmosphere in the room changed from tension to collegiality and mutual respect. Meeting members transitioned from reluctant participants to willing collaborators. Although frustrating, this experience helped me develop my leadership skills within a group of my peers. Without the empowerment I felt from this work-integrated learning experience and the self-efficacy I developed while holding the meetings, I may not have had the conviction to take on the challenging tasks ahead of me.

I NEVER LIKED SCIENCE

Self-study, in the context of doctoral research, centers upon independent learning and exploration to supplement knowledge and gain expertise in areas not covered in formal coursework. Additionally, combining WIL with self-study in research can be a powerful and enriching approach that integrates practical experience with independent learning. This combination allows researchers to bridge the gap between theory and practice, gain real-world insights, and develop a deeper understanding of their research topic. Finally, combining WIL and self-study creates a more holistic and well-rounded learning experience for the researcher, enhancing the impact and relevance of research findings in real-world contexts.

Research for my doctoral dissertation began with my students long before my formal research began. In my science class, I kept hearing my students say, "I never liked science," which confused me as research shows that children are born with an innate "…interest in science and that learning the fundamental principles of scientific inquiry at a young age is critical to success in secondary science courses" (Epstein & Miller, 2011, p. 11). I began having casual conversations with teachers at the elementary level, asking about science education. What I found out was alarming. Educators asserted that they did not feel qualified to teach science, specifically the recently released Massachusetts Science and Technology/Engineering Framework Standards (Massachusetts Department of Education, 2016), and were uncomfortable teaching them. Teachers also cited the lack of science content-specific professional development, which further added to feelings of inadequacy. Studies show that teachers have a significant impact not only on student learning but can shape students' attitudes and behaviors. Additionally, educators play a pivotal role in helping students navigate and make connections between the curriculum and their daily lives. The paradigm of embodied, situated, and distributed cognition (ESDC) suggests that actions and the environment influence learning (Macrine & Fugate, 2022). Teachers' feelings of inadequacy directly influence their ability to teach the subject, which was shown in students' state assessment results.

Armed with this information, I sought out and was accepted to a doctoral program with the hopes of enhancing my knowledge pertaining to curriculum development, educational policies, and instructional practices in STEM subjects. By deepening my knowledge base, I aspired to improve opportunities for teachers to increase their content knowledge and pedagogy of STEM subjects. As I became immersed in my studies, my conversations with elementary teachers became the driving force for my dissertation research. My dissertation aimed to assess the teachers' science teaching efficacy and identify the contributing factors to the development of self-efficacy, specifically at the elementary level.

9 Factors that Influence Elementary Teachers' Science Teaching Efficacy

The following is a summary of my dissertation studies which incorporates WIL experiences and will frame the balance of this chapter.

Bandura's (1997) social learning theoretical framework offered seminal knowledge about an individual's perceived self-efficacy influencing the development of teaching efficacy. Teacher efficacy refers particularly to one's perception of his/her/their effectiveness in generating desired outcomes pertaining to student learning, even when confronted with unmotivated or problematic students (Goddard et al., 2000; Tschannen-Moran & McMaster, 2009; Tschannen-Moran & Woolfolk Hoy, 2001; Tschannen-Moran et al., 1998). Teachers with high levels of self-efficacy are more willing to take risks trying new strategies or techniques, are more organized and more resilient in the face of adversity, and positively influence student motivation, efficacy, and achievement (Henson, 2001). Bandura (1982) asserted that four central tenets directly contribute to the development of self-efficacy: mastery experiences, vicarious experiences, social persuasion, and psychological arousal. Attained through resiliency to overcome obstacles, the construct of mastery experiences builds self-efficacy through perseverance and concentrated, sustained effort.

Conversely, the inability to complete a task or solve a problem can undermine self-efficacy. Vicarious experiences or the observations of others considered role models who successfully navigate challenges positively influence self-efficacy by perceived similarities to the successes of role models. Social persuasion centers upon an individual's verbal persuasion necessary to master activities rather than laboring upon setbacks. Finally, psychological arousal, or personal emotional state, directly impacts how an individual judge his/her/their capabilities and persistence in overcoming challenges (Loach, 2020a, 2020b). Bandura (1982, 1993) postulated that self-efficaciousness ties heavily to the investment of cognitive efforts and knowledge and skill acquisition.

Connections can be made between teacher self-efficacy and WIL. Teachers participating in WIL opportunities can develop a greater sense of self-efficacy as they gain practical experience and apply acquired knowledge directly into their classrooms. Feelings of greater self-efficacy can further lead to greater self-confidence in their abilities, thus leading to greater student achievement. Additionally, teachers who experience WIL may be better equipped to incorporate problem-based learning opportunities for students, building 21st-century skills needed for future career readiness.

10 Relevant Literature

An extensive literature review revealed a large body of research indicating the value of STEM education in early elementary schooling (Kazempour, 2014; Keeley, 2009; Keller, 2016; Morgan et al., 2016). However, further studies show that elementary teachers are underqualified or not adequately trained to teach science (Nowikowski, 2016). Quantitative, qualitative, and mixed methods studies focusing on teaching efficacy beliefs identified factors such as time spent on science content, targeted elementary science professional development, availability and management of science materials, the community's attitude toward science, and participation in science professional learning communities (PLCs) played a pivotal role in building teachers' individual teaching efficacy (Loach, 2020b).

11 Methodology

Employing an exploratory, concurrent mixed methods case study, I collected qualitative data through semi-structured interviews with elementary teachers and quantitative data through demographic surveys and the Science Teaching Efficacy Belief Instrument (STEBI) survey (Riggs & Enochs, 1989) to assess teachers' overall feelings of science teaching efficacy. Study results highlighted several contributing factors to building teachers' self-efficacy in science. These include limited access to science professional development, building facility or technology issues, administration, and socioemotional status (Loach, 2020a, 2020b). Qualitative analysis indicated that teachers had an overwhelming lack of confidence and high levels of anxiety in teaching the 2016 Massachusetts Science, Technology, and Engineering Framework Standards. Citing a lack of professional development before implementing the new frameworks, teachers noted that they needed to gain knowledge of the standards' cross-cutting concepts, practices in science, and pedagogy in teaching science. Additionally, educators emphasized the need for more classroom space to engage students in scientific inquiry and efficiently store science materials. This, coupled with unreliable internet access, impacted planned lessons almost daily. In conjunction with pressures from building administration to adhere to a rigid pacing guide and overwhelming feelings of a lack of support, these factors negatively contributed to teachers' feelings of self-efficacy.

12 Research Findings

Quantitative data analysis (ANOVA) centers upon research questions that look at correlations between science teaching efficacy and the number of years teaching or how belonging to a teaching team influences science teaching efficacy. Although no statistically significant differences were found between science self-efficacy and years of teaching service, there was evidence that participating within a teaching team positively influenced science teaching efficacy. Qualitative data provided a more comprehensive picture of factors that influence the science teaching efficacy of in-service elementary teachers. Codes extracted from participant interviews and observations revealed several categories, including socioemotional, institutional, and environmental factors, teachers' personal feelings, professional practice, and professional development. Through numerous reviews of these categories, four themes related to teaching efficacy became apparent:

1. Socioemotional factors as detrimental to self-efficacy
2. Limitations to teachers' professional practice
3. School facility/internet factors not under teacher control
4. Factors connected with district or building administrations (Loach, 2020a, p. 66).

Based on research findings, several recommendations were made to the district participating in my research study, including:

(1) **The need for ongoing, science content-specific professional development for elementary teachers.** Teachers with access to high-quality professional development (PD) in science are more likely to feel confident in their ability to effectively teach science subject matter, leading to greater feelings of self-efficacy. Targeted professional development and WIL opportunities can help teachers deepen their understanding of science content and concepts, improving the quality of their instruction and leading to better student outcomes. Further, PD and WIL opportunities can enhance pedagogical practices by providing teachers with collaboration opportunities with other educators centering upon new teaching strategies and techniques specifically tailored to teaching science. This can help teachers become more effective in engaging students in scientific inquiry and problem-solving, leading to more active and engaging science instruction. Incorporating WIL into teacher PD can further help schools build stronger relationships with industry partners, which can lead to opportunities for educators and students to engage in work-based learning opportunities.

(2) **Employ a science curriculum coach to support teachers within the classroom** ESD learning theory suggests that learning occurs best through multimodal experiences (Chahine, 2013) when situated in a specific context and grounded in authentic experiences. Informed by the principles of situated learning, science instructional coaches are crucial at the elementary level as they play a pivotal role in supporting teachers in the day-to-day implementation of science curriculum and instruction. WIL research by Darling-Hammond (2008) suggests that teachers who regularly participate in WIL opportunities are more likely to engage with and participate in PLCs. Further, a meta-analysis conducted by Vescio et al. (2008) highlighted a positive correlation between educators' immersion in WIL and participation in PLCs. Findings highlight a synergy between ESD, WIL, and PLCs in nurturing teachers' pedagogy.

Science coaches support teachers with ongoing PD opportunities to deepen their overall understanding of science content and pedagogy. Through coaching, teachers can work to develop and refine curricula aligned to state framework standards and help select appropriate content materials and supplies. Furthermore, science coaches further provide support by co-planning and co-teaching science lessons, modeling effective teaching practices, and giving feedback to teachers. Overall, coaches employ WIL strategies to support teachers in developing effective science lessons grounded in authentic experiences, foster collaboration amongst science teachers, and promote teachers' self-reflection to improve student outcomes in science.

(3) **Support teachers' overall socioemotional health with mindfulness training opportunities to help reduce and eliminate roadblocks to science curriculum implementation.** Research for my dissertation study was conducted in the fall of 2019 and highlighted teachers' low overall socioemotional health. The COVID-19 pandemic of 2020, however, has had a significant and profound impact on the socioemotional health of teachers. Many educators have experienced stress, anxiety, and burnout due to the sudden shift to

remote learning and the high demands of managing hybrid learning environments while being concerned about their health and safety. In order to support teachers' overall socioemotional health, school districts should foster a positive school culture that values teacher well-being and encourages support amongst colleagues. Mental health resources, such as counseling services or mindfulness training, should be offered to help teachers develop strategies for managing stress and prioritizing their personal well-being. Further, districts should recognize and celebrate the successes of students and staff alike to boost morale and create positive school cultures.

(4) **Create a designated science space within the building where teachers can bring their students for science inquiry.** This space should be thoughtfully designed for ease of access for all teachers and students. The room should be large enough to accommodate group activities and experiments and should be designed to encourage inquiry-based learning with flexibility in furniture arrangements. Finally, this space should be equipped with supplies and resources appropriate for grade-level science learning.

(5) **Organize a district-wide professional learning community (PLC) to support all science teachers.** WIL theory can be directly applied to teachers' PLCs by providing a foundation for designing and implementing content-specific, meaningful professional development experiences that apply to teachers' daily teaching practice.

Traditionally, PLCs meet regularly to share knowledge, collaborate, and engage in ongoing learning and reflection in efforts to improve student outcomes. Teachers in PLCs can learn from each other by observing each other's classroom practices, co-teaching, or providing feedback and support to one another. Additionally, WIL provides PLCs with opportunities for collaborative learning, reflection, and innovation. Through engaging in WIL opportunities, educators can share their experiences and perspectives and learn from one another. This can lead to a more profound understanding of pedagogical and content knowledge and strategies needed for effective science instruction. PLCs can also offer a safe space for teachers to share issues that arise in the classroom and collaboratively work to solve them. By incorporating PLCs, districts can create professional development experiences that are relevant, authentic, and connected to teachers' day-to-day work in the classroom, leading to more effective teaching practices and improved student outcomes (Loach, 2020b).

SDL strategies can also be a valuable component of PLCs as they empower educators to take ownership of PD opportunities. In addition, SDL in PLCs can create a supportive environment where educators can feel comfortable trying new teaching practices and reflecting on their effectiveness. Finally, SLD can help educators stay current with the latest educational research and best practices. Overall, WIL and SDL can be beneficial components of PLCs, providing educators with opportunities to take ownership of their learning by fostering a culture of continuous learning and personal development.

The results of my study were shared with district leaders as well as the principal of the school. However, the COVID-19 pandemic was affecting the entire globe at that time. As a result, elementary science education ceased as teachers focused on mathematics and English language arts lessons. Unfortunately, the shutdown of schools caused students to fall behind in curriculum and interpersonal skills. Remote and hybrid learning sought to help students stay on grade level with curriculum. However, a study out of Harvard found that during the 2020–2021 school year, students in the United States in grades three through eight lost approximately twenty weeks of academic progress as a direct result of remote or hybrid learning (Goldhaber et al., 2022). Due to the profound impact of COVID-19 on schools, it is currently unknown if the district participating in my study has taken steps to bolster teachers' socioemotional status or if infrastructure changes were made to help enhance science experiences for teachers and students alike.

13 Embracing New Horizons

After my dissertation defense in April 2020, I felt stuck. I identified a problem of practice I could help fix. However, as an educator, the pandemic also profoundly impacted me. With the constructs of teaching and learning rapidly evolving due to the COVID-19 pandemic, WIL became more prevalent as educators had to learn how to shift their teaching practice overnight. Teaching my eighth graders remotely in the spring of 2020 proved difficult, especially when trying to convey complex topics in science. So, I made a conscious choice to set aside any grandiose plans I had for changing elementary science education and focus on my own teaching practice. In the fall of 2020, I poured myself into my teaching as my students returned to school on a hybrid schedule (and some remotely). I was determined to give my students as "normal" a school experience as possible. District leaders had decided that, at the middle school, students would be assigned to classrooms, and teachers would travel to grade-level classrooms to teach their various subjects. This was done to reduce the number of people in hallways to minimize the spread of COVID-19. However, with a hybrid schedule, remote learners, masks, sanitizer, and students not being able to share supplies, I, like many of my peers, struggled. What ultimately helped me through teaching during the pandemic was my teaching team. At the beginning of the shutdown, we communicated daily through texts and virtual meetings to check on each other's physical and emotional health and share online teaching strategies and resources. We employed strategies of WIL and SDL as we navigated the rapidly changing landscape of teaching and learning. We collaborated on lessons to ensure consistency and continuity for students, especially as they transitioned from fully remote learning to a hybrid, in-person schedule. As situations and teaching guidelines changed, we were flexible and willing to adapt and share workloads. Most importantly, we were there for each other, and the bond we formed during the pandemic is undeniable.

14 Seizing Opportunities

As the 2020–2021 school year was coming to a close, I received an opportunity to create a graduate course to be offered through a local teacher education center and supported by a nearby college. I designed an elementary science content and methods course with my dissertation and elementary teachers in mind. While creating course content, I aligned it with the situated, embedded, distributed learning approach to teacher education, focusing on contextualized, job-embedded, and collaborative learning experiences. Understanding that situated learning emphasizes the importance of learning in a context where knowledge is acquired through authentic learning experiences relevant to teachers' practice, I carefully chose readings, activities, and science content topics to build upon teachers' foundational science knowledge. Teachers address their content weaknesses through coursework while discovering new pedagogical strategies to teach science. Embedded learning integrates coursework directly into teachers' day-to-day work. In doing this, teachers are better able to see the relevance of learning opportunities and are more likely to apply their new knowledge and skills in their classrooms (Courtney, 2018). Distributed learning involves learning opportunities distributed over time and space, leveraging technology to facilitate communication and collaboration. By creating online learning opportunities, I allow teachers to collaborate with colleagues from different school districts, learning from each other's experiences and perspectives. Together, situated, embedded, and distributed learning components support teachers as they acquire knowledge and hone pedagogical skills to enhance student learning outcomes.

Teaching the professional development course is very satisfying as it directly impacts elementary teachers' content knowledge and practice. If my journey in education were to end with this course, I would be satisfied, knowing that I am working to make a difference. However, another major shift in my journey was just around the corner.

In August of 2022, I was contacted by a local university regarding teaching an elementary science course for preservice teachers. This course had been developed over several years by a seasoned professor who had passed away suddenly. With only three weeks until the semester started, the university sought someone to take over the course. Initially, I was concerned about teaching another course while still teaching full-time at the middle school. However, due to the class's schedule, the university agreed to move the course online for one semester. I took the position and immersed myself in coursework to understand the class's scope and sequence. While I enjoyed the flexibility, unfortunately, the online format left me feeling disengaged from students. I needed interactions with my students to help address their individual needs. I struggled to make coursework as engaging and pertinent as possible and wondered about the effectiveness of the course in the online format. I took solace in knowing that the course would be transitioned to an in-person format the following semester. Between semesters, I revised the coursework to reflect my personal teaching style and included meaningful, hands-on science activities designed to deepen students' content knowledge and pedagogy. As the next semester began, I felt much more comfortable and connected with coursework and was starting to enjoy the experience of teaching at the college level.

My students must observe and eventually teach in elementary classrooms, integrating theory into practice, as part of their coursework. These purposeful WIL experiences allow for the integration of teaching theory and practice as preservice teachers are expected to work with teacher mentors to develop and deliver meaningful science lessons and assess students' learning. Further, preservice teachers must reflect on their experiences, noting successes and difficulties. Class discussions surrounding identified problems take place to brainstorm solutions and to further develop students' teaching practice. Coursework for this class has morphed into something entirely unexpected. Students needed more and wanted to learn from my personal teaching experiences and pedagogy. The course has become a quasi-PLC where ideas and strategies are exchanged. Conversations surrounding situations that could arise in day-to-day teaching are infused into our study of science content and methods. Managing challenging student behavior, planning field trips, how to modify lessons to meet individual student needs, and teaching license recertification are some discussion topics brought up by students. Allowing for these types of conversations prepares students for the rigors and expectations educators face daily. These preservice teachers are becoming resourceful, resilient, and better-prepared educators through placements, coursework, and exchanges of practical knowledge.

15 Journeying Forward

The aforementioned WIL and SDL experiences have shaped who I have become as an educator. Am I done developing as an educator? I think not. This study of self has played a pivotal role in identifying and reflecting upon critical personal and professional elements in my life that have shaped my overall self-identity. These experiences morphed my personality and consciousness, allowing me to be adaptable as I continuously seek new knowledge. As new educational research and strategies are brought to light, I will meet them with an open mind and use them to help evolve into the educator I will be in the future.

References

Agostini, D., & Francesconi, D. (2021). Introduction to the special issue "embodied cognition and education." *Phenomenology and the Cognitive Sciences, 20*, 417–422. https://doi.org/10.1007/s11097-020-09714-x.
Bandura, A. (1982). Self-efficacy mechanism in human agency. *American Psychologist, 37*(2), 122–147. https://psycnet-apa-org.umasslowell.idm.oclc.org/record/1982-25814-001.
Bandura, A. (1993). Perceived self-efficacy in cognitive development and functioning. *Educational Psychologist, 28*(2), 117. https://org.umasslowell.idm.oclc.org/10.1207/s15326985ep2802_3.
Bandura, A. (1997). *Self-efficacy: The exercise of control.* W. H. Freeman.

Billett, S. (2020). *Learning in the workplace: Strategies for effective practice.* Routledge.
Billett, S. (2009). Realising the educational worth of integrating work experiences in higher education. *Studies in Higher Education, 34*(7), 827–843.
Bleakney, J. (2019). *What is work-integrated learning?* [Blog Post]. https://www.centerforengagedlearning.org/what-is-work-integrated-learning/.
Chahine, I. (2013). The impact of using multiple modalities on students' acquisition of fractional knowledge: An international study in embodied mathematics across semiotic cultures. *The Journal of Mathematical Behavior, 32*(3), 434–449.
Cooperative Education & Internship Association, Inc. (2022). *History.* https://www.ceiainc.org/about/history/.
Cooper, L., Orrell, J., & Bowden, M. (2010). *Work integrated Learning: A guide to effective practice.* Routledge.
Courtney, S. A. (2018). Teacher educator-embedded professional learning model. *International Electronic Journal of Mathematics Education, 13*(3), 103–123. https://doi.org/10.12973/iejme/2702.
Darling-Hammond, L. (2008). Teacher learning that supports student learning. *Teaching for Intelligence, 2*(1), 91–100.
Dewey, J. (1938). *Experience and education.* A Touchstone Book, Kappa Delta Pi.
Du Plessis, E. (2010). Students' experiences of work-integrated learning in teacher education. *Progressio, 32*(1), 206–221.
Epstein, D., & Miller, R. (2011). *Slow off the mark.* https://www.americanprogress.org/issues/education/reports/2011/05/04/9680/slow-off-the-mark/.
Explore Learning. (2024). *Gizmos.* https://www.explorelearning.com/our-products/gizmos.
Goddard, R., Hoy, W., & Hoy, A. (2000). Collective teacher efficacy: Its meaning, measure, and impact on student achievement. *American Educational Research Journal, 37*(2), 479–507. https://www.jstor.org/stable/1163531.
Goldhaber, D., Kane, T. J., McEachin, A., Morton, E., Patterson, T., & Staiger, D. O. (2022). *The consequences of remote and hybrid instruction during the pandemic* (No. w30010). National Bureau of Economic Research.
Henson, R. K. (2001). *Teacher self-efficacy: Substantive implications and measurement dilemmas.* https://files.eric.ed.gov/fulltext/ED452208.pdf.
Junqueira, K., Matoti, S., & Ronald, O. J. (2011). A comparative study of pre-service teachers' self-efficacy beliefs before and after work-integrated learning. *South African Journal of Higher Education, 25*, 1140–1154.
Kazempour, M. (2014). I can't teach science! A case study of an elementary pre-service teacher's intersection of science experiences, beliefs, attitude, and self-efficacy. *International Journal of Environmental & Science Education, 9*(1), 77–96.
Keeley, P. (2009). *Elementary science education in the K-12 system.* https://www.nsta.org/publications/news/story.aspx?id=55954.
Keller, C. (2016). *Using STEM case studies to prepare today's students for tomorrow's jobs.* https://static1.squarespace.com/static/56fdbc318259b51db19b8496/t/571134c9c6fc081a05deb2f2/1460745421473/Spark-101-Evaluation-Report.pdf.
Kolb, D. A. (1984). *Experiential learning: Experience as the source of learning and development.* Prentice Hall.
Loach, K. A. (2020a). *Factors that influence elementary teachers' teaching efficacy of the Massachusetts Science and Technology/Engineering framework standards: the case of apex elementary school* [Doctoral dissertation, University of Massachusetts Lowell].
Loach, K. A. (2020b). Science in elementary education: Teacher self-efficacy, preparation and student achievement. *Journal of Research in Education, 30*(1), 1–28.
Macrine, S., & Fugate, J. (2022). *Movement matters: How embodied cognition informs teaching and learning.* MIT Press.

Massachusetts Department of Education. (2016). *Massachusetts science and technology/engineering curriculum framework*. Massachusetts Department of Education. http://www.doe.mass.edu/frameworks/scitech/2016-04.pdf.

Mercadal, T. P. (2021). *Self-regulated learning (SRL)*. Salem Press Encyclopedia.

Morgan, P. L., Farkas, G., Hillemeier, M. M., & Maczuga, S. (2016). Science achievement gaps begin very early, persist, and are largely explained by modifiable factors. *Educational Researcher, 45*(1), 18.

Nowikowski, S. H. (2016). Successful with STEM? A qualitative case study of preservice teacher perceptions. *The Qualitative Report, 22*(9), 231.

Panadero, E. (2017). A review of self-regulated learning: Six models and four directions for research. *Frontiers in Psychology, 8*, 422. https://doi.org/10.3389/fpsyg.2017.00422

Pažur Anicic, K., & Divjak, B. (2022). Work-integrated learning in higher education: Student, teacher and employer motivation and expectations. *International Journal of Work-Integrated Learning, 23*(1), 49–64.

Piaget, J. (1972). *The psychology of the child*. Basic Books.

Riggs, I. M., & Enochs, L. G. (1989). Toward the development of an elementary teacher's science teaching efficacy belief instrument. *Science Education, 74*(6), 625–637.

Rusznyak, L., & Bertram, C. (2021). Conceptualising work-integrated learning to support preservice teachers' pedagogic reasoning. *Journal of Education (University of KwaZulu-Natal), 83*, 34–53.

Smith, J., & Ferns, S. (2018). Work integrated learning in teacher education: A pedagogy of experience and learning. *Asia-Pacific Journal of Teacher Education, 45*(5), 441–455.

The 193rd General Court of the Commonwealth of Massachusetts. (2010). *An act relative to the achievement gap*. https://malegislature.gov/Laws/SessionLaws/Acts/2010/Chapter12.

Thornton, K. (2013). Supporting self-directed learning: A framework for teachers. *Research and Practice in English Language Teaching in Asia*, 59–77.

Tschannen-Moran, M., Hoy, A. W., & Hoy, W. K. (1998). Teacher efficacy: Its meaning and measure. *Review of Educational Research, 68*(2), 202.

Tschannen-Moran, M., & Woolfolk Hoy, A. (2001). Teacher efficacy: Capturing an elusive construct. *Teaching and Teacher Education, 17*(7), 783–805. https://doi-org.umasslowell.idm.oclc.org/10.1016/S0742-51X(01)00036-1.

Tschannen-Moran, M., & McMaster, P. (2009). Sources of self-efficacy: Four professional development formats and their relationship to self-efficacy and implementation of a new teaching strategy. *Elementary School Journal, 110*(2), 228–245. https://doi.org.umasslowell.idm.oclc.org/10.1086/605771.

Vescio, V., Ross, D., & Adams, A. (2008). A review of research on the impact of professional learning communities on teaching practice and student learning. *Teaching and Teacher Education, 24*(1), 80–91.

Vygotsky, L. (1978). *Mind in society: The development of higher psychological processes*. Harvard University Press.

The Unlimited Benefits of Work-*Integrated* Learning: Reflections, Shifts, and Other Transformations by an Educational Leader, Improvement Scientist, and Math Pun Enthusiast

Michael Strandberg

Abstract "What is an owl's favorite type of math? Owl-gebra." And what might be an aspiring educational leader's favorite type of learning in the years to come? Work-Integrated Learning (WIL) offers future teachers and school leaders the opportunity to combine real-world experience with the more abstract lessons learned in a classroom to prepare educators not just for the theoretical, but also for the practical applications of the day-to-day life of an educator. My WIL experiences with my doctoral program in educational leadership prepared me for the increased responsibilities of my future roles as Mathematics Department Chairperson and as Assistant Principal of Academics at a high school in New York. The use of WIL through my doctoral dissertation research conducted at my high school taught me how to incorporate WIL during my preparation for future roles in order to continually improve the educational outcomes for all the students at my school. With all its benefits for future educational leaders, WIL warrants a place in the conversation about best educational techniques to consider in devising a learning program, just as the math pun enthusiast in me perhaps deserves a place in the "pun-itentiary" for all the math jokes in the chapter to follow.

Keywords Educational leadership doctorate · Math education · Curriculum · Research · Work-integrated learning

---

M. Strandberg (✉)
Chaminade High School, Mineola, NY, USA
e-mail: mstrandberg@chaminade-hs.org

1 Introduction

"If you're ever feeling a bit chilly in the classroom, feel free to go sit in the corner: it's ninety degrees there." For most of my decade-plus career as an educator, I have begun my classes with this math joke, welcoming my students to a class which would set out to inspire them to more positive perceptions of mathematics; greater interest in science, technology, engineering, and mathematics (STEM) careers; improved achievement in mathematics; and the opportunity to join in laughter together at a weekly math joke that I find online and share.

In order to provide this experience for students, I needed to bridge the gap between the theoretical knowledge I learned through my own formal education and the practical application of this knowledge in the classroom. The innovative approach of Work-Integrated Learning (WIL) enabled me to integrate real-world work experiences with my teaching practice. Evidence from WIL studies indicates that WIL not only enhances academic learning but also shapes career trajectories, fosters personal growth, and strengthens industry-academia collaborations. WIL is "internationally recognized ... as a strategy for ensuring students are exposed to authentic learning experiences with the opportunity to apply theoretical concepts to practice-based tasks" (Ferns et al., 2014). As an educational leader, an improvement scientist, and a math pun enthusiast, I advocate for the incorporation of WIL in academic curricula after experiencing its transformative power.

In this chapter, I will delve into the unlimited benefits that arise from this experiential learning model. Through my personal experiences and professional insights, I will illustrate how WIL has proven its potential to revolutionize traditional education paradigms, leading to profound shifts in the learning landscape.

2 Personal Reflections on WIL

"Why would the student wear glasses in math class? Because it improves division." And why would a teacher choose work-integrated learning? Educators' WIL experiences improve student learning in their classrooms and at their schools.

My professional journey started in the early 2010s. After graduating in three and a half years with an undergraduate engineering degree in Operations Research, I taught mathematics for a year and a half at a public charter school in New Jersey and then for a year at a Catholic high school in New York before returning to teach at my alma mater, an all-boys Catholic high school in New York, where I have been for the past nine years and counting. Along the way I earned master's degrees in mathematics for teaching and in theology.

In my first few years teaching at my alma mater, I took great interest in curriculum, instruction, scheduling, and technology initiatives, in addition to striving to be the best teacher I could be. I jumped at the opportunity to join my school's EdTech Team as we implemented a one-to-one iPad program for our students. I created a spreadsheet to demonstrate that our school could operate a block schedule, with longer periods on alternating days instead of shorter periods every day, ultimately with the intent of encouraging teachers to focus class on student-centered learning activities, instead of direct instruction.

Using my experience of teaching the entire high-school math curriculum in the past, I set out to improve my school's math curriculum. For years, even though eighth graders were taking Algebra 1, we offered ninth-graders the option of taking Algebra 1 again or, through an optional placement test the previous June, Geometry. Since we have an unweighted grading structure, parents had no incentive to put their children through a more challenging course load when many of the top students in each class were choosing to start with Algebra 1. Students would continue on to Geometry their sophomore year and then Algebra 2 and Trigonometry their junior year, when they would spend the first four months of the school year effectively reviewing Algebra 1. The lowest-performing students would then continue on to Precalculus as seniors, where they would learn the same topics a third time.

I engaged in numerous conversations, put together a proposal, and eventually gained approval to change the math curriculum so that all freshmen would start in Geometry (or Precalculus for students who have already taken Geometry). Based on their performance in Geometry, and not an optional placement test, students would be split into Algebra 2 or Precalculus. The Algebra 2 sophomores would continue on to Precalculus junior year and Calculus senior year. The Precalculus sophomores would continue on to a two-year AP Calculus AB or BC sequence, with the option of leaving the sequence after one year to pursue a different AP math elective senior year (ideally with AP Statistics and AP Computer Science A as options), more than doubling our potential AP math participation rate from the old system.

With these meaningful and rewarding experiences providing a glimpse into the life of a high-school administrator, I set out to pursue a doctorate from a university in the Northeast in education leadership, concentrating on STEM education leadership. Through work-integrated learning with my doctoral program, guided by weekly conversations with my dissertation advisor, I developed as a teacher, educational leader, and improvement scientist.

I found everything I was looking for in my doctoral program: classes conducted primarily online with a mix of theoretical and applied learning and the opportunity to learn through experiences at my high school. Before entering the doctoral program, I already had a passion for improving education at my school and the willingness to dedicate the time necessary to accomplish worthwhile educational aims, with a background in teaching and in using mathematical problem-solving and spreadsheets to help achieve goals. However, I knew that there was a tremendous amount of research on effective practices of teachers and administrators, using successful approaches to collecting and analyzing data. I yearned to incorporate this research and data focus into my daily work experiences as an aspiring educational leader.

During my doctoral program, I was able to do just that, pursuing a dissertation regarding my math curriculum initiative. When I began the three-year program, the four-year initiative was at the end of its first year. While the broad strokes of the initiative were set, the work of creating each successive year's new courses still remained, and it would be necessary to evaluate the success of the program and make any necessary alterations. In addition, utilizing existing literature to provide a research basis for the new curriculum would strengthen the initiative.

Through the classes in the doctoral program, I deepened my theoretical knowledge of education leadership and honed my research skills, as I began to put together initial materials for my dissertation and to apply my learning in small ways at my high school. As I completed this coursework, I embarked on the main work-integrated learning experience of my doctoral program, performing research at my high school in order to write the five chapters of my dissertation on the relationship between advanced high-school mathematics course-taking, SAT mathematics achievement, and STEM career interest and perceptions.

About two years into the doctoral program, I wrote the first chapter of my dissertation, in which I identified the problem of practice at my school: the lack of STEM career interest and the differential impact of advanced course-taking on mathematics performance on SAT scores of students enrolled at my high school. I contextualized the problem in the existing research literature, analyzed the problem and its causes, performed a quantitative analysis of student achievement data highlighting the problem of practice, interviewed an assistant principal, surveyed teachers in the math department, and determined research questions and next steps.

Over the course of the third and final year of the doctoral program, I crafted the rest of the dissertation. I conducted extensive research of the existing literature and where my study fit in; outlined the methodology I would use to complete my study; followed this methodology in collecting data at my school, including test scores, surveys, and interviews with current students and recent alumni; analyzed the quantitative and qualitative data from my study; and determined recommendations for my school going forward based on my study.

My personal experiences with WIL transformed my academic journey and career choices, facilitating deeper student engagement and improving the academic performance of my students, while making learning more enjoyable and fostering creativity.

3 Transformations in Learning

"What did the mathematical acorn say when it grew up? Gee, I'm a tree." And what happens to educators who experience work-integrated learning? Through WIL, learners undergo profound transformations. Traditional classrooms are often confined to theoretical concepts, limiting students' understanding of their potential real-world applications. WIL breaks these barriers, allowing students to apply their knowledge in authentic settings, empowering them to connect theory to practice.

In working on initiatives in the past, I would read articles online and would engage in casual conversations with colleagues as I developed my ideas, but everything was done informally. Through the work-integrated learning process of creating my dissertation, I learned how to formally analyze the existing research literature; how to conduct a thorough data analysis, collecting quantitative data and selecting and applying the appropriate statistical test, as well as conducting formal surveys and interviews and analyses of these; and how to use all of this information to determine recommendations for the next steps of a program.

I put my WIL experience to use right after graduating from my doctoral program with a few initiatives at school. In particular, I was one of two teachers at my school to pilot a new teaching style for our math classes, the practices championed by Dr. Peter Liljedahl in *Building Thinking Classrooms in Mathematics* (2020). Liljedahl advises math teachers to put whiteboards on all four walls of the classroom and have students work on thinking tasks at the whiteboards in random groups of three, sharing one marker per group as they solve the task at hand.

Students are energized by standing at the whiteboards to work on problems with their peers, as opposed to sitting down and working independently. Sitting down also can lead to students seemingly hiding during the class period, with the teacher unable to see all of the students' work at the same time. Working at the boards, however, ensures that students know that the teacher and their classmates can see their efforts in class, without singling anyone out. With a single glance around the room, the teacher can see roughly how each of the students in the class is understanding the lesson objective, because there are at most a dozen or so sets of student work to analyze at the whiteboards, compared to potentially upwards of 30 individual student work sets to examine at any given time.

Having one marker for each group ensures that students truly collaborate with each other, as opposed to merely working on problems individually and then checking answers against each other. While one student writes on the board, the other two students point at various writings on the board, share ideas, ask questions, compare and contrast problem-solving methods, and discuss explanations for the work they have shown.

Three students per group keeps the groups small enough that they do not break into sub-groups, and it brings in more perspectives than a group of two would. In addition, randomizing the groups each class for students to see builds student trust that the groups are truly random and that the teacher is not breaking the students into homogeneous groups or groups with some other purpose. Working with different classmates each lesson prevents students from falling into patterns with the same groups regarding which contributions are expected of each student. Ultimately, spending significant amounts of time solving thinking tasks at the whiteboards communicates to students that class is about thinking and learning, not merely listening to and copying the teacher's steps of solving a problem.

WIL offers a shift from passive learning to active engagement. This transformation fosters a more profound understanding and sense of purpose in education, as my students and I found through the initiatives I pursued following my WIL experience.

4 Shaping Career Trajectories

"Why did the $x^2 + 1$ tree fall over? Because it had no real roots." With a foundation of work-integrated learning, teachers and their students will be prepared for whatever may come their way. In fact, WIL has played a pivotal role in shaping my career trajectory.

After I successfully defended my dissertation and earned my doctorate in May 2021, I set out to use the lessons I had learned in the program in my everyday responsibilities at school. At the time, I was teaching math full-time and working with the Assistant Principals' Office to create the school's schedule and assist with various tasks and initiatives. I joined the Instructional Design Team, preparing professional development opportunities and working closely with new teachers to help them develop their teaching practice. In 2022, I became the Director of Academics, Scheduling, and Data, with a reduced teaching load in order to pursue initiatives to improve the school at large with the lessons I had learned from my work-integrated learning experiences.

In January 2024, I became the Mathematics Department Chairperson. As the Math Department Chair, I oversee 15 math teachers directly, observing their lessons several times each year and meeting with them regularly as a department and individually to pursue departmental initiatives and address situations that come up. I review their curriculum and major assessments, and I conduct end-of-year evaluations and meetings with each teacher. I began my first few weeks as the Math Chair by sitting down with each teacher for a half-hour one-on-one meeting to discuss their goals and ideas and how I could best support them from my new role.

I then began my first round of formal observations, using my shadowing experience prior to starting as the Math Chair to guide me. For these observations, I sat in on a full 73-min block for each teacher, taking notes on alignment of the lesson to the instructional purpose, teacher content knowledge and use of academic vocabulary, the intellectual challenge and supportive nature of the learning environment, classroom management, student intellectual engagement, and formative assessment and feedback. Afterward, I met with each teacher for 30 min to discuss takeaways from the lesson and collaborate to create a plan for growth and improvement. Following the post-observation meeting, I fill out a rubric with extensive commentary on the teacher's demonstrated areas of strength and growth, as well as an action item for a teacher to work on over the next several weeks. For this first round of observations, I had a shared action item structure for all teachers in the department, having teachers invite me back into their classrooms a few weeks later to see an aspect of classroom practice deemed an area of focus based on the prior observation.

My second round of observations focused on unannounced informal observations for each teacher. Instead of staying for the entire 73-min block and announcing which day I would observe ahead of time, I stopped by each class for about 20 min and wrote up a shorter report based on my observation for each teacher. The formal and informal observations both provide important information for me in my role as the Math Chair. The formal observations allow me to see teachers at their best, seeing what the ceiling for each teacher is at the moment. Meanwhile, the unannounced informal observations allow me to see more of what is happening on a day-to-day basis in the classroom.

For the third round of observations, the teachers invited me back to their classrooms to see improved teaching practice based on the action items from the formal observations. These informal observations were announced but followed the same shorter reports as in the second round of observations. The additional time required for a third observation in a short amount of time was challenging, but worth it for me in my first year as the Math Chair, providing me with an additional glimpse into each teacher's classroom as I began to learn about each teacher's instructional practice. At a school leadership conference in March 2024, a few colleagues and I came across a video app for teachers to record their classes and fill out rubrics and commentary for their own classes and that of their colleagues. We were so impressed that we decided to buy a schoolwide license for the app. We will analyze the effectiveness of this new app by digging into the data and listening to feedback from the faculty, as I learned to do through my WIL experience of writing my doctoral dissertation. As I wrapped up the third round of observations, my excitement grew at the possibility of using the video app to have teachers record themselves in the classroom responding to an action item from a prior formal observation. Instead of coordinating the proper time within each period to visit each teacher, teachers would be able to record their class and share just the relevant part with me to observe. In addition, teachers would be able to see their own teaching practice and reflect on it. I eagerly anticipate the continued future developments in my observation process over the coming years that will allow me to better support the teachers I oversee.

A few years earlier, I had worked with a former Assistant Principal to create shared planning periods built into each teacher's schedule as part of our six-day cycle. Once every six days, each department would meet for about 35 min to discuss departmental and schoolwide initiatives, plans for the upcoming cycle, and ideas generated by the teachers in the department. On another day each six-day cycle, the teachers of each particular course (e.g., Honors Geometry, Honors Calculus, etc.) meet as a smaller group to discuss the upcoming cycle in the classroom for the course, as well as other plans and ideas generated by the teachers. With my new role as Math Chair came the responsibility of generating the agenda for each cycle's departmental meeting, as well as big-picture ideas for the smaller shared planning periods by course. I created a schedule for the remainder of the 2023–24 school year to facilitate conversations on instructional practice, assessment and feedback, and curriculum, and I set up a structure for intervisitations. Teachers in the department had never as a whole had to visit other math classes. I paired teachers up, created a note-catcher for teachers to jot down low-inference notes, as well as questions and wonderings, and set aside a few weeks for teachers to visit each other's classes. Doing so provided teachers with a new set of ideas from the classes they visited, in addition to fruitful conversations afterward about teaching practice with the colleague they were paired up with. Increasing the number of intervisitations in the coming years will not only help teachers to improve their own instructional practice, but also provide WIL experiences for them to utilize if they pursue instructional leadership roles in the future.

In July 2024, I also became the Assistant Principal of Academics. In this role, I oversee half of our faculty, specifically those in our Mathematics, Science, Religion, Fine Arts, and Financial Literacy departments. Alongside another Assistant Principal, who oversees the other half of the faculty, I pursue schoolwide initiatives and ensure smooth day-to-day operation at the school. I continue to be responsible for the school's schedule each year and various data projects for the school.

Continuing with my dissertation work, I surveyed the next graduating class of students using the STEM career interest and perceptions surveys from my dissertation. In addition, seeing the clear benefits of advanced STEM course offerings for students, I pursued two more courses: AP Computer Science A (to complement our existing AP Statistics course as another senior math elective) and AP Physics C: Mechanics, our first calculus-based physics course. My school offered these two courses for the first time in 2022–23. In 2024–25, my school began to offer AP Computer Science A, AP Statistics, and other courses in place of a fourth year of World Language for interested students, so that students could take an AP Calculus course and an AP Computer Science or AP Statistics course at the same time.

Among the other initiatives I helped to implement at my school, we set up an instructional coaching program for first-year and second-year teachers, in order to provide supportive, non-supervisory instructional assistance through class visitations and structured meetings. In addition, we organized revisions of each course's syllabus to emphasize skills taught and not just content covered.

My school created a new Chief Operating Officer (COO) position in the 2023–24 school year. The new COO began right away to develop a strategic plan by interviewing dozens of stakeholders one-on-one at length and facilitating conversations with focus groups. In addition to participating in the interview and focus-group process, I used the lessons learned in my doctoral research to help with data collection and analysis for the strategic plan. Collecting and analyzing data on the population of surrounding towns and on the academic performance and background of our current and former students will help to inform admissions strategies so that we continue to improve in providing the best learning experience for our students, as we continue to deepen our knowledge of what characteristics prospective students and their families are looking for in making the decision on which high school to enroll at.

The hands-on experience I gained through WIL made me more prepared in the workplace. I look forward to many more years of taking the problems facing my students and crafting solutions to address the problems and consistently improve learning at my school, incorporating extensive research, data analysis, and all the lessons I learned with my WIL experiences.

5 Fostering Personal Growth

"Which country's capital is growing the fastest? Ireland: Every day, it's Dublin." Work-integrated learning can lead to fast growth in teachers' and students' development of essential soft skills, such as communication, teamwork, adaptability, and resilience. These qualities are crucial for success in any field, and WIL has been instrumental in developing these abilities, in addition to technical skills.

For each of my school initiatives described earlier, I completed a deeper dive into researching each topic and I incorporated more formal data analysis with surveys and interviews than I had attempted before my work-integrated learning experiences. For example, with the whiteboard initiative, I interviewed students on their experiences with this new classroom structure, and I surveyed the faculty as a whole through a Google Form to accumulate more information and gauge their interest in potentially incorporating this structure into their own classes, while also holding professional development sessions on using whiteboards effectively in the classroom. After a year with two whiteboard classrooms piloted by the former Math Chair and myself, we expanded to over 20 whiteboard classrooms out of 50 or so rooms in the whole school building just in the following year alone. In 2023–24, I gained approval to purchase and install whiteboards in all the remaining classrooms in the building so that every class would have the opportunity for students to use whiteboards on all four walls of the room each day.

In addition to these initiatives, I have also benefited from WIL in helping to prepare me for my newest roles as the Math Department Chair and Assistant Principal of Academics. A major component of both roles is observing teachers, conducting meetings, and completing observation reports according to Danielson's Framework for Teaching (2007). Rather than merely reading about this framework, I used the autumn months of 2023 to shadow the previous Math Chair in conducting observations, matching the aspects of the lessons to the language of the Danielson rubric, and offering feedback to teachers. Drawing on my experience in my doctoral program with WIL, I knew that the best way to learn how to observe and provide feedback to teachers was to gain experience doing so, under the guidance of someone with expertise. As a result, I sought out additional insights from the previous Assistant Principals and the chairs of other departments. I sat in observations with some of these colleagues of mine to learn from their experiences. By the time I began my role as the Math Chair, I had already conducted several hours of observations and post-observation meetings.

The observation process was not the only responsibility of my future role that I shadowed under the previous Math Chair. In addition, we conducted weekly transition meetings for me to learn how in the role of Math Chair I can better evaluate prospective candidates in the hiring process, review the curriculum, innovate instructionally, evaluate current and prospective textbooks, and shape and edit major assessments.

Learning about the hiring process was essential for the first few months on the job as Math Department Chair. Two positions opened up for the 2024–25 school year. Through the conversations I had with the previous Math Chair in the transition process and through additional discussions I had with the current Science Department Chair, I created a hiring process for the open math teaching positions. I created a job posting for two major networking websites. I received over 100 resumes and applications in March and April 2024. I set up a first round of interviews over video conferencing for the nine applicants I believed to have the most potential for open positions. Out of these nine applicants, I invited the top four for a second round of interviews, including a demo lesson. I set up demo lessons with four different classes of students at my school, including my own class of students for one demo lesson. After observing these four candidates teach demo lessons alongside three other administrators at my school, we met to discuss the lesson and the applicant's candidature. Of these four applicants, I chose two to recommend for hire and was very excited to see them sign for the open positions in May 2024. The conversations specifically on the hiring process before I began as the Math Chair, as well as the shadowing experience as a whole, prepared me for my future role by bringing me closer to the actual situations and challenges I would face on the job.

My experience with WIL has changed how I approach conducting action research at school and evaluating potential schoolwide pursuits. A graphing calculator company reached out to me in early 2024 offering free calculators to all the teachers in my department. I participated in a video conference with the sales representative to learn about the calculator's capabilities for our students and shared what I had learned with my department. After receiving a calculator for each member of my department and passing them out during a departmental meeting, I encouraged each teacher to try out the calculator to see over the course of the next year whether it might make sense to eventually have our students switch from the calculator company we had been working with for decades. I observed teachers using the calculator during class and met with teachers to hear their feedback on the calculator. I look forward to continuing this process inspired by my WIL experiences in the near future to contribute ultimately to a decision on the future of calculators at my school.

Following these recent pursuits, I am excited to see which initiatives I will take up next using the lessons I learned from my work-integrated learning experiences. One characteristic I am already starting to see in my most recent experiences is that I am branching out further from my math background. One of the new teachers I assisted through our instructional coaching program is a World Languages teacher, and I enjoyed working with him in his Spanish classes to improve instructional practice, outside of the math classrooms I have grown accustomed to working in. Now with my role as an Assistant Principal, I am responsible for four additional departments beyond math. In addition, in response to the increased mental health and social-emotional struggles of today's teenagers, I partnered with administrators and guidance counselors to implement a social-emotional learning and character development curriculum to be taught to students starting in the 2023–24 school year. I look forward to continuing this journey of personal growth spurred on by WIL experiences.

6 Strengthening Industry-Academia Collaborations

"What do baby parabolas drink to grow up big and strong? Quadratic formula." And what can forge stronger bonds between educational institutions and industries? Work-integrated learning can provide a platform for meaningful collaborations, enabling academia to stay updated with industry trends and demands. Simultaneously, industries gain access to fresh talent, innovative ideas, and potential future employees, fostering a mutually beneficial relationship.

The alumni at my school have expressed eagerness to have more meaningful interactions with the current students and faculty. My school has long held strong alumni relationships after high-school graduation, with alumni new to the workforce using these connections to learn more about industries and receive opportunities to interview for open positions. As we look to the future, an important goal for the school is to structure additional occasions for alumni to share their expertise and provide WIL opportunities for students and faculty alike. For example, in 2023–24, a renowned author and writing coach who graduated from my high school met several times with the English and Social Studies faculty to look at examples together of how to better coach students to improve their writing. These meetings will impact how hundreds of students experience humanities classes at my high school and learn how to write in the years to come. This opportunity would not have come about without strengthening industry-academia collaborations at my school.

However, the work is not finished. A significant growth area for my school that I have started to assist with is developing a more robust research program. Our Science Olympiad team has finished among the top schools in the state the past few years. However, we only had a few students in each grade completing their own science research projects. We had not won a major science research competition in years. As a student at this school myself, I had an excellent experience completing a research paper with a team to win the Northeast Region in the Toshiba ExploraVision future technology competition and emerge as one of the six national finalists. I wanted the students at my school to have the opportunity to compete in similar contests.

To develop ideas for our research program, I visited two public high schools in New York with reputations for excellent research programs. Each school's research program boasted multiple students who became Regeneron scholars, winners of a prestigious national research competition for high schoolers. As part of these visits, representatives from each school generously shared time and resources to shed light on aspects of their programs that contributed to their present-day success.

Along with a few other educators at my school, I set out to develop a plan for us to develop our own four-year research program. We developed goals and steps to attract students to the program, create a four-year curriculum, and maximize research class time for students given scheduling constraints. We planned ways to utilize our alumni network and our science facilities to improve the experience for our students. We developed an end goal of providing students with the experience of creating their own major research project, conducting the research, writing about the results, and entering competitions and pursuing publications for their projects, regardless of whether it leads to a victory in a competition. The goal is the journey for the students, and additional accolades would be icing on the cake. However, the accolades began right away. In our first year with a revamped science research program, a team of students became one of the winners of the NASA TechRise Challenge, earning them the ability to meet weekly with a NASA engineer to further develop their idea in preparation for a test of a prototype with NASA at the end of the school year.

I had initially thought of high-school research programs as focusing primarily on scientific research, as though the only kind of research was an extension from a science classroom. What I found from the other schools is that social science and behavioral science research are also great options for students. For my school, since we have a math teacher with a Ph.D. in mathematics, we found ourselves in a unique position to add a mathematics research program as well alongside the science research program. Starting as an after-school activity, math research grew in popularity and became a course offering during the school day, similar to our science research program, starting in the 2024–25 school year. In addition, I found myself excited by the opportunity to serve as a faculty mentor for any students interested in education research, given my experience completing my dissertation. It became a full-circle moment, where I would have the opportunity to serve as an advisor for my own students, as my dissertation advisor was for me. I eagerly await the chance to assist students on their own education research projects, helping them to refine the problems and proposed solutions they envision, design research methods, conduct research, analyze data, form recommendations based on the results, write up their findings, and prepare their projects for publication and entry into regional and national competitions. For all our students in the research program, I look forward to witnessing how they benefit from their own work-integrated learning and collaborations with industry professionals outside of our school environment.

7 Embracing the Shift: Challenges and Opportunities

"Why didn't the ancient Romans find algebra to be challenging? Because x was always 10." And why might some educators find work-integrated learning implementation to be a challenge initially? Implementing WIL may involve logistical constraints, resistance to change from leaders and stakeholders, and difficulties scaling these experiences for larger populations of students and teachers. Specifically for the math classroom, a use of WIL is having prospective teachers serve as student teachers in classrooms under the guidance of mentor teachers. This experience benefits prospective teachers by providing them with opportunities to try out teaching strategies with actual students. For the mentor teachers, having conversations about pedagogy with the prospective teachers encourages both teachers to reflect more deeply on teaching practice and on ways to best support students. A challenge, however, is that students may not learn as well in lessons led by the prospective teacher as with the more experienced mentor teacher. Meetings between the prospective and mentor teachers to plan the lesson and the presence of the mentor teacher in the classroom to assist students while the prospective teacher leads a lesson can help to mitigate this concern.

All in all, the benefits of WIL outweigh the challenges. Incorporating real-world experiences into education aids in shaping well-rounded, capable, and successful individuals. WIL develops hard and soft skills for students, teachers, and educational leaders. Increasing the adoption of WIL in school environments will expand these benefits to increase student learning.

8 Conclusion

"Without geometry, life would be pointless," I tell my students each spring, one of my borrowed weekly math jokes, or derivative humor, if you will. From my experience with work-integrated learning, I can say with confidence that without WIL, a graduate program in education leadership would be at least missing a key component, if not completely pointless. My WIL experience transformed my outlook on educational leadership and improvement science, providing me with the tools to engage in any endeavor at my high school with a research focus, formally incorporating existing literature and extensive data analysis into my decision-making. I look forward to using my WIL lessons to continue to transform my high school in the years to follow, shifting my mindset based on the research I conduct, rotating among the data analysis methods in my toolkit, stretching the minds of all the students I encounter, and reflecting on the journey as I go.

References

Danielson, C. (2007). *Enhancing professional practice: A framework for teaching*. ASCD.
Ferns, S., Campbell, M., & Zegwaard, K. E. (2014). Work integrated learning. In S. Billett, C. Harteis, & H. Gruber (Eds.), *International handbook of research in professional and practice-based learning* (pp. 675–698). Springer. https://doi.org/10.1007/978-94-017-8902-8_22
Liljedahl, P. (2020). *Building thinking classrooms in mathematics: 14 teaching practices for enhancing learning, grades K-12*. Corwin.

Math and Maths: Diversifying U.S. Math Instruction with Work-Integrated Learning Through Inclusive Math Pedagogies from England and Spain

Amy Bride

Abstract For the last twenty years, I have taught elementary math in an inclusive classroom in a high-performing school district in the northeast of the United States. Over that period of time, the composition of the students sitting in my classroom has become increasingly diverse. Wanting to better meet the needs of those students, I embarked on a sabbatical research project aimed at improving my cultural competency and expanding my pedagogical toolbox. This project allowed me to visit England and Spain during the 2022–2023 school year to see how math (and maths) is taught. While on this journey, I discovered firsthand how Work-integrated Learning (WIL) theory informs my own learning and teaching, and how it applies equally to students everywhere, as well. This chapter describes my visit to several schools in England and Spain to better understand good math practices in diverse contexts so that I could share my discoveries back home. This chapter further explores the similarities and differences between elementary schools in England, Spain, and the United States with an emphasis on math. Specific to the math lessons are issues of curriculum, organization, structure, and delivery of lessons. In order to get a better understanding of the way schools operate in England and Spain, I visited several from elementary to university level. While there I took ethnographic notes of the experience. The questions I was seeking answers to are the following: *How are lessons delivered? What tools, technologies, strategies, etc. are being used? What curriculum program was being used? What commonalities exist between English, Spanish and North American math pedagogy? How are learning differences addressed in the math classroom? What practices, strategies, tools, systems, etc. would be beneficial to our students in the US?* My visits revealed an interesting comparison between English, Spanish, and North American schools and curriculum. My experience speaks to the power of and the need for more intentional international exchanges and continued conversations around learning in general and math in particular.

Keywords Work-integrated learning · Fourth-grade math · Diversity · Inclusion · Number talk · Number string · Mindset · Interconnectedness · Transnational

---

A. Bride (✉)
Andover Public Schools, Andover, MA, USA
e-mail: Amy.bride@andoverma.us

1 Introduction

> One way to bring students and educators together from around the world is through math because math helps us understand the world — and we use the world to understand math.
>
> —Atweh & Clarkson, Asia Society, January 2023.

Mathematics serves as a universal language connecting people, cultures, and disciplines across the globe. In this chapter, I explore the concept of Work-Integrated Learning (WIL) with the primary goal of demonstrating its relevance to contemporary practitioners. Specifically, I examine its applicability to a teacher seeking a sabbatical for a research project aligned with WIL principles.

In 2022, I independently pursued fieldwork experiences in England and Spain. The purpose of my visits to classrooms in each country was to see how nine-year-old students learn math outside the United States. This fieldwork was intended to improve my professional practice of teaching math back home in my classroom. I became interested in this research after I noticed two important changes in my elementary teaching world. First, over a short period of time, the composition of the students sitting in front of me became increasingly diverse. I wanted to be better able to meet the needs of those students. Second, the way I taught math concepts started to change. According to Randy Bass (2012), such changes to traditional curriculum create a "tension" in learning, where teachers "mov(e) from the instructional paradigm to a learning paradigm" (p. 24). This paradigm shift means that educators are "designing learning experiences" rather than "offering information" for students to absorb (p. 24). My journey to England and Spain was motivated by a commitment to address the needs of my students and experience first-hand math practices through cross-cultural learning and observation.

For the last twenty years, I have taught math in an inclusive classroom to elementary students in a high-performing school district. Far from feeling burned out, this experience has inspired me to learn more about math, as well as the most current teaching methods to better meet the needs of today's diverse learners. This course of study led me to become an elementary math coach. In the role of math coach, my curiosity about math teaching and learning grew beyond the school level. And as a result, in 2022, I embarked on the aforementioned sabbatical research project aimed at connecting elementary school students worldwide by exploring how math is taught transnationally. While on this journey, I discovered the place of WIL theory in my own work, and how it could apply to students everywhere, as well. My guide and bridge to connecting my new WIL experience with my practice comes from *A Practical Guide for Work-Integrated Learning* (2016). My own lived experience as both a teacher and a learner seemed perfectly captured in the guide's Tenets of Experiential Learning Theory (p. 22), which named six core tenets upon which the experiential learning theory is founded (See Fig. 1).

These tenets also apply to elementary school teaching, as well; they represent for me not only what I experienced on sabbatical in England and Spain but what I want my students to experience when learning math.

Tenets of Experiential Learning Theory

1. Learning is a process.	• Promoting student acknowledgement of previous informal and formal learning
	• Student learning is viewed as ongoing
	• Encouraging the modification of ideas or techniques throughout the work-integrated learning experience
2. Learning is grounded in experience.	• Introducing student learning experiences at an appropriate pace and progression
	• Challenging students' preconceptions in light of new experience, theory and reflection
3. Learning involves mastery of all four learning modes.	• Providing students with opportunities to experience, reflect, theorize and apply
4. Learning is a holistic process of adaptation.	• Addressing students' feelings, perceptions, thoughts and actual behaviours throughout the WIL experience
5. Learning occurs when an individual interacts with his or her environment.	• Providing students with experience in the wider real-world environment (e.g., workplace context)
6. Knowledge is created through learning.	• Learning should be individualized to each student
	• Assigning students responsibility over their own learning

Fig. 1 Tenets of experiential learning theory (p. 22)

This international experience allowed me to observe a variety of teaching approaches firsthand, a key aspect of WIL: integrating academic learning with practical work experiences in real-world settings. After having been introduced to recent paradigm shifts in math teaching, I sought to change my practice to include these new (new to me, at least) pedagogical approaches. At the same time, I wondered if other teachers in other countries were having a similar experience teaching math. By good fortune, England and Spain were receptive to my visiting their math classrooms. While there, I was exposed to direct cultural exchanges, observed the hands-on implementation of math instruction, participated in best practice exchanges, had the ultimate professional development experience, and connected the visits with current research and conceptual models. All of this led me to ponder how this data could help inform curriculum policies. In the end, I realized that these experiences underscore the value of global collaboration in enhancing math instruction and continuing to cultivate inclusive pedagogies.

2 Approaches to Teaching Mathematics

Exposure to different approaches to math teaching allowed me the opportunity to compare North American, English, and Spanish teaching styles. The conversations and observations I participated in while visiting England and Spain led me to recognize the common goal teachers share of wanting our students to be successful lifelong mathematicians. The methods to achieve this vary, of course, reflecting cultural nuances, historical influences, and educational philosophies unique to each country. In the United States, for example, there's a strong emphasis on problem-solving and critical thinking, often incorporating hands-on activities and real-life applications to engage students. The English approach focuses on mastering fundamental concepts through structured hands-on experiences. While the Spanish method emphasizes collaborative learning and exploration, encouraging students to work together to discover mathematical principles.

One approach that was present in all of the math classes I visited was getting students to make their thinking "visible" through conversation. Students are constantly being asked to "turn and talk" to fellow classmates or to have a "math chat" and share their thinking. Having students explain how they are solving problems is another aspect of the learner-centered classroom. Other examples that reflects the shift to a student-centered teaching model are Steve Wyborney's Esti-Mysteries (2018) and Graham Fletcher's 3-Act Tasks and Number Talks.

In an Esti-Mystery such as "Beads in a Bowl" (shown in Fig. 2) every student is given a chance to stretch their learning by having an experience with visual representations and clues. Students start by connecting the first clue with a picture and bringing in their background knowledge. A new piece of information with each clue is given and then must be integrated further into the student's thinking. Students must reflect and adjust their thinking around numbers and apply these new ideas to form a new adjusted estimate. Figure 2 shows an example of this with beads in a bowl. The case of the beads pushes students to think about their knowledge of numbers. Having to place the numbers or digits in a specific order forces students to think in terms of place value. The students are taken on this journey starting from the set-up of the beads-in-a-bowl photo to the clue-by-clue build-up of suspense by the effort to narrow in on an answer. In the effort to find the final number students learn about reasonableness and to see possible outcomes. Then, the final clue is the climax that leads to the ultimate reveal. Excitement, enthusiasm, and energy abound in the classroom when narrowing down the possible outcomes in trying to solve each mystery (Fig. 3).

Fig. 2 Esti-mystery: beads in a bowl

How many beads are in the bowl?

As the clues appear, use the information to narrow the possibilities to a smaller set. After each clue, use estimation again to determine which of the remaining answers is the most reasonable.

Write down your first estimate. After each clue, you'll see if your estimate is still a possibility. After each clue, if it is no longer possible write down a new estimate – and be prepared to explain why you chose it.

Fig. 3 Esti-mystery: beads in a bowl clues

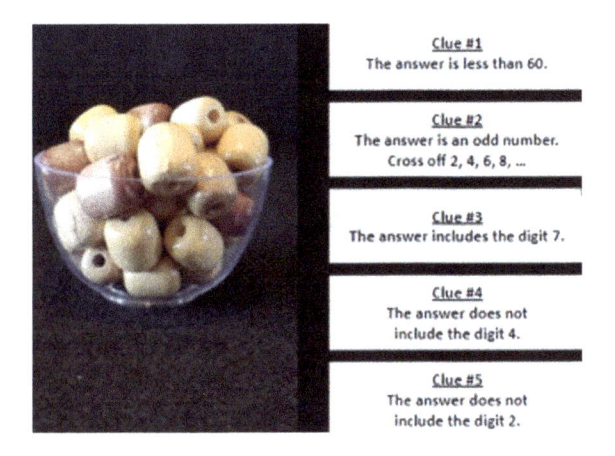

Clue #1
The answer is less than 60.

Clue #2
The answer is an odd number.
Cross off 2, 4, 6, 8, ...

Clue #3
The answer includes the digit 7.

Clue #4
The answer does not include the digit 4.

Clue #5
The answer does not include the digit 2.

Similar to the Esti-Mysteries, the 3-Act Task (in Figs. 4, 5, 6, and 7) is another modern mathematical teaching approach where students are pushed to engage with numbers. Three bits of information are given for which students must find a solution. Like the Esti-Mystery, students have multiple entry points beginning with questions such as "What do you notice?" and "What do you wonder?" regarding figures shown in Fig. 4. Students are then asked to create the question that the task is visually showing them. This is where the sense-making happens, asking students to employ specific vocabulary that leads to enriching discussions.

This dynamic way of inspiring meaningful mathematical conversations among students continues in the subsequent act (Fig. 5). It orients the student to connect with the task, to describe what they see and what they already know, and then to record it on the template seen in Fig. 4.

Next, after viewing Fig. 6, students refine their estimates to accommodate new information. Students are shown an array of Whoppers lined up in groups of ten as a clue. This visual information leads students to use logic, problem-solving, and

1. What did you notice?	2. What do you wonder?
3. Main Question:	
4. Estimate:	5. What information do you need?
6. Show your thinking:	

Fig. 4 3 act task template

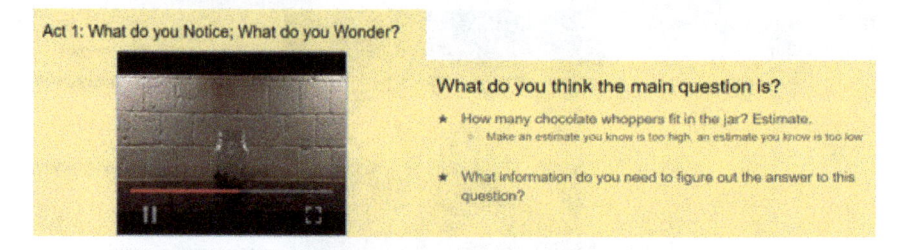

Fig. 5 3 act task: act 1: whoppers in a jar

Fig. 6 3 act task: act 2: whoppers in a jar

computation when shown five bags of Whoppers with 19 individual whoppers in each bag. The students are then shown 16 Whoppers left over from the final bag that did not fit in the jar, so students then have to have to decrease the total by that amount.

This process of figuring out the total number of malt balls in a jar is a representative example of the movement teachers are looking for along the Five Representations model shown ahead in this chapter, where Act 1 shows the concrete manipulative

Fig. 7 3 act task: act 3: whoppers in a jar

phase and gives context that is interesting to students. Act 2 gives visuals to create more context and discussion. Act 3 offers ways to find the answer. This problem can be solved using a concrete model and/or an equation representing abstract thinking. Figure 7 reveals the solution to the Whoppers task. Again, students are exposed to mathematical thinking that students can build on when learning future concepts.

In the final act, the Whoppers are arranged in an organized way called an *array*. Arrays, introduced in later lessons, can help better prepare students to grapple with such concepts as *area* and *perimeter*, fostering mathematical connections that students can employ to construct their own learning and expand vocabulary. In all these tasks, I have found that it is pivotal to make math concepts authentically accessible to all students, considering their cultural heritage and/or ability level. This approach served as one way to create a comfortable learning environment for students, and, for me, the benefits of teaching math in this manner became apparent.

Building on the foundational skills established through the tasks mentioned earlier, I want to introduce another approach: *Number Strings* (Fosnot, 2007). Number Strings consist of a series of slides designed for students to continue building number sense skills by manipulating numbers through pictures or by mental math. The most significant impact comes from the discussions generated by sharing strategies for finding answers. One example that can demonstrate this approach is a string of addition facts. Although the slides are presented individually, it's easy to observe the progression from a double number to a near double.

The problem string for Grade 4, starts like this:

$125 + 125$
$125 + 124$
$125 + 126$
$126 + 127$

As the year progresses, the number talks evolve to include more math standards-based questions, such as this Grade 4 fraction example pictured in Fig. 8.

Once students understand the concept, they are able to learn these algorithms because the steps will make sense and logically fall in order.

The hands-on observations and active participation in Esti-Mysteries, 3-Act Tasks, and Number Strings underscore the importance of finding new and innovative ways to

Fig. 8 Who has more number talk: primary bliss teaching common core aligned adding up friendly numbers

WHO HAS MORE?

Sam and Liam each had 12 tadpoles. Sam noticed that $\frac{3}{4}$ of his tadpoles had changed into frogs. Liam noticed that $\frac{2}{3}$ of his tadpoles had changed into frogs. Who has more frogs, Sam or Liam?

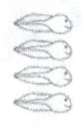

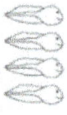

teach these concepts. It was clear to me in my school observations how such classroom activities allow students a holistic way of interacting with and discussing numbers. These methods enable students to be responsible for their own math learning. In my own desire to learn more about math while in England and Spain, I myself talked through many math problems such as the ones mentioned, and the experience was engaging and enlightening for me, both as a teacher and a learner.

3 Cultural Exchange of Mathematical Ideas Between the U.S., England, and Spain

Traveling to England and Spain offered many moments of experiential learning and personal insights that I never could have gotten over, say, a Zoom screen, insights I could only get by visiting in person. There is a corporeal, embodied, sensory experience one has, such as the intake of new food and the many smells associated; there is the feel of the air on one's skin, and experiencing underfoot what the terrain of a country feels like. Socially, there are mannerisms and values related to time and conversation styles that emerge. Amid all these sensory stimuli, I entered the classes and engaged with students and teachers.

I visited five schools in England, from elementary to university level, to better understand math practices in different settings. In Spain, I visited four elementary schools with my focus being to observe nine-year-olds in math class. Every teacher participated in discussions about math as a subject, the teaching of it, the successes and pitfalls. We talked about the commonalities between elementary math teaching in the U.S., England, and Spain. We noticed that our cultures have similar mathematical expectations of our elementary students based on similar standards. We also discussed the format and structure of lessons in whole group, small group, and individual pieces within lessons.

The atmosphere, or culture, created during each observation was different. Some teachers preferred that I remain a silent observer at the back of the room. One teacher in Spain asked me to work with a small group doing one of small group option called "corners." Another teacher asked me to come to the chalkboard and show how I would solve a problem using an open number line during a number string portion of a lesson. Each of these exchanges, it felt to me, could only happen in person in the context of these particular classrooms.

4 Hands-On Implementation of Math Lessons

The importance of context emerged as an anchor for me when watching the implementation of math lessons. Since I do not speak any language other than English, I had an added language challenge—and thrill—in Spain. I got to experience what a non-native-learner's math class looks and feels like. I used the visuals, texts, and students as my guides to understand what concepts and tasks were being asked of me to understand. At times, the English words were more confusing than Spanish, as in the case of the word "scheme." Eventually, I realized the English word "scheme" used in the educational setting context meant "curriculum," thus, proving how important context is to learning. The same is true, it seems to me, in the implementation of math lessons.

Like the number string mentioned earlier, there were some repetitive pieces offered in a sequence that allowed me to work out the meaning for myself—as was the case when doing computation. Spanish students were learning triple-digit addition and subtraction when I visited their classes. Spanish teachers were using models like the open number line to solve large number addition and subtraction problems. During a "Laboratorie" lesson the question posed was $285 + 257 = ?$ Two students shared that they wrote open number lines. One counted from 257 on to get to 285. The other used compensation to add 30 and remove 2. This example gives a glimpse into what a successful elementary math community looks and sounds like. It gives students opportunities to show their work, validates their math reasoning, and provides opportunities to use math language to make their thinking "visible."

In England, I observed a fluency routine that helped students build multiplication and reasoning skills. The class started by counting by multiples of 8 or using arms to show angle measures. This fluency routine went as follows: The teacher held a long rubber tube with Post-it notes equally spaced along the tube with the numbers 0, 8, 16, 24, up to 88 with a couple of gaps. Students, in chorus, said each multiple of 8 until they reached a gap (appearing at number 72) by stating the multiplication fact as a sentence. Starting with "8 times 0 is 0," "1 times 8 is 8," "2 times 8 is 16," etc.

Teacher: How did you know 9 times 8 is 72?

Student: I knew it because 8 times 8 is 64. So I added another 8.

Another Student: I knew it because 8 times 10 is 80, so I subtracted.

Another personal takeaway from my exposure to math lessons abroad was Board work. Students are invited to the board to show a solution and convey an idea. If the student can't provide a correct solution, the teacher impresses upon the students that by making a mistake on the board, they have actually helped others not to make the same mistake again. What I saw were problems posted on the front wall class whiteboard that got solved by students as others watched. American students write on the Smartboard and/or individual whiteboards to share their work by placing it under a document camera that projects to the Smartboard. In Spain, the students solved problems by coming up to the large class whiteboard and/or chalkboard. What was remarkable about Spain's board work is that the students clamored to solve problems on the old-fashioned chalkboard. When I asked about the chalkboards, I was told that they kept them because "the kids love them." I have since learned that the teachers also felt writing on and copying from the board was an effective learning tool. They argued that writing gave students time to use their bodies so that they kinesthetically feel and absorb and process the information. In turn the students then internalize concepts in a more organic way.

Witnessing counting aloud both individually as students and in chorus with the full class, a practice used in all the programs I observed, reminded me of how valuable this technique can be. At times, it sounded like a song of skip counting, up and down by 10's in one case. In England, I sat in on classes where counting and vocabulary reinforcement was repeated in chorus with the words "say multiple," for example, followed by the definition. The whole class was led up in this manner to the teacher's intended purpose and focus for the lesson, in which students were asked to use the scaffolds and guidance provided to solve work individually or in pairs.

5 Sharing Best Practices

The value of a visual model was made clear to me several times during these lessons. Experiencing math from the student perspective with a language barrier led me to rely on different models. In one case, the Spanish Division Diagram (see Fig. 9) was a model that unlocked some of my fixed thinking around division and money. This diagram was helpful in showing where to place the numbers. And despite the language differences, the labels had enough cognates to make sense for me. The backslash at the bottom tells the reader that it is the final answer. All of this was conveyed to me through one picture rather than many words spoken in a language I didn't speak. I feel this demonstrates yet again the universality of math. This example also provided me with some background information when shopping.

In England and Spain, notations for money are different than at home in the States. The comma and the decimal point are switched. Initially, I had a sticker-shock feeling when I looked at prices and thought many items were quite expensive. Though soon

Fig. 9 Spanish division diagram

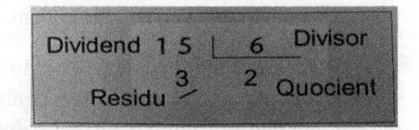

it became clear to me to mentally adjust to switching the comma and the decimal point. And when I saw this division example, it further helped me to adapt as I came to accept the different notations.

In addition to visual models, seating was highlighted in England. The math manual in England even makes a point to state that seating is to "be in a way that the student has direct eye contact with the teacher." Even more interesting is the emphasis on the atmosphere in the room being serene and even lighthearted and humorous. This served as another reminder to me of the importance of the classroom atmosphere, as well as an insight I gained teachers in the British classroom streamlined their delivery of lessons. The students responded positively to these relatively small tweaks.

Such classroom experiences proved so instructive for me as a teacher. Another useful element I observed was the synchronicity of the adults in the English classroom. Despite having three adults in the room, the flow and atmosphere of the classroom was highly functional and productive, like a well-oiled machine. Each adult had a vital role. The "Lead" teacher is up in front of the class, leading the lesson. And when, for example, the Lead shares a vocabulary word, the adult in the "Reactive" role adds that word to the word wall. Then the "Re-teach" person is there to work with any student who needs clarification—either on the specific problem at hand or on the overall operational concept. This triad model is pre-planned, so the execution is seamless, and all students have access, if needed, to adult support. They were in lockstep with each other, and the routine was meaningful as students knew where to look and what to expect. I found their preparation to work together so harmoniously to be most impressive.

Another pedagogical nugget to be shared back home occurred in Barcelona. The Spanish math program employs creativity in some of their lessons, where the idea of a narrative, or story, behind the math was emphasized. One teacher opened the lesson with a slide projected on the Smartboard (see Fig. 10). He went on to tell a story to match the slide.

The teacher says, "I was walking in the park over the weekend. I saw some dogs with spots like this. Altogether I saw 20 spots. How many dogs did I see on my trip to the park?" Students talk in groups and write on whiteboards using "guess and check" strategies. The slide was a valuable visual tool in helping me to understand

Fig. 10 Dogs with spots slide

what was being said. Beyond that, students enjoyed the story as an engaging way to think and reason.

Another creative idea I found from my WIL experience in Spain is to extend the math period, spending a longer time exploring concepts with various methods and tools: video, class discussion, manipulatives, and working in pairs and sharing ideas aloud in a session that lasted almost two hours. During that visit, the teacher said they were going to do an "adventure" lesson with "La Geometria en L'Art Kandinsky." The teacher opened with a video projected on the Smartboard of a group of students at an art museum. They stopped to study a painting by the Russian artist Wassily Kandinsky. The students then moved to study a few more paintings by this "expressionista" artist. After the video, the teacher provided some background about the artist and asked students to analyze the painting. The groups of students then shared their observations with the class. The analysis phase generated a math conversation that started building upon the students' ideas of Geometry.

When analyzing the paintings, students were able to share approaches. For example, students labeled shapes, lines, colors, and general observations. Next, groups were given trays of pre-cut shapes and asked to recreate or interpret the paintings together. This task encouraged further dialogue between the students as they created their own versions of the painting by arranging the shapes on the papers. As soon as students finished that, they were asked to return all the shapes and start over. This led to more discussions and interactions. In the end, each student created their own Kandinsky-like masterpiece in their notebook.

There was a lot of value in the discovery part of that lesson. Noticing math in the real world made the lesson believable and relevant to the students. The students' discussions and involvement revealed that the activity felt meaningful to them; one reason for this may have been that, in some ways, this lesson drew on their background knowledge. A related example of this new learning could be both seen and heard: While the students were working on drawing and coloring their own art, they used the recent visual-art vocabulary and demonstrated techniques acquired from ideas of lines of symmetry and adjacent angles within shapes. The session ended with a gallery walk. Not only were the students engaged, but they also learned some Geometry, worked together, shared work with their peers, saw firsthand how it was connected to their real life, and, in the end, established an art/math connection.

Another creative idea I noted from visiting Spain is the idea of "Corners." One commonality between all the schools in Barcelona is a math period for "corners" that occurs one day each week. During this time, students go to corners to choose an optional independent project, play games (non-computer based), or code. These stations are changed monthly to accommodate new learnings and provide new offerings that range from coding to board games to math writing to computation. WIL experiences like these form a bridge for me on my WIL journey, connecting my own professional development as a learner to my pedagogical growth as a math teacher.

6 Professional Development

Professional Development offers teachers the freedom to delve into their passions, by enrolling in specialized classes or programs, immersing themselves in academic literature and online resources to enhance their teaching skills. Traveling to explore new educational environments is, for me, a meaningful and effective way to develop as a practitioner by focusing on and learning about new and innovative ways to better teach math at the elementary level.

In my experience, I've found that the most impactful professional development often stems from self-generated initiatives. For my part, I feel I created the ultimate WIL professional development with these visits where I had the opportunity to push my own boundaries. The steps of my own process maps on squarely with the four basic steps of Kolb's process for developing an experimentation plan: "1. Generate an idea; 2. Determine the strategy for implementation; 3. Implement the idea; and 4. Evaluate and reflect" (2016, p. 110). In my plan, I started with the question of how math is taught in other countries, connected to schools, set an itinerary, completed the visits, and reflected on the experience, which I'll say more about ahead.

As part of my professional development journey, I participated in a course that encouraged educators to create social media accounts over a decade ago. Little did I know that this simple task would lead to significant connections and collaborations with teachers worldwide. By leveraging platforms like LinkedIn and Facebook, I was able to connect with educators in the classrooms whom I later visited during my international travels. Through these interactions, I discovered shared interests and common concerns in math teaching, leading to fruitful exchanges of ideas and resources like current literature and trends in teaching.

But one resource in particular helped me focus on my WIL-integrated travel-research experience: Carol Dweck's book *Mindset* (2008). In it, she describes the impact that one's own thinking has on our potential for growth. Dweck's theory of how our perception of our abilities in any task seems to the WIL philosophy, to the ways in which people think about themselves and their relationship to any given subject, in my case: math. During my journey, I met a student who came to embody this principle. Her name was Lucy, a 4th grader who proclaimed when she first entered our classroom that she was "just not good at math and never had been." In uttering these words, she implied that no amount of exposure and effort would change that since she was not lucky enough to be born with the math gene that would make her effortlessly good at math. She exhibited what Dweck calls "a fixed mindset" (p. 6), believing that math skills are "innate," (p. 6) and thus she would always be "deficient" in math (p. 6). Dweck would say it is her beliefs and self-perceptions that limit her.

Dweck's book is popular in the education community. Professional development sessions have been devoted to teaching the differences between her theory of the two mindsets. The alternative to having a "fixed" mindset, Dweck asserts, is one where you perceive that you were born with "ability," a way of being that allows for ideas to change and develop in the mind. Dweck's avers that students can build their knowledge and skills and achieve a growth mindset. A growth mindset is a way of being where one's "talents can be developed through hard work, good strategies and input from others" (p. 31). Having a growth mindset is to know that you may not have the answer but that you can work toward one. This is a conceptual framework she calls the "productive struggle" (p. 24). Not knowing how to solve a problem immediately is part of the "productive struggle" concept. In elementary math, this can look like the 4th-grade number-talk fraction-comparison problem discussed earlier with the frog and tadpoles. At first glance, the answer to the question of which fraction is greater (2/3 or 3/4) is not obvious. With effort and logic, students are able to arrive at the answer without knowing any formal procedure to compare fractions. This is what is meant by "productive struggle." It is an empowering way that students are able to combine their own background and logic to solve problems in math. Just like those students having a productive struggle in learning fractions, teachers too benefit from their own productive struggle when building their math knowledge, confidence, and pedagogy.

To instill in my students a respect for lifelong learning in mathematics, I constantly endeavor to build on my own passion for the subject and expand my personal research to incorporate many areas of development, from Carol Dweck's work to inclusive and culturally relevant teaching methods. Collaborative WIL initiatives (such as the project that is the topic of this chapter) present a promising avenue for fostering joint research projects aimed at evaluating the effectiveness of inclusive math pedagogies across various educational contexts and geographical domains.

What has become obvious from the many exchanges, discussions, and observations I have had during my sabbatical is that math needs to be clear, contextualized, and made relevant for students in order to develop a math-thinking mindset and problem-solving skills. The conceptual frameworks needed to teach such skills and educate the diverse population of new students entering my classroom in the United States has come to me by way of my transnational research projects in England and Spain.

All of the various elementary school math lessons I have learned about have similar goals; the countries I visited value math in similar ways. And yet, we come to the teaching of it in different ways. The target for all math conceptual understanding models seems consistent everywhere I visited: Each country wants to build mathematicians who are curious and engaged mathematical problem solvers. In his book *Making Numbers Count* (2022), Chip Heath says "We encounter numbers lots of times in a given day. Our economy, our schedules, our transportation systems, our household management, everything we do is based around numbers. We can choose to be involved with numerical decisions or stay in the dark, but we can't actually opt out" (p. 62). A successful mathematics program creates a space for students to "opt in," to learn math so they can flourish both in and out of class. This is the junction where effective math teaching intersects with how policies and curriculum are designed.

7 Policy and Curriculum Development

My lived experience as a global researcher has made me believe that effective math teaching that is sustainable requires a holistic approach to policies and curriculum. As far as policies related to teacher preparedness go, the inclusion of WIL cultural immersion experiences is a perfect place to start. Teacher preparation programs in England most often include a WIL immersive piece. Participants anecdotally reported that the experiences of visiting Hungary and The Gambia as part of teacher training made them better educators as a result. Their comments are also reminiscent of the impact of WIL on teachers in the guide with the Nipissing University students (p. 60). Including WIL in university programs is one policy that would positively impact teacher preparedness.

The integration of WIL has been proven, by my own example, to be invaluable. Janice Orrell (2018) states that there is considerable evidence of the positive impact of authentic work-based participation. She further states that students who participate in these experiences develop their "professional identity … advance their theoretical knowledge and transferable skills" (p. 1) so they can communicate effectively. The value of WIL extends beyond any classroom.

Ideally, the WIL spirit and ideals can be achieved post school years. In service veteran teachers also deserve the rewards of creative learning experiences outside their daily educational setting. Since I could not find such a program, I created it, planned it, proposed it, embarked on it, and learned from it. I would encourage educational policy makers to include this kind of travel and research in teacher contracts because as Alan Schoenfeld's Cultural Surround graphic shows, the complexities of allowing cultural experiences to merge with school math class conditions for the teacher and students is strong. This includes mathematical thinking, the learning environment, and the cultural surround. The ripple-effect conditions exist within each one of us, whether we are a teacher working to create meaningful math learning for our students or a student learning math.

At the center of Fig. 11: Alan Schoenfeld's Three Expanding Circles is the idea that thinking mathematically is a vital piece of math and having the "growth mindset" (discussed earlier) is helpful in persevering through problems and in the social interactions that accompany math.

But, of course, school is not just about math. It is about making connections and being flexible in how you perceive yourself, how you perceive math, and how you perceive others. In order to be flexible, students must be open-minded.

The outer circle on Fig. 11: Schoenfeld's three expanding circles explore culture in relation to making math equitable. As students and teachers learn new techniques, they begin to know themselves better intellectually and academically, developing the confidence they need to succeed as mathematicians. build the capacity to recognize how issues are interconnected across the globe. These exchanges teach how to adjust our thinking and create a bridge between self-centeredness and empathy, which plays a key role not only in mathematics but in getting along with others.

Fig. 11 Alan Schoenfeld's cultural surround

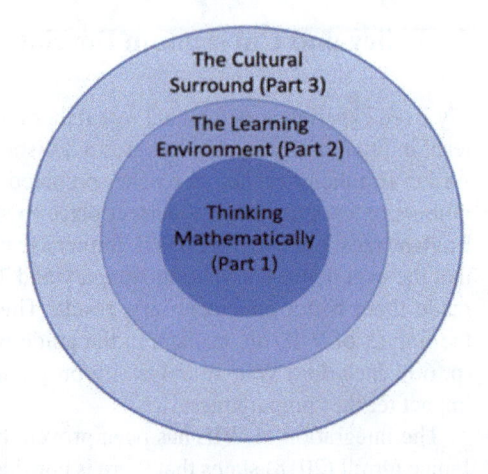

- The Cultural Surround (Part 3)
- The Learning Environment (Part 2)
- Thinking Mathematically (Part 1)

Ultimately, the concept of math identity plays an important role in current and future math instruction. A student's daily experience is created by a teacher's knowledge—both of math and of the world.

8 Conclusion

In keeping with the WIL guide of merging theory with practice, I traveled to England and Spain to see how other teachers in other countries were also trying to stay relevant in teaching math to nine-year-old students. Also, in keeping with the WIL guide, I acted on it by investing my time, effort and resources. The benefits of the personal and financial risks I took to create this self-directed WIL experience have proven to be worth the risk. As I continue to process and reflect on my experiences, I am left with the belief that my experience has shifted my thinking in transformative ways that will benefit my colleagues, students, global communities and myself. The different math approaches I witnessed and experienced pushed me to expand my own understanding of math and the world by allowing me to see other perspectives and ways of teaching. Now, I am excited, not only to share what I have learned, but to build student and teacher math enjoyment through other WIL-informed field work.

My trips to England and Spain were only the starting points. Those visits instilled in me the idea that I need to continue traveling and researching, in order to answer my question of how best to meet diverse student needs. Next, I want to build on the relationships and new learning gained by visiting England and Spain to create a sustainable math network. This hub will have many spokes of engagement for teachers, students, families, and communities. One spoke is to increase the number and type of visits to include WIL-informed exchanges for other veteran teachers like me. Another spoke is to establish communication between students in different countries.

Since my first trip to England, I have also grown as a visitor observing math lessons. During my first school visits, I would check the permissions regarding student safety and the rules for adults in school. This was helpful in establishing whether or not it was ok to take notes or photos and the like. With permission, I started using a peer-observation tool adapted from the Lucy West book *Agents of Change: How Content Coaching Transforms Teaching and Learning* (2013). For those teachers who wanted to see my notes, I quickly noticed that the peer tool proved to be too cumbersome to be effective for collecting and sharing. A simple form listing the time and what the students and teachers were doing was a better tool for me to use when taking notes during observations.

I also connected with a university professor in England and one in the U.S. These consultations helped me learn more ways to gather information about math teaching and learning. One idea was to query students and teachers about math and learning through an anonymous survey. I made a teacher math survey and a student math survey, translated it and brought my new surveys back with me on a second trip to Spain.

Continued collaboration with England, Spain, and beyond is the next step to maintaining and building a network of connections. In the end, relationships are all there are—starting with our relationships with ourselves, our relationships with math, and our relationships with the world. It is a privilege not only to teach math to our many students but also to continue building math relationships around the world.

References

Atweh, B., & Clarkson, P. (2002). Globalized curriculum or global approach to curriculum reform in mathematics education. *Asia Pacific Education Review, 3*(2), 160–167.

Bass, R. (2012). Disrupting ourselves: The problem of learning in higher education. *Educause Review*, 23.

Dweck, C. (2008). *Mindset: The new psychology of success.* Ballantine Books Trade Paperback Edition.

Dweck, C. (2016). *What having a growth mindset actually means.* Harvard Business Review.

Fletcher, G. (2022). *Graham Fletcher's 3 act task file cabinet.* https://gfletchy.com/; https://gfletchy.com/3-act-lessons/.

Fosnot, C. (2007). *New perspectives on learning.* https://newperspectivesonlearning.com/.

Heath, C. (2022). *Making numbers count: The art and science of communicating numbers.* Avid Reader Press.

Orrell, J. (2018, April). Work integrated learning: Why is it increasing and who benefits? *The Conversation.* https://theconversation.com/work-integrated-learning-why-is-it-increasing-and-who-benefits-93642.

Schoenfeld, A. H. (2022). Why are learning and teaching mathematics so difficult? In M. Danesi (Ed.), *Handbook of cognitive mathematics* (pp. 10–11). Springer.

Stirling et al. (2016). *A Practical Guide for Work-Integrated Learning, HEQCO,* Ontario.

West, L., & Cameron, A. (2013). *Agents of change: How content coaching transforms teaching and learning.* Heinemann.

Wyborney, S. (2018). *Steve Wyborney's Esti-Mysteries.* https://stevewyborney.com/category/esti-mysteries/.

Work-Integrated Learning in a Value-Based Course

Maggie Perumal

Abstract The world today is in dire need of human values education. People, therefore, need to get back to basics, to realize the dream of a world in which the human values of truth, love, peace, right conduct, and non-violence thrive and prevail. Sri Sathya Sai value-based education is designed to emphasize the practice of the 5 core human values of truth, right conduct, peace, love, and non-violence, and their sub-values in daily life. This is enhanced by the application of the 5 transformation or teaching techniques of silent sitting and meditation, prayer and quotations, storytelling, song and music, and group activities, which assist in the holistic development of the individual. This study focuses on the use of Work Integrated Learning (WIL) to unfold human values in the students. The author discusses her experiences as a course coordinator and facilitator/trainer of the Sri Sathya Sai Education in Human Values (SSSEHV) Introductory Course over the last 5 years. The impact of the WIL components on the students and the community members demonstrated its transformative power to spread positivity and the five core human values to the people they interacted with. This is the principle of resonance, which is emphasised in the course.

Keywords Human values · Work integrated learning · SSSEHV

1 Introduction

Sri Sathya Sai Baba, a world philosopher, and teacher, is the founder of the Sri Sathya Sai Education in Human Values (SSSEHV) programs. The philosophical cornerstone of Sathya Sai Education is the concept of Sri Sathya Sai Educare. Sri Sathya Sai Baba says (Sathya Sai International Organisation, 2024), "Educare has two aspects, the worldly and the spiritual. Worldly education brings out the latent knowledge about the physical world. Spiritual education brings out the inherent divinity in man. So, both worldly and spiritual education is essential, without which human life has no value".

M. Perumal (✉)
Sri Sathya Sai Institute of Educare South Africa, Durban, South Africa
e-mail: Maggie@srisathyasai.org.za

© The Author(s), under exclusive license to Springer Nature Switzerland AG 2024
I. C. Chahine and L. Reddy (eds.), *Educators' Work Integrated Learning Experiences*,
https://doi.org/10.1007/978-3-031-65964-5_16

The Sri Sathya Sai Institute of Educare—South Africa (SSSIESA), offers various levels of the SSSEHV courses. For this chapter, I will be focussing on the WIL component of the SSSEHV Introductory Course.

A newborn baby comes into the world like a blank canvas. Underneath that canvas lies a beautiful soul in which the human values of truth, right conduct, peace, love, and non-violence reside. If those values are brought to the fore immediately that child will grow up to be a shining example of a true human being—gentle, loving, well-mannered, full of peace, always truthful, and with no inclination to violent behaviour. Can you imagine a world filled with such human beings? (Shah, 2006).

The current state of the world where corruption, greed, violence, rape, murder, robbery, drugs, bullying, etc. co-exist is testimony to the fact that the world needs fixing. Incorporating work-integrated learning (WIL) into human values-based programs can help students develop not only as skilled professionals but also as ethical and responsible individuals. These values lay the foundation for a sustainable and inclusive work culture that benefits both students and the organizations they join (Sathya Sai Educare, 2024).

2 Why the Need for Value-Based Education?

Man, today stands at a crossroads, as he helplessly witnesses the strange paradox that has engulfed the world. One side is full of new milestones of man's conquest of matter and space, and the other shows a directionless quest for elusive peace and happiness (Sathya Sai International Organisation, 1999). While the domain of comfort is expanding endlessly, the one for whom they are intended is becoming increasingly unhappy (Albert, 2019). I have found that students who complete the SSSEHV Introductory course have shifted their traditional beliefs, family dynamics, and spiritual inquiry. Their focus has moved away from preoccupation with financial gains and compulsive acquisition of material goods and services in search of a higher standard of living. They have incorporated values in their everyday life and bring them to the fore during daily interactions (Jumsai, 1997).

The online certificate courses provided by the Sri Sathya Sai Institute of Educare South Africa (SSSIESA) have given people from all walks of life an opportunity to be skilled in the practice of Educare by applying the principles of Sathya Sai Educare Philosophy in their homes, workplaces, schools, and community programs (Jumsai & Burrows, 1991).

In the late fifty's, addressing students, Sri Sathya Sai Baba said: *"The present system of education aims at making you breadwinners and citizens, but it does not give you the secret of a happy life, namely discrimination between the real and the unreal"*. Again, on 12th September 1963, He said: *"Education is not for mere living, it is for life, a fuller, a more meaningful, a more worthwhile life. There is no harm if it is for gainful employment but the educated must realize that existence is not all and that gainful employment is not all. What is needed today is that we should live a life of good quality. The fostering of sterling character and good conduct is the need of the world*" (Sathya Sai Educare, 2024).

I firmly believe that there is more to education than mere regurgitation of facts and figures and that education should also address the intellectual, emotional, physical, psychological, and spiritual domains of the human personality (Taplin, 2002). The shift towards more holistic learning will result in the development of a well-rounded individual through whom human values will blossom. The SSSEHV programs through WIL provide exactly for this gap in learning.

3 Aims and Objectives of the SSSEHV Introductory Course

The overall aim of the SSSEHV courses is to allow students to undergo self-transformation through the practice of the transformation techniques and values to cope with the demands of life and to strive to be exemplars, role models of excellence, and agents of positive change in their workplaces, homes, and social circles.

The training fosters the realization that the answer to society's problems and the nurturing of peace and love in the world will occur through raising the consciousness of the participants. The SSSEHV course outcomes are:

(1) To develop knowledge of the philosophy of Sri Sathya Sai Education in Human Values (SSSEHV).
(2) To enable participants to clearly understand the process of self-transformation.
(3) To develop the ability to unfold human values in personal, professional, and family life.
(4) To develop the ability to practice the 5 Transformation techniques in any educational setting, be it informal or formal.
(5) To make a personal commitment to strive to become an exemplar of universal human values.
(6) To document student experiences with online learning through feedback on assignments and the course as a whole.

In addition, the course attempts to restore discipline and harmony and bring about positive changes in schools, homes, and the workplace by focusing on the practice of basic human values. Through WIL students are allowed to engage in face-to-face activities which allows them to actively practice the Educare principles and bring out their inherent values.

4 The Philosophy of Educare

The word 'Educare' means to bring out that which is within—in Latin it means "to elicit". To bring out means to translate them into action. It is a process of deep understanding of values and knowledge and implies imparting this knowledge to learners.

Table 1 Comparison between secular education and Educare[1]

Secular education	Educare
Worldly (materialistic)	Heart centred
Focuses on survival	Focuses on harmony with creation
Results in greed and aggression	The outcomes are love and compassion
Allows one to demand one's rights	It allows one to realize one's responsibility
It is an outward journey	It is an inward journey
Geared towards gathering information	Geared towards transformation
Offshoots are pride and ego	Offshoots are humility and awareness

It is the blossoming/unfolding of inherent values that brings about transformation, that is, from selfishness to selflessness. Educare illuminates the consciousness within us (SSSIESA, 2022).

Sri Sathya Sai Baba explains Educare as follows:

"Educare is essentially spiritual education, whereas education relates to worldly and physical matters (superficial and changing). Educare is the acquisition of knowledge that results in the transformation of the heart and mind and leads to the power of discrimination (Baba, 1990). Educare implies bringing out inner thoughts and acting according to them. It results in the realization of the true self. An action program of self-development so that one can improve one's leadership potential to the maximum extent." (SSSIESA, 2023). Table 1 compares and highlights the difference between secular education and Educare.

4.1 Harmony of Head, Heart, and Hands

Dr. Margaret Taplin, in her book on *Teacher Survival,* wrote "Educare teaches two important ingredients for life. One is that whatever thoughts come into our heads we should think about and examine in our hearts before we act. This is referred to as 3HV, the harmony of head, heart, and hands. The other is concentration and inner stillness. The main ingredient, though, is love, and through love, individuals are helped to become self-reliant, self-confident, self-sacrificing, and eventually self-realized" (Taplin, 2002).

SSSEHV has been successfully implemented through formal and informal programs e.g., in schools, workplaces, and community organizations across the world. Formal education provides an opportunity to apply the principles of Sri Sathya Sai education at the primary, secondary, and tertiary levels whereas informal programs can be applied in personal, family, community, and work situations.

Assignments for WIL given to the students were both formal and informal. This was aimed at bringing out the latent values within the students thereby

---

[1] Original to author

Table 2 Selfless service project[2]

Ass. No.	Topic	Requirements	Possible service projects
1	Selfless service project The purpose of this project is to inspire the spirit of selfless service in students taking this course	Undertake a mini selfless service project to improve the lives of other humans, animals, or the environment To be done in own time and not during working hours. Minimum of 6 h to be spent on the project. The program of activities and motivation for doing the project must be included in the report In their reports, students are required to explain the impact of the project on themselves as well as on their target group. They have to document the challenges they faced and how they overcame them	Serving the poor, sick, needy, animals, learners with learning disabilities, or the environment Possible service projects could include gardening projects to provide for the homeless or disadvantaged, online tuition programs for disadvantaged learners, and service to the environment e.g., recycling, cleaning up of the environment, etc.

allowing them to experience self-transformation. Assignments focus on experiential learning, ongoing self-audits, quizzes, and practical application of the core values, transformation techniques, and core tenets of Educare in different settings.

Two major formal assignments were given which involved work-integrated learning. The first was a selfless service project in the home/community/ workplace/ school environment. The second was planning and implementation of a value-based lesson in the classroom or workplace.

5 Selfless Service WIL Project

5.1 Methodology

The selfless service project requires students to go out into the community, environment, workplace, society, etc., and perform an activity with no expectation of personal gain or reward, conducted willingly and out of the goodness of their hearts. The assignment is described in Table 2.

Some of the activities included feeding schemes for the underprivileged, beach clean-ups, community or school recycling projects, Go-green projects, free medical camps, free community education/literacy programs, and helping at an animal shelter. This project opens the eyes and hearts of students to the harsh realities of the world.

---

[2] Original to author

They begin to appreciate their comforts and learn not to take things for granted. The change in the heart of the student can be explained using the heart, head, and hand (3HV) concept for critical decision-making described by Margaret Taplin above. Very often our actions are a result of responses coming from the brain/head with little or no consideration for the consequences thereof. The 3HV principle provides for a re-routing of the thoughts by first consulting with the heart before acting upon the thought. This means that the outcome of the action will be one that will not cause harm but rather benefit the giver and the recipient/s.

One of the key goals of this value-based course is to reduce the ego- the feeling that "I am the doer" or "the world revolves around me". This project provides an ideal opportunity for students to minimize their egos. When conducting this project, participants begin to focus on the needs of others rather than their own. In this way, the ego is diminished.

5.2 Findings

Students generally enjoyed this assignment as it was practical and allowed them to include others like family members or friends to be part of this project. The element of sacrifice that was necessary due to the selfless nature of the assignment, humbled students and gave them a deep sense of satisfaction, achievement, and gratitude.

For students who opt to get involved in a community feeding program, the change in heart occurs when they confront other humans who are less privileged than them. Feelings of kindness, compassion, empathy, caring, sharing, sacrifice, respect, etc. are brought to the fore. This could be a life-changing experience for the student. They learn how to bring happiness to others by making personal sacrifices and placing a ceiling on their desires to fund the activity.

In each of the examples of projects, students applied the 3HV principle during their choice of activity. For example, getting involved in a recycling project meant making a conscious decision to save the planet by cutting down on the use of single-use plastic, reusing or re-purposing plastic containers/items, or not placing unwanted plastic in garbage bins but rather collecting them for recycling.

Participants thoroughly enjoyed the activity as evidenced by the reports on the positive impact of this activity on themselves as well as the recipients of the selfless service assignment.

This is the response of one student on the impact of doing a community reading program with children from an informal settlement:

> Humbleness of a simple task like reading to young children was a true gift. Made me commit fully to spending the Saturday afternoon contributing to teaching these young children to read. I am now a full-time volunteer teacher every Saturday reading to Grade 2 learners. The love I receive from the children with the hugs every time I arrive at the Centre is priceless and fills joy in my heart.

The values of humility, dedication, and love are elicited in this project.

Another student got involved in a community feeding programme and this is her response:

> I was overwhelmed at first, however when I got involved in the activities, everything would fall into place so easily. I cooked a pot of biryani in a deck for the first time, and to dish that hot meal out and distribute it made me very happy. Having to see the gratitude of children was the greatest reward. This has made a lasting impact on my life, and I wish to continuously serve those around me in whichever way possible. This has also impacted my family, as everybody at home would assist and want to be involved in the packing of hampers or serving. (Fig. 1a, b)

This project brings out the values of satisfaction, gratitude, and empathy.

The next response is from a student who is an educator. Her project involved creating a fun and safe environment through soccer training for underprivileged children through the 'Kicking through soccer training program'. This is her response: *"Personally, seeing the children off the street and being active in sports made me feel self-fulfilled. I feel fortunate to work with many children at school, and I can continue to motivate them on the path of righteousness. The Kicking Through Life program motivated me to help the children in the community. Having to train the children inspired me to make a difference in their lives. Seeing the success of the project, I am motivated to continue with the program. However, I may introduce other sports and a literacy program at the latter stages."*

The values of caring, sacrifice, and commitment are brought out in this project.

The following response is from a student who chose to serve hot meals at a shelter for the homeless.

> This was an extremely fulfilling experience. Many recipients joined the queue for a second time as receiving a hot meal is not a regular occurrence. They mostly get sandwiches. Just goes to show that we're living in paradise compared to many people in our country. I was grateful for this opportunity to serve, as I will now be assisting at Denis Hurley regularly. They were very appreciative of the meals. Hopefully, this act of kindness showed them that they are loved and cared for. I've built a relationship with some of the people as I've been

Fig. 1 **a** Meal preparation, **b** hampers

there on 3 occasions thus far. Handing of the meals is coupled with a smile and an exchange of a few loving words as well.

This student's response came from the heart, and he was able to empathize with the recipient's neglected circumstances. This act also inspired him to continue offering his services.

5.3 The Reason Why WIL is Appropriate for This Assignment

All the components of Educare as described in Table 1, are brought out during this activity.

Heart-centred. This project opens the hearts of students to the harsh realities of the world. They begin to appreciate their comforts and learn to not take things for granted.

Harmony with creation. When doing beach clean-ups or go green projects participants identify with and appreciate the beauty and bountifulness of nature.

Love and compassion. Feelings of love and compassion are aroused for example, when providing food for the underprivileged or participating in community upliftment programs.

Realizes one's responsibility to society. Students begin to shed their selfishness and get involved in working together for the betterment of society.

Inward journey. In doing this project students undergo retrospection and re-evaluate their purpose in life. This leads to a positive transformation, where the offshoots are *humility and awareness.*

6 WIL Lesson/Workplace Plan

6.1 Methodology

The second formal assignment that students carried out, involved creating and implementing a Lesson plan or Activity plan. The description is given in Table 3.

The transformation techniques are silent sitting or meditation (compulsory), prayer, quotations and affirmations, group singing, storytelling, and group activity. A schoolteacher would prepare a Lesson plan, while someone who works in a corporate or business environment would prepare a Workplace plan. Students who do not fit into either of these categories would prepare an activity plan to be carried out in the home or community.

Table 3 Lesson/workplan

	Topic	Requirements
2	Lesson/activity plan The purpose of this project is to help the student on his/her journey of transformation and provide the opportunity to transform others in the process by integrating values and implementing the transformation techniques in their respective situations (work, personal life, or home)	Prepare and present the lesson plan or activity plan using some or all the five transformation techniques and complete a report based on the outcomes

Once the plan is approved the student must deliver the lesson or carry out the planned activity to the target group. This group could be learners, co-workers, management, family, community outreach members, etc. Students are required to collect evidence such as photographs, videos, testimonies, assessments, feedback, etc. while engaging in the lesson/activity as well as after completing the activity. The evidence must be included in the report. Other requirements for the report are:

- To observe changes in behavior/attitudes etc. in the target group as well as in themselves and make a note of them.
- To determine whether the objectives have been achieved or not and to provide evidence or explanation for this.
- To determine the impact of the lesson/activity on the student as well as their participants/target group.

6.2 Findings

In the 2023 cohort of 13 students, 10 students completed a lesson plan, and 3 students completed an activity plan in the home environment. In the final online assessment, students had to do an oral PowerPoint presentation based on the methodology, results, and impact of their lesson or activity. Students were able to use the appropriate techniques to deliver the lesson or activity. This assignment enabled students to be more confident in their delivery of lessons or workplace activities whilst indirectly including fundamental human values and transformation techniques to bring about positive changes.

A value-based lesson offered to children in the community on good manners and respect had this impact on one educator:

> Planning this lesson made me aware of the impact that I can have in a child's life by instilling the proper values in them, and executing the lesson made that realization even more real. Seeing the children use what they learned in real life made me appreciate the opportunity that I have to share these values. I noticed that my self-confidence had increased because I was able to make such a difference in these learners' lives. I felt lighter and I felt a certain kind of joy from within.

She used all five transformation techniques to achieve her objectives as described in the book by Packham et al. (2024).

Another student used the techniques of silent sitting, song, and storytelling to have a family bonding session involving board games, which brought out the values of sharing, patience, and honesty. Here, she describes her experience:

> It was an overwhelming experience but one I embraced. I enjoyed the planning and execution. I learned new things e.g., it was the first time I conducted a guided Jyothi meditation. Browsing for the appropriate type of music was also fun, as I explored many genres and options to select from. I was a little nervous on the day as to how the target audience would receive the techniques and the purpose of the activity. However, to my surprise, they all were very involved and appreciated the purpose of the activity. I had to re-set and adjust my attitude accordingly to fit the purpose of the activity (e.g.; I became a little more serious in my approach and tone without losing the loving touch), and by doing so the target audience had also adjusted accordingly becoming more involved, engaged and interacting with purpose. I was extremely appreciative that my target audience had taken the time to participate in the activities, I thanked them and expressed how I wanted to share some of the enlightenments I've learned during the year on this course.

The next student did a lesson with young adults on putting a ceiling on their desires (COD) to not waste food, time, money, and energy. The lesson used the techniques of silent sitting and group activity, which took the form of a discussion session. The feedback received from adults was constructive and they also committed to making at least one change as indicated by Reddy (2021). This is what the student had to say:

> I had about 4 young adults present and their takeaway from the presentation was the waste of time. They made a conscious decision to firstly not sleep excessively which they do out of boredom, and to also limit the social media time. That for me was a win.
>
> I must admit I was nervous about introducing the COD program to the individuals I selected. People can be defensive or take offense to being told how to spend their time and money. So, I was taken aback by how receptive they were, and the positive feedback I received. One 21-year-old called me two days later to tell me she's been waking up at 6 am and finding she has a more productive day. She also thanked me for educating her. Making a difference in at least one person's mind is a success.

Educare Philosophy was exemplified through the lesson/workplan (indicated in Table 1) carried out during WIL as follows:

Heart-centered—The use of the transformation techniques allows the student to connect and engage with the target group firstly at the mind level by preparing them for the activity using silent sitting and/or meditation. Once the mind is settled it becomes easy to appeal to the heart. This is key to having the desired outcome.

Harmony with creation. During this activity, students are mindful about what resources they use and not to encourage waste.

Love and compassion. Each lesson/workplan is required to focus on a specific core value and sub-value(s) which will be elicited through the transformation techniques. By focussing on values in their lesson/workplan the focus is not just on completing the lesson but rather on including educare principles. It is a well-thought-out plan, which has the interest of the target group at heart.

Realises one's responsibility to society. An educator's role is to bring out the best in his or her learners. The youth of today must be trained to become good leaders of the future generation. Value-based lessons constantly hammer home the message that we must lead virtuous and moral lives. Through these value-based lessons, the teacher fulfills his/her role "in loco parentis".

In the workplace, the introduction of value-based work activities changes the shift from a corporate culture that focuses primarily on financial and technological advancement to an organization that cares for and respects its workers.

7 Informal Assignments

Two informal assessments namely a Human Values Self Development exercise and a spiritual self-audit were given.

7.1 WIL Human Values Self Development Exercise

In this assignment, students must identify their core human value strengths and weaknesses by completing 3 Tables and calculating their highest score. Their two highest scores are the human value strengths that they explicitly and naturally draw upon the most. The other core human values are their hidden strengths. When they are in touch with their strongest core human values, they can then use them to reach into themselves to bring out the remaining core human values.

There are three sections to this assignment. In Section A, three tables of values were given to determine their human value strengths. In the first table, students were able to determine which expressions of the Human Values they were most aware of in their day-to-day work. In the second table students determined which expressions of the Human Values they primarily drew from when they had opportunities to learn, grow, and see things differently in their work. In the third table students were able to determine which expressions of the Human Values they felt contributed most to their success at work.

Students used the following Guidelines for the interpretation and application of results concerning their strongest core value/s:

If you are strong in **Truth**, you can use that strength to bring out your natural ability to be authentic (Righteousness), self-confident (Peace), pure at heart (Love), and broad-minded (Non-violence).

If you are strong in **Righteousness**, you can use that strength to bring out your natural ability to be sincere (Truth), contented (Peace), forgiving (Love), and helpful (Non-violence).

If you are strong in **Peace**, you can use that strength to bring out your natural ability to be objective (Truth), disciplined (Righteousness), compassionate (Love), and fearless (Nonviolence).

If you are strong in **Love**, you can use that strength to bring out your natural ability to have integrity (Truth), follow your conscience (Righteousness), be equanimous (Peace), and respect others (Non-violence).

If you are strong in **Non-violence**, you can use that strength to bring out your natural ability to be honest (Truth), dutiful (Righteousness), patient (Peace), and kind (Love).

In Section B, students were tested on the practice of the human values of truth, right conduct, peace, love, and non-violence in their relevant field.

This was a self-exercise to test understanding. Students were required to list one example of how they could express each of the Human Values at School/Work/Home. They also had to describe any practical challenges and strategies they used to overcome these.

In section C, students were given a practice and reflection exercise for a week, to unfold values. The task required them to record for 7 days their participation in doing a random act of kindness, speaking softly and lovingly with everyone, and practicing silent sitting for a minimum of 5 min each day.

Through this assignment, students become more aware of their innate human value strengths and have the opportunity to practice the values they are not so strong in.

7.1.1 Findings

The practice of the 5 core values for the first five days was very challenging and students were able to gauge their progress on this spiritual journey and understand how much greater effort was required for further progress. Students were able to identify their strongest human values and acknowledged their challenges in practicing the core human values of Truth, Right Conduct, Peace, Love, and Non-Violence. As the course unfolded, they were able to adopt some of the techniques provided to overcome these challenges. These findings are supported by various authors (Taplin & Lingli, 2021) (Figs. 2 and 3).

7.2 Spiritual Self-Audit

This Spiritual Self-Audit is a personal tool that serves to assist one in tracking the transformation of one's character. The tool is meant to facilitate reflection and prompt the student along his/her spiritual path. Students are required to respond to the same set of questions 3 times during the course; one at the beginning, the second in the middle, and the third at the end of the course. In this way, both students and assessors can determine whether there was any significant shift or progress related to their spiritual growth, which is one of the main outcomes of this course. The self-audit covered 4 main aspects namely, daily spiritual exercises, character development, leadership, and mind and sense control.

VALUE	PRACTICAL CHALLENGES	STRATEGIES TO OVERCOME CHALLENGES
Truth	Sometimes being straight forward is difficult, especially when you are given additional duties to perform at work.	I need to stand up for myself and only accept tasks that I can manage.
Right Conduct	Doing the right thing is sometimes not always possible.	Strive to always use Swami as the ideal.
Peace	When drivers cut in front of you.	Practice breathing exercises whenever this happens rather than agitation and frustration.
Love	To love those who indulge in wrong actions.	Try to forgive which is very difficult.
Non-Violence	Killing of insects or creatures.	Overcome my fear of them thereby not allowing them to die.

Days 1 to 5 exercise tested the student's ability to practice the core values of Truth, Right conduct, Peace, Love, and nonviolence in his/her daily interactions.

Day 6 exercise on moderation of food and sleep was a discipline to instill a ceiling on desires.

Day 7 exercise helped to bring about healing and forgiveness.

Fig. 2 Sample of a response to Section B—practice of human values

7.2.1 Findings

A sample of a completed Spiritual Self-Audit (Fig. 4) displays the student's experiences on two aspects, namely daily spiritual exercises, and character development.

The purpose of the spiritual self-audit was for students to do continuous introspection and evaluate their progress on this spiritual journey. This was well received by students as indicated by the following comments:

> "The self-audits helped me to identify my weaker points which I am still working on." "The self-audit assignments involved practice, reflection, and introspection. It aimed for excellence." "The self-audits assisted me to measure my transformation throughout the course." "I also enjoyed the self-audits, and it helped me to continually reassess my actions and make sure they were in line with what was expected of me as a spiritual aspirant."

As can be seen from the comments, the self-audits achieved the course outcome to make a personal commitment to strive to become an exemplar of the universal human values.

8 Impact of Integrating WIL into the SSSEHV Introductory Course

The course empowers students with good leadership skills (an essential component of the course), but also to practice servant leadership during their WIL. In servant leadership environments the leader/manager encourages innovation, empowers employees with relevant and necessary skills to develop leadership qualities, and ensures the

DAY	TASK TO DO	Y or N	My Experience/Learning
DAY 1	Speak the Truth today. Do not Lie. Do not utter Truth which harms someone.	N	I had to inform an employee that the company no longer grants loan requests which hurt the person, but I had to be the one to relay this message.
DAY 2	Apply your discrimination to everything you do today. Apply the filter of 'Right conduct' to every thought, word, and deed of yours.	Y	I received R100 extra from a customer today who paid a huge amount of cash. Despite it being only R100 I informed my manager and felt good about doing that as I knew that Swami is watching me.
DAY 3	Try to search for 'Peace' today. Can you find it in an object, or a person or at a place? If YES, has that object/person/place always given you peace? Try to meditate today, or at least try to sit down silently for 20 minutes. If you can, do not talk to anyone for 6 hours today and practice silence.	N	I was unable to remain silent for 6 hours. There was always something that needed my attention and hindered my state of peace.
DAY 4	Be extra compassionate today. Give the extra smile, the extra helping hand to anyone and everyone. Just for a day, try to be as selfless as you can! Love as much as possible and as many as possible - through your thought, word, and deed	Y	I was kind to people that I encountered. I allowed people right of way on the road.
DAY 5	Don't be violent for a day – in thought, word, and deed. Practice non-violence towards yourself and towards others. Practice living today without any thought and feeling of envy and anger towards anyone today.	Y	I was very mindful of every action of mine, and I was able to achieve this feeling of satisfaction and contentment.
DAY 6	Practice moderation in food and sleep today.	Y	Ironically it was the weekend and I had visitors over. I had to cut down on my weekend sleep to prepare in advance for the visitors. BY the time I was done there was no time for an afternoon nap or even sit down to a proper meal.
DAY 7	Re-establish an old relationship or form a new bond, based on pure, selfless love. Talk to someone today whom you have not spoken for a long time – a friend, family, your teacher, or anyone! Specifically, connect with your parents or children today, spend some good time with them today and make them Happy!	Y	My friend is going through some difficulties and recently I have been very busy and neglecting her because of my busy schedule. I made some time today to check in on her to see how she was doing which really made her feel special.

Fig. 3 Sample response to Section C—practice and reflection exercise. This required willpower and perseverance. Many students completed the tasks successfully and were pleasantly surprised at the change in their behaviour and attitude

well-being of those around them through nurturing and caring rather than being a "boss". So, students who work in a business environment or a school would benefit from this as they would learn to be self-sufficient and more productive. These value-based courses help students demonstrate characteristics such as empathy,

DAILY SPIRITUAL EXERCISES	Never true of me	Rarely true of me	Sometimes true of me	Often true of me	Always true of me
DATE	DATE	DATE	DATE	DATE	DATE
I'm making a deliberate effort to improve my relationship with God					26/02/2023 15/06/2023 09/10/2023
Mostly I pray when I am in difficulty	26/02/2023 15/06/2023 09/10/2023				
When I pray I spend some time thanking God					26/02/2023 15/06/2023 09/10/2023
I practise some of the prescribed exercises			15/06/2023 09/10/2023	26/02/2023	
CHARACTER DEVELOPMENT/ UNFOLDING VALUES		**My Life Is My Message**
When I am faced with moral dilemmas I look to spiritual knowledge and surrender the problem to God for resolution					26/02/2023 15/06/2023 09/10/2023
I do not speak ill of others especially in their absence.				26/02/2023 15/06/2023 09/10/2023	
I get angry		09/10/2023	26/02/2023	15/06/2023	
When another driver does something				26/02/2023 15/06/2023 09/10/2023	

Fig. 4 Sample of a completed spiritual self-audit form

listening, supervision, and commitment to the personal growth of others (Sathya Sai International Organisation, 2024).

> Two of the core tenets of the Educare program are unity of all faiths and unity in diversity. These topics help students see the world as one big family and this eliminates prejudices based on race, creed, color, religion, gender, etc. When students engage in their selfless service projects or compile their lesson/work/activity plan they are expected to look beyond these traits when choosing their target group. If the selfless service involves environmental awareness this influences them to see how dependent we are on nature and the environment. The values of protection, nurturing, and interdependence come to the fore.

Assignments cater to the application of the core principles of Educare such as values integration, use of the transformation techniques, and practice of unity, purity, and harmony of thought, word, and deed in their relevant settings (home, workplace, community, among others). This ensures that students obtain first-hand experience of the positive aspects of the courses. Mentors are readily available to obtain feedback and guide students in terms of their progress.

9 The Future of Value-Based Education

The course has been well received by students who have testified to their positive changes, behaviour, and attitude after completing the course. The testimonies provided by students on their WIL experiences, confirm the positive effect of the course in their lives. It is therefore essential to forge ahead and continue to provide these courses annually, to keep the momentum going.

On a personal level, I strive to apply the educare principles in my own life, so that I may deliver the programme with full faith and passion. I can testify that I have become more patient, forgiving, loving, and tolerant. My transformation allows me to see the benefits of this program. I firmly believe that I have become a well-rounded individual who has reached the stage of being content with what life offers. I constantly do a self-audit and rarely complain about anything. I check the way I interact and communicate with others, have fewer desires, and show more compassion and understanding, using every opportunity as an educare moment.

The age in which we are living has many challenges and pitfalls that are indirectly related to the erosion of human values (Baba, 1999). The Sri Sathya Sai Education in Human Values Certificate courses have been life-changing experiences for many students who have been inspired, like myself, to make a U-turn in their lives resulting in a great improvement in their personal, family, and work relationships. This calls for alternative approaches to teaching (Kaliannan & Chandran, 2010). The practice of human values in their daily lives using the five transformation techniques is a recipe for character development and a better world for all.

References

Albert, F. (2019). Sri Sathya Sai Education in Human Values. All the depth of integral education for the 21st century. *The Journal of Progressive Education, 12*(2), 99–118. https://doi.org/10.5958/2229-4422.2019.00009.4

Baba, S. S. (1990). *Summer showers 1990: Indian culture and spirituality*. Sri Sathya Sai Books and Publications Trust.

Baba, S. S. (1999). Valedictory function of first Sri Sathya Sai seminar on values. Sri *Sathya Sai Speaks, 32*.

Jumsai, A. N. A. (1997). *The five human values and human excellence*. The Institute of Sathya Sai Education.

Jumsai, A., & Burrows, L. (1991). Sathya Sai education in human values handbook for teachers. Sathya Sai Foundation of Thailand.

Kaliannan, M., & Chandran, S. D. (2010). Education in human values (EHV): Alternative approach for holistic teaching. *Educational Research and Review, 5*(12), 802–807. http://www.academicjournals.org/ERR. ISSN 1990-3839 © 2010 Academic Journals.

Packham, R., Taplin, M., & Francis, K. (2024). *How values education can improve student and teacher wellbeing: A simple guide to the education in human values approach.* Routledge.

Reddy, L. (2021). Light meditation and other silent sitting techniques. In S. Parahakaran & S. Scherer (Eds.), *A human values pathway for teachers.* Springer. https://doi.org/10.1007/978-981-16-0200-9_4

Sathya Sai Educare. (2024, May 27). Sri Sathya Sai Educare—Route to global peace and happiness. https://sssbalvikas.in/courses/group-iii/5elements-its-relationship-with-man/

Sathya Sai International Organisation. (1999). Human values and education divine discourse by Bhagavan Sathya Sai Baba. https://www.sathyasai.org/discour/1999/d990726.html

Sathya Sai International Organisation. (2024, May 27). Human Values and Education, Divine Discourse by Bhagavan Sathya Sai Baba. https://www.sathyasai.org/discour/1999/d990726.html

Shah, S. (2006). Towards Human Excellence. Sri Sathya Sai Education for Schools. Book 6. Short Plays (Skits) On Values, Institute of Sathya Sai Education. https://www.amazon.com/Towards-Excellence-Sathya-Education-Schools/dp/B0018BYMRW#detailBullets_feature_div

SSSIESA. (2022). SSSEHV introductory course learner guide, South Africa.

SSSIESA. (2023). SSSEHV intermediate course learner guide, version 2, South Africa.

Taplin, M. (2002). *A compilation of papers by Dr. Margaret Taplin.* Institute of Sathya Sai Education of Hong Kong. https://www.ssehv.org/files/0301en/Integrating%20Educare%20into%20Mainstream%20Schools-TOC.pdf

Taplin, M., & Lingli, L. (2021). Teachers' perceptions of silent sitting as a buffer to their problems. In S. Parahakaran & S. Scherer (Eds.), *A human values pathway for teachers: Developing silent sitting and mindful practices in education* (pp. 125–150). Springer Nature. https://doi.org/10.1007/978-981-16-0200-9_11